THE LIVES
OF THE
CONSTITUTION

THE LIVES
OF THE
CONSTITUTION

Ten Exceptional Minds that Shaped
America's Supreme Law

Joseph Tartakovsky

ENCOUNTER BOOKS
New York • London

First American edition published in 2018 by Encounter Books, an activity of Encounter for Culture and Education, Inc., a nonprofit, tax exempt corporation.
Encounter Books website address: www.encounterbooks.com

Manufactured in the United States and printed on acid-free paper. The paper used in this publication meets the minimum requirements of ANSI/NISO Z39.48–1992 (R 1997) (*Permanence of Paper*).

All images sourced from Wikimedia Commons.

FIRST AMERICAN EDITION

LIBRARY OF CONGRESS CATALOGING-IN-PUBLICATION DATA
Names: Tartakovsky, Joseph, 1981–
Title: The lives of the constitution : ten exceptional minds that shaped
    America's supreme law / by Joseph Tartakovsky.
Description: New York : Encounter Books, 2018. | Includes bibliographical
    references and index.
Identifiers: LCCN 2017039034 (print) | LCCN 2017039283 (ebook) |
ISBN 9781594039867 (Ebook) | ISBN 9781594039850 (hardback : alk. paper)
Subjects: LCSH: Constitutional law—United States. | Constitutional
    history—United States. | United States–Politics and government—History.
Classification: LCC KF4550 (ebook) | LCC KF4550 .T37 2018 (print) |
DDC 342.73–dc23
LC record available at https://lccn.loc.gov/2017039034

Interior page design and composition by BooksByBruce.com

To my parents,
Dr. Anita Friedman and Igor Tartakovsky,
who constituted me in every respect.

Contents

OVERTURE

The Constitution's Third Century

Every nation has a founding myth. The Bushmen of Africa claim they emerged from a hole in the earth; the Iroquois of America say they descended from a gap in the sky. The Romans had Romulus and Remus; the Israelites a covenant in the Sinai desert. Other foundings involve monsters, gods, floods, and planetary prodigies. The American story, then, at first glance, is not very promising: it's a bunch of legal documents. Yet our tale has the compensating virtue of emerging not out of mysterious antiquity, but out of provable fact. We have something rarer even than the supernatural: the documentary record of a nation rationally created. "We have it in our power to begin the world over again," wrote Thomas Paine, an early enthusiast for the task. "A situation, similar to the present, hath not happened since the days of Noah until now." The Founding Fathers, the time-tested carpenters of our ark, were great enough for myths to gather around them. But the truth of our origin remains a matter of recollection, not imagination.

America's greatest contribution to world civilization has been in the art of establishing and preserving free republican government. By now we've had the longest practice on earth. Our national regime has operated uninterrupted since 1789, through even a civil war. During that time, France, a country that, like us, makes bold claims about having lofted the banner of world liberty, has advanced from its First to its now Fifth Republic, with two Napoleonic empires, a monarchy, and a Vichy puppet regime in between. I think that the United States Constitution has endured, I should say right up front, because it is the finest ever written. It is terse enough to fold into a paper airplane. It is rigid enough to restrain excesses and flexible enough to accommodate innovations. And it is based on principles true in theory and workable in practice.

But the story of our Constitution cannot be told merely as an account of a legal charter. It must be told as a story of human beings. I try to follow, humbly, the biographical method of Plutarch on the Greeks and Romans, Samuel Johnson on the English poets, or Lytton Strachey on the Victorians, all of whom proved that you could best capture a civilization by following some of its prominent members in their adventures through it.

I chose ten individuals whose large thoughts and unafraid deeds all teach something crucial about the American Constitution. The first two figures in this book, Alexander Hamilton and James Wilson, began their services to the Constitution while it was still a glimmer in their far-sighted eyes. Hamilton, an island orphan, led the drive for a new Constitution, then breathed life into it as Washington's most trusted advisor in its shaky first years. James Wilson was a Scottish immigrant whose blazing intellect made him a philosopher in thought and a colossus in debate at the Constitution's drafting and ratification in 1787 and 1788. The heavy-browed Daniel Webster defended the Constitution as a politician in the first generation to follow the framers, though the generation after him would wade through rivers of gore to vindicate the cause he championed.

Stephen Field, a Gold Rush lawyer who became a fiery Supreme Court Justice, presided in the heady days when post–Civil War America first flexed its industrial might. I call in two Europeans—both lofty Viscounts, no less, in their peerages—to examine us and our Constitution in the searching way that only foreigners can: Alexis de Tocqueville, in the first half of the 19th century, and James Bryce, in the second. Woodrow Wilson, hard-driving and prolific, took the White House in 1912 at the height of a reordering of American law now called the Progressive Era. Ida Wells-Barnett was a one-woman army who fought a lonely moral and journalistic war against anti-black violence and misogyny between

Reconstruction and the Jazz Age. Robert Jackson was a dapper and quite deadly lawyer who offered the most enduring defenses of President Franklin Delano Roosevelt's crisis powers during the Great Depression and Second World War. And the late Antonin Scalia, son of a Sicilian immigrant, was a Supreme Court Justice whose feisty brilliance defined today's battle lines over the Constitution.

Each of them had a hand in conceiving, drafting, and ratifying the Constitution, or in interpreting, challenging, amending, preserving, or applying it to radically new conditions. They are linked to one another, and to us, by the fact that we, too, in our peculiar circumstances, continue to have the necessity and opportunity to make for ourselves a more perfect Union. There are crucial differences between the founding lawmakers and those who followed, but all ages require the same spirit. The historian Clinton Rossiter put this too perfectly to paraphrase:

> The one clear intent of the Framers was that each generation of Americans should pursue its destiny as a community of free men. We honor them most faithfully, and do our best to make certain that other generations of free men will come after us, by cherishing the same spirit of constitutionalism that carried them through their history-making adventure. The spirit of the Framers was a blend of prudence and imagination, of caution and creativity, of principle and practicality, of idealism and realism about the governing and self-governing of men. In the constant regeneration of this spirit of 1787 in American public life rests the promise of a future in which our power is the servant of justice and our glory a reflection of moral grandeur.

We know that these Framers did not derive their principles *from* the Constitution. It didn't yet exist. There was something outside of and anterior to the Constitution. So it remains. We possess a constitutional culture, a mosaic of doctrines, moods, sentiments, temperaments, and traditions.

We internalize the guarantees of the Constitution without bothering about its precise words. Most American schoolchildren, for example, know that the president is above the army and that the police cannot crash into your bedroom for their amusement—even if these youngsters can't identify the constitutional clauses that make it so.

We see that a constitution's words are hollow without a culture that reveres them. Russia's constitution, like ours, purports to secure the freedoms of speech and press. But few Russians cared a kopeck when Vladimir Putin, in 2001, seized the last independent TV station—a modern-day reenactment of the First Amendment's fear of the king seizing dissident printing presses. Such an act, attempted here, would have had Americans bursting with virtuous rage.

We believe that even acts that the Constitution allows can still violate our constitutional conscience. Franklin Roosevelt's own Democratic Party in 1937 killed his "court packing" plan, his attempt to add justices to the Supreme Court until he had a majority that would stop striking down his laws. Democrats did so not because his plan offended the Constitution's letter—it didn't—but because his proposal transgressed its spirit. Our constitutional character, not our Constitution, asserted itself.

And we know that individuals create constitutional meaning despite having no formal role in constitutional amendment or interpretation. Three generations of suffragists labored to create a climate to force the enactment of the Nineteenth Amendment, which gave women the right to vote, though they had no hand in drafting that amendment, or even died, like Susan B. Anthony, many years before it was ratified. Women like her created the Constitution that we have, and the meaning that we ascribe to it, even if they never wrote or voted for a syllable of it.

The proposition of this book is that the success and perpetuation of our Constitution depends on many things, but ultimately it must rely on the people and their unforced fidelity to the constitutional character that pervades our national existence. The Constitution runs on patriotism, good sense, decency, compromise, and a love of order. Every generation of Americans, then, must return again to the Constitution, apply it to their distinct predicaments, and pass it on intact to the next generation. That is the great and unending drama of American life.

The Constitution, despite its political and spiritual dimensions, remains in other respects a statement of law, and so this book, I forewarn the reader, contains more judicial decisions than may be safe for children or those with histories of high blood pressure. But I find that constitutional law, even in the hands of lawyers (a tribe to which I belong), is complex but never occult. Lawyers get paid to think about the meaning of the Constitution, yet heaven help us if we are the *only* ones who do so.

Just look at what the English professors did to English literature. Reading old court decisions, alone, as the means of grasping the Constitution is like smelling dead flowers—doctrine with all the scent and color and life withered away.

That's because understanding the Constitution is impossible without marking the influence of experience, politics, culture, and technology. It is true that the Constitution's purpose is, in part, to immunize us against fickle or headlong change, yet the stamp of these forces is unmistakable. For instance, the most perennially fraught fault line in all constitutional law is the division of power between the state and federal governments. The unbroken trend has been toward federal predominance. If the men of 1787 could summon us to the great constitutional convention in the sky, and demand to know why, despite their care and calibration, we have interpreted their handiwork to go so much further in federal aggrandizement than they imagined (excepting probably Alexander Hamilton and a few others), we might explain: "Gentlemen, consider what happened: steam power, automobiles, air travel, and the internet knit us together. Crises like the Civil War and Great Depression strengthened us at the core, in Washington, D.C. Over time states addicted themselves to federal largesse and, in turn, surrendered authority for cash. The intermittent globalization of your day so accelerated that we came to rely on a unified and hence nationalized authority to deal not only with problems you knew, like transatlantic trade and foreign diplomacy, but also ones you didn't, like mafias, toxic pollution, railroads, and cyberwarfare. It turned out that partisan loyalties—in which you gave us a fine head start—overcame most other forms of political identification. And, finally, after a few generations, our pride in the Stars and Stripes came to overshadow our pride in state flags. We can only say, in our defense, that the life of the document has been inseparable from the life of the people."

Our constitutional adventure is marked by an astonishing continuity—the Constitution binds us, literally, to the past—but also by a healthy measure of bumbling, accident, botchwork, and struggle. I think the forefathers believed there was no other way by which to resolve the Constitution's meaning. "It is not to be wondered that doubts & difficulties should occur in expounding the Constitution," said James Madison, after nearly a half-century of reflection on the document. "A settled practice, enlightened by occurring cases and obviously conformable to the public good, can alone remove the obscurity." Well, we are now in the Constitution's third century. We've lived under it, with it, and in it, for about nine generations. We've settled many practices and removed many obscurities. So far as I can tell, only the Constitution's Third Amendment, which outlaws the old British practice of "quartering" Redcoats in private homes, remains untouched by time, and must await a foreign invasion for an occasion to elucidate it. And still some developments would surprise even those who expected surprises. In 1788, Madison and Alexander Hamilton published the *Federalist*, a collection of essays that today is considered authoritative on the Constitution as understood by its first interpreters. Yet even they did not anticipate many defining elements of modern constitutional life, good or bad: they told us the Commerce Clause would prove uncontroversial; they did not imagine the influence of parties on every aspect of law and politics; and they dismissed concerns about a runaway judiciary.

A final theme of this book is that the best antidote to hysteria is a good dose of history. "It is much easier to alarm people than to inform them," said William Davie, a North Carolina founder, in 1788, when the Constitution was being debated for ratification. Since then the Constitution has been pronounced dead so often that a tally of its obituaries is a job not for historians but mathematicians. In this book you will find that earlier eras suffered worse strains and faced deadlier enemies than ours. Most constitutional crises are acute but not, thankfully, unprecedented. If history is to a people what memory is to an individual, the past gives us a sense of proportion and a chance to avoid repeating our worst stupidities. I expect that many readers will disagree with certain conclusions of mine, but I hope that everyone finds some calming heresy in this book.

It is worth remembering, as we reach back to our origins, that the day in July 1776 when a few daring patriots agreed to affix their names to a scroll declaring America independent was a day of terror and loneliness. Today the Fourth of July is a happy holiday of parades and potato salad. But for our rebel ancestors it was a moment in which they braved the gallows of treason and exposed their children and villages to ruin and death. Never should we lose that sense of solemnity, that consciousness of ever-present peril. For as the Founders of this very unmythical nation understood, far better than we, no human creation, however finely wrought, is permanent.

BUILDERS

1765–1804

ALEXANDER HAMILTON

I

ALEXANDER HAMILTON

A War Ends and a Constitution Begins

In the winter of late 1783 the bells pealing in Albany and Manhattan to celebrate the peace between the renegade colonies and his semi-sane majesty must have sounded, to loyalists, like death knells. A half-million souls across the colonies stayed true to George the Third; in New York alone, in 1776, loyalists had amounted to nearly half the state's population. Alexander Hamilton, a Wall Street lawyer in his late 20s, understood why New York's patriots, a fever for vengeance crackling in their blood, were now robbing, exiling, hamstringing (disabling by cutting that muscle), and murdering those they called traitorous "parricides." The war had been fratricidal and eight years long, our longest until Vietnam, and no place was occupied longer than New York City. New Yorkers saw their homes burned, streets denuded of trees, churches used as stables; they saw 11,500 friends and family die on reeking East River prison ships, bones still washing ashore a decade later. It was a time of crisis, and precisely what Hamilton needed to uncoil the powers that would make him loved and feared. He was meddlesome, imaginative, audacious, overbearing, pragmatic, indiscreet, charming, and tireless. He spoke with a confidence so unwavering that one might have supposed he had returned from the future.

Alexander Hamilton was shaken by the cruelties of his countrymen, who had discovered that duly enacted laws could ruin a hated minority faster than street reprisals. A statute from 1784 authorized the sale of seized Tory estates. Philipsburg Manor in Westchester, alone, was parceled out to 287 new landowners, averaging 174 acres apiece. Another law "forever" disenfranchised most Tories for "holding principles inimical to the Constitution," though it mercifully exempted minors and the insane. When the 1783 Trespass Act encouraged patriots to sue Tories who had moved into the houses or used the businesses of patriots, an alarmed Hamilton began taking loyalist cases. Those breathing revenge, he felt, really only coveted a neighbor's house or the chance to eliminate a creditor or business rival, and for these unworthy motives New York was violating the treaty Americans had signed with Great Britain and risking the peace that the nation as a whole had achieved.

But most of all Hamilton feared what New Yorkers' persecutions said about their character. "[W]e have taken our station among nations," he wrote, in early 1784, under the pseudonym Phocion, but now behaved like the dishonorable Greek tribe who pledged to return an enemy's prisoners only to execute them and return the corpses. He closed with a warning: "The world has its eye upon America," but if our misbehavior showed that the "bulk of mankind are not fit to govern themselves," then with the "greatest advantages for promoting it, that ever a people had, we shall have betrayed the cause of human nature."

⟋⟍

The island of Nevis, a mountainous 36-square-mile speck in the Caribbean where Alexander Hamilton was born in 1755, looks like a jungle paradise. But for inhabitants, the azure waters lapping white sands, the drowsy palms and laughing parrots, probably seemed meager compensation for the earthquakes, hurricanes, pirates, isolation, malaria, and crime. "While other founding fathers were reared in tidy New England villages or cosseted on baronial Virginia estates," writes Ron Chernow in his 2004 biography of Hamilton, Alexander "grew up in a tropical hellhole of dissipated whites and fractious slaves." Hamilton regularly witnessed auctions of sugar-cane slaves, with buyers who arrived with branding irons to sear living skin. He was entrusted at age 14 as a clerk for a local merchant. A letter shows Alexander reporting to his boss in stream-of-consciousness style: "I sold all your lumber off immediately at £16 luckily enough, the price of that article being now reduced to £12, as great quantities have been lately imported.... Indeed, there must be a vast consumption of this crop—which makes it probable that the price will again rise—unless the crops at windward should fall short—as is said to be the case—whereby we shall stand fair to be overstocked." Alexander managed shipments of mules and codfish, calculated currency exchanges, advised captains to arm against buccaneers. It was an unmatchable apprenticeship in the centrality of trade, credit, and commerce to the fate of nation.

Alexander Hamilton's life had strikingly modern touches. He was the son of a single mother who worked as a shopkeeper. When she died, Alexander, and his older brother James, both teenagers, were left alone and disinherited. The remainder of his Nevis family life was one sad fact after another. The town judge had to buy Alexander shoes for his mother's funeral. Years later, at his wedding to Eliza Schuyler, the daughter of a powerful New York patroon, not a single family member appeared on his side. Hamilton had everything against him, except the prodigious intellect that led a few local merchants to pay his way to King's College in New York City. He arrived on the continent in 1773, said a biographer, slight and slim, with a "bright, ruddy complexion; light-colored hair; a mouth infinite in expression, its sweet smile being most observable and most spoken of; eyes lustrous with meaning and reflection, or glancing with quick canny pleasantry, and the whole countenance decidedly Scottish in form and expression."

In 1776 he dropped out of college—another admirable modern touch—to take command of 68 men as a 21-year-old artillery captain, braving British fire (recklessly, some thought) and supplying his troops at his own expense. He soon became a staff officer to George Washington, the beginning of a historic two-decade alliance. The sonless Washington called the fatherless Hamilton "my boy," and fellow officers remembered "Call Colonel Hamilton" as Washington's instinctive utterance when important news arrived. Hamilton could write more forcefully than anyone, spoke the French of our allies, and handled politicians like a diplomat. Hamilton was also the sort able to find time between negotiating prisoner exchanges and dodging cannon-fire to begin a systematic study of economics. He filled an artillery notebook with items one might expect to interest a

future Treasury Secretary: how Hungarian corn is six times cheaper than
English corn, for instance, or that goats might be profitably raised for
skin and hair in the South. His self-education would make him the most
learned founder on finance, rivaled only by his friend Gouverneur Morris,
a hilarious, peg-legged cynic who was so intellectually akin to Hamilton
that Hamilton invited Morris, before Madison, to co-write the *Federalist*.

Hamilton's political views arose from his wartime service. He thought
that America's headless, incompetent Congress got Americans killed.
Congress was trying to fight a war by legislative committee, such as by
setting prices and ordering troop movements, all directed by constantly
rotating, often corrupt personnel. General Washington's supplies allowed
his untrained men to fire only two practice rounds before engaging skilled
Redcoats. Charles Willson Peale, later famed as a painter, recalled how
after the Battle of Princeton, to save his exhausted men from another
night of hunger, Peale begged door to door until he had enough beef and
potatoes for their meal. "[N]othing appears more evident to me," wrote
Hamilton, midway through the war, "than that we run much greater risk
of having a weak and disunited federal government, than one which will
be able to usurp upon the rights of the people."

The states had been loosely allied since 1781 under the Articles of
Confederation, which created not a government but a treaty between
independent sovereigns. It functioned like the United Nations: a frequently chaotic gathering of "delegates" representing effectively separate,
self-interested nations, empowered only to issue non-binding resolutions,
and wholly inept at maintaining peace. James McHenry, an Irish-born
surgeon who served at Valley Forge with Hamilton, wrote his old com-
rade that bold measures were difficult with a "people who have thirteen
heads each of which pay superstitious adoration to inferior divinities." It
is no wonder that many of the most committed future Federalists—the
name for the nationalist party that would come to govern during the first
decade and a half under the U.S. Constitution—were ex-officers. John
Marshall, later the fourth Chief Justice of the Supreme Court, confessed
that his captaincy during the war instilled in him his habit of "considering
America"—not Virginia—"as my country."

Hamilton, as the war was winding down, laid out the choice before
the country in a six-part essay series he signed "Continentalist." We could
become a "noble and magnificent" federal republic, he wrote, "closely

linked in the pursuit of a common interest, tranquil and prosperous at home, respectable abroad," or we could stumble on in our "diminutive and contemptible" course, as a "number of petty states, with the appearance only of union, jarring, jealous and perverse, without any determined direction, fluctuating and unhappy at home, weak and insignificant by their dissensions, in the eyes of other nations." His choice was obvious, but he was unsure about whether the crumbling American alliance would even hold. After the war he urged George Clinton, New York's formidable governor, who had privateered against France at 16 and invaded Canada by 20, to hand out land to officers to entice their settlement in New York—just in case the state had to fend for itself. Some veterans, said Gouverneur Morris, "anticipated with horror the moment when they might be called on to unsheathe their swords against each other."

In the late 1780s Greenwich Village was still a village and Long Islanders were farmers, but New York City was already, in ethnic and religious terms, the most diverse city in North America. It was full of merchants and gazettes. Yet streets also thronged with crippled men, widows, and bankrupts; hundreds of soldiers returned from war only to be jailed for debt. Rampant were suicides, counterfeiting, thefts of whole flocks of sheep. No state, Hamilton felt, better illustrated the need for a federal constitution to unite the states and so bring order and prosperity. But having shaken one foreign ruler, no state was less eager to accept another. New York State, in fact, became the great drag on the continental project. When Congress relocated to New York City in 1785, the state's refusal to find office space for it forced the legislature to lease a tavern.

Governor Clinton declared that the act of "confederating" with other states under a single government was unnecessary: the future Empire State had fertile lands, commanding waterways, and choice ports that brought the state a fortune in tariffs and taxes. New York City was probably the entrepôt to half the goods consumed in Connecticut and New Jersey. Connecticut, in the early 1780s, had bravely declared that it would allow free trade between the states in the hope that New York would follow suit, but by 1787 it found itself annually paying £100,000 of coerced "tribute" into New York's pockets. An infuriated Nutmeg State sought to block all exports to New York and to deny its ships landing. New Jersey, for its part, enacted retaliatory tariffs against New York. New Yorkers, particularly the farmers at the heart of the anti-union movement, loved how this income permitted the state to keep land taxation light.

The U.S. Constitution was drafted in Philadelphia in summer 1787 and sent out to the states for ratification, to take effect if nine ratified. Eight states had already ratified by the time New York even *began* its convention to consider ratification in Poughkeepsie. George Clinton's anti-Constitution partisans were glad to let other states go first. Hamilton, the acknowledged leader of the pro-Constitution forces, also favored delay: with only a third of the convention delegates believed to be friendly to the proposed Constitution, he felt that his side's only hope was that ratification by other states would shake Clinton's moderates. The state was split between the southernmost counties, led by a commercial New York City, and upstate farming counties, led by Albany, whose leaders prayed, as Clinton's nephew put it, that from "tax gatherers, standing armies, navies, placemen, sinecures, federal cities, Senators, Presidents and a long train of et ceteras Good Lord deliver us." Hamilton calculated rightly. Midway through the Poughkeepsie convention, New Hampshire and Virginia signed on. The question for New York then shifted from approval of the Constitution to whether to isolate itself, militarily and commercially, by staying out of the new union. There was genuine fear that if the state kept out, Staten Island would peel off and join New Jersey, and New York City and Long Island would link up with Connecticut. So the Constitution came to New York, by vote of 30-27. Hamilton's decisive influence in the close-run affair led some exuberant Manhattanites to propose that New York City be renamed "Hamiltonia."

Presidential candidates today, even after two unbroken centuries of elections, find it hard to avoid doomsday talk about America's survival. When Americans in the 1790s spoke this way, it had the merit of being true. The physical downfall of the fragile new government under the Constitution—the "experiment," as that generation liked to call it—was altogether possible in an age when an unluckily placed boulder in a river, as George Washington found, could still stop the movement of an American president. In 1792 Hamilton found it "curious" that "[o]ne side appears to believe that there is a serious plot to overturn the state Governments and substitute monarchy to the present republican system," while the other "firmly believes that there is a serious plot to overturn the General Government & elevate the separate power of the states upon its ruins." He was in a position to know: the opposition force that inaugurated our two-party system arose as an anti-Hamilton party.

Hamilton was named the first Secretary of the Treasury, at age 34, and served for five and a half years. In December 1790, after the government had been in effect for a matter of months, Virginia's legislature declared that Hamilton's first major economic initiative—to have the federal government absorb state war debts—was not just unconstitutional but "fatal to the existence of American liberty." The Father of his Country was still largely untouchable, so Hamilton took the heat, much in the English tradition of attacking the minister, not the king. Jefferson, as Secretary of State, started in privately with President Washington on how his fellow cabinet member had secret plans for a homegrown monarchy, which he, Jefferson, thought self-evident especially in the way Hamilton "shuffled" around millions of dollars. In 1792 an exasperated Washington urged a truce between Hamilton and Jefferson, whose intensifying warfare—"daily pitted in the cabinet like two cocks," Jefferson recalled—was "tearing our vitals," in Washington's words, at a time when the nation was "encompassed on all sides" by enemies.

The U.S. was then a long thin strip of a country, like Israel or Chile, wedged up against a sea that it did not control, on a coast and continent roamed by three European empires. Above all were the behemoths England and France, whose clash kept the world at war for the rest of Hamilton's life and left Europe strewn with the carcasses of overthrown regimes. America felt the crushing strain of a small besieged African nation trying to survive the Cold War. At first Hamilton was amused, if uneasy, when the revolutionary French Republic made him honorary citizen "Jean Hamilton" in 1792. A few months later Parisian radicals beheaded Louis XVI, our ally from a decade earlier. By then hysteria and delirium had broken lose stateside. Better to have the United States "erased from existence than infected with French principles," cried the Federalist Oliver Wolcott, Jr., who would succeed Hamilton as Treasury Secretary. Jefferson, by contrast, saw the "liberty of the whole earth" turning on the success of the "Jacobin" cause, adding, with customary sangfroid, that "rather than it should have failed, I would have seen half the earth desolated." John Adams recalled that in spring 1793, 10,000 people took to Philadelphia's streets, day after day, threatening to "drag Washington out of his house, and effect a revolution in the government, or compel it to declare war in favor of the French Revolution."

Hamilton dreaded that the U.S. would stumble into a war with Europe during his entire public career—first France in 1793, then England in 1794, then France again in 1797. These were wars, he felt, that we were perilously unequipped to fight. France installed or sponsored puppet "sister republics" in the Netherlands, Germany, Switzerland, and Italy. Hamilton, as time wore on, came to believe that revolution-exporting France had American sympathizers prepared to "cut off the leading Federalists and seize the government." In 1797, after the stabilizing Washington was succeeded by the less balanced Adams, and the French-American Quasi-War began, the British foreign secretary wrote that the "whole system of American government" seemed to be "tottering to its foundations."

Then the 1800 election returned a tie between Jefferson and Aaron Burr so fraught and volatile—Jefferson eventually won on the 36th House ballot, by two votes—that Pennsylvania and Virginia, emotions at a boil, began arming for an anticipated struggle. That election was an extraordinary event in history: the first transfer of national power between rivals after a popular, periodic election in the recorded history of our violent species. Today we know parties cede ground back and forth like football teams. The founders did not, which is why they so often could not distinguish disagreement from disloyalty. It is no exaggeration to say that for stretches in the 1790s, a good portion of Americans thought revolutionary France more true to the cause of 1776 than Alexander Hamilton and even George Washington. The party wars of that decade were so unbearably intense, Jefferson recalled, that lifelong friends crossed streets to avoid meeting.

Hamilton was a man constantly in motion, like a shark that must keep swimming to breathe. A friend remembered a publisher in Hamilton's study at home, waiting to take *Federalist* essays "as they came fresh" from Hamilton's quill, composed between breaks in his law practice. Hamilton eventually wrote under so many pen names that he may have been, says biographer Ron Chernow, the "foremost political pamphleteer in American history." At one point Hamilton began a 38-part series under the name "Camillus," to debate the Jay Treaty in 1795 between the United States reached for familiar kingly precedent that Washington felt obligated, in his draft First Inaugural address, to remind his people that he was child-less. True, he did wear a ceremonial sword and ride in a cream-colored coach attended by liveried servants, but the republican reality was cap-tured by an Englishman who visited him in 1795 in Philadelphia—and found the old warrior domiciled in a simple brick house, near Fourth Street, next to a hairdresser's shop.

Hamilton was interested not in superficial titles but action. In ghost-writing Washington's 1796 Farewell Address, he knew he spoke Wash-ington's mind when he wrote that the "real danger in our system is that the general government, organized as at present, will prove too weak rather than too powerful." Both Washington and Hamilton knew from the war that no legislature could ever match the concentrated intelligence, speed, and discipline of an official who is always on duty—one reason that even today the President works in the same building that he lives in. Federalist preoccupations were soon tested when, in August 1794, 7,000 "whiskey rebels" marauded through western Pennsylvania, setting up mock guillotines and burning the homes of tax officials—the largest incident of armed resistance to federal authority until the Civil War. The rebels considered Hamilton's Excise Act a new Stamp Act, but to Ham-ilton the Excise Act was the second-largest source of federal revenue. Hamilton two years earlier had tried to lower the rate in conciliation, but now rebuffed, energy kicked in.

Hamilton wrote detailed advice to Washington on the number of troops needed and ordered army blankets, medicine chests, and mus-kets, even specifying the materials to be used for jackets. Hamilton had a martial-romantic streak and at night roamed the camp in which federal forces gathered against the rebels. When one soldier complained, Hamilton took the gun himself and paced until relieved. He believed public trust to be essential to durable government. When Pennsylvania militiamen riding to meet the rebels killed two citizens, he rebuked Pennsylvania's governor: troops "cannot render a more important ser-vice to the cause of government & order," he said, "than by a conduct scrupulously regardful of the rights of their fellow citizens and exem-plary for decorum, regularity & moderation."

President Washington believed it of "infinite" importance to get right the precedents he was setting on the many questions the Consti-

and Great Britain, then two days later began a second series, as "Philo Camillus," defending "Camillus," a cascade of words that led Jefferson to exclaim to Madison that Hamilton was an army "within himself." That was when he wasn't writing for others. An editor recalled that when he needed material, he would visit Hamilton late at night. "As soon as I see him," the editor said, "he begins in a deliberate manner to dictate, and I to note down in short-hand. When he stops my article is completed." Hamilton's habit of constantly mumbling to himself suggests an almost unmanageable mental ferment. Hamilton's father-in-law once wrote Hamilton's wife to report, in amusement, that a shopkeeper refused to accept a large bill from Hamilton, in the belief that he, the shopkeeper, would be faulted for taking a madman's money. "I have seen him walk before my door for half an hour," the shopkeeper said, "always talking to himself."

Hamilton was built for national executive work. He declined nominations for New York Governor (too parochial), U.S. Senator (too many colleagues), and Chief Justice of the U.S. Supreme Court (too boring). His writings vibrate with words like "energy," "vigor," "efficiency." He wanted to give government "new life," to have it conduct its business "with dispatch, method, and system," to see the "well-proportioned exertion of the resources of the whole." He saw limits, too. When he read the draft Sedition Act in 1798—which allowed the jailing of administration critics—he rebuked its authors. "Energy is a very different thing from violence," he said. "Let us not establish a tyranny." He even seemed to gainsay the views of George Washington, who had written Adams's Secretary of War, from his retirement at Mount Vernon, to warn against bringing "professed Democrat[s]" into the army. Hamilton thought that putting party above merit forfeited an opportunity to create friends to the government.

The presidency, the stage on which Hamilton would strut, was a new office for Americans. What was the vague "executive power" created by Article II of the Constitution? In 1789 Hamilton's friend James McHenry told Washington, "You are now a king, under a different name," and sent wishes that Washington might "reign long and happy over us." John Adams bridled that Washington would be called, simply, "President," and not his "Most Benign Highness," since there were "presidents of fire companies and of a cricket club." So many Americans tution was silent on. He was acutely aware that his acts would obtain pseudo-constitutional status. Among the precedents settled by twelve years of Federalist rule, largely in Hamilton's favor: Could the House of Representatives demand the President's confidential papers on foreign affairs? On this Washington, as always, sought the advice of Hamilton (who, sorely in need of income, had returned to private law practice a year earlier). Washington thanked Hamilton for confirming that Washington was right to refuse the House's request and indeed "to *resist the principle*." Could legislators investigate executive officials—the first to receive such an honor, in fact, being Hamilton himself? Trumped-up accusations drafted by Jefferson and Madison challenged Hamilton over his management of loans in 1793. Hamilton was exonerated and would be, again, after another investigation in 1794. Hamilton himself, even on questions of presidential authority, got a practical education. In a *Federalist* essay, for instance, he doubted that Senators would actually use their advice-and-consent power to try to influence the president's picks; in fact, senatorial "recommendations" to Washington started rolling in immediately.

When the First Congress asked Hamilton to report to it on economic policy, Congress began the tradition of executive initiative in legislation. Hamilton in 1790 and 1791 produced three major "reports," on debt and taxes, a national bank, and manufacturing. These foundations of the American school of economics established Hamilton's influence in his time more than any other achievement. Congress's skeptics—mostly among the anti-Hamilton party, now called the "Republicans"—were not charmed by what they received. "Some say the Secretary's Reports are like Smith's Treatise on the Wealth of Nations," said one, accurately, adding, "We do not come here to go to school." The Report on Public Credit was dense enough that most lawmakers probably forgave themselves for declining to read it. Hamilton went through specific duties for Hyson tea, green tea, souchong tea, and bohea tea, before informing Congress that he had mostly "omitted details . . . to avoid fatiguing the attention of the House." Hamilton also drafted laws, decided congressional committee memberships, and arrived early at sessions to lobby the Speaker. Another Congressman scolded him for "seem[ing] to take the whole Government upon his shoulders" and for speaking the "language of a Frederick of Prussia, or some other despotic prince."

"The sacred rights of mankind are not to be rummaged for among old parchments or musty records," wrote a young Hamilton, in an exquisite passage. "They are written, as with a sunbeam, in the whole *volume* of human nature, by the hand of the divinity itself, and can never be erased or obscured by mortal power." But he knew that officeholders did not spend their days reaffirming sacred rights. Even the most worshipful parsing of Locke and Montesquieu yielded little about how to run a post office. Hamilton had pondered the "practical business of government" for over a decade before the Constitution took effect. He subscribed to the couplet of Alexander Pope, his favorite poet—and, more even than Shakespeare, the semi-official poet of the American founders—who wrote:

> For forms of government let fools contest;
> Whate'er is best administer'd is best.

Hamilton observed at the Poughkeepsie ratifying convention that governments as exotic as Sparta's ephori or the tribunes of Rome had succeeded. One might add that the great Qing, Ottoman, and Bismarckian empires also owed their conquering superiority to administrative effectiveness, not to liberalism. Hamilton worried that our Constitution, as framed, lacked "energy," but he intended, through invigorating administration, to prove it worthy of the "affection of the people."

Leonard D. White, the historian of American administration, wrote that Hamilton was not only the "greatest administrative genius of his generation in America," but "one of the great administrators of all time." Under Hamilton the Treasury Department became the largest, richest, most efficient enterprise on the continent. Hamilton began with 39 employees, fewer than a large northern shipyard of the day. By 1801 it made up more than half the total civilian federal government, embodied in 1,615 field officials: army and navy accountants, loan commissioners, customs collectors, revenue surveyors, land-office receivers, district attorneys, deputy postmasters, marshals, Indian agents, coastal seamen, and lighthouse keepers. This was the machinery of a modern state, even if, in size, it was a fraction of Cleveland's government today. The State Department, by contrast, after a decade, remained content with ten employees. Its paper operations were confined to a single desk, which kept letters from foreign governments in two pigeonholes on the right side, and foreign treaties in a pigeonhole on the left.

Enemies saw Hamilton as creating an *imperium in imperio* that threatened liberty. Hamilton saw just the opposite: a robust Treasury Department was necessary to *protect* rights. He felt his opponents did not grasp that less government usually does not mean less oppression of property, but, to the contrary, less security for it. Lax enforcement, for instance, gave customs evaders an advantage over those who paid their dues. On his second day in office, he demanded customs returns from his staff—figures that pinpointed the smuggling still pervasive from colonial days when, said Fisher Ames, a leading Massachusetts politician, it was "considered rather as meritorious than criminal." From his childhood Hamilton knew the tricks by which skippers evaded the king's men, from rowing goods ashore in the dark of night to false entries that turned a hogshead of brandy into a barrel of cheap rum. He was not timid about flexing what he saw as his constitutional power to impose registrations, licenses, permits, and fines or to found the fleet of customs interceptors that became the Coast Guard. He also pioneered economic interventionism by the government when he proposed that Congress subsidize nascent manufacturers to help them catch up to European rivals.

And then there was the Bank of the United States. His wife Eliza, in her old age, told a visitor: "He made your bank. I sat up all night with him to help him do it. Jefferson thought we ought not to have a bank and President Washington thought so. But my husband said, 'We must have a Bank.' I sat up all night, copied out his writing, and the next morning, he carried it to President Washington and we had a bank." The bank's creation probably seemed this sudden to opponents, but for a decade Hamilton had called for an institution to do things like ensure a uniform currency, expand the money supply, and service debt. He claimed, in a famous legal opinion to Washington, that the Constitution, read with "liberal latitude," conferred an "implied" power to erect a bank, no less than if the Constitution actually used the word "bank." To many, banks still seemed aristocratic evils. One Virginian planter swore that he would no more be caught going into a bank than a whorehouse.

Hamilton was so far ahead of his time that achievements of his are still being uncovered. Three financial historians claim, based on a Hamilton letter that came to light in 2005, that Hamilton all but saved the center of the nation's economy by inventing the techniques that today's central banks use to manage a crisis. In 1792, the U.S. faced its first financial panic; Hamilton, over several weeks, steadied nerves with a series of creative lender-of-last-resort operations and open-market purchases. He fired off missives to subordinates with instructions like scrawled ticker tape: "[l]et deposits of stock be received to an amount not exceeding a million—six per cent at par three cents at 10 shillings on the pound and deferred at 12 shillings. . . ." He had no staff statisticians or economists, let alone historical cycles for them to study.

Buzzwords like "innovation," "visionary," "democratic," and "revolutionary" clot politicians' speeches today, but in Hamilton's time they were insults. "Democracy," to Federalists in particular, certainly in their pessimistic moods, did not mean stable majority rule—that was the quite separate concept of "republicanism"—but anarchy. It meant the politics of ignorance, jealousy, and fear. It meant policies as flighty as feathers in wind and voters busily redistributing other people's property to themselves. One of the most enduring charges against the legacy of Alexander Hamilton is that he was anti-democratic. Hamilton did say many things about what he once called the "unthinking populace" that one would not care to repeat at an Iowa caucus. Behind the closed doors of the Philadelphia Convention, for instance, he said ordinary Americans were "turbulent and changing; they seldom judge or determine right." Back in public, at the Poughkeepsie convention, he proclaimed us fortunate that the "minds of the people are exceedingly enlightened and refined." Yet the truth is that most leading statesmen of the age spoke fearfully of the "masses" and many were far more disparaging than Hamilton.

Hamilton wanted not a monarch but an executive with the muscle, prestige, and legitimacy to withstand all perils. Elitism and revulsion at bad laws were part of his perspective, but so, too, judging by the frequency of allusion in letters, was experience with actual mobs. Americans of the late 18th century were addicted to the burning of effigies—better, I suppose, than the old European head-on-a-pole. An American of Hamilton's time had a fair chance of seeing a drunken mob in full swarm: a theater immolated, say, or men tortured with scalding tar. Hamilton twice fended off a violent crowd: first, during the war, to allow a loyalist teacher of his to escape at King's College, and again years later, when his head was bloodied by a rock as he spoke in defense of the Jay Treaty on Wall Street. Police forces did not yet exist; mobs were not only deadly but often unstoppable, except by a counter-mob or militia.

The great philosophical realists David Hume (whom Hamilton loved) and Thomas Hobbes (whom Hamilton did not), when pressed, both preferred a monarchy to a republic, on grounds that no king was as deadly as a civil war, considered an ever-present risk in republics. Hamilton said no such thing. Instead he only echoed classic statements of Whig philosophy, like *Cato's Letters* (1720–23), where power was likened to fire: if controlled, it gave light and warmth; if let loose, it scorched and destroyed. "[T]oo much power leads to despotism," wrote Hamilton, but "too little leads to anarchy, and both eventually to the ruin of the people." This theme—that a government must have power to preserve order, because without order there is no liberty—was his preoccupation. He dismissed, in a 1792 letter to Washington, the monarchical accusations against their Federalist party, by arguing that Americans would not accept a king until demagogues, with their cries of "danger to liberty," first discredited republicanism. Therefore, Hamilton continued, it was those who urged commotion and contempt for public order (he had Jefferson in mind) who were the "true artificers of monarchy." Among the ironies of his life was being accused of monarchism by men like George Clinton, who was addressed as "Your Excellency" during his 21-year reign over New York, and who had been chosen by an electorate so narrowed by sex and property qualifications that only about 6% of the population could vote. Democratic skepticism, in short, was not a Hamiltonian trait, but an American one.

Jefferson's first inaugural address in 1801 was excruciating for Hamilton. "[W]e may now safely dispense with all the internal taxes," along with tax collectors and other federal offices "too multiplied," Jefferson said, to count. More terrifying yet, for Hamilton, was that the army and navy were to be basically disbanded; to Jefferson, the only "competent" force against invasion was the "body of neighboring citizens, as formed into a militia." Hamilton blasted what he called Jefferson's promise of "emancipation from the burdens and restraints of government" and his alarming "sacrifice of constitutional energy." Jefferson got what he wanted. "During the opening decades of the nineteenth century," says Gordon S. Wood, the United States government was "weaker than at any other time in its history."

Hamilton died eight years before the War of 1812, the realization of his nightmare. The Republicans controlling Congress, believing a standing military inherently tyrannical, even refused James Madison's request to add two assistant secretaries of war—at the very moment, incredibly, that they voted *for* war with England. Hamilton's enemies had abolished his bank and revenue stream and so left the nation unable to pay its $50 million debt; Treasury Secretary George W. Campbell resigned when the U.S. defaulted. The Jefferson–Madison policy of peace through unpreparedness—Jefferson abolished 319 naval offices in his first year in office—touched President Madison intimately: in 1814, his White House home, minutes after his wife fled with a famous portrait of Washington, was torched by British soldiers.

Hamilton's own worst mistakes arose because he had no non-public life. He could not imagine the national destiny without a heroic role for himself, and, more problematically, he could not hold his tongue about that destiny or his role in it. This led him to bring on the first national sex scandal—against himself. In 1797, a Republican journalist hinted that money Hamilton had sent to a speculator was evidence of insider dealings by Hamilton; Hamilton decided to prove that he was a corrupt spouse, but not a corrupt official. He published a long self-exposé of what was actually a yearlong affair with an unstable prostitute and the hush money he had paid to her pimp husband. Hamilton's wife Eliza must have loved reading her husband declare that by confessing adultery he "wipe[d] away a more *serious* stain," meaning, for Hamilton, the stain that could discredit his superintendence of the nation's finances.

Another self-inflicted wound took the form of Aaron Burr's bullet, in the duel that killed Hamilton in 1804. Hamilton once told his oldest daughter: "If you happen to displease [a person], be always ready to make a frank apology." But when Burr demanded an explanation of Hamilton's denunciations of him—Hamilton had basically campaigned against Burr in 1800 as a man whose true "theory" of government is "despotism"—Hamilton began a series of elaborate refusals either to admit or deny his remarks. Reading these posturings with Burr today reminds one of a tropical-bird dance and its ritualized ducking and puffing. Sophisticated contemporaries recognized duels as comic relics of an aristocratic age of "honor," secret stipulations between two men to permit them simultaneously to attempt assassination of the other. A year before the duel, Washington Irving, America's first celebrity satirist under the Constitution, proposed in New York's *Morning Chronicle*—a paper partly owned by Burr—that a more rational alternative to covert gunplay was to sell tickets to the "show," as in the days of gladiators, since duelers, after all, fought only for "fear of being branded with the epithet of coward."

Hamilton, ahead of his time in so many ways, was retrograde in this. In a statement written privately to justify his decision to fight Burr, he wrote that "considerations" of honor and the "ability to be in future useful" forced him to conform to "public prejudice." He meant that if he was perceived as wimping out, he would lose, as we say today, his credibility. President Adams had made Hamilton an army general, and if there came a bid by states at secession (perhaps led by Burr himself), war with Europe, or another Whiskey Rebellion, what soldier, he seemed to reason, would march behind a confirmed jellyfish? He had reasoned so before. Years earlier he told colleagues that he acted with such fanatical scrupulousness as Treasury Secretary in order to deny Republicans room for attack and thereby "keep myself in a situation best calculated to render service." This turn of mind in fact showed as early as age 14, when he told a friend that he would "willingly risk my life, though not my character, to exalt my station."

In the years before his duel, his mood was often one of mixed despair and bafflement. "Mine is an odd destiny," he told Gouverneur Morris. "Perhaps no man in the U[nited] States has sacrificed or done more for the present Constitution than myself," he continued, yet despite all the neglect and persecution that was his reward, he found himself "still laboring to prop the frail and worthless fabric." Some suggest that his encounter with Burr was suicidal. But he wasn't so gloomy in his last years that he couldn't brilliantly litigate, in New York courts, the *Croswell* case, which helped establish truth as a defense in libel, or to prepare for future influence by starting the *New York Post*. The whole *point* of the duel was to ensure that Hamilton could stay in the game. The duel, then, reveals not disillusionment with public life but how wholly enveloped Hamilton was in it: a healthy man, aged 49, was convinced that his duty to be "useful" to America overrode his separate and, one might think, equally strong duties to his wife and seven children, whom he would leave in poverty, or his obligations to clients and creditors, another acute concern found in his last letters.

The reaction to Hamilton's murder among his old comrades shows how sincere the political hate was. Years later John Adams still asked why he should forgive the attacks Hamilton made on him merely because Hamilton died "with a pistol bullet through his spinal marrow." Stories floated that Burr received an "ovation" at a Republican dinner in Petersburg, Virginia. Yet Republicans owed Hamilton. Hamilton despised Jefferson, and in fact had been personally friendly with Burr, but Hamilton's fear of Burr's dangerous tendencies and adventurism led him to derail Burr's presidential bid—prevailing on the Delaware Congressman whose necessary abstention led to Jefferson's victory—because, as he said, the "public good must be paramount to every private consideration." Burr, later tried for treason after heading up a military expedition bound, apparently, for Mexico, confirmed Hamilton's judgment. "I charge you to protect his fame," said Gouverneur Morris at Hamilton's funeral, to a city stilled by shock. "It is all he has left." Then he asked his listeners not to engage in mob violence.

American constitutional history can be reduced, if one must, into warring "Hamiltonian" or "Jeffersonian" traditions: the builder of order versus the exalter of liberty; consolidated energy versus "states' rights"; a Constitution of growth, flexibility, and creativity versus a Constitution of constriction, rigidity, and caution. There is wisdom in journalist Walter Lippmann's call for a truce: "To be partisan today as between Jefferson and Hamilton is like arguing whether men or women are more necessary to the procreation of the race." But the parity that this implies has never existed. Jefferson has always overshadowed his archfoe, and Hamilton has been persistently denied his due. Until we recognize that the sweep of American history has been infinitely more Hamiltonian than Jeffersonian, that we quote Jefferson but follow Hamilton, I say, let the war of legacies continue.

D.H. Lawrence once told his wife: "Frieda, if people really knew what you were like, they would strangle you." The line comes to mind in considering Americans' attachment to the tall, mystical Virginian polymath.

Like the Lawrences, we are joined with Jefferson in a bond, for better or worse. Our debts to him justify many rays of the aura of reverence he has basked in for two centuries. He was the most soaring, eloquent founder, possessed of a shape-shifting gift for giving voice simultaneously to the convictions of both Left and Right. How else to explain, for instance, that Franklin Delano Roosevelt, the great state-builder, erected a marble temple to the icon of state-minimalism, a man whose contemporary intimates, when they opposed a memorial to Washington, actually put on record their abhorrence of monuments as a trapping of imperialism? The idealized statue-Jefferson will never be dislodged from its shrine on the Potomac, but touching idols, as Flaubert said, does have a way of leaving gilding on the hands.

When Hamilton built his home in what is now Harlem, it rested amid lightly wooded hills and colonial cowpaths, nine miles north of the city. It was the only home Hamilton ever owned; he was otherwise a lifelong renter and early Manhattan commuter. (Those modern touches springing up again.) Hamilton, the supposed banker-elitist, put up a modest two-story home, using hard-won legal fees, in the distinctly American "Federal" style, and named it the "Grange," probably in homage to the seat of his Scottish forebears but that also happens to be the old English word for the dwelling of a yeoman farmer. Jefferson, by contrast, the New World agrarian, chose an Italian name, Monticello, for the Palladian neoclassical mansion that he built with inherited wealth. Today Monticello, privately owned, proudly and fittingly, advertises that it receives no ongoing federal funding. But Hamilton's Grange is a National Park, belatedly created by Congress after New York State lagged, again fittingly, to support it. Its website sheepishly invites people to visit the home of this "controversial" founder. Thousands do. But millions visit Monticello.

Nevertheless, Jefferson's stock has sunk in recent years, largely because of his record on race. Jefferson denounced Hamilton as a closet monarchist while himself ruling as king over a self-contained mini-village, with its generations of vassals (some 600 slaves in his lifetime), who, he said, "labor" for my "happiness." Some criticize Hamilton for writing about child labor in his report on manufacturing while forgetting that Jefferson actually used it. When around 1818 Jefferson noticed a spate of deaths among the black "little ones," he ordered lighter duty for mothers, whom he believed were neglecting their children as a result of work duties. His reason for lightening the burden, however, as he wrote to a neighbor, with unforgettable creepiness, was that "a child raised every 2 years is of more profit than the crop of the best laboring men."

Jefferson did not understand the economic forces reshaping the country because he was not part of that economy: he didn't need banks because his assets were in flesh; compound interest had little appeal because his capital increased through procreation. Jefferson, the supposed man of science, concluded that black inferiority was "not the effect merely of their condition in life," though they did improve, he felt, when their blood was "mixed" with that of whites. Hamilton was the better naturalist where it counted: in 1779 he praised a scheme to raise black battalions because it would prove that perceived black inadequacy was the result of their "want of cultivation" and the "contempt we have been taught to entertain" for them.

Jefferson's politics were "tinctured with fanaticism," said Hamilton, but he predicted that Jefferson, once possessed of authority himself, would "temporize" with his principles to "promote his own reputation." Hamilton was right. At the very moment in 1786–87 that Hamilton was trying to bring order to America, Jefferson, in one of his many proto-Leninist outbursts, welcomed a farmers' rebellion in Massachusetts by declaring that the "tree of liberty must be refreshed from time to time with the blood of patriots and tyrants"—"tyrants," in this case, referring to Massachusetts state officials. Yet once in power, when President Jefferson faced his own "rebellion" along the Canadian border, he instructed New York's governor to "crush these audacious proceedings, and to make the offenders feel the consequences of individuals daring to oppose a law by force." Jefferson, in his "Kentucky Resolutions," urged states to threaten disunion in response to the Sedition Act signed by John Adams, on grounds that the act suppressed political expression. But as president, now under criticism himself, Jefferson secretly urged state officials to bring a "few prosecutions" of Federalist newspapers, even identifying one to "make an example of." Jefferson characterized Hamilton as an English lackey—a curious description for a combat veteran who had spilled English blood—before himself overseeing a ruinous, unconstitutional, and now-forgotten embargo policy that treated northern merchants as cruelly as George III ever dared.

President Jefferson at one point asked his Treasury Secretary, Albert Gallatin, to ransack the archives for evidence of Hamiltonian wrongdo-

ing. "I have found the most perfect system ever formed," Gallatin supposedly reported back. "Any change that should be made in it would injure
it. Hamilton made no blunders, committed no frauds." That didn't stop
Jefferson from continuing to accuse his rival of criminality during the
22 years by which he outlived Hamilton. In an 1816 letter to yet another
successor to Hamilton in his old post of Treasury Secretary, Jefferson
suggested expelling commercial types "as we do persons infected with disease." That sincere proposal, I think, reveals the squire-savant's deepening
horror that his rival had pulled it off: Hamilton took a country with no
past and planned its future. A simple measure of Hamilton's entitlement
to regard as more relevant than Jefferson is that Hamilton's preoccupations—lively commerce, an intimidating military, watchful monetary
stewardship—are today the boasts of every State of the Union speech.

What is remarkable, in the end, is not only what Hamilton achieved
but how precisely it was spelled out in his "Continentalist" essays of
1781–82, at a time when most American leaders had only vague intuitions
about what ought to be done for the country. The 1780s are written, in
relief, in clause after clause of the Constitution that Hamilton fought
for. No longer could a state like New York, for instance, ignore treaties
or trammel trade, because the Constitution made treaties supreme over
state law and gave Congress power to regulate commerce between the
states. Hamilton operated at a time, it must never be forgotten, when his
opposition denied that the United States even had the power to construct
a lighthouse.

Hamilton's origins exposed him to disparagement as a foreigner—or,
as John Adams said, a "creole" and a "bastard brat of a Scotch peddler."
Hamilton concealed even from friends his squalorous upbringing,
a humiliation to this most self-made of self-made men. Yet today
these facts give his achievements even more heroic dimensions. This
isle-to-eminence history, and his enlightened views on race, made the
time ripe for Lin-Manuel Miranda's celebratory half-rapped musical
about the "founding father without a father" to take Broadway like a
Nevis storm. The play, a sort of Parson Weems tale but with historical
integrity, initiated the biggest popular Hamilton revival since Gertrude
Atherton's *The Conqueror, Being the True and Romantic Story of Alexander Hamilton* (1902). Yet the undervaluation of Hamilton continues to
haunt him, even in the one place where he might have expected better.
In 2015, the 76th Treasury Secretary announced the planned removal

of his greatest predecessor from the face of the $10 note—part of an attempt, he said, to honor our "great leaders." The secretary, whose staff apparently failed to brief him on the concept of irony, made the statement while standing in front of Hamilton's statue. A groundswell of opposition, happily, forced a reversal.

Hamilton's own assessment of his accomplishments, in late 1798, was this:

> In some things my efforts succeeded, in others they were disappointed—in others I have had promises of conformity to lay the foundation of future proceeding the performance and effect of which promises are not certainly known to me. The effect indeed cannot yet be known. The public mind of the country continues to progress in the right direction.... [T]he country will ere long assume an attitude correspondent with its great destinies, majestic, efficient, and operative of great things. A noble career lies before it.

My favorite Hamilton story is from Talleyrand, the legendarily corrupt French foreign minister who simply couldn't fathom how Hamilton, a *finance* minister of all things, should have to resign for lack of cash. One night, in Manhattan, Talleyrand passed Hamilton's office and was shocked to glimpse the lawyer toiling by candlelight. "I have seen a man who has made the fortune of a nation laboring all night to support his family," he said. This eminently American scene makes all the more jarring a remark Hamilton let slip in his last years of anxiety about his fate, and his country's: "[T]his American world," he said, "was not made for me." Perhaps that America was not. But *this* one is.

JAMES WILSON

2

JAMES WILSON
The Philosopher of Philadelphia

T he worst thing to happen to the Founding Fathers was
for them to become known as the "Founding Fathers," as
a bloc of brother-statesmen supposedly united in hearty
comradeship. We are daily informed that the latest legislative or judicial
outrage would have the Founders "rolling in their graves." But the only
reason the Founders have to roll in their graves is the frequency with
which they are said to be rolling in their graves. A consecrated mode of
American argument is to rustle up a quote from an illustrious founder,
declare an aspect of current policy inconsistent with it, and call it a day.
But it is among the Founders that we find the first of the great constitutional collisions that recur perpetually. Their intense disagreements not
only are far more illuminating than their agreements, but their clashes
often reveal that apparent departures from the "framing" are nothing
more than belated agreements with one founder over another. Take the
career of James Wilson, the most philosophical framer, and also one of
the most tragic.

There is practically a cottage industry devoted to lamenting the neglect of James Wilson. The authors of a book called *America's Forgotten
Founders* (2008) asked over a hundred scholars of law, politics, or history
to list and rank the most "underrated" founders. They found that Wilson,

from a roster of 73 men, "easily topped the list." Other long-suffering fellows in underappreciation have seen their reputations restored. John Adams got an HBO miniseries and Alexander Hamilton a Broadway hit. Adams signed the Declaration of Independence, and Hamilton the draft Constitution, both impressive enough feats, but James Wilson, so central was he to America's documentary soul, remains one of only six men to sign *both*.

This is not to suggest that Wilson has lacked for partisans. His, in fact, have been among the most fanatical. In 1907, Lucien H. Alexander, a lawyer in Wilson's adoptive hometown of Philadelphia, proclaimed that one day Americans would recognize two great figures—just two—from the revolutionary era: James Wilson, "whose brain conceived and created the nation," and George Washington, "who wielded the physical forces that made it." Alexander helped manage the "James Wilson Memorial Committee" that exhumed Wilson's remains from an unmarked plot in North Carolina and returned them to Philadelphia. Alexander, alive to every opportunity to restore the Wilson name, witnessed the opening of Wilson's casket and saw, in a shapely jawbone, proof of Wilson's "strength and determination of character." Theodore Roosevelt's Attorney General said at a belated memorial for Wilson that it was "one of the mysteries of history, which I have not been able to solve, why his fame has not kept pace with his service."

Later Americans would attribute it to the paucity of surviving Wilson letters; some to his ignominious end; others to his chilly personality. My own answer is that the muses of history lay their wreaths on dash and symbolism—and Wilson didn't win wars like Washington, discover electricity like Franklin, draft declarations like Jefferson, frame banks like Hamilton, guide courts like Marshall, or dominate legislatures like Madison. His was peculiarly a life of the mind. He knew no greater joy than strolling in the light-filled groves of contemplation. In his labors to justify the United States Constitution by every fact of human nature and eternal order, Wilson was the closest the Founding had to an Aristotle. A role like that does not make for HBO specials, but no better man existed for the more enduring task of constitution-making.

James Wilson was born in 1742 on a farm in the shire of Fife in the Scottish Lowlands, a region of cold clear lochs, misty pastures cropped by shaggy Angus cattle, and uncommonly good education. By day, at grammar school, young Jamie studied Virgil and Euclid. By night, before a peat-moss fire, he parsed Latin sentences or listened to his father read from Calvin's Bible. At 14, Wilson began at St. Andrew's College, where he received, each morning, a half-loaf of oat bread and a pint of beer before tucking into a formidable regimen that included Newton's natural philosophy, Locke's psychology, and the epistemology of Francis Hutcheson, David Hume, Bishop Berkeley, and Lord Shaftesbury. He imagined himself as a future tutor, perhaps even a secretary to a lord, until he was lured by glowing accounts from Scotsmen living in America. He sailed for the New World in 1765, but not before becoming the only founder known to golf.

Wilson made his way to Philadelphia, full of coffeehouses and clean streets, whose inhabitants, wrote Washington Irving, were a "uniform, straightforward, clockwork, clear-headed, one-like-another, salubrious, upright, kind of people, who always go to work methodically, never put the cart before the horse, talk like a book, walk mathematically, never turn but in right angles, think syllogistically, and pun theoretically." Perfect, in other words, for James Wilson. He was convinced that we inhabited a rational, balanced universe and that truths about it could be discovered in his overflowing library. He undertook to learn the law, filling notebooks with doctrines of English and ecclesiastical law, legal forms, and maxims from Cicero. He steeped himself in the great common-law writers like Coke, Kames, Bracton, and Hale, and devoured treatises on constitutions and governments.

Soon he struck out for Reading, a town of 1,000 people and 31 taverns, and later moved further west to Carlisle, a frontier of endless land litigation. Wilson grew prosperous handling property disputes—80% of the average colonial lawyer's practice—and his income was augmented by his marriage to an heiress named Rachel Bird. His devout Calvinist mother wrote, with alarm, at his temporal success. By 1775, with the revolutionary movement at white heat, Wilson recruited farmer-battalions before being sent, that May, with Benjamin Franklin, to the Continental Congress, where Wilson served through much of the chaotic 1780s. Wilson began as a moderate, writing a report calling for a return to lawful

British rule. But in July 1776, he broke the Pennsylvania delegation's tie in favor of declaring independence. America cast out into an unmapped, shoreless sea, without a constitution.

There are certain eras in history when the hesitant human race bursts forth into a period of achievement and creativity so magnificent that it exceeds the combined centuries preceding it. To a golden roll that includes Athens under Pericles, Florence under the Medici, England under Elizabeth, comes, I believe, Philadelphia in the 1770s and 1780s, under the American rebels. The era's culminating event was the Constitutional Convention held in Philadelphia in summer 1787, on the eleventh anniversary of the start of the Revolution. When Wilson, now 44, learned that the brightest lights from the continent were to assemble at the Pennsylvania State House, blocks from his home, it must have seemed to him the moment he had been preparing for his entire life: a chance to design a government on "pure" and "correct" principles, to use two favorite Wilson adjectives.

The Convention began with 55 mostly eminent statesmen, the majority planters, merchants, and lawyers by trade, deliberating in secret, voting by state delegation, and gathered, as Virginia's Edmund Randolph said as it began, with the mission of "preventing the fulfillment of the prophecies of the American downfall." These reformers ranged from confident nationalists who lived in large states like Wilson and Virginia's James Madison, to small-state skeptics like Oliver Ellsworth of Connecticut or William Paterson of New Jersey, who thought, as Ellsworth said, that men like Wilson, in their proposals for a bold new constitution, were "razing the foundations of the building when we need only repair the roof." Some kept a sphinxlike silence, like George Washington. Others, like Elbridge Gerry of Massachusetts, kept up a tense, irritating hand-wringing. And Benjamin Franklin kept up spirits with his disarming wit, at one juncture observing that a failure to include a power to impeach presidents left assassination as the sole method of premature removal. Over a hundred increasingly trying days, in a room cozy enough for conversational voices, but also often sweltering and fly-swarmed, the delegates took some 500 votes on all aspects of a government.

By 1787 Americans had more experience writing constitutions than any other society in history. Seventeen such charters had been adopted in the previous decade; some 20 Philadelphia delegates helped write their states' constitutions. In this specialized art, Wilson struck fellow delegates in Philadelphia as practically unrivaled. "Government seems to have been his peculiar study," reported a Georgian delegate, "all the political institutions of the world he knows in detail, and can trace the causes and effects of every revolution from the earliest stages of the Grecian commonwealth down to the present time." Wilson, for instance, knew that the Holy Roman Empire gave its Diet powers of regulating coin, constructing fortresses, and preventing one principality from imposing tolls on another, or that United Netherlands could appoint and receive ambassadors, execute treaties, and raise armies. This helped make Wilson's influence on the gathering, in the words of Max Farrand, who compiled the Convention's records, "second to Madison and almost on a par with him," adding that in respects Wilson was "Madison's intellectual superior." Most of the delegates had views about what a proper government looked like, sometimes strong ones, but as V.S. Naipaul observed, a great many opinions does not necessarily add up to a point of view. Wilson, by contrast, helped guide the debate through his luminous sense of how the various pieces might fit together and what theoretical basis justified each one. He made 168 speeches during the debate, more than any other man save Gouverneur Morris. Most evenings, Wilson was back in his study, making notes from old friends like Cicero, Vattel, Montesquieu, Locke, and Burlamaqui.

The nearest the delegates had to a "party line" was an allegiance, shared almost to a man, to a philosophy known as the "natural law." The well-thumbed acquaintances of Wilson's study were members of this tradition. Their apostolic succession began in classical Greece and Rome, continued through the scholastic Middle Ages, and climaxed during the Enlightenment. The natural law's teaching is that, just as physical laws like gravity create uniformity in the material world, so, too, are there fixed facts of human nature that allow conclusions about rights like liberty and property that are as true in modern Wichita as in ancient Sumeria. The central fact of the natural law is human equality, which meant, as Wilson wrote, that "one man, equal and free, cannot be bound by another, who is no more." For most of history, he continued, the origin of legitimate political power was, like the Nile, considered mysterious or divine. But humanity at last discovered that no government is rightful unless founded on this sublime principle. In practical terms, this means that just government must rest on majority rule.

Wilson was a true believer in power to the people. A contemporary called him "enthusiastically democratic," which was less praise than caution about Wilson's radicalism. This conviction pervaded Wilson's performance at the Philadelphia Convention. Thinkers of the founding generation typically either feared the turbulence of the "masses," and so sought strong government to stabilize it, or feared the tyranny of government, and so embraced strong popular control to restrain it. Wilson was virtually unique in his simultaneous faith in majority rule *and* a muscular regime. During the debates, delegates like Connecticut's Roger Sherman or even Virginia's George Mason called for power to be as distant as possible from the herd, prone as it was, they implied, to dangerous stampedes. Wilson replied that free government, like a pyramid, could rise to noble heights, and be the most unshakeable of edifices, so long as it had the broadest base.

On most questions Wilson favored a maximum of equality and a maximum of popular rule. He wanted Senate elections by popular vote, and not, as the Convention eventually decided, through election by state legislators. In this view Wilson had some allies. But when he went further to propose direct election of the *president*, without devices like an electoral college, he stood practically alone. Wilson argued that the xenophobia in putting office-holding limitations on those born abroad gave the Constitution an "illiberal complexion" and discouraged "meritorious foreigners." He seems even to have gotten emotional when he disclosed the "mortification" he felt, as Scottish-born, at possibly "being incapacitated from holding a place under the very Constitution which he had shared in the trust of making." He opposed proposals to restrict the power of future western states, which frightened delegates as destined one day to outnumber the 13 original states.

Wilson's belief in the people's will collided, most fatefully, with the question that nearly broke up the Convention: whether representation in the Senate would be proportional to population, as in the House of Representatives, or by state delegation. Small states like Georgia and New Jersey and even tinier Delaware (whose population was not even twice that of the city of Philadelphia), feared that Pennsylvania, New York, and Virginia, awash in money, people, and prestige, would dominate the new government. So real was the suspicion that, in what seems to me the Convention's low point, on June 30, Gunning Bedford, Jr., Delaware's Attorney General, announced that small states, "[s]ooner than be ruined" by a new Constitution, would look to "foreign powers" for help. No one fought more militantly against the notion of representation by state than Wilson. He argued, sometimes heatedly, that it betrayed the sacred principle of equality. If Pennsylvania, he asked, with 431,000 people, had the same weight in the Senate as New Jersey, with 173,000 people, would this not make each man in New Jersey 2.5 times more than his Quaker State brother?

Wilson lost the fight, in the so-called "Great Compromise" that passed by one vote: the House would be constituted by population, and the Senate by two members from each state. But the imbalance Wilson identified was real, and it's far worse today. A California Senator represents 40 million; a Vermont Senator represents 625,000. A Vermonter, then, has 64 times more voting power in the Senate. California, Texas, and Florida, which together make up well over a quarter of the U.S. population, get six Senate seats. The smallest 31 states comprise another quarter of the population—yet have 62 Senate seats.

The delegates drew on many sources, from their personal take on human nature and readings in symbolic history—edifying each other regularly, for instance, about the fates of Catiline, Cromwell, and Caesar—but above all they jousted and persuaded each other by reference to their experiences in their home states. Wilson's Pennsylvania was particularly instructive. A quarter-century earlier, in 1776, Pennsylvania adopted an oddball constitution, the most radical in the colonies, with novelties like a twelve-man executive branch (operating like a present-day city council) and an annually chosen, single-chamber legislature that had to consist, as the constitution charmingly provided, of "persons most noted for wisdom and virtue." At the 1787 Convention, the fight over the executive branch, Wilson said, was the longest running. Delegates debated whether the term of office should be two years, or four, or seven, or even fifteen; they weighed whether officeholders should be eligible for reelection; they pondered the likely effects of election by the people, or by state governors, or by Congress. But especially fraught was whether the president should not be a "he," but a "they." Wilson was the first to move that the executive "consist of a single person." Madison noted a "considerable pause ensuing," as everyone looked to the reaction of Franklin, who presided at the 1776 Convention that invented the many-headed executive. Franklin observed that it was a "point of great importance and wished that the gentlemen would deliver their sentiments on it." This kicked off days of debate in which a single-person president was declared by opponents to be the "fetus of monarchy," and alternatives proposed, like a three-man executive with one representative from each of the northern, southern, and middle states. Wilson's single-president position won by a 7-3 vote.

In mid-July, not long after the great compromise, the Convention adjourned to let a five-man "Committee of Detail," as it was called, reduce the dozens of decisions made to that point into a working draft. Wilson was on it. The result was the prototype of our Constitution—a bit longer, and with much work still ahead, but there, in essence. It started with a preamble, and moved on to congressional, then presidential, and finally judicial powers. Wilson was the man most responsible for ensuring this architecture.

Many of Wilson's personal experiences in Pennsylvania made their way directly into the Constitution. To him we probably owe the clause that constitutionalizes the law of treason, the one crime specifically defined in the Constitution. Wilson's special interest here arose in 1778, when he returned from the Continental Congress to practice law in Philadelphia and found patriots bringing vengeful wartime prosecutions for treason. He decided, like Alexander Hamilton, and at considerable personal risk, to serve as criminal defense counsel for 23 men, saving all but four from the gallows. In one, Wilson, defending an elderly man charged with guarding gates for the British, pointed to a statute of Edward III, from 1351, that made an "overt" act the only permissible proof of treason. Wilson's antiquarianism did not save this client, but, in the Committee of Detail, Wilson had a chance to insert a provision that, after revision, would double the requirement of King Edward by requiring *two* witnesses to the same overt act. What we know as the District of Columbia was, for Wilson, also born of harrowing experience. In 1783, Wilson, back in the Continental Congress as a legislator, saw 400 unpaid soldiers, furious with the do-nothing body, mill outside the State House, hand around libations, shout obscenities, and point muskets at the delegates inside. A defenseless Congress appealed, pathetically, to the Commonwealth of

Pennsylvania for help. This persuaded Wilson and others that the new government needed a ten-square-mile "district" independent of any state's protection.

In the end, the Convention delegates were at once engaged in a raw power struggle and in prophecy about what institutional arrangements would best ensure a free and durable government. They balanced doctrine against experience, hope against fear, action against inertia, interest against interest, and creativity against risk of popular rejection. The final result differed from what any attendee imagined. Wilson, like virtually every delegate, disagreed with aspects of the draft. But he accepted it as a many-handed weave of compromises formed, he said, of "heterogeneous materials" in a spirit of "mutual concession." He had no reason to expect, however, that Pennsylvanians back home would be so filled with this spirit of amity.

❦

As soon as the Convention produced its draft, Wilson rallied Pennsylvania's Federalist forces—or "Wilsonites," as one enemy called them—to make his state the first to call for a ratification debate. An anti-ratifier accused Wilson's allies of tolling Philadelphia's bells for a whole day, after Congress transmitted the draft to the states for consideration, to "strengthen the deception" that Congress approved of it. Accusations of bad faith intensified, and Pennsylvania would in fact have the most bitter, violence-marred ratification debate of all. The main reason was that the Quaker State was particularly riven by class antagonisms. For a decade the "Republicans," composed of the Commonwealth's eastern mercantile and financial elite—Wilson among them—had warred for power against the "Constitutionalists," who tended to be Irish-descended, agrarian, and live in the state's west, especially past the Alleghenies. When ratification won in Pennsylvania, anti-Constitution rioters in Carlisle burned "James the Caledonian" in effigy, for want of ability, as some hoped, to secure the genuine article.

James Madison to the end of his days insisted that to interpret the Constitution, Americans had to look to state ratifying conventions—in places like Richmond, Boston, and Poughkeepsie—not to the Philadelphia conclave. "As the instrument came from them," he said of the Philadelphia delegates, "it was nothing more than the draft of a plan, nothing but a dead letter, until life and validity were breathed into it, by the voice of the people, speaking through the several state conventions." Wilson would come to speak not only for pro-ratification forces in Pennsylvania, but such forces everywhere. "I am bold to assert," he said in his "State House Yard" speech in October 1787, that the proposed Constitution "is the best form of government which has ever been offered to the world." This was the first public defense of the Constitution by a member of the Convention. The summary version of the speech became, according to historian Bernard Bailyn, the "single most influential and most frequently cited document in the entire ratification debate." Washington himself recirculated it, adding, in one letter, that Wilson was "as able, candid, & honest a member as any in Convention." The speech, in a sort of chain reaction, was reprinted in virtually every state and served as the crib-sheet for most subsequent pro-ratification arguments. (By contrast, the evidence of the influence of Hamilton and Madison's *Federalist* essays outside of New York, writes Pauline Maier, in her history of ratification, was "sporadic at best.")

One reason for Wilson's impact was that, in a national explosion of pamphleteering that threatened the nation with premature deforestation—essays so proliferated, wrote an observer, that many "are not read by either side"—Wilson's speech, in crisp, cool tones, confronted forthrightly the proposed Constitution's main vulnerabilities. These included the countenancing of a standing army ("I do not know a nation in the world," Wilson said, "which has not found it necessary and useful to maintain the appearance of strength in a season of the most profound tranquility") or the supposed desire to "annihilate" the states (Wilson replied, among other things, that there could be no elections for presidents or Senators without states). A prominent Pennsylvanian accused the "lofty" Wilson of deserving a well-known mob attack on his home in 1779—an incident that left six or seven dead and that was brought on by Wilson's defenses in the Philadelphia treason cases. Wilson was also charged with "despising what he calls the inferior order of the people," by critics unaware of how hard Wilson, himself the child of farmers, fought at the Convention, in private, to empower this people.

Wilson made the first major speech at the three-week Pennsylvania ratifying convention. He explained the struggle the drafters faced (in that very room) and later admitted his dislike, for instance, of Senate representation by state. Many objections to Wilson's positions proved hysterical, such as the fear that the Constitution "effectually abolished" civil jury trial or that it would destroy America's freedoms "until they shall be recovered by arms." On the other hand, some seem prescient, such as the suspicion that the federal plan contained "seeds" whose growth would one day cast a "deadly shade" over states, or the prediction that the Constitution would prove deceptively difficult to amend. As at the Convention, references of varying relevance were made to Montesquieu and Hume, Caligula and Nero, modern Denmark and Poland.

Charles Page Smith, author of a 1956 full-length biography of Wilson—the first, in fact, ever written—found Wilson painstakingly systematic in the ratification fight. Wilson noted, by number, every speaker's objections to the proposed Constitution and cross-referenced them with a master list. He produced entries like: "This government is and was intended to be an aristocracy. No. 34, 35, 38, 82, 115, 134, 148, 150, 151, 219." Each number represented an instance when the argument was asserted. Wilson was able to track the frequency of argument and expose contradictions (e.g., judiciary not sufficiently independent, judiciary powers too extensive). Wilson was a large, imposing man, at least six feet tall, stout and ruddy-faced, but with a forbidding demeanor and a tendency to bookish utterances. This struck some as an "aristocratic" bearing—one contemporary said he looked like he was "stooping backward." This made him a favorite target. One ally felt it necessary to explain away Wilson's "lofty carriage" as the result of an effort to keep his spectacles on his nose. "Lofty" was a word frequently applied at the time to Wilson: to enemies, it conveyed his supposed "dictatorial" manner and condescension, and to friends, it seemed to commemorate what they saw as his elevation of tone and thought. Wilson's scholastic reputation was so formidable that when an opponent—an Irish-born ex-weaver from the backcountry—successfully contradicted Wilson on a peripheral issue about jury trial in Sweden, Wilson's enemies gloated as far away as New York.

The sorest point of all in the ratification debate was the Constitution's lack of a Bill of Rights. Pennsylvania had almost a spiritual commitment to bills of rights, ever since William Penn, in 1682, had the honor of issuing North America's first one. Wilson insisted, in an argument that jars many today, that a bill of rights against the federal government was actually dangerous. It was impossible to enumerate *all* the rights people had, he said, and if an attempted enumeration of them was incomplete, "everything not expressly mentioned will be presumed to be purposely omitted." The central counterargument, made most forcefully by John Smilie, a leading Pennsylvania anti-ratifier, was that without a bill of rights, Americans had no "criterion" by which "it could be easily and constitutionally ascertained how far our governors may proceed."

Yet I think Wilson was correct that the Bill of Rights' first eight amendments—the ones dealing with individual rights—would come to be, in the minds of people and particularly judges, something like a complete catalogue. Today, a person challenging an act of the federal government will squeeze his claim under one of those eight provisions, without reference to some "unenumerated" right. Wilson, for instance, warned that special protection for the "press" (as the First Amendment would eventually provide) would imply power over publishing never given by the Constitution. Sure enough, these days, a newspaper is better off complaining about a tax not as beyond any taxation power but as an infringement of its freedom of speech. This is the presumption Wilson feared: instead of asking whether government *has* the power, we ask whether the Bill of Rights *withdrew* it.

Pennsylvania ratified second, after Delaware, but Pennsylvania was the first ratifying state that was large, populous, and divided. Doubters and waverers in later-ratifying states were heartened by Pennsylvania's victory (by a vote of 46 to 23). It gave ratification early momentum. Yet even with this boost, the Constitution narrowly made it in Massachusetts (187 to 168), Virginia (89 to 79), and New York (30 to 27). I sometimes wake in the middle of the night, in a cold sweat, with the terrifying suspicion that, had all states voted on the same day, nationwide, the Constitution would have been rejected. It seems entirely possible that if Wilson had faltered in Pennsylvania's forensic struggle, as Charles Page Smith said, anti-Federalist obstructionism (which was considerable) might have won a delay tantamount to victory. Wilson in Pennsylvania, then, was as indispensable as Hamilton was in New York seven months later.

As the new government took shape in April 1789, James Wilson wrote President-elect Washington to inform him, bluntly, that "my aim rises to the important office of Chief Justice of the United States." It was a profound disappointment when Washington chose John Jay instead and made Wilson a mere associate justice. Wilson unquestionably was a superior lawyer, but Jay was popular in New York (where the government first sat) and had served as a diplomat and spymaster during the war. These experiences well befit the captain who would steer the new judiciary out of port. Wilson also had one problem fast becoming the curse of his existence: crushing debt. Post-revolutionary men of means, nearly without exception, poured their free capital into land, since commerce was crippled in postwar depression and interstate rivalry and because manufacturing was primitive. But Wilson's over-investment was infamous. Benjamin Rush, the famed Philadelphia doctor, lobbied Vice President John Adams for Wilson as Chief Justice but felt that he had to acknowledge the "deranged state" of Wilson's financial affairs.

Foundational questions were inevitably the work of the Court's first years. In *Chisholm v. Georgia* (1793), the first constitutional case decided by the Court, Wilson wrote: "'The United States,' instead of the 'People of the United States,' is the toast given. This is not politically correct." Wilson was still trying to get Americans to see themselves as the nation's sovereign power. (The *Yale Book of Quotations* calls this the first recorded use of the phrase "politically correct.") Judicial opinion-writing brought out the pedant in Wilson. In *Chisholm* he managed to reference, to take just a sampling, Elizabeth I, the "justly celebrated Bacon," Columbus, Isocrates, and Hénault's "excellent chronological abridgement of the History of France." In his eight years on the Court Wilson only wrote about 20 pages' worth of opinions, but we have a sense of what type of judge Wilson was: unlike any other. I suspect that it was in contradistinction to Wilson's assaultive pedagogy that John Marshall formed his plain style, often requiring no authority more esoteric than what "every man finds in his own bosom."

The explosive question in *Chisholm* was whether a citizen could sue a state in another state's federal court. Governments, from an old English doctrine that we inherited, typically can't be sued, so on *Chisholm* really rested the question of whether the States remained "sovereign." Wilson and a majority of the Court's five justices said that states *could* be sued, pointing to a clause in the Constitution that seemed to allow it. Suits against states, many over war debts, began immediately nationwide. The roar of protest brought on the Court's first crisis. Georgia's lower house passed a bill providing that any federal agent who tried to enforce the Court's decision would be "declared guilty of felony and shall suffer death, without benefit of clergy, by hanging." The next day a constitutional amendment was introduced to immunize states from suits by residents of other states. In 1795 it was ratified as the Eleventh Amendment.

Other kinks in the new government's functioning received straightening in these early days. In *Hayburn's Case* (1792), the members of the Court bucked Congress's attempt to saddle judges with administering veteran pensions. Before the Constitution, judges had been looked on as "magistrates" able to perform non-judicial duties like census-taking. But the new justices felt limited by the Constitution to "business" of a "judicial nature." They told Congress, for the first time, that one of its laws was unconstitutional. "To be obliged to act contrary" to Congress's wishes, by striking down one of its laws, wrote Wilson and one other justice, rather prematurely, "excited feelings in us, we hope never to experience again."

⤜⤛

In 1791 James Wilson began a magnificent series of lectures that, in a career unjustly neglected, constitutes his *most* neglected achievement. The lectures, when compiled posthumously into a book, would comprise some 800 pages discussing virtually the entirety of American's legal fundamentals, from theoretical topics like the origins of society, to the federal government's practical workings, on to finer points regarding juries, corporations, and criminal punishment. The chapters on the American theory of government, in particular, are to my mind the best ever written. It was Wilson's ambition to displace, forever, William Blackstone, the British jurist whose brick-sized *Commentaries on the Laws of England* (1765–69) was then the *vade mecum* of English-speaking lawyerdom. Wilson felt that his lectures would be his masterwork. In attendance at the opening lecture—the first important law course under the new Constitution—were President Washington and Vice-President Adams, members of Congress (now reestablished in Philadelphia), state legislators, and sundry admirers.

In his lectures Wilson was ready to take on the canonical writers of the past in order to illuminate the character of our novel form of government and Wilson's bracingly optimistic view of it. Blackstone, Thomas Hobbes, John Locke, and Edmund Burke, as imposing a set of thinkers as one can find this side of 5th-century Athens, all believed that men and women created what we call "society" by surrendering some degree of their natural liberty in exchange for the security that government provides. Most delegates at the Philadelphia Convention probably shared this view. But Wilson saw this as an application of feudalism: obey the king in return for his strong arm. In fact it was a profound mistake, Wilson wrote, to see government and individual freedom as antagonistic. The simple reason was that we have *more* liberty under a government than outside of one. A government's laws restrict us, to be sure, he said, but every citizen "will gain more by the limitation of other men's freedom, than he can lose by the diminution of his own." He meant, for instance, that in the anarchic "state of nature," you are free to steal from your neighbor; but, then again, he is free to steal from *you*. Life without the security that government provides, as proven by the short, violent misadventures of cavemen or Mad Max, is one of unceasing fear. Today, those huddled in their homes in gang-infested Chicago neighborhoods where police dare not go do not, I suspect, feel liberated by this absence of authority.

To the contrary, claimed Wilson, we willingly accept this authority. In a characteristic passage, he asked why anyone would bristle at the thought of "obedience" to the law? Our safety is not endangered by such obedience, he said, because there is no greater security than to be governed only by laws that you helped make. Nor is our freedom infringed by obedience, he continued, for no man is free who lives in fear. An epigraph from Cicero, attached to Wilson's works by one of his sons, summed it up: "We are slaves to the law, that we may be free." Wilson's take on government cast its light, for him, on everything the state might do. To Wilson, legislation promoting "the arts, the sciences, philosophy, virtue, and religion" was not some external force imposing moral goodness on citizens, but the people choosing to bless themselves. Government is not a necessary evil, but a necessary good. If all men were angels, he might have responded to Madison, government would still be necessary.

The "genuine science of government," said Wilson, was still in its "infancy." But a thrill runs through his lectures in contemplating that it would be Americans who would work out the practical problem with popular sovereignty. This is that political power cannot be exercised personally in a population as numerous and dispersed as ours; there is no vast assembly ground for us all to congregate in and deliberate, constantly, on thousands of questions. The solution is to delegate power for a certain period, on certain conditions, to a certain number of persons—what we call "representative" democracy. Yet "[i]n the whole annals of the Transatlantic world," Wilson said, "it will be difficult to point out a single instance of its legitimate institution." England was no exception. Like us, said Wilson, it had three branches, but its executive branch was a king or queen whose power derived from "divine" election or inheritance, not a vote. The crown appointed the judges, so the judicial branch, too, was equally beyond popular control. The only place the principle of representation even began to show up was in Parliament. But one half of it, the House of Lords, was chosen by heredity or territory, and the other half, the House of Commons, was returned by an electorate no more than a sliver of the people. (In fact, less than a fifth of adult males.) Wilson admired details of the British system, for instance the law of William III that secured judicial independence through life tenure, which the U.S. Constitution borrowed. He just felt that England's lordly judges had little to teach us about peculiarly American innovations like the separation of powers, federalism, and a judicial power to invalidate laws.

The tone of the Lectures is dignified, engaging, and cheerful. Scarcely a lecture passes without quotation from the likes of Shakespeare, Lucretius, Aristotle, and Alexander Pope. Wilson wore his learning more lightly once he doffed his judicial ermine. The year 1791 also saw the publication of James Boswell's *Life of Samuel Johnson* and Thomas Paine's *Rights of Man*. For the 18th century Wilson's prose style is remarkably fluid and readable. He lacks the playfulness of Addison, the witty snap of Chesterfield, and the momentum of Johnson, but the Lectures nonetheless reflect Wilson's piercing clarity. He could also turn a phrase. On kings: "In the attempt to make one person more than man, millions must be made less." On unity: "[U]nion is a benefit, not a sacrifice." On separation of powers: "The legislature, in order to be restrained, must be *divided*. The executive power, in order to be restrained, should be *one*."

That last quote sounds like something out of the *Federalist*. The joint authority of Hamilton and Madison will always overshadow Wilson, but their respective works are hardly competitors. The *Federalist* moves in quick, polemical strokes. Wilson, by contrast, invites us on a sunny, pleasing journey, calmly sailing over time and space, examining man, society, and equality. Law, at its best, was for him not a compromise between jangling interests but a faint terrestrial echo of a universal symmetry. Where *Federalist* #51 saw ambition checked by ambition, Wilson saw generosity aided by generosity. Even something as mundane as presidential appointments, Wilson felt, could act like a "fragrant and beneficent atmosphere" and "diffuse sweetness and gladness around those, to whom they are given."

Wilson's erudition allowed him a steady flow of amusing illustrations. A typical sentence might condemn New York State for requiring judges to retire at age sixty, when, he notes, the Spartans deemed no man fit for high office *until* sixty. He mocks timidity about new legislation by recalling that the ancient Locrians required a citizen who wished to propose a law to appear before the assembly, with a cord around his neck, and explain his reasons; if those reasons were found wanting, he was instantly strangled. He finds that the Privileges and Immunities Clause in Article IV of our Constitution nicely imitates Rome's easy and generous incorporation of foreigners—a policy, Wilson was quick to add, also approved by Francis Bacon and Machiavelli. (Before ratification, the Pennsylvania legislature printed 2,000 copies of the draft Constitution in English—and 1,000 in German.)

But Wilson's most peculiar principle came not from England, but Scotland. His education was perfectly timed to follow the flowering of the Scottish Enlightenment. This saw Hutcheson, Hume, Adam Smith, and others make Edinburgh and Glasgow the most interesting intellectual centers in the West for a generation. But for Wilson, above all, stood Thomas Reid, the philosopher and father of the "Common Sense" school of philosophy. Wilson took from Reid the fascinating notion that we possess a sort of sixth sense, called the "moral sense," that lets us detect right and wrong as immediately as our eyes register light and dark or as unerringly as our tongue distinguishes bitter from sweet. We simply *feel* right and wrong, Wilson wrote, "in a manner more analogous to the perceptions of sense than to the conclusions of reasoning." For example, he asked, when a feeling of resentment, pride, or shame swells up within you, do you really have to *think* about why you feel that way, or is the sensation instinctive and instantaneous? Modern science goes far to confirm this 18th-century intuition about moral hardwiring. A Brazilian neuroscientist recently identified a part of the brain that flares when it hears particularly of moral offenses, like punishing an innocent. This view of a "moral sense" pervaded Wilson's thought and led him to an embrace of man that made him unlike world-weary grumblers around him, muttering of human folly and frailty. Wilson's unusual constitutional psychology moved him to predict that, one day, civilization would acknowledge that "mankind are all brothers," and act like it. Until then, he admonished Americans to observe justice toward Indians, receive foreigners of good character as citizens, protect the rights of conscience, and work to improve the minds of citizens.

This last concern—citizens' character—was a Wilson preoccupation. He liked to remind Americans that self-government not only *gave* us more than any other government, but it *required* more of us, too. In an oration celebrating the Constitution's adoption, Wilson told a sea of Philadelphians, ship cannons firing in the distance: "In battle, every soldier should consider the public safety as depending on his single arm; at an election, every citizen should consider the public happiness as depending on his single vote." A citizen had to exercise his rights, he implied, or others would, on his behalf—politicians, judges, bureaucrats. This is why the law, in its rudiments, had to be the concern of all. "There is not in the whole science of politics a more solid or a more important maxim than this," he wrote, "that of all governments, those are the best, which, by the natural effect of their constitutions, are frequently renewed or drawn back to their first principles." And if, heaven forbid, our constitutional culture were ever corrupted, the end would be near: "For a people wanting to themselves, there is indeed no remedy."

❧

In 1795 and 1796, Wilson was twice more passed over for Chief Justice. Washington may have been right to suspect that Wilson's financial entanglements might impede his service on the Court. Wilson made business deals while riding circuit and sought to reroute judicial travel to coincide with these dealings. Wilson's disappointment in being denied the coveted post was immense, but not fatal. The same cannot be said of his speculations, especially those in land. Wilson had at times controlled millions of acres. In the mid-1790s a scheme that he developed to attract Europeans makes him, so far as I can tell, the first American master-plan developer. He imagined immigrants conveyed to a "house already built, a garden already made, an orchard already planted, a portion of land already cleared, and grain already growing or reaped," all to let them start anew without risk of starving first. He was honest but overextended. Through the late 1790s he worked feverishly to hold together his flimsy empire. "The only difference between George Washington's speculations and Wilson's," says scholar Richard Samuelson, "was that Washington's were successful." Plus Wilson, unlike Washington, did not own slaves to keep him afloat. The panic of 1796 finally ruined him. But until that time Wilson had been one of the wealthier men in America, on paper at least.

Now judgments from creditors piled up; men began to wonder openly about how long he would avoid arrest. It finally came in 1797. By then his larder was empty, his rent was in arrears, and his tailor refused to supply his beloved children with new clothes. Benjamin Rush observed that the man who once made Cicero and Coke his daily study now stupefied himself with novels. He died in August 1798, aged 55, haggard and hounded, in a bleak inn in North Carolina, where he fled to avoid creditors. He owed former Convention-mate Pierce Butler alone some $197,000 — millions today. Wilson's failing was less a moral one — he did not cheat anyone, for instance — than a tragedy born of Wilson's congenital enthusiasm, a good deal of greed, and an era of economic instability. Over time he convinced himself that his land ventures assisted in the great unfurling of American life and law over the continent; he felt that he could serve his pocketbook and patriotism together. Wilson was in fact just one of ten of the 55 delegates to Philadelphia in 1787 who met calamity in financial distress or bankruptcy.

James Wilson, unlike most of the heroes of his library, was able to submit his principles to the probation of practice. Yet the strain of real politics did not weaken his faith in the people's wisdom, as they did for so many others at the Convention. Where skeptics sought a government that diffused the people's dangerous "democratical" spirit, Wilson embraced that spirit. His faith in Americans' love of law and our good character led him to advocate government as a common enterprise guided by a moral people, not government solely as the balance wheel of a multiplicity of hostile interests, always at each other's throats. Madison is Wilson's only rival to the title of the Convention's philosopher. But in remarkable respects, later generations would deliver victory to Wilson in fights that he lost in his own time. Wilson imagined that we would one day have the sort of president who soared above faction, a "man of the people," in his words. The Seventeenth Amendment, in 1913, belatedly vindicated

Wilson's plea for Senate elections by popular vote, not by state legislators. When he opposed restrictions on western states, he evinced a belief that, however uncouth and unschooled, men were never to be ruled without their consent. Wilson's writings are virtually free of aspersions about mobs, even though one had almost murdered him. Wilson held fast to a faith in the mass of people to erect for themselves a house of order, dignity, and happiness. It was, in part, Wilson's Reidian belief in man's moral sense—the inner constitution, written on the soul itself—that gave him this confidence. Man is not wolf to man, or at least not merely so, for a divine light, as sure as sight and sound, guides us. This instinct also convinced him that one day Americans would turn themselves to the "great principles of humanity" and liberate America's slaves.

Wilson's stamp on the Constitution lives on in one last beautiful way. The opening line of the draft Constitution at one point ran, "The people and the states of New Hampshire, Massachusetts, Rhode Island," and so on. Wilson, in the Committee of Detail—I think quite deliberately—changed "the people and the states" to "the people *of* the states," and prefixed "we," so that it came to read, in yet another draft, "We, the people of the states. . . ." One final tweak (probably by Gouverneur Morris) produced the immortal opening of "We the People." "[T]he force of the introduction to the work must by this time have been felt," said Wilson of these three clarion words and the Preamble, at the Philadelphia ratifying convention. "It is not an unmeaning flourish. The expressions declare, in a practical manner, the principle of this Constitution."

It is fitting that Wilson was born abroad, since the "People" he envisioned was never a matter of blood or land, but of principle and character. Wilson believed that he was acting for the "citizens who in future ages shall inhabit the vast uncultivated regions of the continent." But he glimpsed even more distant horizons. "By adopting this system," wrote Wilson, "we shall probably lay a foundation for erecting temples of liberty in every part of the earth." So they did, at least in imitation, even 200 years later, in the preambles of constitutions worldwide: "We, the people of Mongolia" (1992); "We, the Polish Nation" (1997); "We, in the name of the Tunisian people" (2014). History was being made right in front of James Wilson and he marveled, on the first Fourth of July under the Constitution, in 1788, at what had been achieved: "A people free and enlightened, establishing and ratifying a system of government, which they have previously considered, examined, and approved! This is the spectacle, which we are assembled to celebrate; and it is the most dignified one that has yet appeared on the globe."

FIGHTERS

1814–1897

Daniel Webster

3

DANIEL WEBSTER

The First Generation after the Founders

O n July 4, 1828, a 90-year-old Charles Carroll, the last
surviving signer of the Declaration of Independence,
turned the first spadeful of earth in the construction of
the Baltimore & Ohio Railroad. "I consider this among the most important acts of my life," he told the crowd, "second only to my signing the
Declaration of Independence, if even it be second to that." But to Daniel
Webster, then a mostly unknown, middle-aged United States Senator
from Massachusetts, both acts were part of one grand, unprecedented
revolution. "[We] proceed with a sort of geometric velocity," Webster
wrote, "accomplishing for human intelligence and human freedom more
than had been done in fives or tens of centuries preceding." Webster's life
would come to stand for the proposition that if Americans honored their
founding principles, they were destined to a prosperity and greatness that
would stun the world—but that honoring those principles would take a
full complement of civic and moral virtues.

The America into which Webster was born, in 1782, was a Third
World country. So isolated was his family's dwelling in his native New
Hampshire, he recalled, that "when the smoke first rose from its rude
chimney, and curled over the frozen hills, there was no similar evidence

of a white man's habitation between it and the settlements on the rivers of Canada." His parents knew the frontier terrors of midnight Indian raids, gray wolves, and digging for potatoes with icy fingers. In 1813, when New Hampshire first sent him to the House of Representatives, the nation's per capita gross domestic product was still roughly that of Jordan's or Ecuador's in 2002. Small-town storekeepers kept accounts in shillings and pence, 50 years after the revolution, and it was still cheaper to ship goods across the 3,000 miles of the Atlantic than to transport them 30 miles by wagon on America's unpaved, stump-littered roads. We were a notably filthy people, too. In 1832 a New England doctor could still complain that four out of five of Webster's constituents did not bathe from one year to the next. Not that doctors, for their part, had much to boast of. As Webster lay ill in his final days, the diagnosis by one of Boston's leading physicians was that the statesman had a "mortal disease in some one of the great organs of the abdomen, but that, after the most careful examination, he could not tell in which of them it was, with any considerable degree of confidence." He prescribed a regimen of all-purpose leeches and brandy.

Daniel's devoted yeoman father, Ebenezer, mortgaged his farm to send his son, at age 15, to Dartmouth College. Daniel wasn't a scholar—like most minds of the first order, he read by inclination, which ran to poetry and history. But a prodigious intellect was evident. There is a story that he once startled an instructor by memorizing, in one evening, 700 lines of Virgil. He soon turned to the law, but he found its dense, disordered treatises only marginally more stimulating than the plow. "A 'student at law' I certainly was not," he wrote, "unless 'Allan Ramsay's poems' and 'Female Quixotism' will pass for law books." On the other hand, actual court trials—some before judges first commissioned by George II—were a leading form of popular entertainment. Webster became a local headline attraction. A court crier in 1807 described one performance:

> When Mr. Webster began to speak, his voice was low, his head was sunk upon his breast, his eyes were fixed upon the floor, and he moved his feet incessantly, backward and forward, as if trying to secure a firmer position. His voice soon increased in power and volume, till it filled the whole house. His attitude became erect, his eye dilated, and his whole countenance was radiant with emotion. The attention of all present was at once arrested.

Webster was drawn from a smaller New Hampshire town to, finally, Boston. He went on to handle an extraordinary 1,700 cases over the next decade: will contests, murder prosecutions, debt suits, maritime disputes, and the rest.

If ours is the era of speechwriters and the teleprompter—a device, said Barbara Tuchman, that "allows an inadequate, minor individual to appear to be a statesman"—Webster's was the golden age of self-composed oratory. Citizens gobbled up extended disquisitions at rallies, dinners, conventions, funerals, barbeques, and parades. Preeminent were the high-toned gladiators who strode the floor of the United States Senate: the sparkling, cavalier Henry Clay of Kentucky; the intense, logical John C. Calhoun of South Carolina; and the blustery Thomas Hart Benton of Missouri, whose voice supposedly shook windows. But no speaker, contemporaries universally agree, mesmerized like Daniel Webster. "[T]o have heard the noble effort [Webster] made... marked an epoch in the lives of those present," wrote Josiah Quincy, Jr., a future mayor of Boston, after he saw Webster defend a judge against impeachment in 1821. "It gave me my first idea of the electric force that might be wielded by a master of human speech." Webster's serious efforts typically ran well over two hours, sometimes as long as four. "I was never so excited by public speaking before in my life," said George Ticknor, a friend of Webster's, after hearing a speech on the Pilgrims: "Three or four times I thought my temples would burst with the gush of blood," he continued. "When I came out, I was almost afraid to come near to him. It seemed to me as if he was like the mount that might not be touched and that burned with fire."

Other observers also reported something otherworldly about Webster. If you encountered him at night in some solitary place, wrote the *New York Mirror*, you wouldn't know whether he was "a demi-god or a devil." His hair was raven black and his skin so swarthy that in college people mistook him for an Indian. Thomas Carlyle, the Scottish historian, at a breakfast with Webster in London, was struck by his companion's "tanned complexion, that amorphous crag-like face; the dull black eyes under their precipice of brows, like dull anthracite furnaces, needing only to be blown." "There was a grandeur in his form," said another contemporary, "altogether beyond [that] of any other human being I ever saw." Webster's costume for important occasions was a black long-tailed coat with shiny gold buttons, white cravat, silk stockings, and a buff-colored vest—an ensemble already at least a generation out of fashion. He "moved through the streets of Washington and Boston," said Irving Bartlett, one of Webster's biographers, "like a revolutionary frigate under full sail." His eyes, large and sunken, appear in photographs less to gaze at you than to penetrate your thoughts. A minister recalled being unable to deliver a sermon when Webster, in the front pew, set "such great, staring black eyes upon me that I was frightened out of my wits."

What established the 36-year-old Webster's reputation as a constitutional lawyer was his four-hour argument to the Supreme Court in the famed *Dartmouth College* case (1819). The case involved a politically motivated attempt by New Hampshire's legislature to convert the private college into a public university under state control. Justice Joseph Story observed of Webster:

> There was a solemn grandeur in every thought, mixed up with such pathetic tenderness & refinement, such beautiful allusion to the past, the present & the future, such a scorn of artifice & rancor, such an appeal to all the moral & religious feelings of man, to the love of learning & literature, to the persuasive precepts of the law, to the reverence for justice, to all that can exalt the understanding & purify the heart, that it was impossible to listen without increasing astonishment at the profound reaches of the human intellect.... When Mr. Webster ceased to speak, it was some minutes before anyone seemed inclined to break the silence.

It resembled religious inspiration, and, for Webster, it was, the Constitution his holy text and George Washington his god. His father Ebenezer, a captain during the Revolutionary War, had personally guarded the General's tent after Benedict Arnold's betrayal. "Captain Webster," Washington supposedly said, "I believe I can trust *you*." Nothing made Daniel Webster prouder.

His generation was the first to follow the founding generation, and he once said of these predecessors that he acted "as if I could see their venerable forms bending down to behold us from the abodes above." A number of founders in fact had beheld Webster, on earth. Webster was a child when Alexander Hamilton arranged America's finances and Webster later had Aaron Burr as a client. He spent five days at Monticello, marveling at an 81-year-old Thomas Jefferson's "fixed hours for everything." Webster regularly called on John Adams when he passed through Quincy. He entered Congress under James Madison—the "wisest of our Presidents," Webster said, after George Washington—even though Webster's first official acts included harsh denunciations of "Mr. Madison's War" against Great Britain.

What made Webster nationally famous was his rejection of the claim, made by Southerners, that when Congress overstepped, states had power to "nullify" federal law—to arrest the operation of federal law—in supposed conformity with the Constitution. Webster debated the issue in 1830 against South Carolina Senator Robert Hayne. Afterward Madison wrote Webster to endorse Webster's "overwhelming" arguments, which must have been gratifying to Webster, since both Hayne and Webster claimed Madison's imprimatur in their clash. The fight began over whether South Carolina could stop the enforcement, within the state, of Congress's protectionist tariffs (which hurt cotton). It soon grew into an existential debate over the nature of our dual state–federal governments. Hayne claimed that every state had the right "to judge of the violations of the Constitution on the part of the federal government, and to protect her citizens from the operation of unconstitutional laws." Webster's reply was so anticipated that Senators in the packed chamber chivalrously yielded their floor seats to women. Friends the evening before found a calm Webster at home, assuring them that he would "grind" Hayne "as fine as a pinch of snuff."

Webster recalled of the speech he made, later known as the "Second Reply to Hayne": "I felt as if everything I had ever seen, or read, or heard, was floating before me in one grand panorama, and I had little else to do than to reach up and cull a thunderbolt, and *hurl* it at him!" A Southern Senator approached Webster immediately afterward and said, "Mr. Webster, I think you had better die now, and rest your fame on that speech." "You ought not to die," said Hayne, overhearing. "A man who can make such speeches as that ought never to die." Webster's address said the question Americans faced was: "Whose prerogative is it to decide on the constitutionality or unconstitutionality of the laws?" If all 24 states individually could decide for themselves what federal law to allow, or not, he continued, it was useless to speak of a national government. In his view the people had created a federal government and gave to the federal Supreme Court, alone, the power finally to judge between the states and the national government on questions of constitutionality. Webster closed in famous peroration:

> When my eyes shall be turned to behold for the last time the sun in heaven, may I not see him shining on the broken and dishonored fragments of a once glorious Union; on States dissevered, discordant, belligerent; on a land rent with civil feuds, or drenched, it may be, in fraternal blood! Let their last feeble and lingering glance rather behold the gorgeous ensign of the republic, now known and honored throughout the earth, still full high advanced, its arms and trophies streaming in their original luster, not a stripe erased or polluted, nor a single star obscured, bearing for its motto, no such miserable interrogatory as "What is all this worth?" nor those other words of delusion and folly, "Liberty first and Union afterwards"; but every-where, spread all over in characters of living light, blazing on all its ample folds, as they float over the sea and over the land, and in every wind under the whole heavens, that other sentiment, dear to every true American heart—Liberty *and* Union, now and forever, one and inseparable!

Webster's son Fletcher afterward wrote him: "I never knew what the Constitution really was, till your last short speech. I thought it was a compact between the states."

Webster had a simple political philosophy: America's glory hinged on fidelity to the "principles of the Revolution." "The great trust now descends to new hands," he told a crowd that included war veterans of 1776, at the 1825 dedication of Boston's Bunker Hill Monument.

> We can win no laurels in a war for independence. Earlier and wor-thier hands have gathered them all. Nor are there places for us by the side of Solon, and Alfred, and other founders of states. Our fathers have filled them. But there remains to us a great duty of defense and preservation.

He was a forward-looking reactionary. This unusual political cast is possible in the first generation after a founding.

Another speech demonstrated the spiritual intensity of his consciousness of the past:

> By ascending to an association with our ancestors; by contemplating their example and studying their character; by partaking their sentiments, and imbibing their spirit; by accompanying them in their toils; by sympathizing in their sufferings, and rejoicing in their successes and their triumphs, we seem to belong to their age, and to mingle our own existence with theirs. We become their contemporaries, live the lives which they lived, endure what they endured, and partake in the rewards which they enjoyed. And in like manner, by running along the line of future time, by contemplating the probable fortunes of those who are coming after us, by attempting something which may promote their happiness, and leave some not dishonorable memorial of ourselves for their regard, when we shall sleep with the fathers, we protract our own earthly being, and seem to crowd whatever is future, as well as all that is past, into the narrow compass of our earthly existence.

This sentimentalism was the secret resource in Daniel Webster's soul. He not only said these things; he felt them. This cause was enough to keep him working twelve-hour days well into his 60s. It fortified him to leave behind, for months at a time, his working farm south of Boston, eventually 1,400 acres in size, called Marshfield (his oxen, he said, were "better company" than Senators), and to deprive himself of his favorite pastime, fishing in New England streams with Shakespeare in his pocket. He continued to serve in office even though it forced him to forego immense lawyers' fees that, later in life, he desperately needed to pay massive debts. Ambition surely was part of Webster's story. But there must be something more to explain the position he took, in 1850, that, as he himself suspected, might forever damn his standing in history.

This was his support in Congress for the "Compromise of 1850." Webster's legacy never recovered from it. That bargain sought, essentially for the last time, to alleviate the sectional tensions over slavery. The North accepted a strengthened fugitive-slave law, and the South, in return, agreed to a free California, a tamed Texas, and a ban on the slave trade in the District of Columbia. Some of Webster's admirers saw a courageous act of union-mindedness and reconciliation. "I wish to speak today," Webster said in his speech defending the compromise, "not as a Massachusetts man, nor as a Northern man, but as an American." But anti-slavery forces, nowhere stronger than in Massachusetts, saw Judas in a cravat. Webster's apostasy, fumed Theodore Parker, the Transcendentalist minister, was a craven "bid for the Presidency." The mystery, however, is that at the Whig Convention two years later Webster got not a single Southern ballot. Many historians chalk up Webster's stance as an instance in which a shrewd politician, despite 40 years in politics, miscalculated. But what seems to me more likely is that Webster really believed that heading off a civil war required the bargain, however repulsive.

Webster never failed to denounce slavery as one of the "greatest evils." "I hear the sound of the hammer," he said. "I see the smoke of the furnaces where manacles and fetters are still forged for human limbs." On a few occasions he purchased slaves their freedom. In thousands of pages of his writings one does not find a word of racial prejudice. What you do find is a sincere belief that an attempt by Congress to strike at slavery would, as he said, "break up the Union just as surely as would an attempt to introduce slavery in Massachusetts." He imagined, as had many founders, that if slavery was prevented from advancing a single inch it would wither and die. But he insisted that if Northerners, in the meantime, ignored the Constitution's Fugitive Slave Clause—a shameful but real part of the document—Southerners would feel entitled to ignore the remainder of the Constitution. And, eventually, they did: the supposed "disregard" of this clause was precisely the ground on which South Carolina, in 1860, in its Ordinance of Secession, claimed a legal right to "dissolve" its "compact" with other states.

Webster labored under challenges that the hallowed forefathers had not. The debate preceding the Missouri Compromise of 1820—which admitted Missouri as a slave state, Maine as a free one, and barred slavery in part of the Louisiana Territory—revealed that the Southern men of Webster's generation had quietly become much more committed to slavery than their parents. Thomas Jefferson's famous sentiment in 1785—that he "trembled for his country" when he reflected on the injustice of slavery—would by 1850, in the South, have got him prosecuted for sedition.

The silky lords of the South loved their plantation palaces, their easeful existence and racial aristocracy. By 1840 cotton constituted 59% of U.S. exports. In South Carolina, half of the population was a form of property. No wonder, then, that Hayne and others fought emancipation as if their lives, or at least their lifestyles, depended on it. Webster, sympathetic in the 1830s, came by 1850 to regard the provocations of William Lloyd Garrison and other abolitionists as hasty, fanatical, and self-defeating. "[E]verything that these agitating people have done," he said, unfairly, "has been, not to enlarge, but to restrain, not to set free, but to bind faster the slave population of the South." Webster never forgave them for their unscrupulous rumor-mongering against him, philandering being the main charge, or the third-party presidential candidate they ran in 1844— James G. Birney of the Liberty Party—which cost Henry Clay the state of New York and thus turned over the White House to the pro-slavery James K. Polk, whose lasting achievement was to add Texas to the slave empire. And whom, Webster asked, did that help?

Webster was of course right to predict that these divisions would tear the country apart. His generation of Whigs tried to save the union through compromise; their heirs, the Republicans, accepted war when the compromises ran out. Yet many historians echo the hostilities to Webster of the New England abolitionists, even while these historians acknowledge that had war broken out in 1850, instead of 1861, the North would probably have been unable to resist a South splitting off into a sort of proto-apartheid confederation. Webster deserves better. His efforts to avert war, if nothing else, helped ensure that when Fort Sumter, in Charleston, South Carolina, was finally shelled and war begun, the North was more populous, more industrialized, and more zealous to extirpate slavery. Thirteen presidents held office during Webster's lifetime. A President Daniel Webster elected in 1836 or 1840 would have been only the third who did not own slaves, after the Adamses.

Robert Remini, in *Daniel Webster: The Man and His Time* (1997), attributes Webster's repeated failure to carry a presidential nomination largely to his overemphasis on imitating a George Washington–like loftiness. Webster thought that the ideal statesman had to be reserved, stately, unapproachable. Oliver Dyer, a Senate shorthand reporter, said that at times Webster "did not even look at the person introduced, but mechanically extended his hand, and permitted the stranger to shake it, if he had the courage to do so." This attitude was fatally out of place in the everyman-idolizing age of Andrew Jackson, where the masses, after ten presidential elections, had learned to feel their immense power. (No matter that Jackson himself was no glad-hander: once, irritated by the attention and crowding, he fled his own reception.) It was more a political pose than an expression of character. Webster, to friends, was known as a hilarious storyteller, an instigator of song medleys, and a hearty drinker (later in life, too hearty). He was also an affectionate father who for years kept a letter reporting that his son Charley, two years old, went around telling everyone that "Pa's gone to Wa'n to make 'peeches." Webster's friend Peter Harvey recalled that when Webster's first wife lay dying, in a friend's home, she told her husband that she preferred the wood fire they had at home to the coal one in her room. Webster, though a houseguest, hired a mason to remove the coal grate and have a wood fire built.

❧

  Aristotle's chief rule of rhetoric is that a speaker must match the mode of persuasion to the audience. In this Webster rarely failed. To a large crowd, he was soaring; to courts, logical; to juries, righteous; to Congress, driving. His youthful prose could at times read like a bad parody of grandiose Augustan poetry (he wrote of soldiers "chilled by the northern blast, their marches traced in blood") or simply be overlong. But the prose of the early 19th century was overwrought and highly ornamented; Webster, by contrast, took pains to develop a style that was taut, forceful, and precise. He studied Cicero, Shakespeare, John Milton, Alexander Pope, Isaac Watts, Joseph Addison, Edmund Burke, and the King James Bible, but his least forgiving teachers were citizen jurors, who taught him that you lose if you dazzle but do not persuade—a result best avoided, he learned early on, by speaking in a "plain conversational way." His secretary Charles Lanman said that Webster delivered "ponderous blows, leisurely inflicted." By this curious phrase he captured Webster's tendency to think in paragraphs, not sentences, which is why so few Websterian lines seem ripe for quotation. But at their best, his speeches are true American music: flags flutter and snap, waves crash in orderly salute on free shores, the rich machinery of a vast continental workshop whirs, clanks, shrieks, grinds, and hisses. Webster's finest tone, serene and majestic, was so internalized that even private letters are free of grudge and heat. "I war with principles, and not with men," he told his son Fletcher.

"Twentieth-century historians have shaken their heads over Webster's inflated nineteenth-century reputation, and well they might," writes Daniel Walker Howe, the dean of Whig Party historians. That Webster was right on most of the controversies of his day—the need for a national bank, the duty to stand with Greeks trying to shake off Turkey, the sin of Indian removal, the error of the Mexican-American War—seems ultimately to count for less than his inability to maneuver his way to legislative victory like the whiskey-and-poker Senator Clay or the fact that his loyalists clustered around Boston and New York City. Webster himself sensed that his legacy would rest on his literary productions. He also felt, at the same time, that these *were* themselves political achievements. When a speech rose to such power that it moved minds, he wrote, it is "something greater and higher than all eloquence—it is action, noble, sublime, godlike action." His speech on "First Settlement of New England" (1820), for instance, shaped the imagination of Northern schoolchildren for generations. "This oration," said John Adams, "will be read five hundred years hence with as much rapture as it was heard." Webster's speeches did for America of the crisis-filled 1830s what Winston Churchill's did for England of the crisis-filled 1930s: they sought to rally the deepest, best instincts of a people before a coming storm.

This is why Webster's supreme speech, in my view, is his 1833 exhibition usually given the title "The Constitution Is Not a Compact between Sovereign States." Superior to his more famous "Second Reply to Hayne," this 1833 speech was political scripture for unionists up to the Civil War. It was provoked when South Carolina, yet again, purported to "nullify" federal tariff laws. Congress retaliated with the 1833 "Force Bill," which gave President Jackson military power to enforce the tariff. South Carolina nullified *that* law, too. It was not mere rhetoric; a year earlier, South Carolina had raised 25,000 volunteer militiamen for the purpose of resistance. In his speech, Webster, with more refinement and vividness than his "Reply to Hayne" three years earlier, laid out precisely how destructive John C. Calhoun's doctrine that states could lawfully disregard federal law could be. One state, he said, might declare an embargo law unconstitutional and prevent its enforcement within the state. Another state might proclaim a tariff law illegal and seek forcible reimbursement of any tariff revenue. A third state, then, could announce its intent to ignore federal laws in protest of the actions of the first two. Calhoun's doctrine, to Webster, reduced the Constitution to a new Articles of Confederation, where one state could again impede the many on national questions. To start down this course, while denying that it would end in "dismember-ment," Webster said, was "to take the plunge of Niagara, and cry out that he would stop half-way down." James Madison again wrote Webster to thank him for a speech that "crushes" nullification and proved the talk of secession, increasingly thrown about by Southerners, to be nothing less than a call for "revolution."

These arguments in political forums, combined with his court vic-tories, made Webster the most influential practitioner of constitutional law in the first half of the 19th century and, pound for pound, probably the greatest in American history. When he first argued to the Supreme Court—he had only to slip downstairs to the Capitol's cramped basement to do so—the justices of the young court had barely begun to examine the Commerce Clause, corporate charters, bankruptcy, eminent domain, admiralty, patents, or copyright. Webster would argue 168 cases there, some while serving as Senator or as Secretary of State. Maurice Baxter, in his study *Daniel Webster and the Supreme Court* (1966), finds that Web-ster's legal legacy was to found a permanent jurisprudence in favor of the security of property rights.

In *Charles River Bridge v. Warren Bridge* (1837), for instance, he plead-ed for the encouragement of private capital investment, and in *Swift v. Tyson* (1842), he championed a uniform national law of commerce. *Dartmouth College* (1819) had ensured the place of corporations as largely untouchable creations of private contract, immune to legislative med-dling. Before that case, the few hundred American corporations mostly served religious or educational missions. But by 1830, there were 1,900 in New England alone, mostly devoted to trade and production. Web-ster's briefs were not mere templates for Chief Justice John Marshall's opinions, as Webster sometimes too casually suggested, but there was a partnership between the two cast-iron Federalists, both thoroughly political contenders against attempts to sap the power of the fledgling national government.

Today only militia-grade libertarians rejoice in the feebleness of the federal government as it existed in Daniel Webster's day. By 1821, after more than 30 years of operation, it still only had 6,914 employees, most of them in the Post Office. (Today it approaches three million civilian employees.) The case of *McCulloch v. Maryland* (1819) was another Webster–Marshall glory. Maryland had tried to tax the Bank of the United States, and the decision declared, in John Marshall's organ tones, that this could not be: the power to tax was also the power to destroy—a line, as it happens, taken from Webster's brief—and so the people of one state could not tax a bank that served the people of all the states. It was an American milestone on the road to federal predominance, but there were many more treacherous miles to go. Six months later, Ohio ignored the decision and enacted an illegal tax more punitive than Maryland's. In 1828, John C. Calhoun, while serving as Vice President of the United States, published a pamphlet describing a procedure he invented by which states could nullify a federal law. The President, John Quincy Adams, to unbend after overseeing an administration daily undermined by his own Vice President, took his exercise by swimming naked in the Potomac. There was no need to fear onlookers in the dismal, half-empty capitol. (Only a few years before a British diplomat reported "excellent snipe shooting" along Pennsylvania Avenue.)

Stephen Vincent Benét's short story "The Devil and Daniel Webster" features Webster winning over a jury composed of the ghosts of infamous men—stranglers, tyrants, pirates, all handpicked by Satan—in order to save a client who signed over his soul. Arthur Schlesinger, Jr., quipped that he could buy the stuff about the devil and the undead, but Daniel Webster, the supreme business lawyer, attacking the sanctity of a *contract*? Schlesinger was right that fiction remained stranger than truth. The American Revolution, Webster said, was "undertaken, not to shake or plunder property, but to protect it." It was the opposite of the later revolutions led by Jacobins, Bolsheviks, and Maoists. Webster saw the purpose of the United States in mercantile terms. "Commerce, credit, and confidence were the principal things which did not exist under the old Confederation," he argued in *Ogden v. Saunders* (1827), an important early bankruptcy case, "and which it was a main object of the present Constitution to create and establish." Webster's prose opens a vista onto a hundred thousand fields bursting in one colorful harvest; flatboats, sloops, scows, and schooners, in long sunlit glistening lines, churning white the Delaware, Hudson, Mississippi, and Ohio Rivers; clogged wharfs, bustling manufactories, merchant houses in New York and Baltimore vibrating like beehives with activity. New technology enabled this explosive commercial power. Steamboats, coming into widespread use, let men, for the first time in history, defy the current. These chugging vessels would evolve, like the first fish to crawl onto land, into railroads. On their newly laid iron rails goods would glide from state to state. Stock markets seized on Samuel Morse's telegraph, which, at long last, let humans across distances decouple the words they wished to communicate to each other from the physical object—paper, papyrus, clay, wax—on which these words had been written.

Stimulating commerce filled much of Webster's time during his two rounds as Secretary of State. Webster served first under William Henry Harrison—who died 30 days into his term, probably of fever, despite his doctors' determined application of castor oil and leeches—and later John Tyler, and finally President Millard Fillmore. "You have many productions, which we should be glad to buy," Webster wrote the Emperor of Japan in 1851, in a typical letter, "and we have productions which might suit your people." Webster believed, in what is a truism today, that international commerce prevents war by making the fruits of trade greater than the gains of conquest. A banker said that diplomat Webster, with his staff of four, "watched our commercial interests more closely and acted more promptly than our merchants themselves." Among the happier circumstances of Webster's life was that his politics coincided so snugly with the interests of his clients at the bar. Shippers, financiers, insurance houses, mercantile companies, and banks had made Webster, in the 1820s, probably the nation's highest-paid attorney.

President Andrew Jackson wheeled into Washington in 1829 in a carriage and rolled out eight years later on a train. This was a train Occupy Wall Street missed by 175 years. Old Hickory was their man: the impetuous bank crusher, the feared and unpredictable enemy of "money power," and a man largely above many niceties of constitutional limitation. (He also enjoyed wagering slaves on horse races and called abolitionists "monsters" who should "atone for [their] wicked attempt, with their lives.") The Whig Party, of which Webster was a pillar, arose in reaction to Andrew Jackson. "It is no matter of regret or sorrow to us that few are very rich," said Webster, in one riposte during his years of Senate opposition to Jackson's populism, "but it is our pride and glory that few are very poor." The word "millionaire" entered the lexicon around 1840, but it was false, said Webster, to speak of "classes" ranged against each other in permanent hostility; there were only Americans, rising and falling together. Webster knew that even unregulated banknotes were better than the absence of banknotes, which, wrote a historian of antebellum banking, meant throwing the people back on a "rag-tag mixture of foreign and domestic coins, land warrants, tobacco warehouse receipts, even animal pelts." Webster thought Alexander Hamilton's financial system "perfect" and that the "history of banks belongs to the history of commerce and the general history of liberty," since no free modern society lacks them.

Democratic presidents like Jackson, Madison, James Monroe, and James Polk had at times all doubted Congress's constitutional power to sponsor "internal improvements," the general term for the dizzying array of waterways, rails, bridges, harbors, bays, ports, ferries, canals, dams, and roads that Americans, sleeves rolled up, were eagerly constructing. But Robert Hayne, speaking for South Carolina's states' righters, offered a narrower vision: "What interest," be asked, "has South Carolina in a canal in Ohio?" It was a fair question in his day. But Webster had an answer: "In war and peace we are one; in commerce, one." The Whig Party was the political home of merchants, manufacturers, bankers, and believers in transformation through conscious economic planning, on both the state and federal levels. A study shows that Prussia contributed 7% of the capital needed to lay its first railroads; in the United States, by contrast, state governments put up 45% of initial railroad investment. The Erie Canal was begun on July 4, 1817, and, within a few years, floated twice the cargo of the Mississippi. Local papers marveled when fresh Long Island oysters appeared in western New York. All Americans, in the Whig view, benefited from this nation-building. "Do we ever hear," said Webster, "that because the intercourse between New York and Albany is advantageous to one of those places, it must therefore be ruinous to the other?" I suspect it would not have bothered Webster in the least to learn that the elegant brick building in Boston that he knew as the offices of Ticknor & Fields, legendary publisher of Nathaniel Hawthorne, Ralph Waldo Emerson, and Henry Wadsworth Longfellow, is now a Chipotle Mexican Grill.

Does Daniel Webster matter today? Polemics, however great, usually die with the circumstances that called them forth. This is true for Webster, most obviously, on the questions of slavery and the virtues of Union. Both were ultimately resolved as live, legal-political questions by the Civil War. But other political disputes that embroiled Webster remain as unsettled as ever, especially his arguments on the scope of the president's authority under the Constitution. These were laid out in a series of cannonades against Andrew Jackson between 1832 and 1835 and remain eloquent tutorials in republican order. On some questions Jackson prevailed, such as in his view that a presidential veto can be exercised not merely from policy disagreements but from constitutional objections, too. On others, Webster won.

He demonstrated that a president has no general power to decline to enforce laws of Congress simply because he thinks them unconstitutional. On this point, Jackson had claimed that his oath to "support" the Constitution meant supporting it "as he understands it, and not as it is understood by others," including judges. "If that which Congress has enacted, and the Supreme Court has sanctioned, be not the law of the land," Webster responded, "then the reign of law has ceased, and the reign of individual opinion has already begun." Some attempts by Jackson to establish that reign, in fact, had ugly consequences. Jackson, for instance, refused to enforce Congress's Indian treaties. When, in 1831, Chief Justice Marshall ordered arguments after Georgia sentenced an Indian to death for murder, the State of Georgia, emboldened by Jackson, ignored the court's writ and executed the man. That was a prelude to the Trail of Tears that occurred under the direction of the Jackson Administration.

Also of lasting value are Webster's legal arguments on the breadth of Congress's power under the Commerce Clause. These prevailed most notably before the Supreme Court in *McCulloch v. Maryland* (1819) and *Gibbons v. Ogden* (1824). It is no accident that those two cases were invoked twelve times in the briefs from both sides during arguments, in summer 2012, over President Barack Obama's Affordable Care and Patient Protection Act. "Almost all the business and intercourse of life," Webster argued in *Gibbons*, "may be connected incidentally, more or less, with commercial regulations." In this sentence Webster anticipated the endlessly vexing problem with the Commerce Clause. That clause gives Congress power to "regulate" commerce "among the several States." The framers conceived of it as a means to create an American free-trade zone among the states. But no congressional power, after decades of failed attempts to limit it, would have such overwhelming effect on the day-to-day lives of Americans.

Some of Webster's boldest arguments prefigure the holdings of the New Deal Court in the 1930s, but it was only in the late 20th century that the Commerce Clause became a plenary power for Congress to enact laws in any area touching, plausibly or implausibly, on buying and selling—including workplace discrimination, child pornography, or the black market in bald-eagle feathers. The swell of the federal government, which is the story of American government, might have staggered Webster, but not altogether have surprised him. The Commerce Clause could not avoid a more expansive construction as states integrated through roads, railways, telegraphs, and cross-border manufacturing. Today, even purchasing the *Collected Works* of John C. Calhoun probably involves a half-dozen states in various stages of editing, publication, payment, and shipping. Webster, in fact, hoped that "completely" internal state commerce might one day largely disappear. His campaign to build up the U.S. government gave him few occasions to speak, however, of the limits of federal power. That's *our* problem.

But even these fights occur within bounds settled by Webster. He killed nullification as a living theory. Bucking at the 2010 Affordable Care and Patient Protection Act, for instance, state Senators in North Dakota introduced a bill declaring that Obamacare's laws "likely are not authorized by the United States Constitution and may violate its true meaning and intent as given by the founders and ratifiers." That hesitant "likely" and "may" concede the truth of Webster's view that only the Supreme Court is empowered finally to decide a federal law's constitutionality. In South Carolina, the doctrinal demi-heirs to Calhoun and Hayne introduced a bill to "render null and void" Obamacare, but far from blocking the law, the bill just withdrew state participation in it—a very different, and wholly constitutional, response.

⊸≫✦≪⊷

Friends said that after his humiliation at the 1852 Whig Convention in Baltimore, at which he placed a distant third, Webster looked "sad and weary." Lower South hotheads had begun to squeak and gibber about a "Southern Confederacy." "To dismember this glorious country!" cried Webster—this was his nightmare. The Union was a "miracle," he insisted, and now it appeared that it would be his generation, the first after the framers, who would fumble it away. Webster had been declawed as a Supreme Court advocate after Jackson named six of the nine Justices, most of them hostile to Webster's positions. "I am tired of these constitutional questions," he told his son Fletcher. "There is no Court for them." Worst of all, family sorrows continued. In 1848, he buried his daughter Julia on the same day that he received the coffin of his son Edward, lost to typhoid fever while serving in the U.S. army in Mexico—deployed in a war Daniel Webster had strenuously opposed. He planted two weeping willows, side by side, and named them "Brother and Sister." Four of Webster's five children would precede him to the grave. Fletcher outlived him, but he was killed in 1862 at the Battle of Second Manassas.

Yet less than three weeks after Baltimore, Webster, now 70, returned to Boston and found himself greeted by roaring applause, fluttering handkerchiefs, and his portrait hanging from balconies. Mothers held up infants so that they might one day say they saw the great "Defender of the Constitution." Webster felt the rumblings of civil war, but his cast of thought in his final months was faithful to the young Webster. "This is the New World! This is America!" he had said, on July 4, 1851, the nation's 75th anniversary. "This fresh and brilliant morning blesses our vision with another beholding of the birthday of our nation; and we see that nation, of recent origin, now among the most considerable and powerful, and spreading over the continent from sea to sea." California had joined the union months earlier, and its rough adventurers, Webster said, already proved themselves more fit for self-government than Cicero's descendants in Italy.

By 1840 the U.S. population caught up with Great Britain's—some 17 million people. Webster saw 13 states added to the union while in office. He personally negotiated, while Secretary of State, the line between New Brunswick and Maine. His parents' generation saw their ships fall prey to European cruisers during the Napoleonic wars, but in 1850 Secretary Webster felt confident enough to tell Austria—which threatened us over our support for Hungarian independence—that the American republic was now spread over a region next to which the "possessions of the House of Hapsburg are but as a patch on the earth's surface." President Washington governed a country of 864,000 square miles; President Millard Fillmore now oversaw some 3 million. Ralph Waldo Emerson said that Daniel Webster was by the end of his life the "representative of the American Continent."

In 1837, on a tour of the west, Webster visited Springfield, Illinois, where he met a 28-year-old Abraham Lincoln. This promising young Whig had steadily absorbed Webster's lines about "the people's government, made for the people, made by the people, and answerable to the people," or how "if a house be divided against itself, it will fall," or that America is the "world's last hope." Lincoln thought Webster's "Second Reply" the "very best speech that was ever delivered." Webster is the link between Federalists like James Wilson, Alexander Hamilton, and George Washington on one side, and Republicans like Lincoln on the other, all believers in energetic national government and broad, confident readings of the Constitution.

Webster's great life-theme was that the inheritance enjoyed by Americans was the most noble and precious imaginable, but that we had to take care to transmit it unimpaired. His writings brim with words like "defend," "maintain," "uphold," "perpetuate," "support," and "preserve." "I profess to feel a strong attachment to the liberty of the United States," said Webster. "I feel every injury inflicted upon it, almost as a personal injury." Contemporaries attested to the almost physical transformation Webster underwent when pleading for the Constitution. But he needed conflict to energize him. This is why Webster's triumphs were all defenses: against New Hampshire's seizure of Dartmouth College; against Jackson's abuses of power; against Southern assaults on the Union. Once these attacks were made and Webster rose to the defense, he was nearly invincible. Not even his enemies seemed willing to deny this. This country never knew a President Webster because he was a creature of resistance, of preservation, of guardianship. He was fitted to oppose, not to direct. Yet when the fate of America depended on him, as it did in profound degree, he did not fail.

STEPHEN FIELD

4

STEPHEN FIELD
Civil War and Uncivil Justice

I f Herman Melville could spin out a half-dozen novels from a
few years of seafaring, and Samuel Clemens convert his stint
on a steamboat into an entire persona, then their contemporary, Stephen J. Field, best known today as the second-longest-serving
Supreme Court justice in history, was entitled to refashion his 15 years
as a Gold Rush lawyer into a lifetime of philosophy. His youthful experiences would make him one of the most uncompromising defenders
of the sanctity of property rights in the era of Vanderbilt and Carnegie,
supposing he had any rivals at all. But his is a reputation darkened by a
puzzling indifference to the other rights revolution of his era, the slow,
painful, and ultimately failed struggle to guarantee black citizens their
dignity under law.

In 1776, as America was declaring independence, Spanish priests and
soldiers were founding an outpost above an immense Pacific bay, later
called San Francisco, after Saint Francis, patron saint of merchants. These
two events united providentially in the life of Field, who, as a 33-year-
old attorney, sailed through the Golden Gate in 1849, if not exactly to
strike it rich, to provide legal services to those who might. San Francisco,
Field wrote in his memoir, was "strange and wild," a Babel-like bazaar of
exuberant gold-hunters from "every nation under Heaven," many living

in canvas tents on the city's sand-swept hills. It was the moral and geo-graphical opposite of his childhood in Connecticut and Massachusetts, under a brimstone preacher father (Stephen heard three sermons each Sunday) and mother whose name, "Submit," suggests something of the family's brand of Puritanism.

"I had always thought that the most desirable fame a man could ac-quire was that of being a founder of a State," Field said, "or of exerting a powerful influence for good upon its destinies." His first chance came when he sailed north to a primitive and yet-unnamed encampment just outside the Sierra Nevada foothills. Within minutes he acquired land on a handshake. If this colony of dreamers and wanderers was to succeed, Field told a few dusty bystanders, it needed a government to record deeds. The ambitious easterner stood for election the next morning. "The main objection urged against me," he recalled, "was that I was a newcomer. I had been there only three days; my opponent had been there six." But Field won and became the "First Alcalde of Marysville," an office under Mexican law, derived from the Arabic *al-qadi*, or judge. The unwashed prospectors and trailblazers chose "Marysville" as the town's name, to honor a Donner Party survivor hailed as the town's most beautiful woman, gallantly forgetting that she was also the town's only woman. Field was tall and trim, peering out from blue-gray, bespectacled eyes, in a surtout and frilled stock, already curating a long unkempt beard that would forever make him look like a miner with a Ph.D.

"I knew nothing of Mexican laws; did not pretend to know anything of them," confessed the new Alcalde, "but I knew that the people had elected me to act as a magistrate and looked to me for the preservation of order." A tale, perhaps tending toward the tall, has Stephen Field pre-siding in a whiskey saloon in a suit against suspected claim-jumpers. The assorted gamblers clear out for trial, then resume their card games when the jury leaves to deliberate, and then again vacate for the verdict. When the defendants lost, their lawyer took a frontier appeal, urging his clients to resist the verdict "at the point of the knife." Twenty revolvers, most of them drawn by jurors, suddenly glint in the parlor. But what impressed the crowd most was the conduct of the judge. Stephen Field

drew from his breast pocket an eight-inch Bowie knife, placed its back between his teeth, and from its holster drew a Navy Colts revolver,

cocked it, and placing its muzzle within six inches of the offending
counsel's head—hissed at him the command, "Eat those words, or
damn you, I'll send you to hell." The counsel meekly said "I eat . . . "
The judge then said to the two miners, "Jumpers, you are dishonest
men, this Bar don't want you on it. If you or your counsel are here
at sunrise tomorrow morning, you will never leave the Bar again—
Court is closed."

Field, the only law northwest of the Yuba River, grasped intuitively that the
security of property was Marysville's vital concern. Thieves were punished
more severely than murderers. He once had a stealer publicly whipped
(secretly hiring a doctor to be on hand) because, faced with a mob, it was
"the only thing that saved the man's life." If horses or pouches of gold
could vanish without prompt justice, the whole precarious system would
collapse. Marysville was thick with "desperate persons, gamblers, black-
legs," Field boasted, "yet the place was as orderly as a New England village."

⊸୨୧ତ⊸

The ancient Greek writer Hesiod, a contemporary of Homer, was the
first to posit the existence of a golden age before private property. His
myth was refined as a theory in Thomas More's *Utopia* (1516) and Jean-
Jacques Rousseau's *Second Discourse* (1755), and it failed spectacularly in
practice, in settings as diverse as Indiana's New Harmony and the Leninist
steppe. Generations of anthropologists, archaeologists, and historians
have hunted in vain for proof of a complex society where all goods were
owned collectively. They fail because humans, to put a fine point on it,
need a food supply, and this necessity led our hunter-gatherer forebears to
assert claims on specific territories, killing or frightening away trespassers.
Property claims intensified when humans settled down 10,000 years ago
to tend the soil, arduous work whose fruits, not to mention vegetables,
take time to mature. Some say that ancient Israel is the first country from
which we possess firm evidence of private land ownership. "Cursed be he
who moves his neighbor's boundary stones," commands Deuteronomy.
The Lord, it appears, is no socialist.

Neither is the typical American. John Locke's *Second Treatise* (1689),
the closest thing we have to a national theory of property rights, said

that private possession arose from two facts: first, the earth's offerings, in the beginning, belonged to no one in particular; and, second, man must preserve himself. So a red apple was free for the plucking, but once you snatched it—or "mixed your labor with it," as Locke put it—it was yours. The only obligation you had was to leave enough for others. "Nobody could think himself injured by the drinking of another man," Locke wrote, "though he took a good draught, who had a whole river of the same water left him to quench his thirst." Then one fateful day, Locke continued, mankind discovered a "little piece of yellow metal" and, lo, the age of enough gave way to an age of hoarding and war. Locke called the "wild woods and uncultivated waste of America" the world's leading example of the uncorrupted state of nature.

Gold Rush California stumbled through Locke's stages of development in about five years. In 1848, 5,000 placer miners were sifting California's icy Sierra streams. But by the ingathering's peak in 1853, 250,000 American, Australian, Chilean, Mexican, and Chinese jostled, sometimes murderously, among the pines and mineral fields. The astonishing thing is how quickly they rediscovered the wisdom of Deuteronomy and Locke. Property regimes called "mining districts" arose spontaneously. In Tuolumne County, for instance, a gold miner could stake a claim, by all means, so long as he didn't cordon off more than he could actually mine actively; his claim was generally marked simply by leaving his pick and shovels in the holes.

Before the U.S. acquired the California territory, in 1846, the Mexican government granted large semi-feudal ranchos, usually based on crude sketches of oak trees and rivers, to wealthy "Californios" who were supposed to guide the land's development. At mid-century some 700 of these men held about 13 million sun-drenched acres, some 14% of the vast terrain, perfect for cattle ranches or fragrant orange groves—all without appearing to put any of it to use. This problem confronted Stephen Field in two jobs that he acquired in his steady rise, first as a lawmaker for Yuba County and then as a justice of California's Supreme Court. The young Justice Field quickly got a reputation for blending English common law and his own sense of good policy in decisions that favored landowners over squatters. "There is something shocking to all our ideas of the rights of property," he wrote in 1859, describing a view that actually shocked very few locals, "in the proposition that one man may invade the possessions of another, dig up his fields and gardens, cut down his timber and occupy his land, under the pretense that he has reason to believe there is gold under the surface." Field knew how the German-born Swiss John Sutter—in fact Field's former client—had watched helplessly as his estate was denuded within days of the legendary Eureka moment in which gold was discovered near Sutter's mill. (Some intruders crept by night onto his estate and erected sheds using wooden screws, to avoid the hammering that would alert Sutter's patrols, only to claim the next day that they had been there all along.) Field saw that if property rights hinged on nothing more than the will of those who emerged upright from the melee, the richest veins of gold would go to the most brutal, rapacious, and well armed. Upholding the flimsy, suspect Mexican land grants was, in his view, still better than legitimating plunder.

Field also came to believe that in a legal order that guarded property rights, the rewards typically went to clever, audacious individualists. He imagined that their enterprises would carry society forward and, eventually, benefit all. Not least among these destiny-minded men was Field himself. He had sat for five and a half years as California's Fifth Chief Justice when his name reached President Lincoln through his brother David Dudley Field, a prominent New York Republican who, years earlier, helped escort the still-beardless Illinoisan to the podium at Cooper Union for a famous speech. Lincoln saw in Stephen Field a loyal and capable War Democrat, who gave Lincoln the opportunity to make a handsome bipartisan gesture as well as to link a turbulent California to D.C. through the appointment of the Supreme Court's first Westerner. Field joined the Court in 1863, a month and a half before Gettysburg. He found the capital a muddy camp swarming with officers, politicians, and camp followers. Confederate cannons were audible in the distance.

After the Confederacy surrendered at Appomattox, the proscription against secessionists began. In 1865, Missouri, a state that suffered some of the bloodiest infighting, declared that any person who had expressed "sympathy" with the rebels was forever disabled from work as a lawyer, preacher, corporate officer, teacher, or official. Meanwhile Congress barred any attorney from federal courts who could not swear that his Union loyalties never failed. In *Cummings v. Missouri* (1866) and *Ex Parte Garland* (1866), both of these laws were declared unconstitutional by the Supreme Court, with Field writing the decisions, his first major opinions as a justice in Washington. "The theory upon which our political institutions rest is, that all men have certain inalienable rights," he wrote in *Cummings*, "that among these are life, liberty, and the pursuit of happiness; and that in the pursuit of happiness all avocations, all honors, all positions are alike open to everyone." The decisions broke 5-4 on straight party lines—the antebellum Democrats, including Field, against the Republicans, who in *Ex Parte Garland*, for instance, insisted that Congress had the power to "prevent traitors [from] practicing in her courts." But it was not, for Field, a purely partisan decision. He was here introducing his lifelong project: to convert the Declaration of Independence's phrase "pursuit of happiness" into a functioning, if unwritten, clause in our Constitution, and serviceable to annul what he saw as unjust legislation.

As a young lawyer Field had been disbarred by a California judge with whom he had feuded. The terror of being legally denied the right to do the only thing he knew how to do had been the partial inspiration for a debtor-relief law that Field supported as a California legislator; the law exempted bankrupt miners from the forced sale of their tools to pay their debts. So long as you could work, Field seemed to think, there was hope. An ex-Confederate colonel told Field's brother Henry that as a result of *Ex Parte Garland* "my limbs were unbound." Field's argument in the case has deep philosophical roots. Shakespeare gave his best natural-law speeches to Shylock, a despised outsider who argued, in a Venetian court, against legal disability. "You take my life," Shylock pleaded, "when you do take the means whereby I live." What Field did was to constitutionalize the sentiment. He claimed that "pursuit of happiness" and "property" were legally synonymous.

Field's grandest exposition of this "right to labor" was his dissent in the *Slaughter-House Cases* in 1873. These cases arose when Louisiana banned all butchery in New Orleans for 25 years—except, that is, by a single company called Crescent City. A thousand meat-cutters, in a sort of early class action, denounced the new law as old-world monopoly. But the Supreme Court accepted Louisiana's claim that the law was a "health" regulation to keep slaughter's effluvium downstream. The butchers' challenge had been brought under the Constitution's Fourteenth Amendment, which had been introduced after the Civil War by Republicans above all to ensure that no state could abridge a black citizen's rights. The justices' real fear in the case, however, plainly stated by the

Lincoln-appointed Samuel F. Miller, was that the shiny-new amendment would "transfer the security and protection of all the civil rights...from the States to the Federal government." Actually, making the United States the final guarantor of such rights *was* what most Republicans wanted, since states had proved incompetent at the task. But a majority of the nine justices, every one of them born under Presidents Jefferson or Madison, still believed that states were the primary repository of protection for civil liberties. They were simply unready for a revolution in federalism that would reverse these traditional roles.

But not Field. He claimed, in his dissent, to see the "real character" of the Louisiana law in the fact that it made the *only* place to prepare meat—for 250,000 souls, in parishes covering a thousand square miles, for a quarter-century—a single building owned by a single company. What the government gives, he implied, it can take away, and in fact a decade later Louisiana did revoke the monopoly. Puffed up by this vindication, Field later delivered, in a case called *Butchers' Union* (1884), an annotated Declaration of Independence. It is surely a high point in the Supreme Court's 600 volumes:

> "We hold these truths to be self-evident"—that is, so plain that their truth is recognized upon their mere statement—"that all men are endowed"—not by edicts of emperors, or decrees of parliament, or acts of congress, but "by their Creator with certain inalienable rights"— that is, rights which cannot be bartered away, or given away, or taken away, except in punishment of crime—"and that among these are life, liberty, and the pursuit of happiness; and to secure these"—not grant them, but secure them—"governments are instituted among men, deriving their just powers from the consent of the governed." Among these inalienable rights, as proclaimed in that great document, is the right of men to pursue their happiness, by which is meant the right to pursue any lawful business or vocation, in any manner not inconsistent with the equal rights of others, which may increase their prosperity or develop their faculties.

Field quoted Adam Smith, long an oracle for Field, who had written that the "patrimony of the poor man lies in the strength and dexterity of his own hands, and to hinder his employing this strength and dexterity in what manner he thinks proper, without injury to his neighbor, is a plain violation of this most sacred property." Field, like his brethren, would not include among these lawful vocations female lawyering (*Bradwell v. Illinois*, 1872) or liquor distillation (*Bartemeyer v. Iowa*, 1873), but ever sensitive to property rights, Field alone objected in *Mugler v. Kansas* (1887) to part of a dry law that let officials destroy bottles and utensils that were used in illegal distillation. His ground of dissent was that these items could be repurposed for, say, medicine. For Field, it was just another application of the principle behind the California law that guaranteed that whatever else creditors took from a broken miner, they left his tools, and his shot at recovery.

Field was a lonely character on the Court. Between 1873–87 he was one of only two Democrats. (The other was the incomprehensible, Buchanan-appointed doughface Nathan Clifford.) Almost by necessity, then, Field pioneered the use of concurrences and dissents to self-consciously frame a body of interesting but ineffectual shadow jurisprudence (much like Justice Clarence Thomas today). Other justices shared Field's views on the right to work, especially Noah Swayne, an Ohio Quaker, and Joseph Bradley, a New Jersey business attorney, as well as on railroads, like John Marshall Harlan, the Kentucky ex-slave owner. But Field's clarity and missionary zeal distinguished him from his colleagues on the Court of the 1870s and 1880s, a rather long-winded bunch that redeem themselves largely by their magnificent facial shrubbery, above all Morrison Waite's angry-pitchfork beard and George Shiras's sumptuous chops, the envy of every Bengal tiger.

It was during the Gilded Age, the years roughly between 1870–1900, that American capitalism matured into its modern form. In 1865 the spire of Wall Street's Trinity Church (where Alexander Hamilton lay) still overshadowed the merchant houses across the street. A Manhattan financier who made his fortune after the war recalled the time when Broadway was a cattle trail. The period from 1865 to 1898 was the longest stretch in U.S. history without an organized war (excluding Indian campaigns), and with nowhere to direct the massive industrial energies called forth by the Civil War—textile mills, foundries, shoe factories, lumberyards—the chief business of America became business. Rudyard Kipling, visiting in the late 1880s, wrote bemusedly of Yankee preachers who spoke with "imagery borrowed from the auction-room." There's an impressive roll-call of men born in the 1830s—Carnegie, Rockefeller, Wanamaker, Studebaker, Deere, Julliard, Pabst, Pullman, Swift, Hill, Gould, Morgan—who all came of ambitious age in the 1860s and '70s.

Stephen Field saw that these men were inventing modern corporations as we know them: publicly traded entities with thousands of employees spread across regions, and hierarchies of professional managers devoted to squeezing out better performance. Field also saw that resistance to their power came from the chief losers of the new industrial economy, namely farmers, still the largest single profession, but burdened by the need to sell simultaneously with neighbors, pressed by competition from abroad, and utterly dependent on railroads, the most fearsome new titans. Henry George, the economist who wrote the famous *Progress and Poverty* (1879)—an illustration of his theories led to the board game Monopoly—said that railways sought to "name governors, senators and judges almost as they name their own engineers and clerks." In an era before conflict-of-interest rules, Leland Stanford saw nothing untoward in serving both as the Governor of California and as the Chairman of the Board of the state-subsidized Central Pacific Railroad. His lobbyists operated a "museum," devoted to the railroad's glories, in the California capitol building.

The *San Francisco Examiner* in 1879 uttered what was already a cliché about Stephen Field when it blasted his "ardor to serve the great corporations." It is true that Field sided reliably (though not always) with big business. But his real ardor was for the *men* behind those companies: the farsighted risk-takers, like Leland Stanford, who had first hit it big in mining and grocery sales. These were men, in Field's view, who had, through personal efforts, enabled themselves to trade in their bandannas and jeans for frock coats and ribbon neckties. The Fourteenth Amendment guarantees due process and equal protection to all "persons," and when, in 1883, Santa Clara County argued to Field, riding circuit, that corporations were not "persons" under the Constitution, Field was practically scandalized. Behind every corporation, he said, a mere legal vehicle for holding wealth, were "living human beings whom it represented." Field was no social Darwinist, to invoke that much-overused term, nor did he care to link material and moral worth. But to attack corporations was, for him, to attack private property. Billions were invested in countless ventures, he wrote, an aggregate of wealth that "keeps our industries flourishing, and furnishes employment, comforts, and luxuries to all classes, and thus promotes civilization and progress." To annihilate capitalists, in the words of Yale's William Graham Sumner, then the Stephen Field of academia, "would be like killing off our generals in war." No one knew better than Field how comprehensively businessmen had sponsored the rise of his beloved Pacific empire. For Westerners in fact were "rugged individualists chiefly in their dreams," writes historian H.W. Brands. But outside of those dreams they were "likely to draw paychecks for digging in corporate mines, plowing corporate fields, or chasing corporate cattle."

Field was right that the Constitution was designed, within limits, to protect these endeavors from populist assaults. James Madison recognized that in our government the "real power lies in the majority of the community, and the invasion of private rights is chiefly to be apprehended, not from acts of government contrary to the sense of its constitutions, but from acts in which the government is the mere instrument of the major number of the constituents." Before the Bill of Rights that Madison compiled was added in 1791 to safeguard printing presses and the right to remain silent, the concerns of the original 1787 Constitution, in clause after clause, were to forbid economic redistributionism. Nearly half of the provisions in Article I, Section 10 — the portion of the Constitution primarily devoted to limiting state powers — strip states of authority to coin money, issue credit, dilute debt repayment, or impair contracts, the chief means by which majorities in the 1780s waged class warfare. In these clauses Field saw a sphere of liberty as sacred as free speech.

But by the mid-1870s voters had begun to approve new forms of experimentation to bring corporations to heel. Field, now a veteran judge in his 60s, saw the same constitutional blasphemy he had battled in California. In *Stone v. Wisconsin* (1876), the Court first upheld a so-called "Granger" law, named for their purported origins in farmers' granges, that began issuing out of Illinois, Wisconsin, Iowa, and Minnesota. This particular Wisconsin law let the state replace a railroad's prices with "reasonable" official rates. Field was outraged; his concern was not extortionate pricing by railroads but depriving them of their just rewards and deterring future investment by them. "Does anybody believe," he wrote, in another Granger decision, that railroads would have laid their track "had they been informed that, notwithstanding their vast outlays, they should only be allowed, when it was finished, to receive a fair return upon its value, however much less than cost that might be?" When in the *Sinking Fund Cases* (1878) the Court upheld a law of Congress that obligated railways to sequester 25% of their income to pay their debts, Field let loose in his best gadflyish editorial style:

> I am aware of the opinion which prevails generally that the Pacific railroad corporations have, by their accumulation of wealth, and the numbers in their employ, become so powerful as to be disturbing and dangerous influences in the legislation of the country; and that they should, therefore, be brought by stringent measures into subjection to the State. This may be true; I do not say that it is not; but if it is, it furnishes no justification for [this statute]. The law that protects the wealth of the most powerful, protects also the earnings of the most humble; and the law which would confiscate the property of the one would in the end take the earnings of the other.

Stalin and Trotsky were born within a year, but Field already knew of Karl Marx and the Paris Commune; he had also read anxiously of the Great Strikes of 1877, in Baltimore, Pittsburgh, Omaha, San Francisco, and St. Louis (where the Marseillaise was sung). In opinions he almost never referred to socialism by name, but privately he urged President Grover Cleveland to appoint "conservative men" who would resist radicals seeking to "break down all associated capital by loading it with unequal and oppressive burdens."

The cry of radicals, and not just radicals, was against "monopoly." Field was among the first American judges to anatomize that slippery word. In *Munn v. Illinois* (1876), the Court let Illinois, as a matter of constitutional law, set the prices charged by private grain warehouses, over the warehouses' claim that doing so infringed their property rights. Chicago was the "gateway" between western grain-producers and eastern markets, reasoned the Court, and so the law was the same sort of intercession allowed against, say, a man who had a "virtual monopoly" on a river crossing because he owned both banks. The fallacy, for Field, was that the river monopolist did not *build* the riverbank, but merely privatized a feature of nature that formerly belonged to all. Hence in *Illinois Central v. Illinois* (1892), Field, for the Court, undid a law that dedicated Lake Michigan waterfront to a railroad. The "harbor of a great city," he said, could not "pass into the control of any private corporation."

Field's insight was that everything depends on distinguishing wealth that came from artificial advantage and wealth that derived from foresight. In *Spring Valley Waters-Works v. Schottler* (1884), the Court allowed San Francisco to lower the rates charged by a privately owned water company. Field, dissenting angrily, saw a company that had risked millions to build waterways yet now faced the "monstrous injustice" of seeing its investments put at the "absolute mercy of an irresponsible public sentiment." He invoked Locke's principle of acquisition by labor: San Francisco could allow a company to gather water, just as it could allow divers to collect pearls on the seafloor or trappers to gather furs on the plains—but San Francisco could not then stand aside until the hard work was done, then snatch the gains. In his memoir Field wrote that his adoptive San Francisco prided itself on a generosity "not infrequent when exercised with reference to other people's property."

❧

But there was, in fact, a point at which San Francisco's generosity ran out. In 1848 the news of gold had reached China before it hit New York or Boston. A pamphlet circulating in the Canton province enticed peasants with tales of the "gold mountain," a land, it advertised, "without mandarins or soldiers. All alike: big man no larger than little man." The Chinese were instantly popular with railroads. Unlike the Irish, generally, they were cheap and obedient; blasting power, a Chinese invention, was second nature; and they drank tea instead of whiskey. Once, after Irish masons went on strike, Charles Crocker, a railroad king, called in Chinese workers. When his foreman scoffed at their ability to take over the stonework, Crocker replied: "Didn't they build the Chinese wall?" By 1871, California had some four workers for every job, yet the Chinese kept pouring off crowded steamers, mostly young men content to work for a fraction of customary wages. White rowdies soon waged racial war across much of the West. "Down at the Little Yuba River shot a Chinaman," wrote an excited young tax collector in Stephen Field's old district. "Had a hell of a time."

In the 1870s, California's Democrats swept the legislature on an anti-Chinese platform. They were stunned when Justice Field, one of their highest-ranking members, began ruling for the Chinese while riding circuit (which, under the procedure of the time, let him decide cases without the rest of the Court). In *Ah Fong* (1874), Field struck a law that let California commissioners refuse landing, in their discretion, to the "lewd and debauched" from foreign countries. Field was not impressed when 21 young Chinese women were detained at port. "I have little respect for that discriminating virtue which is shocked when a frail child of China is landed on our shores, and yet allows the bedizened and painted harlot of other countries to parade our streets." In a case called *Quong Woo* (1882), Field voided a San Francisco ordinance requiring Chinese seeking to operate a laundry to first obtain the approval of twelve white citizens. The "pursuit of their vocations," said Field, could not depend "upon the favor or caprice of others." In *Ho Ah Kow* (1879), Field encountered San Francisco's infamous "pigtail ordinance," which required the hair of male prisoners in city jails to be clipped to a uniform one inch. Yet everyone knew, wrote Field, that this supposed "sanitary" regulation was in fact a means of "wanton cruelty" against Chinese men, who wore long braids out of piety. It was no different, he said, than serving pork to Jews in prison. "When we take our seats on the bench," he continued, "we are not struck with blindness, and forbidden to know as judges what we see as men." Years afterward grateful Chinese in San Francisco would greet his annual arrival at the Palace Hotel, hoping to glimpse the "Protector of the Chinese."

These sojourners from the Chinese empire were also mistreated by Congress and by Field's colleagues on the Supreme Court. In *Fong Yue Ting* (1893) the Court held that America's 93,445 unregistered, Chinese non-citizens—among the "vast hordes," said the Court, "crowding in upon us"—could be summarily deported at Congress's command. Field exploded. He cursed this approval of inhumane "despotic power" and later wrote friends to propose that Congress pack the court to achieve a "proper" result. (Later that year, the Cleveland Administration nevertheless found itself lacking both the resources and will to enforce the law; thus *Fong Yue Ting* averted descent into the circle of hell occupied by cases like *Dred Scott* (1857), which said that blacks could never be citizens, and *Korematsu* (1944), which said that Japanese-Americans could be put in camps.)

The supreme puzzle in the career of Stephen Field is his contrasting indifference to the plight of Southern blacks. He does not seem to have been personally hostile to blacks, for his time, and he opposed slavery, unlike his slave-owning brother Matthew. But his callous, often dishonest opinions will forever bar him from the pantheon of the greatest freedom-minded judges. In 1865 four million slaves became four million citizens. The task of integrating such a large, unprepared population was immense. "These niggers will all be slaves again in twelve months," a Mississippi planter hissed to a Yankee officer. "You have nothing but Lincoln's proclamation to make them free." White Southern humiliation at the inversion of the natural racial order curdled, for many, into vengefulness at the moment they peeped through their windows and saw armed black men in Prussian blue coats and forage caps marching through Savannah, Richmond, and Charleston.

The South's "Redemption," its answer to Reconstruction, took shape in Black Codes that included forced labor contracts, some requiring that freedmen address employers as "master," or slave-like punishments such as the chain gang for uttering "abusive" language toward whites. Dixie vets in slouch hats, riding by torchlight, and mobs breathing moonshine, alike tingled to avenge any rumor that a black man laid unwelcome hands on a white woman. After the war the Constitution was amended. The Thirteenth Amendment, ratified in 1865, prohibited slavery. The Fourteenth Amendment, in 1868, outlawed the deprivation of rights without due process and the unequal protection of law. The Fifteenth Amendment, in 1870, forbid the denial of the right to vote on the basis of race. Yet unregenerate rebel lawyers, pandering Governors, and vicious sheriffs conspired, over time, to mock America's hopes for a new constitutional beginning.

The Supreme Court played a cringing part, too. This flowed from the belief, held by every justice, that the states had preeminent jurisdiction over crime and punishment and that the Bill of Rights had little to say about it. In *United States v. Cruikshank* (1875), Chief Justice Morrison Waite crippled federal rights enforcement by quashing an indictment against the perpetrators of Louisiana's 1873 Colfax Massacre, in which as many as 81 defenseless black Republicans were slaughtered by whites. Waite's rationale was that the Fourteenth Amendment "adds nothing to the rights of one citizen against another," but instead forbid only violations by the state government. (The Fourteenth Amendment provides that "No *State* shall" commit the forbidden acts of violating due process or enforcing laws unequally.) Even the humane, creative John Marshall Harlan, author of immortal dissents in the *Civil Rights Cases* (1883) and *Plessy v. Ferguson* (1896), felt compelled to join a unanimous Court in *United States v. Harris* (1883), as it struck part of a federal anti-Klan law from 1871, being enforced in Tennessee, on grounds that the Fourteenth Amendment did not bear on "private"—read: Klan-led—invasions of rights. Tennessee and the Southern states, in their tender solicitude for black rights, would be left to handle the problem.

The *New York Times*, despite its still-hardy Republican credentials, denounced the Civil Rights Act of 1875 as "startling proof [of] how far and fast we are wandering from the principles of 1787." Blacks were left in a nightmarish legal netherworld, unprotected by states, unprotectable by federal authorities. The South steadily grew more brazen. By 1899, a black man named Sam Hose, accused of killing his employer and raping the employer's wife, was tortured and immolated alive in Newnan, Georgia, before a few thousand spectators arrived in town for the occasion. A reporter heard a conductor cry, "Special train to Newnan! All aboard for the burning!" Charred chunks of his body were sold as souvenirs in a local grocer's store. The U.S Attorney General refused to investigate on grounds that the case had "no federal aspect."

Federal protection for Southern blacks slowly receded. The 1876 presidential election, contested and razor-thin, purportedly led to a compromise between Republican candidate Rutherford B. Hayes and Democratic candidate Samuel J. Tilden, in which, in return for Tilden's concession, the U.S. would withdraw the last federal troops from the South. This delivered the South to Democrats for a century. Meanwhile, the Republican Party, which had once united its anti-slavery and pro-business wings, saw the latter come to predominate. In *United States v. Reese* (1875), a black voting-rights case, only Justice Ward Hunt, a forgotten New Yorker who dissented four times in ten years, spoke up for "timid, ignorant, and penniless" blacks helpless against "the wealth, the influence, and the sentiment of the community."

Field and his brethren were right that federal courts would eventually strip from states the final say over criminal justice. But the catalyst was not Washington, D.C.'s aggrandizement but the decades of almost rabid determination, by a significant part of Southern society, to oppress those with differently pigmented skin. The federal government finally summoned the will to re-intervene in limited ways in the 1930s, bore down hard in the 1960s and '70s, and today makes the extirpation of racism an art form. In 2013 the ever-suspicious Equal Employment Opportunity Commission sued BMW when the automaker's plant in South Carolina refused to hire felons, alleging that the company's policy, though technically race-neutral, nevertheless had a "disparate impact" on black workers.

The problem with Stephen Field is that even on a Court busily undoing the work of the great Republican Congresses, Field outdid himself. The most indefensible decision in his career was his dissent (along with the other Democrat, Nathan Clifford) in *Strauder v. West Virginia* (1880). A West Virginia law kept all blacks from jury service. The Court blasted the statute as "practically a brand upon [blacks], affixed by the law, an assertion of their inferiority." In defending a law that did precisely what the Equal Protection Clause meant to outlaw, Field drew on a distinction between "civil rights," such as the right to work or hold property, and "political" rights, like the right to hold office or sit on a jury—the latter a "purely local concern." The distinction was common in 19th-century legal treatises but today seems artificial and absurd, for what do liberty and property mean, really, without the possibility of a trial by one's peers? In *Virginia v. Rives* (1880), Field wrote that "every day's experience" told him that black men in a Virginia county got fair trials, though no member of their race had ever been allowed onto a jury. What happened to the judge that Field earlier described who was not "struck with blindness" on taking the bench, the judge who saw masked bigotry for what it was?

For Field there were simply two Fourteenth Amendments. In a series of black-rights decisions Field construed the amendment so narrowly as to make it meaningless—the very error he accused the Court of falling into when it came to economic rights. The *Slaughter-House* majority had concluded in 1873 that the Fourteenth Amendment did not "radically change . . . the relations of the State and Federal governments." Field vilified this position—until he adopted it. In *Ex Parte Virginia* (1880), another case considering a state's power to keep blacks off juries, Field suddenly agreed that the amendment did not intend a "change so radical in the relation between the Federal and State authorities." The white Louisiana butchers got his aid; black defendants could rot. In *Ho Ah Kow* he rebuked San Francisco's anti-Chinese law as "unworthy of a brave and manly people," yet with equally imperiled black rights, Field swung into full states' rights mode. In hot, spasm-like opinions, he lectured readers on the "humiliation" of Southern sovereignty under meddling federal civil rights laws. One can read only so many encomiums to liberty inspired by the plight of the Southern Pacific, with its infinite legal resources, before a sensation of disgust arises in that so little of this was seen by Field as fit to apply to blacks, who were outgunned, encircled, and terrorized.

Perhaps Field, a Northerner who went West, never saw black mistreatment firsthand as he did with the Chinese. Certainly he received no corrective insights from his brother Henry, a preacher and popular travel writer, whose book about a trip to the South brimmed with naïve and unconvincing remarks about freedom bringing "new light into those dark African faces," an account that echoed prewar accounts of grinning sambos. Field was preoccupied with Yankee–Dixie reconciliation, but given the South's unapologetic manias, this mostly meant appeasing racial supremacists. Field lamented in his memoir that what might have been a "simple and just" liberation led to "stringent measures" against whites.

Field biographers like Carl Swisher, in *Stephen J. Field: Craftsman of the Law* (1930), and Robert McCloskey, in *American Conservatism in the Age of Enterprise* (1951), attributed Field's states' rights trumpet-blasts to his growing presidential ambitions. Yet this fails to explain why Field defied California Democrats over the railroads and Chinese, when he must have known that his positions would cost him the one state essential to any nomination of him. Field felt that his position as a standard-bearer of the Democrats' conservative wing would be his appeal. "Sound in Doctrine, Brave in Deed" ran his 1880 campaign slogan, but the effort sputtered. By the time of his second bid in 1884, California refused even to forward his name at the national convention. "Tilden first, Thurman second, and Field never," they said, still smarting from Field's pro-Chinese decisions and his denunciations of those, as Field told a friend, who were trying to "commit the Democratic party to the lawlessness of confiscation and the chaos of communism."

In truth Field was never built for politics. A capacity for bargaining and a thick hide were foreign to an iconoclast like Field, who acted with a moralizing certainty that some chalked up to his minister father. This quality lent his opinions their force and lucidity, but it also gave Field an astonishingly vindictive nature, which intensified, as most personal qualities do, with age. When Grover Cleveland appointed a Californian over his objection, Field sent the president a petulant letter that enclosed press clippings to support his views, as if Cleveland cared. Field's memoir has a special section called "The Annoyances of My Judicial Life" with testy, resentful chapters like "The Moulin Vexation" and "The Hastings Malignity," attacking at length insignificant and probably insane plaintiffs from years past. There is something wincingly small about a public figure of such long and eminent service indulging these petty grudges, yet they nearly double the book's length.

A society rarely recognizes its gains as they pile up. Much of the enduring literature from the 1870s and '80s teems with regret for most aspects of capitalism. Mark Twain and Charles Dudley Warner satirized crazed speculators in *The Gilded Age* (1873). Henry Adams wondered anonymously whether our institutions were worth it in *Democracy* (1880). Edward Bellamy's socialist sci-fi *Looking Backward* (1888) fantasized about the glorious day when private profit gave way to "men at Washington" who would "direct the industries of the entire nation." Bellamyite "Nationalist Clubs" drew in doctors, lawyers, and journalists, one of whom crowed that they had begun to "unite the farmers with the toilers of the city." Hammer-and-sickle themes figured menacingly in the farmer-powered People's Party of 1892, which, unsatisfied with Granger laws, declared that the "time has come when the railroad corporations will either own the people or the people must own the railroads." They also made Trotsky-like demands for public ownership of telephone and telegraph companies. Their candidate, ex-Union General James B. Weaver, carried five states and 8.5% of the vote.

Only in the 20th century would historians and economists discover that, sometime around 1880, America quietly became the richest nation in history. Americans enjoyed kerosene lighting, humanity's most diffuse land ownership and highest real wages, a stock market dispatching capital from shore to shore, and refrigerated railroad cars that brought fresh meat to New England or fruit from the sun-warmed coasts of California and Florida to the kingdoms of snow. Marxism never stood a chance here. It has no appeal to farmers who turn their own soil, or laborers who can afford their own houses, and who both resolutely refuse to see themselves as anything but "middle class." America's march to prosperity wasn't slowed by the unprecedented absorption of so many immigrants that, by 1890, 21 million, a third of the population already here, arrived from abroad or had parents who did.

If Field is remembered today, it is mostly in conservative and libertarian legal circles, as an early champion of *laissez faire* and ultimately the laissez-fairest of them all. But a legal movement whose first rule of jurisprudence is faithfulness to a law's text should beware. The late Justice Antonin Scalia would have given up his beloved Italian opera before writing, as Field did in the *Legal Tender Cases* (1871), that "fundamental principles of eternal justice" condemned a federal statute even though Congress was "not restrained by any express constitutional prohibition." The words "pretense" and "disguise" were Field's telltale death sentences for laws that offended him. If he perceived a sinister economic-discriminatory or anti-competitive motive—as he did, for instance, alone among his colleagues, in *Powell v. Pennsylvania* (1888), a decision that upheld a state's ban on margarine, a law suspiciously friendly to the powerful dairy industry—no amount of lawmaker protestation about public-health dangers could persuade Field otherwise.

In other words, Field was the sort of guardian-judge who is very dangerous unless you happen to agree with him. Everything in the law is a matter of degree and Field had a notably undeveloped sense of subtlety. Any inching toward regulation was liable to strike him as a bold stride toward tyranny. Sometimes he was far-seeing—in *Munn* he predicted still-controversial rent control—while at others he was alarmist: in *Stone v. Wisconsin* (1876), he said that a railroad-rate law would "justify the legislature in fixing the price of all articles and the compensation for all services." But despite all of his excesses, which, it must be said, were considerable, Stephen Field made one permanent contribution to our jurisprudence: the lesson that a judge must remain ever-vigilant against supposed "health" or "safety" laws that mask unlawful economic favoritism. Today these laws often lurk in the crevices of multilayered statutes or in obscure licensing regimes. What Field believed a judicial duty is largely neglected or eschewed, but every now and again the watchful Fieldian eye snaps open. In 2013, for example, a federal appeals court struck down a Louisiana law permitting only authorized "funeral directors" to sell funeral caskets; after a handful of Benedictine-monk carpenters showed that the law had no plausible purpose but to enrich industry insiders. These Louisiana carpenters succeeded where the Louisiana butchers, in the *Slaughter-House* case, 140 years earlier, had failed.

The octopus-like corporate conspiracies, real or imagined, which led Field's enemies to pass crude laws against large businesses, are today controlled by antitrust divisions, Securities and Exchange Commission litigators, and extensive public-utility codes. Nowadays the issue of sanitary butchering in *Slaughter-House* would, it seems to me, be resolved as a straightforward zoning matter. On the other hand, the "centralized" federal government that Field also sometimes dreaded is our reality. In 1896, John Pierpont Morgan single-handedly lent the U.S. government the cash it needed to avoid default. By 2013, J.P. Morgan's bank was the most regulated institution in the world, with 8,000 "compliance" officers, investigations by at least seven federal agencies, and billions in annual legal expenses. I imagine Field, witnessing all this, and nodding his approval at the 2009 Tea Party movement, which for a time represented the very American phenomenon of a popular movement that takes to the streets for fiscal restraint. (Yet Field would also have frowned at any populist, anti-corporate overtones.) Great endeavors today require concentrations of capital as much as they did in 1890, but instead of robber barons we have Mark Zuckerbergs and Sergey Brins—T-shirted, high-tech capitalists who are young, hip, and philanthropic enough to make entrepreneurship almost as bohemian as being a blog-poet.

A reporter watching the Supreme Court arguments over the constitutionality of the federal income tax in 1895 described the 78-year-old Field as "awe-inspiring and dignified," like "one of the old prophets." His chest-length beard was by now positively biblical; his eyes blazed at the communistic tendencies of legislators. The prophets of Israel, however, were not distinguished for their nuance. Field, too, near the end, was a castigator, a forecaster of sinking society and ruin. "The present assault upon capital is but the beginning," he growled in *Pollock v. Farmers' Loan* (1895), the decision on the income tax. "It will be but the stepping-stone to others, larger and more sweeping, till our political contests will become a war of the poor against the rich." We might be glad that Field, in his crankiest moments, so underestimated his people's resistance to this perpetual campaign theme. It helps, too, of course, that the formidable William Jennings Bryan and his "Cross of Gold" speech (1896) have long since simmered down into the banalities of a Jonathan Edwards's "Two Americas" (2004) or Bernie Sanders's "Reverse Robin Hood" (2016).

Just as it seems right that George Washington, like a Moses, would die in 1799, never to cross into the century whose future he assured, so does it seem proper that Field died in 1899, never to learn whether capitalism and democracy could truly coexist in America. He had been at the center of legal life for 40 years, the most unreconstructed free-marketer ever to sit on the Supreme Court, presiding, no less, over the youth of our market enterprise—fitful, unregulated, unjust, and finally prosperous beyond imagining. In 1938, after the New Deal's triumph, his successors on the Court famously announced that they would henceforth have precisely the opposite concerns of Stephen Field: racial equality would be jealously guarded; economic equality would be left to the vagaries of majorities. Field, then, confounding though he was, supplies something we have lost. "It should never be forgotten," he said on the Constitution's centenary, "that protection to property and persons cannot be separated.... Protection to the one goes with protection to the other; and there can be neither prosperity nor progress where either is uncertain." Like the prophets, Field spoke to posterity: "I have long since ceased to expect [praise], feeling confident that at some future day my services in support of order...and of the great institutions of society, will be recognized and appreciated."

INTERLUDE FROM ABROAD

1835–1888

ALEXIS DE TOCQUEVILLE

JAMES BRYCE

5

ALEXIS DE TOCQUEVILLE AND JAMES BRYCE
Europe Visits at Mid-Century

Alexis de Tocqueville was born, in 1805, into antique Norman gentry whose forebears squeezed their peasants and fought for kings. These nobles were exempt from certain taxes; they enjoyed the right to bypass lower courts; and they inherited the best pews in church. The Tocqueville family kept at their chateau, in the Manche district of Normandy, some 3,000 crop-devouring pigeons that had long infuriated their farm laborers. When Alexis's father Hervé returned from ten horrific months in Robespierre's prisons, he found the birds dead. Four of nine arrestees from Hervé's family survived the Reign of Terror, by a matter of days. The strain of hearing prisoners shriek as they were dragged to their beheading turned Hervé's hair white at age 21. He began a lifelong habit of napping between 3 and 4 p.m., the hour of death at which his jailer summoned a handful of victims to feed the guillotine. Years later, when his son Alexis stood for a seat in Parliament, opponents warned voters that Alexis—still a landed *comte*, or count, though he declined to use the title—would bring back the pigeons.

The kings, in fact, would return first. Alexis, just like his legendary great-grandfather Malesherbes, his famed uncle Chateaubriand, and Hervé, began his career in the crown's service, in Alexis's case under the restoration government of Charles X. Alexis was a *juge-auditeur*, a sort of apprentice prosecutor, at Versailles. He enjoyed the practice of law, he told a friend, though he confessed that "my inadequacy makes me despair." The work grew distasteful as the king's popularity declined. Tocqueville once had to report young workers simply for shouting "*Vive L'Empéreur!*", which got them prison terms. The king seemed to Tocqueville to be unfit for modernity, playing evening whist as protestors against him massed. Yet in 1830, when Tocqueville witnessed the king's carriage flee Paris at dawn, for the last time, the royal escutcheons concealed by mud, he wept: "I felt, even to the last, a residual, hereditary affection for Charles X." Tocqueville, pale, slightly built, with a dignified aloofness in his manner, and more than a touch of frost, sensed that it was time for a change. He arranged for a grant to himself, to report on American prisons, with his fellow *juge-auditeur* Gustave Beaumont, and the two friends, still in their twenties, booked passage. "When one sees one's fellows in danger," Tocqueville wrote to a relative, "it is a duty to try to rescue them." It was never the *Americans* who needed rescuing, and that is the key to the epic that his journey produced, the great work known as *Democracy in America*.

The premise of the book, published in Paris in two hefty volumes in 1835 and 1840, is that equality, as the living principle of government, was coming like a sky-high wave to sweep away unrooted monarchs and drown any lingering rouge-and-champagne nobles who failed to give way. Each nation had to determine for itself whether the transition would end in bloodshed or prosperity. "[I]n America I saw more than America," Tocqueville began. "I sought there an image of democracy itself . . . I wanted to become acquainted with it if only to know at least what we ought to hope or fear from it." Emphasis, one soon learns, on the fear. "My object in writing my book," he told a critic who, Tocqueville felt, had missed the point, "was to exhibit the fearful possibilities which are opening before my contemporaries . . . and thus to inspire those efforts of the heart and the will which alone can fight them, to teach democracy how to know itself and then to govern and direct itself."

Over 271 days, beginning in May 1831, Tocqueville and Beaumont visited 17 states and walked, galloped, floated, or steamboated across 7,300 miles. They wore out silk gloves flirting with shippers' daughters at lower Manhattan balls and chatted in French with refined Unitarians in Boston's

Beacon Hill. They gaped in horror as hungry, broken Choctaws were forced across an icy Mississippi in a silent death-march. They saw what 13 million people with centuries of inherited experience in agriculture could grow with an infinitude of valleys and pastures in a territory five times France's. Years later, in Algiers, he found that its market labyrinths and incessant hammering reminded him of Cincinnati. He saw literate pioneers read *Henry the Fifth* in log cabins insulated by moss and dirt. He chuckled at the "American Museum" in New York whose *pièce de résistance* was a bunch of stuffed birds. He scarcely knew what to make of the bears he saw chained outside dwellings in Pontiac, Michigan, for use as guard dogs.

In France, he said, we "still mix debris from all ages in our opinions and tastes," yet here, in America, was a society "only being born." Born, too, with a sort of evenness among all in wealth, education, and cul-ture—the central fact, he said, from which all else in the country radiated. Tocqueville quickly noticed that equals, like magnetic filings, instinctively drew together into "associations" for purposes of public-spirited self-help. America had no fire departments, he observed—not quite accurately, if Benjamin Franklin can be believed—and yet house fires were extinguished faster than in Europe because eager neighbors rushed in. At first he was bemused to hear that 100,000 American men pledged to eschew liquor, which seemed to him a strangely public admission of a personal failure, until he realized that the customary French approach would have been for the men individually to petition a minister to take ownership of cabarets across the realm. When a highway was obstructed, or a new school need-ed, talkative mini-congresses sprung up to improvise, without appeal to the state. (In a litigation I once came across a political circular issued by the "Fresno United Church Women's Sub-Committee on the Problem of Lotteries.")

Tocqueville marveled at this localism. It made government invisible, self-sustaining, durable. The lack of such a quality seemed to him the chief reason why New World cities with French origins, like St. Louis, New Orleans, and Duquesne, withered so many leagues from Paris. Both American and French governments were centralized in a capital (or rather, in the America of 1831, in Washington, D.C., plus 24 state capitals), but unlike France's top-down prefectures and sub-prefectures, the American administration of power was diffused. A typical state might demand a tax, but a town assessor apportioned it, a local tax collector levied it, an elected treasurer received it, and a nearby court heard complaints about it. Each separate office, filled by some neighbor or other, could gum up an attempt at oppression. Tocqueville has a disproportionately long chapter on the way that New England towns bred a private self-reliance and initiative with efforts that cumulatively surpassed, he found, what their officialdom could do. "A good government's greatest care," he wrote, in one of his many wishes for his mother country, "should be to accustom the people, little by little, to do without it." Tocqueville had seen the future, and it worked.

Also hard at work, to his surprise, was the humble American magistrate. In France, cushy posts were prizes hunted by ambitious college graduates eager for easy prestige and lucre; in America, such rewards were almost entirely reserved to the private sector. Most elected high officials actually kept their day jobs, like New York Governor Enos Throop, who toured Tocqueville and Beaumont through his modest working farm. Beaumont, a keen observer himself, wrote that where a Louis XVI demanded every punctilio of deference to him, while in his sacred presence, for an American politician even to *hint* at a sense of superiority was political suicide. "The President of the United States occupies a palace which in Paris would be spoken of only as a handsome private mansion," Beaumont said after their visit at the White House with President Andrew Jackson. Inside they saw no guards, no courtiers, just the man, alone, who poured them — himself — glasses of Madeira. They had to call him *mister*, added Beaumont, "as we would a man on the street."

Back on those democratic streets, they found no fixed hierarchies, no noble titles, no rigid "stations" in life. All dressed the same; no one bowed; it was good-mornings all around. In Canandaigua, New York, a wide-eyed Tocqueville saw a district attorney shake hands with a prisoner. Everywhere he observed workers (not "servants") chat amiably with their "boss" (never "master"). He watched waiters sit down alongside patrons once guests were served. These were things to catch a nobleman's eye, a vantage that also explains *Democracy in America*'s chapter-length longueurs on aristocratic preoccupations like primogeniture and the selection of a spouse on the dubious basis of love.

Meanwhile, Tocqueville omitted discussion of subjects that did not seem to him to illuminate France's democratic destiny. This turns out to

comprehend a great deal: not only abolitionism, universities, and literature (he might have mentioned Washington Irving, William H. Prescott,
William Ellery Channing, or James Fenimore Cooper), but emblems
of early American-ness like industrialization, manufacturing, banking,
technology, and railroads. Tocqueville's fellow Frenchman Michel Chevalier, also on a government grant to report on America, wrote *Society,
Manners, and Politics in the United States* (1838), a book that saw what
Tocqueville missed about America's commercial explosion. Tocqueville
mistook American capitalism for a grubby, monotonous materialism that
distracted from art and other high flights of soul. Chevalier, by contrast,
rightly described capitalism as merely the economic expression of the nation's devotion to individual liberty. (Chevalier also echoed Tocqueville's
famous prediction that the U.S. and Russia would one day each sway the
fate of half the globe.)

Nor did Tocqueville spend much time on white racial bigotry toward
a large domestic black population, another problem that France did not
have. He left that to Beaumont, whose *Marie, or Slavery in the United
States* (1835), was one of the first abolitionist novels based on slavery in
North America. It is the self-portrait (and rather a poor one) of an ad-
venturesome French nobleman who learns of a Baltimore beauty whose
secret was to have a single drop of black blood; once exposed, she dies
from the shame and ostracism. "Now I understand you egotistical Americans," says the disillusioned pseudo-Beaumont, "You love liberty for
yourselves. A race of merchants, you sell the liberty of others!"

The apparent hypocrisy of most Americans had already long exasperated the English, at least since Samuel Johnson asked, in 1775, "How is it
that we hear the loudest yelps for liberty among the drivers of negroes?"
Another English observer was Dame Frances Trollope, mother of the
famous novelist, whose *Domestic Manners of the Americans* (1832) is the
most vinegary, entertaining encounter one could imagine between a
high church Tory snob and the new American people. Trollope, for one,
refused to be lectured by Thomas Jefferson, the author of the "warlike
manifesto called the Declaration of Independence," when his "especial
pleasure" was to quaff goblets of wine at Monticello "tendered by the
trembling hand of his own slavish offspring." All men, she felt, including
white ones, were scarcely created equal. Trollope was shocked when she
was scolded by her cook for suggesting that the cook eat separately in

the kitchen ("You'll find that won't do here!"). Later she was rebuked for suggesting that not every American child might one day become president. On entering the slave states, however, she felt "immediately comfortable" at the recognized roles and accustomed servility. The American "fable" of equality took its most insolent, scandalizing form, she wrote, in a conversation that her husband overheard between a "greasy fellow" lost to history and President-elect Andrew Jackson, then steamboating his way from Tennessee to assume the White House:

> "General Jackson, I guess?"
> The General bowed assent.
> "Why they told me you was dead."
> "No! Providence has hitherto preserved my life."
> "And is your wife alive too?"
> The General, apparently much hurt, signified the contrary, upon
> which the courtier concluded his harangue, by saying, "Aye, I thought
> it was the one or the t'other of ye."

Back in England, after such effrontery, the only question for His Majesty would have been the stocks first or straightaway on the first ship to Australia. Jackson simply had to take it. These were America's teenage years, awkward, moody, over-assertive, with an adolescent's blend of high judgmentalism and even higher ignorance. "I expect your little place of an island don't grow such dreadful fine corn as you sees here?" a patriotic milkman asked Frances Trollope. "It grows no corn at all, sir," she replied. "Possible! No wonder, then, that we reads such awful stories in the papers of your poor people being starved to death."

Americans had high hopes when the great England-basher Charles Dickens arrived, in 1842, for what he announced would be a 2,000-mile tour over "soil I have trodden in my day-dreams many times." "His mind is American—his soul is republican—his heart is democratic," declared the *New York Herald*, bestowing an honorary citizenship that was, it turns out, prematurely conferred. Dickens came prepared to ridicule, since he came everywhere for that purpose, but the caricature of his American experiences, many finding their way into *Martin Chuzzlewit* (1844), dripped, even for him, with a genuine, unrelieved disgust. He described our thoughtful politics ("friends of the disappointed candidate had found it necessary to assert the great principles of Purity of Election and Freedom of Opinion by breaking a few legs and arms"); our charming etiquette ("Sitting opposite to them was a gentleman in a high state of tobacco, who wore quite a little beard, composed of the overflowings of that weed, as they had dried about his mouth and chin: so common an ornament"); our illuminating journalism ("Here's... the *Sewer*'s exclusive account of a flagrant act of dishonesty committed by the Secretary of State when he was eight years old"). Yankees took credit, in his presence, for the ocean and wondered why the Queen did not personally reply to taunting letters they had sent her. The tendency to correct British pronunciation probably drove Dickens nuts. The only evidence to suggest that he didn't wish to abolish the America of 1840 was that his non-fiction travelogue, *American Notes for General Circulation* (1842), was fair and in places even generous; he was particularly bowled over by the intelligent humanity he saw in Boston's Asylum for the Blind and in the uplifting way proud working women in Lowell, Massachusetts, seemed to manage their own newspaper.

By the time James Bryce, a Scottish historian, lawyer, and politician, published his masterpiece, *The American Commonwealth*, in 1888, it was a matured, sobered country that spread before his bearded, donnish gaze. Bryce, born in Belfast in 1838 and raised on the Irish shore, was well suited to undertake a complete survey of America. He was independent-minded and unquenchably curious. As an Oxford aspirant, he had rejected Church of England tenets, then required for admission at Trinity College, and won admittance anyway; some called it the "triumph of liberalism" at the university. He trained as a barrister but was more interested in law's historical aspects. A book on the Holy Roman Empire earned him Oxford's Regius Chair of Civil Law, which he held for almost 25 years. Meanwhile he served as a Liberal in the House of Commons, and in Gladstone's cabinet; later he was the first member of the House of Lords to decry the genocide in Armenia, a country he visited as a mountaineer. Queen Victoria, expressing a universal impression, called Bryce "one of the best informed men in all subjects I ever met." Americans were charmed by his cheery manner and enthusiastic admiration for their country during his service from 1907–1913 as Ambassador to the United States. So popular was Bryce in his mission to unite the U.S. and U.K. that, until Winston Churchill in 2013, Bryce was the only British statesman honored by a bust in the U.S. Capitol. The monument stands in the Senate wing and reads "James, Viscount Bryce, Friend and Ambassador to the American People and Interpreter of their Institutions."

American Commonwealth, all 1,500 pages of it, required Bryce to make three transatlantic trips between 1870 and 1884. His first visit left him with a "swarm of bold generalizations," he said, half of them discarded upon his second visit. This was a swipe at Tocqueville, part of Bryce's gentle but determined campaign to unseat the Frenchman as the supreme European expositor of America. Bryce admired Tocqueville's genius and said that Tocqueville wrote "one of the few treatises on the philosophy of politics which has risen to the rank of a classic." But despite the French aristocrat's scientific pretensions, Bryce continued, "it is really a work of art rather than a work of science, and a work suffused with strong, though carefully repressed emotion."

Tocqueville, his heart in Paris, wrote Bryce, could not see the "truth that the American people is the English people." It was not just America's institutional mimicry, like appointing judges for life or requiring money bills to originate in the lower house. For Bryce, even Tammany bosses reminded him of Anglo-Norman vassalage and the supposed American spirit of patient striving was nothing, he felt, if not a middle-class English value. (One suggestion of the special kinship: you know Italian-Americans or Irish-Americans, but how many friends of yours identify as "English-Americans"?) Bryce sought to give readers a social scientist's reliance on hard figures together with the legal historian's attention to precedent, by contrast to Tocqueville, who, he said, only had gleaming aperçus and "theories ready made." Bryce was on to something. Tocqueville is canonized by political-philosophy professors as the peerless metaphysicist of democracy. But historians cite him with caution.

Bryce, like Tocqueville, saw a land and a people living out the "type of institutions towards which, as by a law of fate, the rest of civilized mankind are forced to move, some with swifter, others with slower, but all with unresting feet." And for years, Bryce's *American Commonwealth*, always careful, generally engaging, but frequently textbookish and overlong (it cries out for abridgement) contended with *Democracy in America* as the "best" book written on America. But today Alexis de Tocqueville's eclipse of James Bryce is complete. Some attribute this to the miracle of a 26-year-old with halting English having peered into America's soul more deeply, some say, than anyone before or since. The better explanation is that Tocqueville had a mind of astounding penetration and subtlety, to be sure, but more than that he was a nonpareil stylist whose highly quotable, sweeping generalizations ("In no country on earth..." is a common one) and genius for prediction allowed his work to become an infinitely adaptable, if occasionally self-contradictory, grab bag of pensées.

This grace that launched a thousand quips was part of Tocqueville's conscious artistry. "Show me the books which have remained, having as their sole merit the *ideas* contained in them," he wrote a friend in 1834. His notes disclose that in his research Tocqueville reviewed volumes on the Delaware Indian Lenape language or American foliage, and dense statute books, yet his final product was still one of soaring abstraction. The corresponding neglect of Bryce has been unjust. For it was Bryce who, more accurately than Tocqueville, traced how the guiding axiom of American political theory, equality—we say "theory," but our natural-rights philosophy treats human equality as a fact—ran through our Constitution, in surprising ways that broke not only with English practice but with all human antecedents.

"I talked to everybody I could find," wrote Bryce, "not only to statesmen in the halls of Congress, not only at dinner parties, but on the decks of steamers, in smoking cars, to drivers of wagons upon the Western prairies, to ward politicians and city bosses." Bryce, like his French predecessor, found that a spirit of equality "rules the country." Of course this equality did not mean that every man had a mind as sharp as his neighbor's, or strove as hard in business, or played violin equally well, or rose to the same height, or kept a pocketbook of equal girth. It meant, rather, that human worth would not be measured by genealogy; that the banker's daughter sat in class aside the carpenter's son; it meant, as Bryce put it, that some were not "porcelain" and others "earthenware." Tocqueville and Bryce lived and died under monarchs whose heads graced the coins of the realm while they reigned, yet here was a country whose president was no likelier than an assistant pastry chef to adorn a two-cent stamp. In America hereditary heads of state or inherited legislative seats were not only spiritually intolerable, or as illogical to us as hereditary mathematicians (in Thomas Paine's words), but specifically unconstitutional in a half-dozen respects. The Constitution, for instance, prohibits the federal and state governments from granting titles of nobility; a president, U.S. representative, or U.S. senator can only take office if personally elected; and the Constitution limits the qualifications that can be imposed on office eligibility to age, citizenship, and residency. Here, no peasants groaned under permanent feudal neglect, excepting Southern blacks.

Equality requires a government of popular sovereignty. This in turn requires popular participation. Bryce estimated that the number of Americans involved in politics in a day-to-day, professional sense—federal, state, and local legislators, officeholders, party workers—was in the hundreds of thousands. In England that "inner circle" was about 4,000. All adults males voted in the U.S. (blacks in the South again excepted), compared to less than two-thirds of males in Britain. And where a resident of Manchester or Liverpool might vote once a year for a town councilor and once every four years, on average, for his member of the House of Commons, Americans seemed to live in polling booths. Bryce considered it absurd that a 1906 Chicago ballot listed 334 candidates for positions like state treasurer, trustee of the University of Illinois, sanitary-district administrator, judge of the county court, judge of the probate court, clerk of the circuit court, sheriff, school superintendent, Congressman, state senator, and so on, with no end in sight. On the other hand, Bryce observed—for weighing trade-offs was his forte—this never-ending burden of evaluation and selection "educates the citizen in his daily round of civic duty, teaches him that perpetual vigilance and the sacrifice of his own time and labor are the price that must be paid for individual liberty and collective prosperity."

But there was nothing, not even close, said Bryce, to a presidential election, the quadrennial carnival of madness, three parts gleeful anger, one part unadulterated nonsense, that seized every American mind for a few months in election years. (Tocqueville called it a "period of national crisis.") Where else on a single day, Bryce asked, did tens of millions collectively entrust the world's greatest office to one man? What kind of crazed people, he wondered, composed campaign novelettes "wherein lovers talk about tariffs under the moon"? He said that he could never imagine 800 barristers marching from London Bridge to South Kensington shouting themselves hoarse for Gladstone or Disraeli.

But what struck both Tocqueville and Bryce was how, despite the screaming fever of American elections, a paradoxical steadiness and moderation seemed always to prevail in the end. Extremists were never elected; everyone calmly trudged to work the next day with colleagues whom, a day before, they firmly believed were willing to destroy the union. Tocqueville saw the answer in what is translated awkwardly as "mores," or the "whole moral and intellectual state of the people." In one of his finest chapters, called "Why Great Revolutions Will Become Rare," Tocqueville confessed himself startled by the "singular fixity of certain principles" that endured in America, unaffected by the tumult. True, bakers and miners seemed to feel that it was more honorable to earn their keep rather than vote it to themselves from wealthy employers; to be sure, a hearty commercial spirit taught Americans to value bargaining and compromise. But there was also an abiding sense, he said, that the Americans' fundamental law gave Americans something true and good, and though ordinary laws might spring up like ugly weeds, Americans dared not touch the "principal" law; this alone could threaten their "peaceful and lukewarm atmosphere." And so, he wrote, on the fate of demagogues:

> It is not that [Americans] resist him in an open manner with the aid of studied combinations or even by a premeditated design of resisting. They do not combat him energetically, they sometimes even applaud him, but they do not follow him. To his impetuosity they secretly oppose their inertia; to his revolutionary instincts, their conservative interests, their homebody tastes to his adventurous passions; their good sense to the leaps of his genius; to his poetry, their prose. He arouses them for a moment with a thousand efforts, but soon after they get away from him, and, as if dragged down by their own weight, they fall back. He exhausts himself in the wish to animate this indifferent and distracted crowd, and finally he sees himself reduced to powerlessness, not because he is defeated, but because he is alone.

This is beautifully expressed, but incomplete. It describes effect. How about cause?

This was where Bryce, ever attentive to institutional form, excelled his Gallic rival. What made presidential elections so hot, momentous, and costly, Bryce said, was the immense power that flowed from what he considered America's great structural innovation—the disentanglement of the executive and legislative branches. In England, the executive branch, the so-called "government," is "formed" of sitting parliamentarians. But the Constitution forbids an American legislator in Congress from simultaneously holding executive "office." In the president, alone, for four long years, is reposed the entirety of executive power. The president appoints his branch's top officials, starting with his cabinet (or "ministers," as the Constitution has it), whom Congress can interrogate, harry, defund, or impeach, but never dismiss. This makes the election of this one single man a winner-take-all proposition. Bryce's answer to Tocqueville's chapter on the American distrust of revolution was entitled "Why Great Men Are Not Chosen Presidents." In a presidential election, Bryce said, the task was to find the man best fitted to hold together the largest coalition. This meant inoffensive, serviceable men, smart and capable, but who had the empty-vessel quality needed for broad alliances that great men did not. (Not one of the 20 presidents since Madison, said Bryce, would have been famous had he not been president, except Grant, and only Lincoln displayed "rare or striking qualities.")

This is where the Constitution's structure enforces moderation. In a winner-take-all system, party unanimity and coherence are the key to victory. Parties, in turn, tack to the center, where, by definition, most voters live. A third party or splinter movement, always radical or idiosyncratic in some way, usually draws off votes from one of the two largely equipoised mainstay parties, whose incentive is to return breakaways to the fold by co-opting their positions. If the fractured party cannot, the other party, the one that maintained its cohesion and moderation, wins. In the 1880s, Prohibitionists cost Republicans elections by siphoning Republican votes; single-issue Greenbackers inflicted similar wounds on Democrats. Theodore Roosevelt's insurgency assured the defeat of the GOP, nominally led by William Howard Taft, to Woodrow Wilson in 1912. The outsider Robert La Follette sunk John W. Davis against Calvin Coolidge in 1924. The eccentric Ross Perot guaranteed Bill Clinton's victory over George H.W. Bush in 1992. And so on. In European parliaments, by contrast, political coalitions form *after* the election, and not, as here, before; a few seats won by a fringe party can still earn it a portfolio, like the ministry of the environment. Thus the Constitution's design, by handing electoral victory to the broadest coalition, ensures that there will only ever be two permanent parties in America, and moderate ones at that.

Tocqueville wasn't interested in parties, but perhaps he might have been, had he noticed that the centripetal pressure to capture the White House meant that, in America, parties never formed, as in Europe, around fraught and irresolvable divisions like class (permanently rich vs. perpetually poor), mode of government (monarchist vs. imperialist vs. republican vs. radical), or, deadliest of all, faith (Protestant vs. Catholic). Both Democrats and Republicans had wealthy patrons and poor ones, voters from states large and small, coastal or plains, and adherents of all religions. America has had its Old World flare-ups, particularly in hostility to Catholics or foreigners, but elephants and donkeys could still always dine together or even, if in the mood, intermarry. In America, in short, a party based on a single demographic or cause is usually extreme, and, in a two-party system, these hot little streams dry up unless they merge into the large, cooling river of a majority.

Bryce noticed, as Republicans and Democrats drove to the vague, all-things-to-all-men center, that political rhetoric devolved into "two or three prejudices and aversions, two or three prepossessions for a particular leader or section of a party, two or three phrases or catchwords suggesting or embodying arguments." He failed, as had Tocqueville and countless other Europeans, to elicit the precise difference between the parties:

> When an ordinary Northern Democrat was asked, say about 1880, to characterize the two parties, he used to say that the Republicans were corrupt and incapable, and would cite instances in which persons prominent in that party, or intimate friends of its leaders, had been concerned in frauds on the government or in disgraceful lobbying transactions in Congress. In 1900 he was more likely to allege that the Republican party is the party of the rich, influenced by the great corporations, whereas the Democrats are the true friends of the people. When you press him for some distinctive principles separating his own party from theirs, he may perhaps refer to Jefferson, and say that the Democrats are the protectors of states' rights and of local

independence, and the Republicans hostile to both. If you go on to
inquire what bearing this doctrine of states' rights has on any pres-
ently debated issue he may admit that, for the moment, it has none,
but will insist that should any issue involving the rights of the states
arise, his party will be, as always, the guardian of American freedom.

The range of legitimate dispute in America, in other words, is measured in inches. "I have yet to hear anyone," Tocqueville said in a letter,
"whatever his social rank, publicly express misgivings about the republic
being the best of all possible governments." (In France, by contrast, he
said, intellectuals discovered daily some previously unknown eternal law
of government.) That settles a lot. It leaves us, by European standards,
with a mostly moderate left and a largely temperate right. Genuine policy
fights, as time has wound on, rage mainly over minutiae. The burning
question in 1831, when Tocqueville made footfall, was "Can South Carolina nullify a federal tariff?" When Bryce visited in the 1880s, it was closer
to "Shall we have a 20% tariff on wooden screws?" Today the *Washington
Post* might analyze tense questions like, "Should this tariff power rest with
the U.S. International Trade Commission, the U.S. Trade Representative,
or just be given a logo and christened as a new agency?" Boring it may be,
but the losers of American elections have little motive to jail opposition
leaders or roll tanks into public squares.

⚜

In one way or another, the preeminent question that lured both Tocqueville and Bryce, the question that ultimately made America so interesting, was: Did the people create the regime, or the regime the people?
On this turned the question of whether the American government was
a model for all humane nations, as some said, or whether America was
exceptional, as others insisted. Law, custom, and sheer fortuity are too
tangled to unravel this in any complete way, but it seems true that law,
in its most basic sense, has ensured American prosperity more than any
non-human factor like land or climate. Tocqueville noted—as had Daniel
Webster, whom Tocqueville met—that Spanish South America had lush
valleys and long coastlines, like us, but, unlike us, despotism and disorder. Since 1945 we have three times seen a single people, with a single

culture and history, cut in two by war and placed under vastly different legal regimes—West and East Germany, North and South Korea, China and Taiwan. One group produces BMWs and Samsungs, the other Stasis and starvation.

The precise effect of a written charter is complex. Bryce lived to 1922, just long enough to witness the birth of the Soviet Union, whose 1918 constitution promised "freedom of expression to the toiling masses" and "real freedom of conscience." The Tsarist Constitution of 1906 had at least been honest; it began: "The supreme autocratic power is vested in the Tsar." The United Kingdom famously has no written Constitution. Yet Bryce saw something peculiar about our piece of parchment's effect on the American mind:

> Someone has said that the American government and Constitution are based on the theology of Calvin and the philosophy of Hobbes. This at least is true, that there is a hearty Puritanism in the view of human nature which pervades the instrument of 1787. It is the work of men who believed in original sin, and were resolved to leave open for transgressors no door which they could possibly shut. Compare this spirit with the enthusiastic optimism of the Frenchmen of 1789. It is not merely a difference of race temperaments; it is a difference of fundamental ideas. . . .
>
> The spirit of 1776, as it speaks to us from the Declaration of Independence and the glowing periods of Patrick Henry, was largely a revolutionary spirit, revolutionary in its faith in abstract principles, revolutionary also in its determination to carry through a tremendous political change in respect of grievances which the calm judgment of history does not deem intolerable. . . . But the spirit of 1787 was an English spirit, and therefore a conservative spirit, tinged, no doubt, by the hatred to tyranny developed in the revolutionary struggle, tinged also by the nascent dislike to inequality, but in the main an English spirit, which desired to walk in the old paths of precedent, which thought of government as a means of maintaining order and securing to everyone his rights, rather than as a great ideal power, capable of guiding and developing a nation's life. . . . [R]everence for the Constitution has become so potent a conservative influence, that no proposal of fundamental change seems likely to be entertained.

And this reverence is itself one of the most wholesome and hopeful elements in the character of the American people.

At times, to Bryce's regret, Americans pushed this spirit of restraint beyond even what the Constitution required. One exception to his almost complete admiration for America was what he saw as the utter foolishness of Americans in refusing to elect House members outside of their congressional districts, even though the Constitution actually requires only that a candidate reside in the *state*. If ten great House leaders *in potentia* all lived in Philadelphia, nine would be out of office. In England, talents like Lord Palmerston, Earl Grey (he of the famed tea), and Viscount Castlereagh could lose an election and then without missing a fox hunt reenter through the door of some far-off, unvisited province. Bryce represented greater London and northeast Scotland without any need ever to change residence. Tocqueville didn't once visit his constituency in Manche, Normandy, before his 1849 election.

Harriet Martineau, a thoughtful English liberal and writer, in many ways the anti–Dame Trollope, wrote in *Society in America* (1847) of a visit to a rusticated James Madison, at his Virginia estate, where Madison told her that America had been "useful in proving things before held impossible." Madison, in referencing the naysayers of republican democracy, may have had in mind Plato. That aristocratic ex-wrestler witnessed one of mankind's first attempts at self-rule in Athens—and how it led to his mentor Socrates being forced to take hemlock—and later came to warn that in democracies even the mules prance about in their refusal to obey. Yet here was the first nation to embrace the truth that legitimate political power emanates from the people, and its formative act was thoroughly to bind itself by a specimen of legalism. Even the mechanism for amendment proved more constraining than imagined: some 2.5% of voters can, in theory, block a constitutional alteration. Thomas Cooley, the underappreciated 19th-century Michigan justice who wrote the great treatise *Constitutional Limitations* (1868), and also served as one of Bryce's chief correspondents, said the U.S. was

not so much an example in her liberty as in the covenanted and enduring securities which are intended to prevent liberty degenerating into license, and to establish a feeling of trust and repose under a beneficent government, whose excellence, so obvious in its freedom, is still more conspicuous in its careful provision for permanence and stability.

This was a government so shot through with built-in conflicts, political tugs-of-war, and sluggish procedure, that a philosopher from Jupiter, said Bryce, reading over a draft of the Constitution, would pronounce it unworkable. The strangest feature, to Englishmen, was the one Bryce thought its chief achievement, its separation of the executive and legislature branches. "Dear me," I imagine a skeptical Londoner asking, for some reason a George Bernard Shaw look-alike (as was, for that matter, James Bryce), eyebrows aloft, "Do you mean that when a president and the Congress are of hostile parties, there is legislative stalemate, unless one party enjoys a supermajority in Congress? And isn't it a touch confining to disallow your president from dissolving Congress and calling new elections? And who *does* manage foreign policy? Your Secretary of State host dinners as freely as our Foreign Secretary, but the silverware can be rolled up in a trice by the chair of your Senate Foreign Relations Committee. Rather odd, no?"

"What has struck me most up to now," Tocqueville wrote, in a letter from New York, "is the artfulness with which the public and private interest are made to advance the same goal." How was this accomplished? When "people make [law] themselves and are able to change it as they see fit," Tocqueville found, "[e]very man regards himself as having a vested interest in public safety and the exercise of laws." Bryce agreed that it was awkward to feel oppressed when virtually every top official was a person you voted on, and where every statute bound you as well as everyone else in sight. Dickens, in *American Notes*, described an interesting instance of how egotism was converted into virtuous behavior. He attended a White House ball hosted by President John Tyler, a man who personified mediocrity tapped for coalition-building. (Though, to be fair, a man who sired 15 children must have serious passions other than politics). Tyler's event was open to the public; in England, such occasions, mingling the classes, produced rowdy, resentful affairs. But here Dickens saw only order. All of the attendees "appeared to feel that he was a part of the Institution," he said, with wonder, and "responsible for its preserving a becoming character."

The notion that by serving oneself, one serves the whole, was a fixture of 18th-century thought. It appeared in Alexander Pope's poetry ("Man, like the generous vine, supported lives / The strength he gains is from the embrace he gives") and Adam Smith's economics ("It is not from the benevolence of the butcher, the brewer, or the baker that we expect our dinner, but from their regard to their own interest"). Yet the zeal with which Americans pursued this principle, especially in making their livings, amused Europeans. These curious people "put a sort of heroism into their manner of doing commerce," said Tocqueville. A sailor would brave storms, repair his ship on the high seas, and drink brackish water, he said, all in order to sell a pound of Chinese tea one penny cheaper than his English rivals. He continued:

> The American inhabits a land of prodigies, around him everything is constantly moving, and each movement seems to be progress. The idea of the new is therefore intimately bound in his mind to the idea of the better. Nowhere does he perceive any boundary that nature can have set to the efforts of man; in his eyes, what is not is what has not yet been attempted.
>
> The universal movement reigning in the United States, the frequent turns of fortune, the unforeseen displacement of public and private wealth—all unite to keep the soul in a sort of feverish agitation that admirably disposes it to every effort and maintains it so to speak above the common level of humanity. For an American, one's entire life is spent as a game of chance, a time of revolution, a day of battle.

Bryce's landlady during a stay in a Colorado mining town offered him an "option" on her mining claim if he spread the word about it in London. The "heroes and leaders of the commercial world," he wrote, far from being despised, sit on a "pinnacle of fame which fires the imagination of ambitious youths in dry goods stores or traffic clerks on a railroad." Americans, though prudish, did not object to unwed men and women strolling together, Tocqueville informed his sister-in-law, since the "tête-à-tête is normally spent talking about the price of wool and cotton." Every honest job, for Americans, merited respect. Beaumont was struck by how a Governor or Secretary of State would speak without embarrassment of his brother the grocer or his cousin the salesman. (I once received an airport shoeshine from a man who, learning I was an attorney, handed me a business card identifying his other profession as a "commercial resolution expert.")

Competition, risk, enterprise, gambles, possible bankruptcy—Americans took fearlessly to these things. When Dickens wrote that Americans resembled the "melancholy ghosts of departed book-keepers, who had fallen dead at the desk: such is their weary air of business and calculation," he didn't imagine that the efforts of talented, unsung technicians—engineers, accountants, programmers, small investors, scientists, and other minor Edisons—would enable Dickens's great-great-grandchildren to fly in tubes using aerodynamics discovered by two brothers in Ohio or to broadcast themselves at light speed on iPhones designed in Cupertino. Money-madness has an upside, as the investors say, and, at its best, an upside that reorders American life more thoroughly than any mere president could do.

༄

America had its ugliness, too—for Tocqueville, above all, America's supposed intolerance of minority opinion, what he called the "tyranny of the majority"; for Bryce, the almost comical corruption of cities. But they also found that a self-governing body politic, like the human bodies that compose it, is self-healing. The shameless boasting in the 1830s and '40s that made Americans sound like the first draft of North Korean minders—"What are the Great United States for, sir, if not for the regeneration of man?" emits a general in *Martin Chuzzlewit*—that phase fell at Antietam and Gettysburg. Yet the unique and (for Bryce) inspiring American optimism remained. "They are proud of their history and their Constitution," he said, "which has come out of the furnace of the civil war with scarcely the smell of fire upon it."

Tocqueville's homeland was not so lucky. In 1836, at the outset of his public career, and between volumes of *Democracy in America*, he swore to his friend Eugene Stoffels that he would try to "persuade men that respect for the laws of God and man is the best means of remaining free." The next 20 years proved that many of his countrymen preferred their pikes and tricolors. The July Monarchy did what Tocqueville said was impossible: in 1831 it permitted 166,583 citizens to vote, and, by 1847, still only

241,000—out of a population of 30 million. When 97% of adult males are excluded from the franchise, only force remains for them to have their way. (Tocqueville himself did not support universal male suffrage until 1851.) Throughout the 1840s Tocqueville corresponded both with radical socialists like Proudhon ("property is theft") and landed nobles (including his family members); as a member of parliament, he saw firsthand how each illiberal tendency provoked and radicalized the others.

In 1848, while riding to the Chamber of Deputies, Tocqueville witnessed a mob tear apart a troop of gendarmes before nearly turning on him. "You say it is the triumph of liberty," he raged to a friend afterward. "It is liberty's last defeat. . . . No, I tell you, it is the same as always; as impatient, as thoughtless, as contemptuous of the law, as easily led by bad example and as reckless as its fathers were." Hugh Brogan, Tocqueville's biographer, writes that the Man of La Manche was always an "active, improving conservative, even if he hung the word 'liberal' round his neck." As yet another upheaval loomed—France saw seven revolutions in 60 years—Tocqueville's reactionary impulses quickened. The word "order" came to dot his letters. His speeches on workers' welfare were heckled by leftists. "For me the Republic is, above all, the reign of the rights of each man," he said, in an election circular, "guaranteed by the will of all; it is profound respect for all types of legitimate property."

His chance to be Founding Father of France's Second Republic came in 1848. He was appointed to a drafting committee for a planned constitutional revision. But glancing around the room, he said in *Recollections*, his memoir of the 1848 revolution, the conventioneers "bore very little resemblance to the men, so certain of their objects and so well acquainted with the measures necessary to attain them who, sixty years before, under Washington's chairmanship, so successfully drew up the American Constitution." The French delegates fell out over the most basic principles and worked hastily under revolutionary conditions. He watched in growing despair as they "little by little buil[t] up the whole machinery of government without properly taking into account the relative strength of the various wheels and the manner in which they would work together." Tocqueville, the preeminent French student of democracy, failed first to carry his proposal for an electoral college, an idea taken from the U.S. Constitution, then really lost heart when the committee rejected his call for bicameralism. By now he feared the "socialism at the gate" more than any throne within it. His concessions to égalité were made in the interests of order, not philosophy: "I thought it best to treat the French people like those madmen whom one should be careful not to bind lest they become infuriated by the restraint." Spoken like a true man of the people.

But then again, his experience showed that a Parliament packed, as was France's, with an explosive mix of Bonapartists, anarchists, bourgeois republicans, Bourbon legitimists, Orleanists, and Saint-Simonian socialists is no lawn party. Nor could it last. In 1851, Louis Napoleon, France's first elected president, undertook a *coup d'etat* to extend his term by a decade. Tocqueville, weary but determined, rushed with fellow legislators to the Palais Bourbon—and into the bayoneted hands of waiting troops. He was marched to prison, alongside, he said, the "elite of France in education, in birth, and in talents." Here he was with the "notables" that he believed, all along, were entitled to rule France, now crowded together like geese. "The Duc de Broglie and I tore our chickens with our hands and teeth," he recalled, lying on a floor "strewed with mattresses and statesmen." As the shadows lengthened that day I imagine it crossed Tocqueville's mind that, across the Atlantic, the Americans that he had met in what seemed a lifetime ago were carrying on in their dogged, practical way, not reading Locke but living it, while he was left to ponder life, liberty, and the pursuit of aristocracy on the wrong bank from power.

The two tracks of Tocqueville's life—his literary career with, most famously, *Democracy in America* and his history of France, *The Old Regime and the Revolution* (1856), and his political career, including an able five-month stint as France's foreign minister—never converged as he hoped. He had often succumbed to an intense gloom and a perfectionist self-doubt; pessimism now set in for good. "No longer do I hope to see the establishment in our country of a government that is at once lawful, strong, and liberal," he wrote to Stoffels. "That ideal was the dream of my whole youth, as you know, and also of the days of my prime, which have already gone by." He felt his political career a failure, but sensed that it might have been glorious within a stable, flourishing *ancien régime*. The "loss of our aristocracy is a misfortune from which we have not even begun to recover," he wrote, in 1854, five years before his death, from tuberculosis, at age 53.

The government that Tocqueville preferred, had he resettled, say, in Boston, was something like Hamiltonianism with the addition of a hereditary principle. He thought the coming of the Federalists "one of the most fortunate events" in the birth of the union, since they "struggled" against the inclinations of the masses; the Constitution, he said, was a "lasting monument to their patriotism and their wisdom." Neo-Jeffersonian idolaters (especially touchy Southern ones) of the charismatic General Andrew Jackson, the most Napoleonic figure to be born outside Corsica, are derided in *Democracy in America*. His attack on Jackson is a notable departure from his book's practice of never insulting American politicians by name. Some critics take this as proof that Tocqueville was duped on arrival by toothless Federalist elders. But Tocqueville naturally distrusted a movement that admired the French Revolution that executed his family. His spirit inclined to property-respecting parties of order. He wouldn't have minded a constitutional king, so long as true rule was in the hands of the "most enlightened and moral classes of society," as he wrote to his cousin from, of all places, Yonkers. His class would be a balance wheel against irresponsible scepters and covetous masses, in a sort of managed democracy. Only an aristocrat, an unpersuaded friend, I conclude, could have written *Democracy in America*.

⁂

There are two forms of patriotism: the kind you have because you were born in a country, and the kind you have because you weren't. The uncommon potency of the latter comes because its adherents know, from life in their homelands, the alternative, and imagine how narrowly they escaped lifelong misery. With this comes gratitude and a willingness to defend their sanctuary. Generations of men and women have found that they were born American, but in the wrong country. They recast in Hungarian, in Swahili, in Vietnamese, the Latin motto adopted by some patriots of 1776: *ubi libertas, ibi patria*, where there is liberty, there is my country. And they keep coming. Between 1820, the decade before Tocqueville arrived, and 1909, as Bryce sent his last edition to print, some 27 million souls flooded into the U.S. Today 40 million live here who were born in other countries. This includes two of eight living Secretaries of State, America's diplomatic face to the world—as astonishing a sign as any of America's commitment to the principle of equality. Apple Computer, Facebook, eBay, and Google were all co-founded by immigrants or sons of immigrants. A few years ago, a first-generation Portuguese-American Congressman, who owns a rural dairy farm in California, and who co-founded Congress's Sikh Caucus (to honor a large constituency), told me that he publicly debated a challenger entirely in Spanish. He supposed that it was the first time a debate between congressional candidates took place in a foreign tongue.

How do the foreign-born become American? Tocqueville told a story of a Frenchman, a radical and a "great leveler" at the time of the 1789 French Revolution, who resettled in rural Pennsylvania only to become a planter and ardent discourser on the importance of property rights. But otherwise Tocqueville mostly missed America's irresistible pull of assimilation. Not so James Bryce:

> The schools, the newspapers, the political institutions, the methods of business, the social usages, the general spirit in which things are done, all grasp and mold and remake a newcomer from the first day of his arrival, and turn him out an American far more quickly and more completely than the like influences transform a stranger into a citizen in any other country.

There is still something more, something flowing from the country's organic principle. Being an American requires no particular accent, religion, or birthplace; no one can say what an "American" looks like. It's different in countries not consciously founded on the Anglo-Scottish Enlightenment. A Turk in Germany or an African in Sweden, to many locals, will never *really* be a German or a Swede. But here, no matter your origins, wrote Abraham Lincoln, those who embrace our Declaration of Independence's faith in equality can claim an American lineage "as though they were blood of the blood, and flesh of the flesh, of the men who wrote that Declaration." Then, to take formal citizenship, the Americans already here ask only that you keep faith with the Constitution and abide by our laws. In this way did Americans come to constitute a new people on the face of the earth.

G.K. Chesterton, after a visit, wrote that America is the "only nation in the world that is founded on creed." The first, but not the last. The

Republic of Cuba, the Islamic Republic of Iran, and the Democratic People's Republic of Korea are quite creepy. Their hypocritical invocation of a mode of government that America proved possible—the "Republic" in their official names—is an unintended tribute to the truth that there is no alternative. But only the American creed liberates. Immigrants keep coming. Even great French and English men of letters who set forth in part to make war on America became converts. Michel Guillame Jean de Crèvecoeur, the Normandy-born imperial French lieutenant, resettled in New York and wrote the celebrated *Letters from an American Farmer* (1782) to describe how America replaced multiple ethnic identities with a single civic one. Two centuries later, almost to the year, Christopher Hitchens, the Portsmouth-born anti-imperialist Trotskyite, alighted in Washington, D.C., only to leave it a votary of what he considered the last radical faith standing, the American cause. This notion that all men are created equal has created a rather pleasant place to live, all things considered. As Tocqueville said, near the close of his great meditation that will be ever disputed but never displaced, in one of those of alluring phrasings that seem at once a statement about the past and a prediction of the future, the "great revolution that created it still endures."

DREAMERS

1885–1931

WOODROW WILSON

6

WOODROW WILSON
The President of the Progressives

Woodrow Wilson was the first U.S. president to send millions of Americans abroad to fight. He was the first president with a Ph.D., and, totally coincidentally, the first whose collected works reached an extraordinary 68 volumes. He was also the first president to hold regular press conferences, the first to visit the Pope at the Vatican, and the first to put Jewish-Americans on the United States and New Jersey Supreme Courts. He was *not* the first president to throw the opening pitch at a Major League baseball game— that was his immediate predecessor, William Howard Taft, in 1910—but Woodrow Wilson was the first who, earlier in life, had coached a college baseball team.

Firsts, however, take on an inevitably sinister cast in America when it comes to our Constitution. When the Sorbonne in Paris, after the First World War, bestowed its first honorary degree in seven centuries on the man it called "Wilson the Just," the *New Republic* speculated that Wilson might be in violation of the Constitution's Titles of Nobility Clause, which forbids federal officials from receiving any "title" or "present" from a foreign state. In 1913 Wilson became the first president to address Congress in the flesh since John Adams, in 1800. Wilson thus broke a 113-year tradition begun by Thomas Jefferson, who refused to approach

Congress, he said, "from the throne," like an English monarch. A senator denounced Wilson's attempt to "influence legislation" as a breach of the Constitution's separation of powers. "I am very glad indeed to have this opportunity to address the two Houses directly," Wilson began his speech, "and to verify for myself the impression that the President of the United States . . . is a human being trying to cooperate with other human beings in a common service." He was not the first president to leave the United States while in office—Teddy Roosevelt inspected the Panama Canal for a few days in 1906—but Wilson was the first to travel for an extended period. His trips to Europe after World War I, in fact, lasted nearly seven months. An outraged senator introduced a resolution declaring Wilson's departure a "palpable violation" of his constitutional duties and a forfeiture of his power.

Wilson took these charges of unconstitutionality the way J.P. Morgan took money-management tips from the kid selling lemonade. Before Wilson assumed political office, first as New Jersey's Governor and later as a two-term President, he had spent 25 years as a professional scholar of the American Constitution. He knew that his favorite founder Alexander Hamilton had said, mere years after ratification, that it had already become "too much a fashion with some politicians" to dress up partisan objections as constitutional ones. Woodrow Wilson's career would show that it is in fact perilous to read the Constitution too rigidly, for rigid things crack. "The Constitution was not made to fit us like a straightjacket," he said. "There were blank pages in it, into which could be written passages that would suit the exigencies of the day."

❧

Thomas Woodrow Wilson was born in 1856, in Staunton, Virginia, and raised in Georgia and the Carolinas. His first memory was from before his 4th birthday, "hearing someone pass and say that Mr. Lincoln was elected and there was to be war." His uncle, a scientist, was one of the first academics fired for belief in Charles Darwin. This uncle also served as the Confederacy's chief chemist, overseeing munitions manufacturing. Wilson's father's parents were Scots-Irish, and his mother Scottish, leaving "Tommy" with no American-born grandparents. Though the son, grandson, and nephew of Presbyterian preachers, Tommy was drawn to politics, in particular constitutional politics. At age nine he drafted a mini-constitution for his little league team; later he wrote charters for a yacht club, a literary society, and a debate club. After a false start in law, he entered academia, with a doctorate from Johns Hopkins, and taught at Bryn Mawr and Wesleyan before a famed two-decade stint at Princeton as professor and then the college's president.

Throughout his life Wilson was dogged by an image of aloofness and cerebrality, an impression not diminished by his lantern-shaped head, pince-nez, and output of some dozen works of political science and history. But he had a "contagious interest" in life and learning, a Wesleyan student recalled. "I can see him now with his hands forward, the tips of his fingers just touching the table, his face earnest and animated, many times illuminating an otherwise dry and tedious subject by his beautiful language and his apt way of putting things." A year into his first term as U.S. president, Wilson told the National Press Club that "I have never read an article about myself in which I have recognized myself, and I have come to have the impression that I must be some kind of fraud . . . that I am a cold and removed person who has a thinking machine inside." He added: "You may not believe it, but I sometimes feel like a fire from a far from extinct volcano." The lava would bubble up regularly in his life. A. Scott Berg, one of Wilson's biographers, recalled exclaiming to himself, after reading thousands of Wilson's frothy love letters, first to his wife Ellen, and later to his second wife, Edith: "This is Woodrow *Wilson?*" Berg was not the first intimate of Wilson to be surprised by Wilson's intense emotionalism. After Wilson asked Congress to declare war on Germany, Wilson's secretary remembered that Wilson returned to his office and sobbed "as if he had been a child."

Intellectual work, too, had its emotional aspects for Wilson. "I have a passion for interpreting great thoughts to the world," he said, as a young man, in one of many signs of his political ambition. He would write two books on American constitutionalism, the first of which, *Congressional Government* (1885), published at age 28, inaugurated his national reputation as a constitutional theorist. He hoped that the book would show "our constitutional system as it looks in operation" and "result in something like a revelation to those who are still reading the *Federalist* as an authoritative constitutional manual." The great theme of Wilson's political philosophy was captured in a 1913 speech in Philadelphia to dedicate the building where the first Congress sat. "The men who sat in this hall, to whom we now look back with a touch of deep sentiment," said Wilson, "were men of flesh and blood, face to face with extremely difficult problems." He continued: "Do not let us go back to the annals of those sessions of Congress to find out what to do, because we live in another age and the circumstances are absolutely different; but let us be men of that kind; let us feel at every turn the compulsions of principle and of honor which they left...let us remind ourselves that we are the custodians, in some degree, of the principles which have made men free and governments just." Elsewhere, more pointedly, Wilson said that he had contempt for the timid types who "want to consult their grandfathers about everything."

Remarks like these lead many today to peg Wilson as "hostile" to the founders. But he saw his approach as obedient to them. Not only did Wilson, over 40 years of writing, speak reverentially of the founders, this son of Virginia even called himself a "Federalist" who favored strong, central government and dismissed Jefferson as "not a thorough American because of the strain of French philosophy that permeated and weakened all his thought." He suppressed criticism of Jefferson of necessity upon entering Democratic politics, but the first clues to his later political positions are revealed in his unguarded academic days. He spoke ill of the narrow-minded Andrew Jackson; praised proto-Republican nation-builders like Henry Clay and Daniel Webster; and wrote worshipfully of Abraham Lincoln as the "supreme American of our history," about whom, Wilson added, he found "something absolutely endless." Wilson's pro-Confederacy passages in early writings seem the stuff of birth and prejudice; his pro-Union passages, the result of education and conviction.

No self-styled historian, moreover, was ever so preoccupied solely with the future. Wilson said he wrote his five-volume history of the United States "not to remember what happened, but to find out which way we were going." What he found was the occasionally forgotten fact that our constitutional tradition did not begin with the Constitution. The American government, founded a century before his first book on it, Wilson felt, was just an "adaptation of English constitutional government," with its monarchical elements left on the cutting-room floor. Its framers, he said, were essentially "progressive Englishmen." Even to *get* to

1787 required a generations-long "drill in order and in obedience." Wilson saw no reason to think our forward march would end.

One of Wilson's favorite tropes was to say that the founders believed in a "Newtonian" theory of government, in which the apparatus of checks, balances, and branches was spoken of as if ruled by unalterable orbits and gravitation, whereas Americans had since learned that the Constitution "falls, not under the theory of the universe, but under the theory of organic life." "It is accountable to Darwin," he said famously, "not to Newton." Wilson incorporated this line into stump speeches. But it is misleading, because the call for evolutionary change in an organic society, long before Charles Darwin made it a vogue concept of Wilson's day, was associated with Edmund Burke—the Irish statesman whom Wilson declared to be, in politics, his "master" and the "authentic voice of the best political thought of the English race." No president before or after has ever spoken more frequently of Burke. Burke was the broad-shouldered defender of the unwritten English Constitution who believed, in Wilson's account, that governments changed "by slow modification operating from generation to generation." A lot, in fact, like Charles Darwin's Galapagos tortoises.

Wilson wasn't particularly consistent with his Newton–Darwin metaphor; Alexander Hamilton is called a Newtonian *and* a Darwinian in the same book, and Wilson denominates men one would think thoroughgoing Newtonians, like John Marshall and Daniel Webster, as organic-Constitution Darwinians. That roster of statesmen suggests that what Wilson actually had in mind was a defense of bold new uses of government power of the sort those men promoted. The idea of organic life and its bodily "organs" also captured Wilson's view on how government's branches should cooperate (more below) and, for added benefit, needled traditionalists who harassed him, as they had his uncle, for his refusal to repudiate Darwin. The Darwin metaphor, in short, was not a repudiation of the framers, but a literary device used by Wilson to convey his take on how to honestly interpret their handiwork.

When Wilson decorated his first house, he had his wife Ellen, a talented artist, draw portraits of Gladstone and Bagehot (Wilson was a hardcore Anglophile), along with Daniel Webster, his father, and, of course, Edmund Burke—with no Charles Darwin in sight. Wilson saw the statesman's task as updating American life in an evolutionary way, in order, actually, to head off revolutionary breaks. "If I did not believe that to be progressive was to preserve the essentials of our institutions," he said, "I for one could not be a progressive."

⟨∽∘≻⟩

What was "Progressivism"? Historians still struggle to define it, except to agree, broadly, that it was a diverse national response to the strains of industrialization and urbanization between 1890 and 1917. Chronologically, it followed the Populist movement and preceded the New Deal, with links to both, yet also distinct from both. It enacted Populist priorities of the 1880s and '90s like the eight-hour workday and direct primary, but in tones that were calm and middle-class by contrast to the frantic, farmer-led Populism. Progressivism contained multitudes. Some Progressives wanted to increase the power of ordinary citizens to vote on everything, others to confine a maximum of decision-making to experts. Progressives like Jane Addams, the Chicago social worker, eagerly embraced immigrants, while others, like California Governor Hiram Johnson, fought to keep them out. Socialists like Eugene Debs thought Progressives stole his platform, while Progressive anti-socialists, who were far more numerous, saw their movement as checking America's leftward drift. Progressive philosophers like John Dewey imposed Darwin on every student; William Jennings Bryan, Wilson's first Secretary of State, ended his career, in the Scopes Monkey Trial, trying to defend American students from Darwin.

Many of Progressivism's proposals were commonsensical, like organizing Boy Scout troops (whose federal charter Wilson signed in 1916) or building playgrounds, instead of jailing street urchins with adults for playing stickball in Hell's Kitchen. Many Progressive reformers were apolitical, like William T. Harris, the St. Louis school superintendent who pioneered the K-8 scheme, or Dr. Hermann Biggs, the New York Board of Health doctor who introduced diagnostic tests for cholera. Progressives included sons of poverty like William Bauchop Wilson, who worked at age nine in mines only to oversee the abolition of child labor as Woodrow Wilson's Secretary of Labor, as well as scions of mining wealth like William Randolph Hearst, who won a term in Congress in 1902 on the slogan "Congress must control the trusts," then began hosting lavish parties in D.C. where guests left with solid-gold pins bearing his portrait. Progressive-era initiatives that remain ubiquitous and controversial today include environmental conservation, zoning, and limits on corporate political spending. The Constitution between 1913 and 1920 was amended four times—to add an income-tax power (1913), direct election of Senators (1913), Prohibition (1919), and female suffrage (1920). But just as importantly, the Constitution avoided dozens more proposals that failed to gather steam, from the broad and structural, like the 1912 Democratic Party platform's call for a single, six-year presidential term, to the specific and crotchety, like a Louisiana Senator's proposal in 1914 to ban remarriage after divorce.

What Woodrow Wilson recognized, however, was that if political Progressivism were traceable to any one phenomenon, it was the monumental imbalance between a private business sector that had surged since the Civil War, reaching staggering proportions by 1890, and primitive modes of government, skeletal and passive, that hadn't even begun to catch up. Wilson told a group of bankers in Denver in 1908 that the "most striking fact about the actual organization of modern society is that the most conspicuous, the most readily wielded, and the most formidable power is not the power of government, but the power of capital." "Men of our day," he continued, "have almost forgotten what it is to fear the Government, but have found out what it is to fear the power of capital." Between the Civil War and World War I, the prototypical business was owned by a single man, run with his nephews and maybe a few journeymen, limited in range to a county or two. Yet his business was increasingly being displaced by corporations, some large and some gigantic; a railroad might employ over 100,000. The biggest and scariest corporations were called "trusts," the most titanic of which, U.S. Steel Corporation, controlled 213 manufacturing plants and transportation companies, 1,000 miles of private rail, and the world's largest coke, coal, and ore holdings. Similar concentrations arose with telegraphs, shipping, oil, electricity, cotton, tobacco, whiskey, and sugar. Around 1905, insurance companies alone saw returns of $613 million, more than the annual budget of the U.S. government.

Wilson thought the best businessmen praiseworthy, the sort who in other times and places might have been emperors. But he was not above using fearful abstractions for political gain. What alarmed Americans was not only the power of syndicates to cheat them or to corrupt legislatures or rule as invisible masters, but the fear that getting ahead with hard work, in the old way, seemed increasingly out of the question unless you had a few million lying around to build a foundry or maintain a research division. (Still today we retain a measured distrust of the very largest corporations and a special solicitude for "small business owners.") Despite this rapid change, said Wilson, government remained stuck in an age when all it was expected to do was to "put on a policeman's uniform, and say, 'Now don't anybody hurt anybody else.'" Nowhere were the consequences of this disconnect more evident than in America's big cities.

By the end of the 19th century, the U.S. had 76 million people and 38 crowded, disorderly cities whose population surpassed 100,000. These metropolises seemed like grimy, overheated boilers, screws rattling, shrieking, spitting steam—all beneath your cramped parlor. But the city dweller, as Robert Wiebe wrote in *The Search for Order* (1967), "could never protect his home from fire or rid his street of garbage by the spontaneous voluntarism that had raised cabins along the frontier." Woodrow Wilson thought that American cities were "worse governed" than any in Europe except for the Ottoman Empire and Spain. The supreme Progressive chronicler of municipal decrepitude was Lincoln Steffens, later Wilson's friend and ally. Steffens was born in 1866 in San Francisco and moved east to begin as a Wall Street cub reporter, interviewing police about the best methods of clubbing garment workers on strike. Steffens's great insight—which Wilson shared—was that "political corruption was not political, but business."

American cities had traditionally contracted out for bridges, sewers, gas, streetcars, tunnels, roads, water, and street lamps; private businesses, in return for these services, got franchises and licenses. But in an era before cleansing agents like open-bidding laws, public hearings for key decisions, and anti-corruption stings, bribing mayors and aldermen was the easiest path to these prizes. (Even today cities and states can't actually provide their own gas and electricity, but give monopolies to private companies under strict price control.) The companionable Steffens spent so much time with bosses in New York, Chicago, Pittsburgh, Minneapolis, and St. Louis that by the time he came to rake Philadelphia's muck, in 1903, he could tutor the bosses there in best practices. "That would work," one exclaimed, on hearing from Steffens of a clever graft technique. "It's cheap, too, cheaper than our way!" Thus the rise of capitalist dominance, and the ubiquity of bribes, rake-offs, frauds, and levies, went hand in hand, palm in greasy palm.

The Progressive movement, the self-proclaimed opponent of both unrestrained industrialism and the corruption it underwrote, marched from cities to statehouses. In these reigned governors like Albert B. Cummins in Iowa, Joseph W. Folk in Missouri, Hiram Johnson in California, and Frank Lowden in Illinois. But the most famous of all was the feisty, ball-fisted Robert La Follette, Wisconsin's Republican governor (1901–06) and U.S. Senator (1906–25), a man I think of as the Great Badger of Democracy. A clash in his 20s with a local boss over La Follette's bid for district attorney initiated a lifelong mission to break machines, even if, in doing so, he created something close to a counter-machine. At 29, La Follette was elected as the youngest member of Congress, where he met Senator Philetus Sawyer, Wisconsin's most powerful Republican, who believed, according to La Follette, that railroads and lumber companies, "as benefactors of the country," deserved every favor he, Sawyer, might bestow, and that "anything that interfered with the profits of business was akin to treason."

La Follette came to see secret privilege and skullduggery lurking in every committee conference and in every bill. He witnessed land giveaways in enactments for rail tracks that included, in one case, a grant of 828 acres for "terminal facilities." Later, as Wisconsin's governor, he met a state lawmaker who was forced to vote against a railway taxation bill when a railroad threatened to discount his business competitors' rates and so ruin his livelihood. "I have a wife and babies," he wept to La Follette. Woodrow Wilson called La Follette a "very energetic man," which is one way to describe a fellow who, to defeat machine candidates, once stumped across his state for 48 straight days, excepting Sundays, and averaging, he claimed, over eight hours a day on the platform, with time only for one formal meal in a "bottle of good rich milk and two slices of the crust of bread buttered." Two slices were good enough for La Follette's nutrition, but not for his reforms. "Half a loaf, as a rule, dulls the appetite," he said, "and destroys the keenness of interest in attaining the full loaf." Governors, not legislatures, were the hope of the day—a reversal from the founding era—and they promised citizens intelligent expertise, driven by statistics, applied in non-partisan commissions that would depoliticize, say, rates for electricity and freight. The legislation La Follette drafted or inspired in Wisconsin became the Progressive gold standard. Yet in his autobiography, completed in 1912, La Follette happily named imitators in other states but went out of his way to shun Woodrow Wilson. My guess is that La Follette was jealous that it was the Democrat Wilson, not he, who would become the Governor anointed to carry Progressivism to the White House.

In 1907, three years before he was elected Governor of New Jersey, Wilson's views kept him firmly within the conservative wing of the Democratic Party. He criticized William Jennings Bryan from the right and Theodore Roosevelt from a vague states' rights perspective. New Jersey's Democratic boss, James Smith, Jr., thought that the buttoned-up Princeton outsider, with his aura of clean, polished respectability, was the ideal recruit to fend off the more threatening of his party's Progressive urges. Before he entered politics Wilson had derided certain Progressive measures as "essentially socialistic in principle" and warned that "I can resist my neighbor but I cannot resist the government; and when the government is made strong against me and interferes in everything that I attempt to do, then my life is the life of a man enslaved." But once Wilson went on the hustings—where the veteran lecturer excelled—his conservative utterances stopped. Opportunism was surely part of it; Wilson saw the popularity of Theodore Roosevelt's activism and the electoral defeats of non-Progressive Democrats. Wilson won, aged 53, in what was his first race for office. But he believed, quite reasonably, that he had been preparing for the role by his years of studying practical politics. During the campaign, when Republicans called out his lack of experience in office, he challenged any politician in the state to debate any public matter, on any platform.

It remains a mystery how Wilson broke the New Jersey bosses and pushed through so much legislation that even Trenton's veterans were stunned. "After dealing with college politicians," Wilson would say, "I find that the men with whom I am dealing now seem like amateurs." In 1911 he shepherded through laws, many modeled on La Follette's, for a direct primary, workers' compensation and workplace safety laws, as well as a corrupt practices act, commissions to control railroads and public utilities, and limits on campaign spending. He began to call himself a "modern radical," since he wanted, he claimed, to "bring my thinking up to the facts and not drag the facts back to my antiquated thinking." Even after both of New Jersey's houses went Republican, Wilson was still able to enact laws for milk and food standards, establish free dental clinics, and limit women's work to 60 hours a week. Reform was in the air and through it soared the Wilson meteor. In October 1910 he was running a small men's college in New Jersey; by November 1912, he was preparing to escort his wife and three daughters into the White House.

The Progressive Era was an era of crusades that, like many crusades, had some very unholy ends. This was a generation newly enthralled with science, but today's science, as Progressives proved, is tomorrow's pseudoscience. Wilson was one of more than a dozen governors between 1907–17, for instance, who signed laws allowing the forced sterilization of undesirables like "morons," "rapists," and "other defectives." An epileptic woman named Alice Smith, in 1912, challenged New Jersey's law as unconstitutional after New Jersey's Board of Examiners of Feeble-Minded—another manifestation of the new rage for expert commissions—ordered her Fallopian tubes removed to prevent further degradation of the gene pool. Progressives generally assailed courts for clinging to supposedly cobwebbed constitutional interpretations, but in 1913 the New Jersey Supreme Court respectfully reminded Dr. Wilson that under that old-time Equal Protection Clause, the Garden State could not "essay the theoretical improvement of society by destroying the function of procreation in certain of its members." Alice Smith avoided sterilizing surgery, but some 60,000 other Americans, across the country, weren't so lucky.

The "trust"-phobia of the age was harnessed by those with ulterior motives, including the very motive that produced so many of the trusts themselves: eliminating fair competition. Dairymen decried the "oleomargarine octopus," while margarine producers sounded the alarm against the "creamery trust." Chicago's U.S. Attorney called prostitution the "white slave trust," and in 1910, in the Mann Act, Congress asserted control over the interstate movement of women for "immoral" purposes. When the law was challenged as exceeding Congress's authority under the Commerce Clause, the Supreme Court, in *Hoke v. United States* (1913), replied that if Congress could stamp out lotteries, obscene literature, diseased cattle, impure food and drugs—other exercises of power, in a country busy extirpating social evils, which had all earlier overcome constitutional challenges—surely it could stop the "enslavement" of women.

But the single most unfortunate legacy of Progressivism, I submit, was a change in government structure that still disorders many states: the direct-democracy reform known as the "initiative" (part of a triumvirate that also included the "referendum" and "recall"). The "initiative" allowed citizens, in theory, to become impromptu legislators who could act, as in ancient Greece, over the heads of elected representatives and pass laws by popular vote. This was a departure from the American theory of representative government. The initiative first emerged in South Dakota in 1898 and was adopted by 19 states, mostly in the West, by 1918. This new power, it was claimed, let a dissatisfied electorate override useless or buyable legislatures. But others, at the time, observed that if the "people" were so disorganized or indifferent that they couldn't be trusted to elect honest legislators, how were they ready for the more complex act of drafting honest *legislation*?

Woodrow Wilson was a skeptic from his academic days, but he warmed to the initiative during his governorship. In spirit, at least. It seems revealing that, as Governor, he saw through almost the entire Progressive catalogue of reforms—but the initiative was not among them. He thought that with initiatives, by contrast to a bought legislature, you at least had a chance at identifying the hidden hand. But Wilson failed to anticipate how easily the initiative would become a means for the best-funded special interests to purchase statutes. It is child's play to spin a proposed law as designed to "reduce taxes" or "fight crime" or "fix education," before a voter likely to spend 20 seconds perusing it on the ballot before voting for it. "Self-government," Wilson wrote, before public office, "does not consist in having a hand in everything, any more than housekeeping consists necessarily in cooking dinner with one's own hands." Some eccentrics for decades have campaigned for a federal constitutional amendment to create a "national initiative."

⚬⚬⚬

The 1912 election was one of our history's most memorable: it featured a past president in Theodore Roosevelt, a current president in William Howard Taft, a future president in Woodrow Wilson, and a perennial never-president in Eugene Debs. Each candidate, to one degree or another, embraced the name "progressive." Even the most conservative of the four, Taft, called himself a "believer in progressive conservatism" with a record to back it. He was a bigger trust-buster than TR. He urged Congress to limit campaign contributions and expenditures and to tax poisonous phosphorous matches out of existence. He appealed to voters in 1912 by citing his Administration's "wise and progressive" accomplishments, like the creation of a specialized Commerce Court, new regulation of telephone companies, and the establishment of a federal Children's Bureau. And, going further than even Wilson thought proper in commingling the branches, he suggested that Congress reserve seats in its chambers for his cabinet members, who might, he said, "take part in all discussions." But Taft had failed in one cardinal way: as Progressive Republican "insurgents" tried to seize the party from the Old Guard, Taft made too many gestures in both directions. The party ruptured in 1910.

There was a man ready to step once more unto this breach, as Shakespeare said, and set his ever-clenched teeth and stretch his nostrils wide. That man was Theodore Roosevelt: cow-cleaving Dakota rancher, swaggering Cuba war hero, hard-stomping Gotham police commissioner, polymathic author of some 35 books, ripsnorting president at age 42. Friends described him as a two-legged bugle, a man so excitable that he could haul off and slug them at any moment. The real race in 1912 was Wilson against Roosevelt, running as a third-party candidate for the new Progressive Party. Roosevelt thought Wilson looked like an "apothecary's clerk" and told journalists that the scholar-politician struck him as "merely a less virile *me*." Wilson, in turn, called Roosevelt a "great big boy." There was something to both men's observations. TR was canny and eloquent, but a less restrained, less legal-minded version of Wilson. When in 1902 he met constitutional opposition to his plan to seize the nation's coal production during a strike, he supposedly roared: "To hell with the Constitution when the people want coal!" Wilson didn't talk like that. But Roosevelt did say a good deal to prepare the public for Wilson. In 1908, for instance, Roosevelt declared that asserting federal control over interstate commerce was merely carrying out the Constitution's "prime purpose." Doing so hardly fit the charge of unlawful "centralization," he continued, but was instead acknowledgment of the patent fact that centralization has already come in business. If this irresponsible outside business power is to be controlled in the interest of the general public it can only be controlled in one way—by giving adequate power of control to the one sovereignty capable of exercising such power—the National Government.

Roosevelt's popularity helped persuade Wilson that the nation was ready for muscular new federal exertions. In TR's case, these included a reinvigorated Interstate Commerce Commission to regulate railroads; a Forest Service to maintain the federal lands whose acreage Roosevelt doubled to some 230 million; and a Food and Drug Administration, which was then essentially a team of chemists who tested food and the potions that passed for medicine.

During the 1912 election, Roosevelt and Wilson, in the similarity of their policies, were compared to Tweedledum and Tweedledee. "Paternalist" versus "patrician" is more accurate. Both admired Hamilton—Roosevelt called Hamilton the "most brilliant American statesman who ever lived"—and they outdid each other in embracing a vision of strong, consolidated government. "Free competition and monopoly—they're all the same thing unless you improve the condition of workers," thundered Roosevelt, about his plan, called the "New Nationalism." "What I am interested in is getting the hand of the Government put on all of them." "We do not want a big-brother government," replied Wilson, describing his counter-program, the "New Freedom." "I do not want a government that will take care of me. I want a government that will make other men take their hands off so I can take care of myself."

A young Walter Lippmann, the journalist who later all but invented the role of omniscient newspaper columnist, wrote his summation of mature Progressivism, *A Preface to Politics* (1913), during the campaign. He thought Roosevelt "crude" and unfocused where Wilson was "urbane" and able to state "something he has borrowed with more ease and subtlety than the specialist from whom he got it." Wilson seemed a "foretaste of a more advanced statesmanship." Here was a leader who promised hardheaded empiricism but with a self-consciously poetic streak. Wilson told Americans, in his first inaugural, that the new age's feeling would "sweep across our heartstrings like some air out of God's own presence, where justice and mercy are reconciled and the judge and the brother are one." (If this sounds more like Burke than Darwin, it may be because Wilson, I suspect, adapted part of the line from his man Burke.)

Scott Berg calls Wilson perhaps the "least experienced person to hold the highest political office in the land." That depends on how you define experience: true, Wilson was elected president after only 658 days of public service. Yet no president, not even Madison, had turned out a library of systematic constitutional scholarship. This self-apprenticeship gave Wilson the confidence to distinguish between the constitutional and the sub-constitutional, between the few but fixed limits of the fundamental law and the vast range of action permissible within those limits. Original Progressives, like Wilson, are attacked on the right today for "rejecting" the Constitution. But Progressivism is not among the powerful movements hostile to the Constitution, like anti-federalism, secessionism, and strains of abolitionism. Thoughtful Progressives of the era were opposed not to the document itself but to what they saw as outdated interpretations of it. As Herbert Croly wrote in *Promise of American Life* (1909), one of the movement's more enduring book-length statements: "What we Americans have to do in order to fulfill our national Promise is to keep up the good work—to continue resolutely and cheerfully along the appointed path." The 1912 Progressive Party platform appealed, rather inclusively, to both Jefferson *and* Lincoln in proclaiming its mission to "safeguard" the Constitution from "those who, by perversion of its intent, would convert it into an instrument of injustice."

Progressives framed their effort as a recovery of the Constitution. This was nowhere more dramatically shown than in President Wilson's chief contribution to American government: the modern (or, in his view, revived) doctrine of presidential initiative in legislation. He had argued, some 30 years before he became president, in his book *Congressional Government*, that government works best when the White House and the Congress reach out across Pennsylvania Avenue to formulate law together. In office he put this belief into practice. He proposed and shepherded legislation, lobbied lawmakers, or appealed over their heads to the public. This did not make him, as some claim, a "critic" of the separation of powers; it made him a critic of the separation of powers *as practiced* between 1880 and 1912. Then these powers were, for him, a bit too separate. The Constitution had "nicely adjusted, ideal balances," he wrote, but we had arrived at a "scheme of congressional supremacy" in which a "silent and inactive" president left most administration to some 50 standing committees of Congress under domineering Speakers like Joseph G. Cannon and Thomas B. Reed—a terrible form of "government by mass meeting."

This conclusion, joined with his inveterate Anglophilia, drew Wilson to British parliamentary practice. Here a ruling ministry is composed of the stars of the House of Commons. American cabinet members, by contrast, he felt, were "little more than chief clerks" expected to carry out Congress's will. The Constitution forbids executive officers from serving in Congress—which rules out the British model—but in other clauses the Constitution *compels* cooperation between the branches. Article II, Section 3, for instance, imposes on the president a duty to "recommend" measures to Congress. Wilson thought Grover Cleveland the "sort of President the makers of the Constitution had vaguely in mind," a man, he wrote elsewhere, who was the "leader of his party as well as the Chief Executive officer of the Government." House Minority Leader James Robert Mann felt that Wilson's approach to Congress smacked of a "schoolmaster telling fourth-grade school children to be good," but to Wilson, the Oval Office—which Taft built, incidentally—was "anything he has the sagacity and force to make it."

On some points even the doctrinally consistent Wilson continued to develop. He came, in fact, to sound a lot like Theodore Roosevelt. In *Constitutional Government* (1908), his second major book on constitutional practice, published four years before he became president, Wilson called the notion of a federal constitutional power to ban child labor "obviously absurd." Eight years later he lobbied for the 1916 Keating-Owen Child Labor Act. He had long considered women's suffrage an issue to be decided within individual states, but during his second presidential term he came around to support a federal amendment. He even rejected a plank of the platform on which he was elected. The Democrats in 1912 called the tariff unconstitutional when used to protect industry against foreign competition, instead of merely to raise revenue. Wilson was unwilling to contradict Alexander Hamilton on this century-old practice respecting tariffs (even though he broke with 24 presidents on Jefferson's precedent of refusing to appear in Congress). That same Democratic platform demanded that the Constitution be amended to limit the president to a single six-year term. Wilson would not support what he saw as a structural change that stripped a president of the "right to appeal to the people."

Arthur S. Link, who wrote a five-volume biography of Wilson, and edited Wilson's 68 volumes of collected papers, goes so far as to call Louis D. Brandeis the "chief architect" of Wilson's New Freedom. When they first met, in New Jersey in 1912, Brandeis, an attorney in private practice, found the president-elect "eager to learn and deliberate." He became a sort of consigliere to Wilson, including even after Wilson put Brandeis on the U.S. Supreme Court. Brandeis was born in Louisville in 1856, and his first memory, as with Wilson, was from the war, "helping my mother carry out goods and coffee to the men from the North." His father Adolph, a German-speaking Jewish immigrant from Prague, marveled after his arrival that the "hard work of these people is a kind of patriotism. They wear themselves out to make their country bloom, as though each of them were commissioned to show the despots of the Old World what a free people can do." Louis's uncle, a lawyer, translated *Uncle Tom's Cabin* into German and named one son Henry Clay and another Abraham Lincoln. From this uncle, Louis—large-eyed and tousle-haired, with a permanent quizzical expression on his face—chose the path of law. He became a multimillionaire representing department stores and liquor dealers. Some wealthy men liked rare art or yachts, but Brandeis's hobby, he said, was solving social problems. Often he refused fees so as not to be beholden to any side in a lawsuit and thus remain free to serve as "counsel to the situation."

Wilson and Brandeis both occasionally described themselves as conservatives, since, in Brandeis's words, "[t]rue conservatism involves progress." He added that "unless our financial leaders are capable of progress, the institutions which they are trying to conserve will lose their foundation." Both he and Wilson had broad views of constitutional possibility; both saw government as an organism; both had strong states' rights urges (Brandeis, for one thing, opposed the federal regulation of insurance); and both instinctively wanted to keep business out of government and government out of business. Brandeis persuaded Wilson that the crucial task was to restore conditions of commercial competition. This meant faith in antitrust law, the complex body of doctrine that seeks to require businesses in the market to play fair.

The new industrial giants were guilty of some fearsome fee-fi-fo-fumming, but like the beanstalk-dweller who gave Jack a run for his money, something of the fairy tale hovered about them. Some of their consolidations resulted from masterminds stacking corporations like cards. But more often, mergers were attempts by quite unplutocratic businessmen to stabilize chaos by substituting cooperation for competition. It made sense for Massachusetts rail executives to ask in 1875, for instance, before a flurry of mergers, whether their state really needed 62 rail companies. The notion of fixing prices or dividing up market share, far from having the present-day stigma of a "cartel," struck many industrialists as firmly in the public interest. But pushed too far, legislators found, collusion could stifle innovations and inflate prices. Twenty states adopted antitrust laws during the 1880s. The federal Sherman Antitrust Act of 1890 is still in effect—and still infamously vague. In 1912 Wilson condemned the practices whereby a company undersells local rivals to kill them off (today called "predatory pricing") or strong-arms a purchaser into refusing to buy from a rival (now called "refusal to deal"), both banned during the Wilson Administration in the 1914 Clayton Antitrust Act. But beyond this it turned out that separating acceptable bare-knuckled competition from the unacceptable brass-knuckled varieties—the purpose of antitrust law—was harder than anyone thought.

The solution was the Federal Trade Commission, staffed with apolitical professionals and given regulatory powers to investigate and issue injunctions. As with other commissions, the belief was that the agency would exhibit a speed and subject mastery impossible for generalist judges burdened with dozens of various bodies of law. Government's search for efficiency, in this respect, really only emulated private businesses. This was fitting, since private businesses asserted most antitrust complaints and overwhelmingly supported the Federal Trade Commission. Wilson also signed the Federal Reserve Act of 1913, which created a board to oversee our money supply without political interference and check periodic panics, and the first tax under the Sixteenth Amendment, with its admirable rate of 6% on income over $12 million (in today's dollars). These were his first term's lasting contributions to our economic life. They seem modest and uncontroversial today.

In 1916 Woodrow Wilson barely beat his Republican challenger, the statesmanlike Charles Evan Hughes, a former New York Governor with a

Jehovah-like beard who left the U.S. Supreme Court to run. Like Wilson, he also had impressive Progressive anti-boss and antitrust credentials. Wilson declared in accepting the Democratic nomination: "We have in four years come very near to carrying out the platform of the Progressive Party as well as our own." His second-term enactments in its first year alone included the child labor ban; an eight-hour workday for rail workers; and a disability-insurance law for federal civil employees. It was fortunate for Wilson that he always rode hard out of the gate, because his domestic vision was increasingly stung and clouded by smoke drifting over from Europe. Europe's self-immolation began in 1914.

The Great War opened as Wilson's first wife Ellen lay dying. Her death crushed Wilson. But seven months later he met Edith Bolling Galt, a widow; they wed quietly in 1915. A smitten Wilson by that point was writing Galt two or three love letters a day, including one on the day after the *Lusitania* sunk. Wilson's passions roared anew, so much that he took the First Lady on a three-week honeymoon as American ships, and Americans *on* foreign ships, were under regular German torpedo assault. President George W. Bush stopped golfing when the 2003 Iraq War began—it "just sends the wrong signal," he said—but Wilson, a fanatic for the links, kept swinging as Brussels burned. (His incredible feat of 1,200 rounds while in office is another first.) He and Edith were so close that she accompanied him to cabinet meetings and intelligence briefings.

That intimacy eventually facilitated what Scott Berg calls the "greatest conspiracy that had ever engulfed the White House." In October 1919, Wilson, after a speech in Pueblo, Colorado, in support of the League of Nations, suffered the first of a brutal series of strokes. Wilson had years of health issues related to blockages in the arteries to his head, one permanently impairing his left eye while at Princeton; this was why Wilson traveled with a doctor named Cary Grayson. But there would be no recovery this time. Wilson, according to John Milton Cooper, another of Wilson's biographers, became an "unstable, delusional creature." Dr. Grayson and Edith, convinced that solitude would heal Wilson, and that resignation from office would kill him, concealed the incapacitated president from the world.

The Constitution says that if the president is unable to discharge his duties, the vice-president takes over. Wilson, after years of facing mostly dubious accusations of unconstitutional action, had finally committed his first personal violation of the Constitution, though under tragic circumstances beyond his control. Wilson, gaunt and short-tempered, lay in bed for months and received only highly filtered news. By day he napped, went on drives, and sat in the White House rose garden that Edith planted; at night he watched silent films. No cabinet meetings were held for seven and a half months. Commission vacancies lay open. China, Italy, and the Netherlands lacked ambassadors. In 1917, Wilson, under a statute, had taken control of the railroads as a war measure, but now he defaulted on his promise to return them immediately after the armistice. His Secretary of State, Robert Lansing, urged Vice President Thomas R. Marshall to step forward, but Marshall would not, in part because Wilson's true condition was so skillfully hidden. The Bureau of Investigation (later the FBI), already quite out of control during the war—at one point investigating "Arabic hieroglyphs" in a Hearst paper's cartoon as a possible encoding to Germans—managed to grow even worse after the war. An unsupervised Attorney General A. Mitchell Palmer began his infamous raids and deportations, beginning in late 1919, against activists of every shade of Red; one day in January 1920 brought 4,000 arrests in 33 cities. Woodrow Wilson was not competent to stop the rampage.

Yet at one point the crippled president was able to summon his old creativity once more, in a minor but interesting episode by which Wilson sought to overcome Republican Senate opposition to the Versailles Treaty. British "governments," unlike our presidential "administrations," regularly collapse and prompt new elections. Wilson, to determine the popular will over the Treaty in this British fashion, proposed that anti-treaty Senators resign and run again. If reelected, he, Wilson, would resign, along with his vice-president—but not before naming an anti-treaty Republican as Secretary of State. The Secretary, then, in the order of succession, would become president. Wilson, broken and depressed, had little left to offer. After retiring from office he occasionally gave speeches to admirers from his D.C. doorstep. He died in February 1924.

Wilson's reputation is at its lowest point since his death. This is because he forgot to follow his hero Lincoln on the issue of race. John

Milton Cooper said that blacks were "invisible" to Wilson; Wilson also refused to appear before black audiences. Scott Berg calls Wilson's views a "genteel racism." Wilson subscribed to a sort of give-it-time indifference, not a frothing hatred, more of a white Northerner than a white Southerner. Progressives, as a class, were no better or worse on race than other Americans. Wilson used the word "nigger" in speeches, but so did the California-born Steffens, later a Communist. Justice Brandeis's biographer, Melvin Urofsky, marvels that in Brandeis's 23 years on the Court, the paragon of legal Progressivism never once wrote an opinion on a racial issue. When Wilson took the White House, observes Arthur Link, "Southerners were riding high in Washington for the first time since the Civil War." Wilson allowed his cabinet, heavily Southern, to segregate, fire, and demote black civil servants, especially where black men supervised white women. One Navy office put up screens to separate whites and blacks, and Atlanta's postmaster purged 35 black employees. Wilson's erstwhile black supporters, like William Monroe Trotter, confronted Wilson during a 1914 meeting at the White House: "Have you a 'new freedom' for white Americans and a new slavery for your Afro-American fellow citizens?" Wilson reversed some of the segregation after protests, but the truth is that a modern president so progressive on economic equality was also the modern president most regressive on racial equality.

The world the Progressives made was the world after the adjustment and modernization needed to bridge the preindustrial and postindustrial ages. If you live in a state with voter registration, or in a city that owns its bus system or that licenses a company to pick up your trash, you live in the Progressives' semi-socialistic world. Yet from the modern vantage, Progressivism mostly just looks like a reaction to large private enterprise in an era before corporate excesses and brutalities were tamed by well-enforced and sophisticated anti-corruption and antitrust codes, labor laws, activist shareholders, audits, 10-K disclosures, and the rest.

Many modern conservative critics of Progressivism see in that super-heated era the seeds of today's leviathan state, and in Wilson in particular a diabolical corrupter of the framers' work. But virtually none of Wilson's serious critics, it seems to me, wish to roll back Wilson's chief institutional accomplishments: the Federal Reserve Act, Clayton Antitrust Act, and Federal Trade Commission. These legacies of Wilson's Progressivism—a spent force by the time doughboys sailed for the Argonne Forest—were left intact by Wilson's three Republican successors, Warren Harding, Calvin Coolidge, and Herbert Hoover. Come to think of it, has any modern president really disproved Walter Lippmann's 1913 prophecy that party platforms would "grow ever more and more into a program of services"? It was not Wilson but later generations that in fact chose to fulfill so many dreams of the 1912 Progressive platform. That platform demanded an agency to supervise "worthless investments" and "highly colored prospectuses offering stock"; this was signed into law in 1934 by Franklin Delano Roosevelt as the Securities and Exchange Commission. It also called for an agency to fix "safety and health standards for the various occupations"; this was signed into law in 1970 by Richard Nixon as the Occupational Safety and Health Administration.

Giving Wilson too much blame gives him too much credit. The assumptions of Progressivism, in its heyday, were so universal that the writings of leading conservative Republicans could sound awfully like the arch-Progressive Democrat Wilson. Elihu Root, for instance, was a GOP veteran of the McKinley and Roosevelt cabinets (though he backed Taft over Roosevelt in 1912), and an erudite, morning-coated corporate lawyer with impeccable right-wing credentials. In 1913 he published a book-length attack on Progressivism's more strident tendencies, in whose "assault against existing institutions," he said, the "wisdom of the founders of the Republic is disputed." He particularly worried about the vogue new direct-democracy reforms, especially the initiative power. But he recognized that the "organic growth" in our institutions followed from technological and industrial progress. His plea was to "adapt our laws as the shifting-conditions of the times require," without abandoning our fundamentals. For, as he said elsewhere of these adaptations:

> There will be no withdrawal from these experiments. We shall go on; we shall expand them, whether we approve theoretically or not, because such agencies furnish protection to rights and obstacles to wrongdoing which under our new social and industrial conditions cannot be practically accomplished by the old and simple procedure of legislatures and courts.

Or take George Sutherland, an English-born, Republican U.S. Senator from Utah and later one of the Four Horsemen, the quartet of Supreme Court Justices famed for their hostility to the New Deal. In a

1912 essay called "What Shall We Do With the Constitution?," Sutherland called the federal government a "social organism" that was constantly "molding by evolutionary rather than by revolutionary methods the fundamental principles of law and government into appropriate form." He objected to Progressive preoccupations like the initiative—as did Wilson—but mostly Sutherland wanted "restless" reformer types to know that the Constitution, far from impeding social advance, was a "free-flowing stream within whose ample banks every needed reform can be launched and carried." Sutherland thought, again like Wilson, that it was a mistake to think that Congress lacked a power because it hadn't exercised it before.

The Constitution was amended four times during Woodrow Wilson's Administration. Dozens of other amendments were seriously considered, by senior members of both major parties, on a welter of topics, from banning child labor to federalizing the "entire transportation system of the country." This is why the assertion, made most eloquently by Wilson, that the Constitution contained within it all the power and flexibility we needed, helped, I believe, to save it. Americans were persuaded to regard most policy choices as sub-constitutional and therefore to leave the Constitution alone. This spared the document marring repetitions of the mistake of 1919's Eighteenth Amendment, on Prohibition, which wrote into the Constitution the era's anti-liquor fad. (Wilson vetoed the amendment's implementing legislation before being overridden by Congress.) If the amendment craze had taken off, it would have destroyed the Constitution's beauty and simplicity. Wilson sternly rejected the call, made most prominently in the 1912 Progressive Party platform, for a "more easy and expeditious method of amending the Federal Constitution."

It was instead state constitutions that suffered the full depredations of Progressivism's amendment run riot. The initiative power opened the floodgates. Some state constitutions underwent almost constant legislation-like revision until they lost their character as constitutions. Today's California Constitution, for instance, one of the worst casualties of this scribbling itch, is a monstrous 75,000 words (the U.S. Constitution is about 7,300), so endlessly patched up with hundreds of amendments, so internally incoherent and unwieldy, and so determined to cover every subject as a matter of fundamental law that it even specifically discusses taxation of nonprofit golf courses. Things could have been worse, in short, for the U.S. Constitution. It emerged from the Progressive Era respected and unimpaired, having borne all the idealism that the people could muster, and ready to serve a citizenry, in the 1920s, surfeited with reform. "Sometimes people call me an idealist," Wilson told an audience in South Dakota, in 1919, a month before the stroke that felled him. "Well, that is the way I know I am an American."

IDA B. WELLS-BARNETT

7

IDA B. WELLS-BARNETT

Rights after Reconstruction to the Jazz Age

S ocrates is said to have chosen a wife so headstrong that, if he could get on with her, it would prove that philosophy is indeed a form of consolation. Yet perhaps it was his experience with Xanthippe that led Socrates to make the immortal argument for female equality that appears in Plato's *Republic*. It has stood unrebutted these last 2,400 years. Socrates, in response to the conventional prejudice that the home was a woman's place by "nature"—a dangerously slippery synonym for "custom," he noted—he offered what one might call the Parable of the Cobblers. Some men by nature were bald, and others hairy-headed, he said, but this fact was perfectly irrelevant to their capacity to hammer shoes. Likewise, women differed from men in many wonderful ways, but in no respect that disqualified them from a share in political power, or even from ruling men.

Ida B. Wells, a black woman born a slave in Holly Springs, Mississippi, in 1862, could have sympathized with Xanthippe. Wells, too, was called irascible, rebellious, and stubborn. Wells, too, had a thoughtful partner—a leading Chicago lawyer named Ferdinand Barnett, who made her "Wells-Barnett," in an avant-garde instance of feminist hyphenation (and which I'll use even when referring to her premarital days). But it was Wells-Barnett, not her husband, who did the philosophical work.

For several years in the 1890s, according to Wells-Barnett's biographer Linda O. McMurry, no black American, except Frederick Douglass, enjoyed more press attention than Wells-Barnett. Once labeled the "uncrowned queen of the Negroes of America," she rose as a newspaper journalist whose fiery editorials in defense of black rights were cast across the nation like hot embers. When Frederick Douglass died, says McMurry, Wells-Barnett was heir apparent, "better known than W.E.B. Du Bois and more ideologically compatible with Douglass than Booker T. Washington." But black women didn't lead black men in those days. And that is what makes the career of Ida B. Wells-Barnett so memorable: she stood at the intersection of the two great socio-legal contests between 1880 and 1920—the struggles against White Supremacy and against Male Supremacy—and battled both quite successfully.

Ida's father Jim was the son of his master and a slave named Peggy, meaning that Ida's grandfather owned humans. The master's childless wife, still bitter about her husband's liaison years later, waited until her husband died and then ordered Peggy whipped. As a little girl Wells-Barnett remembered her mother pacing the floor anxiously, about something called the Ku Klux Klan. Ida studied to become a teacher in the postwar South when, at age 16, yellow fever killed both her parents within hours of each other. "After being a happy, light-hearted schoolgirl," she wrote in her memoir, *Crusade for Justice*, "I suddenly found myself at the head of a family." To support five younger siblings, each week she rode a mule six miles away to teach, then returned on the weekend to wash, iron, and cook.

Wells-Barnett had an irrepressible sense of dignity that was often aroused to her peril. In 1883, riding a train to Memphis, where she would soon teach, she refused an order to move from the ladies' car into the smoking car. The conductor grabbed her shoulder; she bit his hand. It took three men finally to remove her, as she watched white passengers applaud her humiliation. For Wells-Barnett, unlike for Rosa Parks, no NAACP existed in 1883 to bring a lawsuit, so the 21-year-old hired a lawyer herself, in one of the first suits of its kind in Tennessee. "A Darky Damsel Obtains a Verdict for Damages," read the headline in the *Memphis Daily Appeal*. (The Tennessee Supreme Court promptly reversed her victory.)

Not long after, she was fired by the Memphis school board for her criticism in the press of the inadequate buildings and poor teachers given to black students. By now she had begun regular publication. Friends thought her needlessly confrontational—a theme of her life—but she "thought it was right to strike a blow against a glaring evil," as she wrote in her memoir, "and I did not regret it." Nor should she have, for it forced her into full-time journalism. This eventually transformed her from a teacher of a schoolroom into the teacher of a nation.

The "remarkable and talented young school marm from Memphis," marveled the *Washington Bee*, a black paper, has "developed into one of the foremost among the female thinkers of the race." She wrote for a bewildering number of papers in a newspaper-rich era—the *New York Age*, *Detroit Plain-Dealer*, *Indianapolis World*, *Little Rock Sun*, *Memphis Watchman*, *Chattanooga Justice*, to name a few—on subjects all relating in one way or another to black "uplift." This meant everything from etiquette and homemaking to school-board elections and national politics. In 1887 Wells-Barnett attended the Louisville gathering of the National Colored Press Association, in the year it first accepted female journalists; soon she obtained a leadership position within the organization. "She reaches the men by dealing with the political aspect of the race question," one colleague wrote, "and the women she meets around the fireside." "There is scarcely any reason why this woman, young in years and old in experience, shall not be found in the forefront of the great intellectual fight in which the race is now engaged for absolute right and justice under the Constitution," said another journalist. "[I]f she fails to impress her personality upon the time in which she lives, whose fault will it be?"

❧

The doctrine of the first generation of American suffragists held that Wells-Barnett was twice born a slave: first as a black American, then as a female one. These two burdens of birth were linked in the minds of antebellum women's rights activists, abolitionists all. It was in the movement to free the slaves that women like the Grimké sisters, Lucretia Mott, Lucy Stone, Ernestine Rose, Sojourner Truth, and Susan B. Anthony learned to organize, speak, debate, and petition. More specifically, it was at the World Anti-Slavery Convention, in London in 1840, that Elizabeth Cady Stanton and Lucretia Mott, disgusted by the male refusal to seat female delegates, decided to plot the resistance. It began in 1848 with a hundred radical ladies at Seneca Falls, the hometown of Stanton, whose prolific wit would make her the Voltaire of the movement.

The event that changed Elizabeth Stanton's life was to hear her father, a prominent judge, cry out after her brother's death, "Oh, my daughter, I wish you were a boy!" "I taxed every power," she wrote, "hoping someday to hear my father say: 'Well, a girl is as good as a boy, after all.' But he never said it." She emerged a cross between Betty Friedan and Martha Stewart. She was a rebel who at her marriage ceremony refused to utter the word "obey." Yet she was also a self-described "enthusiastic house-keeper" who needled women for striving to become "artists" while unable to "make a good loaf of bread nor a palatable cup of coffee." Watching her father work taught her the miseries of a law that was created and executed by men alone. Her friend Ernestine Rose reported that in New York a judge imprisoned a boot thief while letting off a wife-beater with a rep-rimand; the difference was that the thief had misused *another's* property. In a different case, a brute who murdered his wife's lover was acquitted for insanity, only to exercise his legal custody power to dispossess his wife of the 12-year-old son she alone had always cared for.

Some women at Seneca Falls thought that demanding the vote would "make the whole movement ridiculous," preferring to concentrate on things like educational rights or divorce laws. But Stanton was already convinced that the "power to choose rulers and make laws, was the right by which all others could be secured." Stanton was a granddaughter of veterans of George Washington's army, and took up her forebears' cry that "no just government can be formed without the consent of the governed." Soon after Seneca Falls, one of the nation's largest circulating newspa-pers, the *New York Herald*, pronounced the women's movement part of the 19th century's "comic history." Men actually paid to attend suffrage gatherings for the high privilege of drowning out female speakers with foot-stomping and boos. It took decades for a majority even of women, outside the suffrage movement, to agree with Stanton that to be voteless was to be powerless, and therefore that suffragism was a form of eman-cipationism. Stanton was endlessly exasperated by women who thought their presence at political rallies immodest while devouring newspaper accounts of their dresses at evening balls.

Yet the tension between political activity and femininity was real for women, Ida Wells-Barnett included. The many targets of her criticism did not include the ladylike elements of her mid-Victorian era and its demure high collars, chaperoned movement, and comfort with viewing life chastely from behind window curtains. In one article from 1888 Wells-Barnett described her "model woman" as possessed of the "preservation of honor," "womanly modesty," and "sweetness of disposition." Wells-Barnett knew that part of the insult intended to her by the Memphis train officials who ordered her off the ladies' car was to show her that, to whites, she lacked the quality of womanhood. When Wells-Barnett, prim and well-dressed, waded into the hurly-burly of political journalism, she was pelted with condescension, accusations of promiscuity, and names like "adventuress," "strumpet," "saddle-colored Sapphira," and, by the *New York Times*, "mulatress missionary." At other times she was praised for her writing's "masculine" force and effectiveness, which she must have felt rather a mixed compliment. Wells-Barnett was at home in her rigid age. She was as determined as any woman to act in an upper-class, even queenly fashion, and to be treated as such, notwithstanding that the classic "feminine virtues"—innocence, delicacy, reticence, coyness—are the antitheses of the political ones. But she understood the dilemma. "I am an anomaly to myself as well as to others," she wrote in her diary.

The fear that many women had of losing their romantic charms—which really meant their desirability for marriage—was played on by politicians as they swatted away proposals for a female vote. U.S. Senator George Vest of Missouri, a former legislator in the Confederate government who, not incidentally, popularized the line that a dog is a man's best friend, said the following in an 1887 debate on whether to recognize female suffrage in the Constitution:

[W]hen I turn from the arena where man contends with man for what we call the prizes of this paltry world—I want to go back, not to the embrace of some female ward politician, but to the earnest loving look and touch of a true woman. I want to go back to the jurisdiction of the wife, the mother; and instead of a lecture upon finance or the tariff or upon the construction of the Constitution, I want those blessed loving details of domestic life and domestic love.

This argument—that politics stripped women of their comeliness—seems to have been the most effective anti-suffrage argument, with both men *and* women, until the very moment, in 1920, that suffrage finally entered the Constitution. Suffragists noted, early on, how arguments like Senator Vest's purported, with overflowing chivalry, to protect women, while keeping man and his interests, as always, at the center. Many of these gallant knights of womanhood fretted that the vote would "mar the beauty" of the women they worshipped—while blocking any legislative effort to prevent the mangling of mothers in overheated machine-rooms or to rescue twelve-year-old girls from ten-hour peonage in cotton mills. Hollow arguments like Vest's were nevertheless far from the only cause of the delay.

Equally important was that the crucial alliance between the women's rights movement and the black rights movement exploded in the late 1860s, during the debates over the Fourteenth and Fifteenth Amendments. These amendments after the Civil War sought to secure to black men the same rights enjoyed by white men, including the vote, but in doing so they actually introduced the word "male" into the Constitution. The great Massachusetts Senator Charles Sumner, a champion of both movements, believed that only one group, between women and black men, could enter the gates of enfranchisement at once. "Suffrage for black men," said a colleague, "will be all the strain the Republican party can stand." The truth, and tragedy, was that the two causes were pitted against each other. An outraged Stanton, an ugly tone creeping into her normally tolerant prose, fumed that illiterate black field hands and bootblacks were now to become an "added power" against the mothers, wives, and daughters of white judges and legislators. Black men would learn, conversely, that white women, whether Southern supremacists or Northern indifferents, could be a counterweight to *them*. Only one group was sure to lose: black women.

"There is a great stir about colored men getting their rights," said Sojourner Truth, the tall, mystical ex-slave who once bared her breasts when a catcaller accused her of being a man, "but not a word about the colored women. And if colored men get their rights, and not colored women theirs, you see the colored men will be masters over the women, and it will be just as bad as it was before." In a tense exchange between two titans of American history, at a suffrage convention in 1869, Frederick Douglass rebuked Susan B. Anthony for her apparent insensitivity to black needs: "when women, because they are women, are hunted down through the cities of New York and New Orleans; when they are dragged from their houses and hung upon lamp-posts," said Douglass, only then would come the "same urgency in giving the ballot to woman as to the negro." A voice in the audience cried out, "Is that not all true about black women?" "Yes, yes," Douglass shouted back. "But not because she is a woman, but because she is black."

Ida Wells-Barnett, like Douglass, and most black women, feared racism more than sexism. It was deadlier. The event that "changed the whole course of my life," she wrote, was the Memphis lynching in 1892 of one of her closest friends, Thomas Moss. He was part owner of the People's Grocery Company, a new outfit that had drawn black shoppers from a rival white grocer named William Barrett. This commercial clash, added to postwar hatreds and a street fight in which black boys prevailed over white boys, eventually led to Moss and two others being dragged outside the city limits, mutilated, and killed. Moss begged for his life with these last words: "Tell my people to go West—there is no justice for them here." Wells-Barnett published searing exposures, in a paper called *Free Speech*, of this and other lynchings. She showed, in particular, how they were abetted by the law itself; Barrett, by some accounts, eventually acquired the People's Grocery Company for an eighth of its value. Her exposés were so embarrassing to Memphians that Wells-Barnett herself drew a mob to her office and was forced to flee forever. Men watched the trains as she escaped, promising to kill her on sight, and she bought a pistol that afterward she always kept in her purse. "I felt if I could take one lyncher with me," she wrote, "this would even up the score a little bit."

The lynching of Thomas Moss illuminated for Wells-Barnett, as in a flash, the nature of lynchings: they were not spontaneous outbursts of murderous white rage but a useful means of terrorizing "Negroes who were acquiring wealth and property." The near-universal excuse by lynchers and their apologists was, as Wells-Barnett wrote, that black men were a "race of rapists." Contact between black males and white females was supposedly what provoked lynchings, before the act, and justified them afterward. White Southerners apparently felt that white men could (discreetly) enjoy the favors of black women, like, actually, Wells-Barnett's grandparents, but the idea, as one black journalist wrote, that there might be a "partiality of white Juliets for colored Romeos," was unthinkable to a majority of them. In one typical frame-up, Wells-Barnett noted, an eight-year-old "rape" victim turned out to be the 18-year-old daughter of a sheriff who discovered her in the room of a black man. But rape claims had the dual purpose of saving the family's honor and better instigating the lynch mob. In response to criticisms by Northern papers of Memphis after the People's Grocery lynching, the *Memphis Appeal-Avalanche*, Wells-Barnett's chief antagonist, defended its citizens by arguing that when an "unprotected woman is assaulted...chivalrous men in the neighborhood will forget that there are such things as courts." Yet in murdering Thomas Moss, Wells-Barnett observed, the lynchers hadn't bothered even to fabricate a rape charge against their victim.

Covering the death of her friend began the journalistic work that made Wells-Barnett famous as an anti-lynching activist, the "crusade" for which she is best known today. Others wrote, like Wells-Barnett, with rhetorical outrage and remonstration, but she cultivated a fact-heavy reportorial style that made her doubly effective. She pioneered the practice of visiting black men accused of crimes, in their jail cells, to get their side of the story; she attended trials to hear white women compelled to accuse black men who in fact had been secret boyfriends; she hired white Pinkertons to investigate in places where she could not go. "We should be in a position to investigate every lynching and get the facts for ourselves," she said. What she found shocked even her: in a given year, despite popular conceptions to the contrary, not even a quarter of lynchings had a sexual assault alleged. Greed, instead, often seemed the hidden, compelling motive.

The Arkansas Race Riot (1920) was a pamphlet she wrote detailing the weeklong mass killing and arrest of black cotton farmers and their families, in October 1919, in Elaine, Arkansas. The aggressors were white competitors of these farmers who resented their victims' attempt to organize to assert their economic power. At the end of the work she calculated the looters' gains: "the white lynchers of Phillips County," she wrote, "made a cool million dollars last year off the cotton crop of the twelve men who are sentenced to death, the seventy-five who are in the Arkansas penitentiary, and the one hundred whom they lynched outright." Wells-Barnett had been the first outsider to arrive in Arkansas to help the condemned men. Their case eventually got to the U.S. Supreme Court, which, in *Moore v. Dempsey* (1923), found the facts so repulsive—such as setting the prisoners' execution date weeks before their trial—that it ordered their case reheard. This was one of the first humanitarian interventions of its kind by the Supreme Court. And it was rare.

Wells-Barnett became a sort of clearinghouse to document lynchdom in order to bear witness to its medieval fiendishness. She reported that, in 1893, in South Carolina, three black men were hanged, "one after another," on a charge of rape, because the crowd said it wanted to be sure it got the "right one." The next year, in Tennessee, after a black man allegedly frightened three white girls on a wagon, Wells-Barnett received an ogreish telegram from a local journalist: "Lee Walker, colored man, accused of raping white women, in jail here, will be taken out and burned by whites tonight. Can you send Miss Ida Wells to write it up?" These taunts rarely provoked Wells-Barnett to depart from her literary style at its best: the unadorned, emotionless, and brutal statement of fact, such as that, in the 20th century, a significant part of American civilization was engaged in the ritualistic "burnings alive of black human beings."

Susan B. Anthony, once called the Napoleon of the struggle for women's suffrage, at first laughed at the idea of votes for women. But subordination by men in her original cause, temperance, convinced her that the moral power of women meant nothing unless backed by the ballot. Eventually she came to believe suffrage the solution to every problem, from war to co-education. Elizabeth Stanton recalled that her friend Anthony's "refrain, 'woman suffrage,'" was "as persistent as the 'never more' of Poe's raven." For decades Anthony traveled at her own expense to speak in halls, lyceums, saloons, barns, legislative assemblies, train depots, constitutional conventions, log cabins, unfinished schoolhouses, congressional committees, or, in one notable instance, on a barge halfway across the Mississippi at midnight. She even spoke to the inmates of an insane asylum. A fellow activist, Virginia Minor, justified this appearance as simply an address to a group of peers, since "lunatics," like women and criminals, were among the select classes of Americans declared by law to be incapable of voting. Anti-suffrage women for years refused to shake Susan B. Anthony's hand and often informed the unmarried campaigner, to her face, that *they* had husbands, thank God, to look after their interests. The Fifteenth Amendment forbid denial of the vote "on account of race." The draft women's suffrage amendment replaced "race" with "sex." For years Anthony watched as what she hoped might be the Sixteenth Amendment, then Seventeenth, and then Eighteenth, came to be known simply as the "Susan B. Anthony Amendment," so wholly had it become associated with her personally. This amendment would be introduced in Congress annually, in vain, for 42 years, beginning in 1878.

Ida Wells-Barnett was Anthony's houseguest after a speaking visit by Wells-Barnett in Rochester, New York, where Anthony lived. "Those were precious days," recalled the younger Ida, "in which I sat at the feet of this pioneer and veteran in the work of women's suffrage." Anthony respected Wells-Barnett's anti-lynching struggle, too. When Anthony's longtime stenographer refused to take dictation from Wells-Barnett—she would not serve a black woman, she said—Anthony immediately told the stenographer to get her bonnet and find new work. But at the tactical level, Susan B. Anthony pushed for women's rights at the expense of black rights. Anthony frankly admitted to Wells-Barnett during her visit that, for the sake of Southern support, she distanced the National American Woman Suffrage Association, or "NAWSA," her movement's organizational vehicle, from black suffragist organizations. Anthony even asked Wells-Barnett: "And you think I was wrong in so doing?" Wells-Barnett said yes: the "gains for suffrage," she was sure, were not worth the acquiescence to the "attitude of segregation."

Wells-Barnett, like Anthony, became a vigorous speaker; in Wells-Barnett's case, on lynching. During one tour through Illinois she spoke in Decatur, Quincy, Springfield, and Bloomington with her six-month-old son in tow. She claimed, plausibly, to be the first woman to take to the lecturing circuit while breastfeeding; she even brought the baby on stage one night, until the baby, hearing but not seeing his mother, began to wail. Susan B. Anthony, during another stay by Wells-Barnett at Anthony's home, chided Wells-Barnett for starting a family. "Miss Anthony, you don't believe in women getting married?" Ida asked. "Oh, yes," Anthony replied, "but not women like you who had a special call for special work. I too might have married but it would have meant dropping the work to which I had set my hand." Anthony's prediction about Wells-Barnett's "divided duty" came true: after Wells-Barnett's second child was born, she essentially retired from public life until her fourth and last child was eight years old. Wells-Barnett's younger daughter recalled that her mother, despite the activist work that made her famous, "firmly believed in the importance of the presence of a mother in the home during the children's formative years."

Susan B. Anthony's successor at the National American Woman Suffrage Association was Carrie Lane, later famed as the great Carrie Catt. She was an Iowa farm girl who became the largely ungarlanded hero of the suffrage movement and one of the finest political strategists in American history. Catt rose to be the five-star general of the mostly female suffrage "army" that, with its yellow ribbons, long dresses, wide-brimmed hats, and unflappable courage, made the final drive to victory in 1920. She was discovered when the Iowa Woman Suffrage Association learned to its astonishment that almost every woman in the town of Mason City, Iowa, where Catt lived, had signed a suffrage petition, though the town had no formal suffrage organization. Carrie's second husband signed a nuptial contract that let Catt devote two months each spring, and two each fall, to suffrage organizing. Nobody did it better. In an 1895 speech at a national suffrage convention in Atlanta, she lamented that suffragists numbered in the millions while the organizational ranks only comprised thousands. Suffragists for the last 40 years had been preoccupied with "education and agitation, and not organization," she continued. "[T]here are States in which there is sentiment enough to carry a woman suffrage amendment, but it is individual and not organized sentiment, and is, therefore, ineffective."

Her brilliant insider's history of suffrage, *Woman Suffrage and Politics* (1923), contains one of the most famous passages in suffrage literature: "To get the word male in effect out of the constitution," she wrote, "cost the women of the country fifty-two years of pauseless campaign." She tallied 56 referendum campaigns; 480 campaigns to urge state legislatures to submit suffrage amendments to voters; 30 campaigns to get national parties to put suffrage planks into their platforms; and 19 formal campaigns in Washington, D.C., with 19 successive Congresses. Millions of dollars were raised and spent. But most heartbreakingly, she wrote:

> Hundreds of women gave the accumulated possibilities of an entire lifetime, thousands gave years of their lives, hundreds of thousands gave constant interest and such aid as they could. It was a continuous,

seemingly endless, chain of activity. Young suffragists who helped forge the last links of that chain were not born when it began. Old suffragists who forged the first links were dead when it ended.

Carrie Catt set out, in her book, to answer the question that she thought would most interest posterity: why did a cause of such "inevitability," she said, whose best recommendation, in the words of a Rhode Island legislative committee in 1879, was that its ablest opponents seemed unable to give a coherent argument against it, remain stalled for so many agonizing decades? I might rephrase it thus: how could it be that the suffrage movement began in earnest in an age when most Americans had galloping horses for transportation, only to end in the same decade that commercial flights began? Catt's conclusion was that even the noblest constitutional rights are won only after passing through the greasy, principle-free meat grinder known as partisan politics. "No party adopts an idea," she told the League of Women Voters in 1921, "until it believes it will gain more votes than it will lose by it."

Suffrage would get entangled over the years with one cause after another, in each stoking the male fear that granting women the vote meant relinquishing ancient prerogatives or present-day advantages. Women, inch by inch, obtained the right to inherit property; the right to be a doctor or a police "matron"; the right to divorce dinner-table despots; the right to throw off groping foremen. The right to cast a ballot, alone, is the only female right that had to be specifically secured in the Constitution. This was not the result of mere cultural paternalism, and its musty prattle about woman's "sphere" or God's plan or the home's harmony. These were all arguments, said Thomas B. Reed, a Maine Republican in Congress whose pro-suffrage views disgusted his own spouse, readily made by Algerians in the habit of storing their veiled wives in dark rooms. What ultimately kept women back, rather, is that traditionalism is often little more than a prejudice, and a prejudice, in turn, is often little more than unconscious self-interest. Ida Wells-Barnett knew this quite well. "[W]hen principle and prejudice come into collision," she wrote, "principle retires and leaves prejudice the victor." Thus custom, taboo, and stigma against women all fell, one after another, except as to voting, for voting was the one right that translated into raw power. It was the one right that threatened political emasculation.

The slow-motion stumble to the Nineteenth Amendment began in quiet, empty Wyoming Territory (population in 1870: 9,118). No interests had yet entrenched themselves there and the lonesome ranchers and buck-skinned mountaineers eagerly welcomed gentler influences. Suffrage passed Wyoming's tiny Senate by a 6-2 vote, with one abstention. A New England preacher, visiting during an election, saw that each time a woman approached the polls a man cried out "Hist! Be quiet! A woman is coming!" But what really illustrated Carrie Catt's thesis was what happened when, in 1890, Wyoming, under firm Republican rule, sought admission to the Union. Democrats resisted the prospect of two new Republican Senators under the pretext of horror at women's suffrage. The House vote to admit Wyoming broke along party lines. Utah in 1870 became the second territory to give women the vote. But in 1887, Congress, in the Edmunds-Tucker Act, stripped Utah of its polygamy, the true target of the act, and woman's suffrage, the collateral damage.

In one election in pre-suffrage Kansas, Catt noted, a suffrage amendment showed strong support. But Populists, though the first national party to endorse suffrage nationally, nevertheless believed, under the pressure of this particular election, that women in cities outnumbered women in the country and feared that these city-dwelling women would elect Republicans. Republicans, by contrast, suspected that there were more rural women than urban ones and, if allowed to vote, they would put the Populists in. So both of these parties in Kansas that year opposed suffrage. New York City's Tammany Hall blocked suffrage for years, fearing that women's promise to "clean up politics" meant its demise. Only in 1917, when the machine became convinced that alienating women was the greater danger, did it stand aside and let suffrage into New York.

Suffrage, like most moral causes, eventually changed from a political liability to support to a political liability to oppose. But even that didn't end the partisanship. By 1913, individual states had enfranchised women in a fifth of the United States; these states, together, elected one-seventh of the House and a sixth of the votes necessary to choose a president. Yet there was still the question, by 1917, of which party would get the credit, among a soon-to-be, 20-million-strong class of voters, for ushering suffrage into the Constitution. Republicans, hoping their pro-suffragism would restore them to power, needed to deny the still-majority Democrats this victory, so maneuvered to block a vote on the Anthony Amendment before the 1918 congressional election. An electoral cycle later, when Republicans had the votes to pass the Anthony Amendment on their own, Senate Democrats now showily urged ratification of the amendment in order to neutralize Republican pretensions as the benefactors of women.

Among the states, the main source of political opposition varied by region. In the Midwest, it was typically the shadowy "liquor interest." This was in fact distillers and brewers as well as allied industries: saloon keepers, hoteliers, bottle-makers, barley farmers, druggists, and coopers, all convinced that women would dry them out. This coalition, long the demon of feminists, invented a hardball version of cigar-wreathed intrigue. Suffragists were alternately depressed and amused by years of documents like the one, in 1913, from the "women" of the "Michigan Association Opposed to Woman Suffrage," which read: "We have women's greatest right—to be free from political medley. . . . We now ask the men of Michigan to defend us and vote NO on suffrage." It was mailed out courtesy of a local Liquor Dealers' Association. The liquor opposition was poised to keep derailing votes for women, by a hundred tricks and stratagems, until finally it was cut off, in 1919, by Prohibition and the Eighteenth Amendment. Those women who opposed suffrage, the so-called "antis"—who minced into public life under the protective cover of their husbands, as in "Mrs. Louis Frothingham" or "Mrs. Horace Brock"—served frequently as lacy camouflage for liquor groups or, elsewhere, states' righters.

In the East, industrial and business concerns often had no principled opposition to suffrage other than anxieties over a new, untested voting bloc and the unsettling prospect of further innovation against the established financial order. Railroads and banks had seen how expansion of voting power in Progressive reforms like the initiative had become anti-corporate maces. Among easterners, there was a strong overlap between those who opposed suffrage and those general anti-reform types who opposed the Sixteenth Amendment's income tax and Seventeenth Amendment's direct Senate elections.

In the South, the fear, as ever, was that enfranchised black women would undermine Jim Crow. Black women, said Susan B. Anthony, also combined the "two most hated elements of humanity." Carrie Catt said that the average Southern Democrat, as late as 1920, was still filled with explosive rage at any mention of woman suffrage. He would not and could not argue the question. His response to all appeals [for suffrage] was a scornful, sputtering ejaculation, "Negro *women*!"

But white Southern suffragists, like Kentucky's Laura Clay, tried to assuage these fears: they argued that giving suffrage to them would double the white vote and so *ensure* white supremacy. But for Southern officialdom, the supreme imperative of keeping out black women justified keeping out white women, too. John Sharp Williams, a U.S. Senator from Mississippi, supposedly said: "We are not afraid to maul a black man over the head if he dares to vote, but we can't treat women, even black women, that way. No, we'll allow no women suffrage. It may be right, but we won't have it." "Not one perhaps in a hundred of them can read or write," said James B. Beck, a U.S. Senator from Kentucky, of black women. "Take them from their washtubs and their household work and they are absolutely ignorant of the new duties of voting citizens."

❧

Ida Wells-Barnett, who relocated to Chicago after fleeing Memphis, was one of the most important figures in America working to ensure that black women would overcome ignorance, real or perceived. Black women had organized on a large scale in the North as early as the 1890s, particularly though "clubs," a now-vanished form of political sisterhood. Wells-Barnett personally founded so many of them that she became known as the "Mother of Clubs." Some, in her honor, were named Ida B. Wells Clubs. In the days before suffrage, her goal, Wells-Barnett said, was to gird black women to "use their moral influence to see that their men voted and voted right." By 1896, the National League of Colored Women, and later the National Association of Colored Women, had a hundred groups among its associational members. At one remarkable gathering, Harriet Tubman, the oldest attendee, introduced to the audience the youngest attendee, Wells-Barnett's first son.

Later, in 1913, Wells-Barnett founded the famed Alpha Suffrage Club, the first suffrage organization for black women. That year women in Illinois got the right to vote for U.S. presidents and local officials—a form of so-called "partial" suffrage that in many states preceded full suffrage. (It was easier to obtain since it didn't threaten state-legislature incumbents.) In 1916, in the first national election where both major parties embraced suffrage, on paper at least, Wells-Barnett supported Charles Evan Hughes over Woodrow Wilson. Three years before, Wells-Barnett was part of a delegation to the Wilson White House to complain about growing segregation in federal departments. She recalled that Wilson "received us standing" and said he was "unaware of such discrimination," but after being shown an order from a cabinet member forbidding white and black clerks from using the same toilets, he "promised to look into the matter."

Wells-Barnett took pride in her business card during this period; it denominated her the national organizer for "Illinois Colored Women." The Alpha Suffrage Club hosted panels, dinners, parades, and receptions for candidates for offices like city judge or county commissioner. Wells-Barnett brought women to Springfield to lobby against a Jim Crow public-accommodations bill and another bill outlawing miscegenation. "[T]he winding through the capitol building of two or three hundred colored women," Wells-Barnett recalled, "was itself a sight that had never been witnessed before." She bought a voting machine and had an election commissioner give her members lessons in electoral procedure. Racial tribalism was the order of the day, and Wells-Barnett sought to elect blacks, as blacks, to office, most famously the Chicago South Side's Oscar De Priest, the first black man elected to Congress in the 20th century. Her club even expelled members found to have worked for the election of white aldermen and published their names as traitors. In 1918, an overheated federal agent labeled Wells-Barnett a "far more dangerous agitator than Marcus Garvey," which was untrue; aside from advocating defensive fire against lynchers, Wells-Barnett never encouraged violence.

It was in working to elect black men that Wells-Barnett encountered a form of opposition unrelated to racism and in some respects even more disheartening, because it was so unexpected: she learned that black men usually choose maleness over blackness. Around 1913 Wells-Barnett organized a door-to-door campaign to encourage black women to take to politics. "The women at first were very much discouraged," she recalled. "They said that the men jeered at them and told them they ought to be at home taking care of the babies." The passages in her memoir where she comes closest to losing her cool are those describing what she saw as short-sighted, self-defeating black husbands and ministers who "not one of them" said a word to encourage black women to take advantage of the vote. The men of her community, she would find, were hostile to the unmanning suggestion that inferiors like women were needed to defend their lives and honor.

Wells-Barnett had long struggled against this perception. In 1911, after Wells-Barnett took a leadership role in the Negro Fellowship League, the group's president said that some among the group's "manhood object to the leadership of a woman." Wells-Barnett replied that she stepped forward because she "could no longer sit quietly by and see the interest of the race sacrificed because of the indifference of our manly men." Anna J. Cooper, a scholar who in 1925 became the fourth black American woman to get a Ph.D., lamented that "while our men seem thoroughly abreast of the times on almost every other subject, when they strike the woman question they drop back into sixteenth century logic." Charlotte E. Ray, thought to be the first black woman to qualify as a lawyer in America, had to give up her practice in the District of Columbia after too few people — black men included — found themselves willing to entrust their legal affairs to a black female.

The second source of enduring disappointment for Wells-Barnett was that, just as black men put sex before race, white women put race before sex, usually to appease the hideous idols of the South, in their suffrage quest for the all-important electoral majority. In 1918, the Northeastern Federation of Women's Clubs, an affiliation of about 6,000 black women, was quietly asked by a higher-up at Catt's National American Woman Suffrage Association to withdraw its request to join NAWSA's ranks. A few years earlier, in 1913, Wells-Barnett was in Washington, D.C., as part of Illinois's delegation to a national suffrage parade. Southern white ladies threatened to boycott if Wells-Barnett and other black women marched alongside them. When her Illinois colleagues asked her to defer to the sensitivities of the lily-white belles, a reporter for the *Chicago Daily Tribune* caught the reaction: "Mrs. Barnett's voice trembled with emotion and two large tears coursed their way down her cheeks before she could raise her veil and wipe them away." She pretended to exit and stand as a spectator. But when the Illinois delegation passed by, she quietly slipped into formation.

The great question for two generations of suffrage leaders was whether the vote was best reached by piecemeal, state-by-state efforts, or all at once by a federal constitutional amendment. The movement split, in 1869, into the Anthony-Stanton National Woman Suffrage Association, and Lucy Stone's rival American Woman Suffrage Association; the tactical difference over state or federal approaches was one cause of the rupture. "It is the business of the States to do the district work," said Anthony, at a convention in 1893, "to create public sentiment, to make a national organization possible, and then to bring their united power to the capital and focus it on Congress." A woman there responded that 25 years in the halls of Congress was enough to show her that they ought instead to "sow the seed of suffrage" back in their respective home states and their state constitutions. The bitter difference of opinion on this state-or-federal question continued to the very end. Only in retrospect did it become clear that the only path, as Yogi Berra might have put it, was both at once.

The state route brought early victories in the free-spirited West: Wyoming (1890), Colorado (1893), Utah (1896), Idaho (1896), and then a second wave before World War I in Washington (1910), California (1911), Arizona, Kansas, Oregon (1912), Montana, and Nevada (1914). Suffrage efforts in the states grew increasingly sophisticated and varied. In the 1910 campaign in Washington, led by Emma DeVoe, a low-level approach was chosen, with women soliciting neighbors, doctors, grocers, and postmen, and asking ministers to preach a "special woman suffrage sermon" on one Sunday. In 1912, in Well-Barnett's Illinois, by contrast, suffragists—fighting for presidential and partial suffrage only—compiled card indexes for every legislator ("card-indexer" became a leading insult from "antis"), noting political leanings, religion, marital status, and the harmoniousness of home relations, if wedded. Legislators were then approached "in a way to overcome their individual prejudices." In later campaigns women also took note of golf partners, drinking habits, and whether a lawmaker's mother or wife was thought to have more influence on him.

Toward the end of the victorious Illinois campaign, which was led by a woman named Grace Wilbur Trout, the pro-suffrage House Speaker was spotted looking "haggard and worn" from relentless opposition. A Mrs. Treadwell arranged a "telephone brigade" of men and women to call the Speaker every 15 minutes for three days to buck him up. During the floor vote, Mrs. Trout personally stood guard to keep hostile lobbyists from illegally oiling into the chamber. In 1915, New York saw a loud and costly campaign led by Carrie Catt that had activists target ethnic communities like Germans or legislative committees like Ways and Means. They made speeches between acts at playhouses and convened an astounding 5,225 outdoor meetings. And they lost big, 553,348 for suffrage, 748,332 against it. Yet—and here is the real lesson—two nights later, they raised $100,000 for the 1917 campaign. That time they won, making New York the only full-suffrage state on the East Coast before ratification in 1920.

For each state victory there seemed a counterbalancing setback. In 1912–13, as suffrage won in Oregon, Arizona, and Kansas, for instance, it lost in the bigger and more influential states of Ohio, Michigan, and Wisconsin. Particularly discouraging were the losses in Michigan and Ohio, generally regarded by suffragists as having been stolen by liquor operatives and collusive officials, largely by ballot-stuffing or ballot-skimming. (California suffragists had avoided that possibility in 1911 by posting detectives at ballot vaults in San Francisco and Oakland.) In states that experimented with granting "partial" suffrage, which often amounted to the right to participate in boring plebiscites on bond measures or school-board elections, low turnout in the elections on these matters gave anti-suffragists supposed proof that women were indifferent to the vote. In 1915, the suffrage cause lost its massive showdowns in New York, described above, but also in Massachusetts, New Jersey, and Pennsylvania, which undermined not only efforts in other states but the federal campaign, too. In Massachusetts, in particular, suffrage went down so comprehensively—losing in every city, except noble Tewksbury, and there, apparently, by one vote—that Bay State women, their cause all but dead, would have no choice but to await the Nineteenth Amendment.

Some suffragists even felt that their *successes* had an undermining effect: wins in Western states suggested, to Northeastern and Southern voters, that a state-by-state approach was a perfectly democratic way to give women the vote, *if* that was what the people, i.e., the men, really wanted. In the South, the slogans of home rule, states' rights, and white supremacy forbid any endorsement of a federal amendment, even though many Southern suffragists watched with despair as their legislators rushed, hypocritically, to federalize prohibition by constitutional amendment. In the end, both the state and federal tracks proved necessary. State victories ensured that sympathetic Congressmen would not fear getting too far ahead of constituents. Meanwhile, state "ground" operations, even in states where suffrage lost chronically, were still necessary for victory when the final federal push for ratification came.

The days before the Nineteenth Amendment was at last ratified had all the shabbiness one could want in a moment of profound constitutional change. Thirty-six states were needed. In Texas, a representative named R.H. Watts declared, "I would rather die and go to hell than vote for woman suffrage." He earned a minute's applause for his statesmanlike sentiment. Western Governors whose states had had suffrage for years refused to call special legislative sessions to ratify, for no better reason than that special sessions were expensive and national ratification seemed likely to happen without them. The women in Carson City, Nevada, provided free room and board to Silver State lawmakers to overcome their untimely penny-pinching. World War I had begun and Western suffragists wrote their Governors to remind them that women, by that time, were voting in elections held by most of our war allies, like the British Empire, Russia, and Belgium, and even in the elections of our war enemies, in Germany and Austria-Hungary. Most sordid of all was the clash to keep Tennessee from becoming the 36th and final state. Lobbyists from around the nation flooded in. The Maryland Men's Anti-Suffrage League, for instance, renamed itself the Maryland League for State Defense and urged Tennessee's legislators to hold fast. In a last act of desperation, two dozen anti-suffrage legislators crossed states lines into an open-armed Alabama to try to break the quorum.

But there were also bright moments in the larger struggle. In January 1918, Frederick C. Hicks, a Congressman from New York, was with his dying suffragist wife when the vote approached in Congress to send the Nineteenth Amendment out to the states for ratification. He left her deathbed in order to vote and returned from Washington for his wife's funeral—all in order to ensure that the amendment passed in the House by 274-136, exactly the necessary two-thirds majority. That October, the bill Hicks voted for lost in the Senate—by two votes—before finally passing, after another try, in 1919. A few months later, in the Tennessee legislature's ratification proceeding, Harry Burns, a 24-year-old lawmaker from rural east Tennessee, switched his vote to support suffrage. In doing so he brought the vote to 20 million American women. His change in heart came after receiving this note from his mother:

> Dear Son: Hurrah, and vote for suffrage! Don't keep them in doubt. I notice some of the speeches against. They were bitter. I have been watching to see how you stood, but have not noticed anything yet. Don't forget to be a good boy and help Mrs. Catt put the "rat" in ratification. Your Mother.

Years later Burns said:

> My mother was a college woman, a student of national and international affairs who took an interest in all public issues. She could not vote. Yet the tenant farmers on our farm, some of whom were illiterate, could vote. On that roll call, confronted with the fact that I was going to go on record for time and eternity on the merits of the question, I had to vote for ratification.

And thus, for one sweet moment, the fate of a nation and a mother's love became one.

The dread of the party chieftains was that enfranchisement would introduce, all at once, a bloc of women voters who would outnumber men. This fear produced the most interesting legal challenge to the Nineteenth Amendment, *Leser v. Garnett* (1922). Here the U.S. Supreme Court rejected the argument that so great an addition to the electorate, forced on a state by national constitutional amendment, destroyed the state's autonomy. But as it happened, politicians relaxed when they saw that women fell out along party lines as inevitably and as reliably as men did. Today it seems obvious that half of humanity would differ on subjects like segregation, alcohol, pacifism, Sabbath laws, capital punishment, and labor reform, just as it differs today, even on "women's issues" like abortion. Women began voting in equal numbers with men in 1956. Since 1966, in terms of sheer numbers, more women have chosen to vote in elections than men.

For Ida Wells-Barnett, the 1920s, her final decade, featured, as for most Americans in fact, none of the boozy disillusionment or carpe-diem raciness of cocktail-sipping flappers and Fitzgeralds. She kept soberly at her work, even as she remained, by the standards of the time, a radical. She broke with the Alpha Suffrage Club to campaign solely for women candidates, a stance that was then a novelty. Another group she founded in 1927, the Third Ward Women's Political Club, had the motto "For Women, of Women, by Women." Feminism, in 1927, was a rare attitude for black women, who, as the social worker Jane Addams said, were "never aggressive, but always ready quietly to walk into the way of opportunity when it is presented." Patronizing this may seem, but it captures the quietism of a class of Americans that W.E.B. Du Bois called the "daughters of sorrow," or that Zora Neale Hurston would soon label the "mules of the world," a group facing more daily abrasions than any other.

Wells-Barnett also maintained a matriarchal devotion to elevating black culture and what she called "respectability." She gave lectures on African-American history, for general audiences, and on modern banking, for women. She groomed black female leaders, whose success, as with her friend Bertha Montgomery, was still mostly confined to positions in places like the County Board of Assessors Office. Wells-Barnett, in her late 60s, traversed Illinois registering black women voters, claiming to have raised their vote by 50%. She wrote pamphlets to influence her cohort, like *Why I Am For Hoover*. "Few women responded as I had hoped," she wrote of her struggle for distaff solidarity. But her efforts restored some of the name recognition she had lost since the 1890s, during the peak of her anti-lynching campaign. She also became the first black woman to run for the Illinois State Senate. But it would be 47 long years before a black woman would actually win such a seat.

"An uncompromising militancy and 'race first' attitude doomed Wells-Barnett's influence in the national suffrage movement," writes Linda O. McMurry in her biography. But Wells-Barnett nevertheless remained among the most influential suffragists in Chicago and in Illinois. More broadly, Wells-Barnett, from the end of World War I to her death, remained vigilant for justice to her people, male and female. She was a being of agitation, confrontation, exposure, and of personal and often lonely efforts. In her memoir she frequently regrets hasty breaks with former friends. This accounts for part of her isolation. But her eclipse was also the result of changing modes of reform. Wells-Barnett, like Elizabeth Stanton and Susan B. Anthony, was followed by disciplined lockstep organizations that were savvy in power-brokering, deal-making, and gradualism—at least until the next wave of upraised fists, whether in the sermons of Martin Luther King, Jr., or, later, in Black Panthers' gun-toting. (Wells-Barnett actually advocated that every black family, for self-defense, keep a Winchester rifle in a "place of honor.") Wells-Barnett in her last years applied the anti-lynching techniques that she had developed in Memphis in the 1890s and 1900s to Chicago police shootings of black youths in the 1920s.

She labored during the despairing nadir of black–white relations, in a generation that could not have conceived, not in its wildest dreams, that in 2015 America's most powerful law-enforcement official, the United States Attorney General, would be held by a black female—and moreover possess the eerie name of Loretta Lynch. On lynching, in particular, Wells-Barnett was responsible for the "awakening of the conscience of the nation," wrote W.E.B. Du Bois, after her death, in 1931, at age 68. He added that her work had "easily been forgotten because it was taken up on a much larger scale by the NAACP and carried to greater success." He was right that the NAACP would be celebrated for doing much of what Ida did, alone, from post-Reconstruction on through the Jazz Age. Wells-Barnett never received prestigious awards, nor did she see all that many victories. It was too early in our history for that. The struggle of her life, then, was much like the struggle for suffrage: of the 68 female signatories at Seneca Falls, only one lived to see the Nineteenth Amendment in 1920. Ida B. Wells-Barnett, like those signatories, began what others would end. Each day's experience reminds us that as the light of day grows, even the brightest stars fade.

Restorers

1934–2016

ROBERT H. JACKSON

8

ROBERT H. JACKSON

New Deals and World Wars

Robert H. Jackson, before he became the greatest lawyer of the Greatest Generation, lived and worked as
normally as the very normal 1920s allowed. He was
born in 1892, in western Pennsylvania, and raised over the border in
Frewsburg, New York, in what a biographer called a "typically American
farm life of the early twentieth century." He was like fellow Americans in
receiving no formal education beyond high school (plus a year at Albany
Law School), which, so far as I can tell, simply gave him less to unlearn
later in life. He was a prototypical "country lawyer" for twenty years,
starting with livestock cases in lamp-lit New York barns, though later
he earned a small fortune (and family vacations to Bermuda during the
Great Depression) from lucrative business cases for local big shots. He
had an engaging demeanor, two fine kids, and a stately white-columned
manor to raise them in. What was atypical about Jackson, however, was
his venture into Democratic politics, in 1911, despite his deep roots in a
thoroughly Republican region of southwestern New York. His clients
thought his politics "harmless and eccentric," he said, but those views
would lead him to Franklin Delano Roosevelt, then a freshman state
senator in Albany. It's always good to be on personal terms with a man
destined to be President for twelve years.

In the 1920s Americans were busy doing very American things like buying washing machines on installment and making movies an in-flight feature and turning out business books that made Moses a "real-estate promoter" and Jesus a "great executive" who with only twelve associates forged a world-conquering organization. Then, in 1929, it all came crashing down into the purgatory of modern America's most atypical decade. "My own feeling," wrote Harold Ickes, a Roosevelt confidant, is that Robert Jackson "is the kind of man we need in our public life if we are to escape disaster." FDR agreed. In 1934 he brought Jackson to Washington as general counsel for the Bureau of Internal Revenue. Within seven years Jackson leaped from directing the Justice Department's tax and antitrust divisions, to Solicitor General (winning 38 of 44 cases in the U.S. Supreme Court), to Attorney General, to Supreme Court Justice.

Today we know that the Great Crash was not as bad as believed nor the New Deal as good, the Brain Trusters not as coherent as advertised, nor FDR as radical. The Great Depression, however, needs no de-mythologizing. In three catastrophic years, 5,000 banks failed. An official saw friends laying sewer pipe in business suits because they couldn't afford overalls and rubber boots. The Detroit Zoo slaughtered its inmates for food. The writer Erskine Caldwell saw on the floor of a Georgia sharecropper's cabin, before an open fire, "two babies, neither a year old, sucking the dry teats of a mongrel bitch." Economic depression is the curse of incumbents—Herbert Hoover's mistake, one wag said, was getting himself elected to the 1928–32 term—but a gift to inheritors. Roosevelt asked Congress for "broad Executive power to wage war against the emergency, as great as the power that would be given to me if we were in fact invaded by a foreign foe." Robert Jackson cheered the bold experimentation, even if he felt some early New Deal forays excessive. Jackson, in a never-finished portrait of FDR, wrote that his patron had "keen political judgments" but little grounding in "economic theory or practice."

Jackson's broad, inviting face, arched brows, and unassuming personality first graced the national stage in the drama of the "court packing" plan, in early 1937, one of the great episodes in constitutional history. Jackson thought the affair—which would prove that even the most popular presidents can fly too high—the symptom of a "bad attack of overconfidence." FDR won his second term in the rout of the century, taking 46 of 48 states. Yet he was the first president ever to see a full term pass without a high-court appointment. (Warren Harding, in two and a half years, got four.) Now FDR watched as a tribunal dominated by Republican appointees, as Jackson characterized it, struck "blow after blow" at his policies. Seven major laws fell in two years. FDR was not alone in seeing a politicized Court consciously undermining his New Deal. Burton Wheeler, a Montana Senator, proposed a constitutional amendment to give Congress power to override Court decisions by two-thirds vote. "I do not want," FDR said, "to leave the country in the condition Buchanan left it to Lincoln."

But FDR introduced what he called his judicial "reorganization" plan on a very disingenuous, un-Lincolnian note. In a message in February 1937 he spoke boringly of the costs and delay of litigation and the senility of many judges. For every justice over 70, under his plan, he would appoint a new one, which meant, unless sitting justices retired, that the Supreme Court could be enlarged by up to six seats. Congress at least a half-dozen times had altered the number of justices (with a potential low of five and a high of ten), but never with additions on the scale proposed. A century earlier Daniel Webster warned that such a move would "dilute the Constitution by creating a court which shall construe away its provisions." Woodrow Wilson thought Congress had power to "overwhelm the opposition of the Supreme Court upon any question by increasing the number of justices," but he had faith in "public opinion which makes such outrages upon constitutional morality impossible by standing ready to curse them."

"I was up in Jamestown," Jackson told Roosevelt, where he learned of the court-packing initiative from local papers. "Nobody knows what you are getting at and nobody knows what your grievance is." Jackson's political instincts, always strong, here surpassed those of the master himself. FDR agreed to pivot and make the case that Jackson, in fact, had already been making. A week before the plan was introduced, Jackson made headlines with a speech that argued that courts hostile to the New Deal were "closing the roads to political compromise" and forcing frustrated Americans onto radical paths. "Out of the breakdown of an attempt at free government which failed to function," he said, "arose Hitler, Lenin, and Stalin." The Constitution, he continued, was just a "general outline of great powers," and it "would be as reckless for the President to steer public policy by precedent," he said, "as to drive in the dark with only a tail light." Jackson would continue to hammer the Court for months. In a 1937 speech, in Carnegie Hall, he declared: "The difficulty with the Court is that it has lost touch with reality, that the actual problems faced by working people...come to the Court through books and printed briefs and lawyers' windy arguments." He insisted that despite their superficial beginnings as lawsuits, major constitutional decisions in the Court were political acts, the sort of "[s]truggles over power that in Europe call out regiments of troops," but that "in America call out battalions of lawyers."

Party lines broke down in a bracing clash between all three branches. Each moved to protect itself as an institution. Chief Justice Charles Evan Hughes wrote a deflating letter denying that the Court was behind on its work. Senator Burton Wheeler, whose own plan Jackson thought more radical that FDR's, said that the president "means to make himself the boss of us all.... [T]his is our chance to cut him down to size." FDR's attempt to tamper with the Court, two Washington journalists reported, "frightened many liberals who feared its use in the future by conservative or semi-Fascist administrations." A Senate committee finally killed the plan as "contrary to the spirit of the Constitution."

But then again, in March 1937, the plan had suddenly become super-fluous: Justice Owen Roberts, in an astonishing flip-flop, voted to uphold a Washington State law indistinguishable from a New York law that he voted to strike down a year before. His vote had been cast weeks before the court-packing plan was announced, but it owed much to the pressure that Jackson and others had laid on the court. From there on the Court began upholding New Deal legislation on municipal debts, taxation, utility regulation, and more—many in cases argued by Solicitor General Robert Jackson. Almost 40 years would pass before the Court again dared to lay a finger on any major New Deal–era legislation.

In his book *The Struggle for Judicial Supremacy* (1941), Jackson offered, even after a cooling-off period, the ultimate legal-intellectual defense of the court-packing plan. Jackson made it seem almost reasonable, an in-evitable response to a Court endangering us all. He also claimed victory. "The President's enemies defeated the court reform bill," he wrote, but the "President achieved court reform." Jackson emphasized as often as he could that the Court's key reversals came *before* Roosevelt appointed a single justice; the Court's membership had seen the error of their ways.

In a speech in 1939, Jackson felt confident enough to proclaim a "constitutional Renaissance." We now revered the Constitution's actual text, he said, not the Court's volumes of commentary on it, as if a painting "retouched by successive generations of artists were to have the successive layers of oils removed and the Old Master itself revealed once again."

☙◆❧

The outcry against the plan, and other New Deal novelties, forced Roosevelt to issue an unusual disclaimer from his vacation home: "I have no inclination to be a dictator. I have none of the qualifications which would make me a successful dictator." He was right. Autocrats worth their saltpeter don't tolerate the degree of punishment he eventually took with the same broad smile. Jackson was suspicious, rather, of those sputtering most hysterically about FDR's supposed proto-tyranny, in the way that the politician who fulminates most energetically about family values usually has the secret mistress. If European-style dictatorship was to come, FDR wouldn't be the harbinger.

How exactly dictatorship *might* come was the subject of Sinclair Lewis's bestseller *It Can't Happen Here* in 1935. Lewis, the first American to win the Nobel Prize in Literature, was married to Dorothy Thompson, who in 1934 became the first American journalist to be expelled from Hitler's Germany. Lewis imagined a mass movement called the "League of Forgotten Men," led by the hokey but charismatic "Buzz" Windrip. He beats FDR for the Democratic nomination in 1936 and then wins the election (and promptly names the defeated ex-president as minister to Liberia). Windrip first demands that Congress amend the Constitution to give him authority to "execute all necessary measures for the conduct of the government during this critical epoch," then serve in an "advisory capacity," while the Supreme Court is to be stripped of power to "negate" his acts. Legislators who balk are arrested by paramilitary "Minute Men." Before long America is a "well-run plantation" of concentration camps and book burnings, and even hardened Communists wax nostalgic for the "Golden Age of Frank Roosevelt." Lewis's novel sold well, but it oversold the danger. Windrip was a Frankenstein of the worst of the left and right, and the onset of despotism in the book is impossibly sudden and deception-free, as if tyranny were not, in fact, a degenerative disease.

(Hitler and Stalin took the helm of their parties in 1921 and 1922, a decade before they became household names.) Yet Lewis was onto something: what perplexed his protagonist, a newspaper editor named Doremus Jessup, was that Windrip was nothing like the "gesticulating Fascists" he saw abroad. Instead he had the "earthy American sense of humor of a Mark Twain" and spoke "beautifully" about "church attendance, low taxation, and the American flag." "That couldn't happen here," someone says of this all-American, apple-pie dictatorship in the offing. "The hell it can't!" Jessup replies. "Look how Huey Long became absolute monarch over Louisiana."

That would be Huey Pierce Long, Louisiana governor at age 34 and later U.S. Senator, and a man who, in the words of his measured but friendly biographer, T. Harry Williams, seemed "in the 1930s to be the first American dictator." In his own autobiography, *Every Man a King* (1933), Long described the origin of his politics in a sort of backwoods communitarianism, seeing an impoverished farmer begging authorities to stop the auction of his home. Reporters visiting the "Kingfish," as Long took to calling himself, found a pudgy, messy-haired prankster with a boyish face. Yet they noted something dangerous and electric about him. He was hilarious, tireless, brilliant, and untouchable. As a lawyer he had argued in the Supreme Court—Chief Justice Taft apparently said that he seldom saw a lawyer with a finer legal mind—but he played the buffoon to perfection. He told Calvin Coolidge, "I'm a hillbilly, more or less, like yourself." Long's techniques ran from mere bullying, like telling legislators that unless they "got right" he would dismiss their relatives on the state payroll, to highly creative, public-interest bullying, such as ensuring that Louisiana had fewer bank failures than any state during the Depression, by strong-arming prosperous banks, on threat of immediate audit, to lend to weaker ones.

But what makes Long endlessly fascinating, and more than simply the ultimate machine boss, was that when it came to homegrown dictators, Long seemed, as the yearbooks put it, most likely to succeed. Before he was gunned down by a physician in 1935, at age 42, his national popularity was second only to that of Franklin Roosevelt. He eschewed the race-baiting and Klan themes of standard Southern politics, and unlike the typical demagogue—which he defined as "a politician who don't keep his promises"—Long delivered to the Bayou State on his pledges of farmer relief, free bridges, and abolition of the poor-suppressing poll tax (thirty years, in fact, before the Constitution's 24th Amendment made it the law of the land).

Long's plan to overtake FDR was to bellow mercilessly about wealth redistribution and shrinking the rich down to "frying size." In 1932, Long became a U.S Senator—while effectively keeping his position as Louisiana Governor—on his "Share Our Wealth" platform. This offered every American family $5,000 by, among other things, a tax confiscating income over $1 million. When Long began undermining FDR in the Senate, the President was spooked enough to undertake some Long-like gambits himself: he dispatched 50 Internal Revenue Service agents to Louisiana under the tax sleuth who brought down Al Capone. Robert Jackson, the IRS's general counsel at the time, was briefed on the case. In spring 1935, FDR told associates that he might have to "steal Long's thunder," and, in the Federal Revenue Act of 1935, he rather did, declaring that the government had a "duty" to "restrict" top incomes "by very high taxes." Jackson got to Washington almost two years before Long was murdered, and the Long effect was as evident on him as other FDR surrogates. On a radio program in 1939, for instance, Jackson, in true Huey Long style, dismissed a respected lawyer's alarm at D.C.'s growing bureaucratic muscle as the complaint of rich men "thoroughly scared" of fair taxation.

But nothing ends domestic policy fights like war. Jackson learned of Hitler's invasion of Poland during a Saturday evening get-together at the White House for poker and cocktails (that FDR mixed for guests himself). Jackson thought that Roosevelt genuinely intended to retire to his estate at Hyde Park after two terms, but that FDR became convinced that leaving the war to an untested corporate businessman named Wendell Willkie, his opponent in the 1940 election, would be a "rather dangerous experiment." Calvin Coolidge's probably apocryphal quip when told that the Army and Navy both wanted new aircraft—"Why can't they just buy one airplane, and take turns flying it?"—represented, in America, a mainstream interwar attitude about limited government that was fast vanishing. Stalin, Mussolini, Hitler, Churchill, Daladier, Blum, and Roosevelt all concluded, to varying degrees, that national survival required national regimentation. Jackson linked the nation's fate to his battle against the Justices over the Constitution's scope. If the U.S. was "able to organize its economy to support its defense today," he said, in

June 1940, "it is in no small measure due to the greater liberty of action won in little-publicized court decisions."

The Japanese masterminds of the Pearl Harbor attack missed the significance of the fact that, by 1920, Henry Ford could already turn out a new car every minute of each day. His ingenuity, now in the service of the American military, led to the Ford plant at Willow Run, Michigan. By 1944 it rolled out a new B-24 heavy bomber every 63 minutes to cloud Japan's rising sun. The Lend-Lease Act, probably the broadest delegation of Congress's constitutional spending power in history, was only possible in a country so wealthy that it could not only erect history's most fearsome war machine at breakneck pace but also supply some $693 billion in today's dollars to 38 countries, including a quarter of British munitions and a third of the Red Army's trucks.

☙❧

If Robert Jackson was the Attorney General under the most powerful president in our history, that would seem to make Jackson, in turn, the most powerful Attorney General in our history. Jackson's responsibility touched on wartime price controls, embargoes, foreign commerce, internal surveillance, alien property, and defense secrecy. Through it all Jackson spoke in his characteristically modest and tolerant voice. When the War Department suggested that his Department of Justice be given expanded powers to wiretap and search, Jackson demurred, on grounds that the "man who today will rifle your desk for me, tomorrow will rifle mine for someone else." Private employers asked Jackson whether they should fire foreign employees. Jackson told them that aliens surely owed us a measure of fidelity, but that Americans, too, had a duty to the aliens, to "earn their confidence and to maintain their loyalty." Yet Jackson would also play a starring role in two controversial events that he would have to revisit postwar.

"What worries me," wrote Roosevelt, in 1939, "is that public opinion over here is patting itself on the back every morning and thanking God for the Atlantic Ocean (and the Pacific Ocean)." By summer 1940 those watery buffers seemed knee-deep. Churchill, his nation stoically holding out alone against Germany, told FDR that if his island fell, the "whole world, including the United States, including all that we have known and cared for, will sink into the abyss of a new Dark Age." But Roosevelt told Churchill that he had to reject Britain's request for some fifty World War I–era destroyers because Attorney General Jackson had advised him, FDR, that under American neutrality laws he was constitutionally barred from aiding a belligerent. Churchill said that he thought the "trouble must be in the Attorney General rather than in the Constitution."

In fact, the trouble was in a lack of creativity, which Jackson and other FDR lawyers soon overcame: they determined that if the U.S. declared the ships obsolete, then "exchanged" them for strategic leases on United Kingdom bases, the transaction could be framed not as a departure from neutrality, but as a purely defensive measure. Jackson wrote an opinion that found it "beyond doubt that present world conditions forbid [Roosevelt] to risk any delay that is constitutionally avoidable." The opinion's most disputed part declared that FDR could send ships to existing belligerents, without violating neutrality, but not *build* ships for sending over. This provoked Edward Corwin—an eminent legal historian of the day who, incidentally, helped devise the court-packing plan—to attack Jackson's opinion as an "endorsement of unrestrained autocracy in the field of our foreign relations." Had Japan and Germany, in 1940, stipulated not to attack us, I suspect more Americans might have agreed.

A year later Jackson issued a second legal opinion justifying another emergency action by the President. In June 1941 workers went on strike at an aircraft factory in Inglewood, California. The administration suspected intrigue by the Soviets, still Hitler's ally. The stoppage threatened to suspend 25% of our fighter-plane production. So 2,500 soldiers marched over to seize the plant. "There can be no doubt," wrote Attorney General Jackson, "that the duty constitutionally and inherently rested upon the President to exert his civil and military, as well as his moral, authority to keep the Defense effort of the United States a going concern." The president, specifically, had a duty to prevent plane construction from being "paralyzed" by a strike, which wasn't really a strike anyway but an "insurrection" provoked by "disloyal" Communists.

What Robert Jackson's destroyer and aircraft opinions had in common was Jackson's claim that, at bottom, the President had no choice. Self-preservation, it turns out, is not only the first law of organic life but a legal conclusion that those burdened with national defense rediscover in every age. "A strict observance of the written laws is doubtless *one* of the high duties of a good citizen," wrote Thomas Jefferson, when once asked whether a president could act "beyond the law." But the "laws of necessity, of self-preservation, of saving our country when in danger, are of higher obligation," he continued. "To lose our country by a scrupulous adherence to written law, would be to lose the law itself, with life, liberty, property & all those who are enjoying them with us—thus absurdly sacrificing the end to the means." Abraham Lincoln, in 1864, had offered the same defense to justify his decision to liberate and conscript 130,000 slaves:

> [M]y oath to preserve the constitution to the best of my ability, imposed upon me the duty of preserving, by every indispensable means, that government—that nation—of which that constitution was the organic law. Was it possible to lose the nation, and yet preserve the constitution?

Jefferson and Lincoln agreed that emergency power was dangerous to use, but sometimes fatal *not* to use. Yet Jefferson thought such acts of necessity to be forgivable transgressions; Lincoln, by contrast, believed that the Constitution permitted any truly necessary act. Much turns on the distinction.

Robert Jackson described one instance in which he felt that FDR went "beyond the Constitution," in Jefferson's sense of the phrase, though the quoted words are Jackson's. This was when Roosevelt built an airport, now Reagan International, without a congressional appropriation. FDR found it pathetic that America was heading into a global war without a serious capital airport—police at the existing airfield had to stop traffic for landings—while Congress gabbed about whether to place it in Maryland or Virginia. Jackson described FDR's move as a sort of victimless crime, since any injury here, technically, was to Congress.

Alexander Hamilton's view was that it was dangerous for a president ever to go "outside" the Constitution. The perils to a nation are "infinite," he said, and every time a government is forced by a defective charter to overleap its bounds, respect for law shrivels. The safest Constitution, then, he thought, was not one of "shackles" but one that allowed self-defense "without limitation." If this view implies that the Constitution firmly limits the courts and Congress, but not the president, the answer must be that the country cannot be irretrievably lost by a failure to decide a lawsuit or pass a law. The delegates to Philadelphia in 1787 did not seem to think it would be necessary to go outside the Constitution. A majority of the framers were veterans, drafting in a time of emergency. Their Constitution recognized the two gravest possible crises—foreign attack and civil war: it speaks three times of "invasion," three times of civil war ("insurrections," "rebellion," and "domestic violence"), and even contemplates martial law in permitting the suspension of habeas corpus. The Constitution cages presidents with bendable bars.

In crises of self-preservation, when law becomes secondary to mortality, the real limit on a president is his character. "The American people can be sure that I will use my powers with a full sense of responsibility to the Constitution," FDR said in 1942. The Constitution subordinates military to civilian rule so that at all times a man elected by the whole nation—the only American so chosen—keeps the helm. Americans could take comfort that a jovial FDR instinctively reached for "charm" before "strength," as Jackson put it. He kept wearing a civilian suit in wartime and admitted, in an early fireside chat, that he knew he wouldn't get a hit "every time I come to bat" but that he would strive for a good "average." Hitler and Stalin, in their pharaonic pomp, did not talk or dress like that, or have a legislature to wrangle against. Congress, even in war, refused some of FDR's requests for laws and at other times overrode his veto when he opposed a law. The good thing about checks and balances, said Jackson, was that they "work as effectively on spite, jealousy, or personal ambition as they do on patriotism or principle."

❧

Pearl Harbor was bombed in December 1941, six months after Roosevelt appointed Jackson, now 49, to the Supreme Court. The former Attorney General said that he felt "frustration and dissatisfaction" at now being removed from the action and stuck in the "back eddy" of the judiciary. But war remained part of Justice Jackson's docket for years. In one case, he agreed that enemy aliens could be summarily deported, even after the shooting had stopped, since it was not for courts to second-guess the president on the danger these aliens posed. Yet in another case, Jackson voted to uphold postwar rent control while sternly cautioning that when the "war power" was invoked to justify measures not usually associated with combat, the "constitutional basis should be scrutinized with care." Jackson's decisions almost always deferred to presidential power on war and foreign affairs.

Yet the very fact that the Court even *heard* such cases reminds us that, in America, judges can call a halt against presidents and generals, but that these supreme commanders can never return the favor. The two court cases that more than any others established Jackson's permanent reputation as a judge, however, would prove that the "war powers" that the Constitution gives to presidents are, in the end, less matters of law and doctrine than of prudence and exigency. These cases may not confirm the Roman adage that the law is silent in time of war, but they prove that the law keeps its head down in time of true national menace.

In 1952, 650,000 union steelworkers went on national strike when mill-owners, after months of negotiations, finally rejected their demand for a wage increase. President Harry Truman, pro-union all the way, declared that interrupted steel production would "jeopardize" troops engaged in the "police action" in Korea. He ordered 86 steel plants seized. The act was an immediately unpopular move by an already unpopular and lame-duckish president. The Court's 6-3 decision, in the case *Youngstown Sheet & Tube Co. v. Sawyer* (1952), rebuked Truman for using the "seizure technique to solve labor disputes." That was a task "for the Nation's lawmakers, not for its military authorities." Three dissenters, in tones reproachful and panicked, seemed stunned that the Court would tell troops to sit tight for the "ammunition upon which their lives depend." The battle royale between the justices catalogued all the rhetorical arguments made in war-power cases. For instance, did the "Founders" believe that unfettered executive action in time of fear was what imperiled the nation — or that the nation was imperiled when such action was *disallowed*? Was the Constitution written by men who feared royal prerogative — or by men who saw Americans die during the Revolutionary War because their regime *lacked* a strong and decisive head?

Robert Jackson rose above the fray to offer what he called a "practical" framework for resolving the case. It was not wholly original, but never was it more elegantly expressed. It remains the only enduring part of the *Youngstown* decision. "[A]nyone who has served as legal adviser to a President" in crisis, Jackson began, knew of presidential power that it was impossible to "say where it begins or ends." A president's acts fell, then, into one of three categories: if he acts under the authority of Congress, his power is "at its maximum, for it includes all that he possesses in his own right plus all that Congress can delegate." If he acts where Congress is silent, he operates in a "zone of twilight" where the balance of power between him and Congress is uncertain. And if he acts in defiance of the will of Congress, his power is at its "lowest ebb," for "he can rely only upon his own constitutional powers minus any constitutional powers of Congress." Between the president and Congress, then, there could be no firm delineation of power, but only overlap and fluctuation.

Jackson found the seizure illegal. He saw an exasperated president, firmly in his third category, ignoring labor law and using brute force to intervene in a "lawful economic struggle between industry and labor," with war a mere cover story. Jackson did, however, depart from his statesmanlike continuum with unsporting rhetoric about how Truman might take "instruction" from the "governments we disparagingly describe as totalitarian." His successor in the position of Solicitor General can be forgiven for suggesting at the court argument that Jackson, as a character in a recently premiered sitcom put it, had some splainin' to do. Exhibit A was Jackson's justification of the airplane-plant seizure by the Roosevelt Administration in 1941.

Jackson figured that Truman's steel seizure would be "laid at my door," he replied, given his role in creating its chief precedent. But he wrote in his *Youngstown* opinion that any similarity between the two seizures was "superficial," since, for instance, one involved Communist subversion, and the other an impasse between loyal Americans. It seems only fair to Truman to note that some of the distinguishing facts that Jackson now identified appeared nowhere in his airplane-plant opinion. But in the end Jackson was right. David McCullough, in his biography *Truman* (1992), called the seizure a "high-handed" mistake provoked largely by anger at perceived profiteering attempts by steelmakers—and not by any genuine military necessity. "I am not alarmed that it would plunge us straightway into dictatorship," Jackson concluded of Harry Truman's seizure, "but it is at least a step in that wrong direction."

But a far more interesting question is this: if a president is willing to submit to a court's mandate, can it really be a crisis? The *Youngstown* Court simply disbelieved Truman's claim of emergency, and, once it did, the case was no longer about constitutional "war powers." The Court's rigid opinion, read literally, is useless as a statement of law, for it suggests that the president cannot act domestically unless a statute first authorizes his action. The viability of such a rule was tested on September 11, 2001, when military brass scrambled fighters to intercept Flight 93 as it barreled toward Washington, after other planes had struck the Twin Towers and Pentagon. Hearings in 2003 held by the 9/11 Commission revealed that no one involved was quite sure where the authority to shoot down domestic airliners came from—one general guessed President George W. Bush—but it certainly wasn't a statute. Flight 93 crashed in a Pennsylvania field before military jets could reach it, 20 minutes outside of Washington, D.C., and its target, the Capitol building, where Congress was in session.

Sometimes even having a statute is no guarantee of legal or moral righteousness. So a second case—and for Jackson, a far more difficult one—would show. America's sense of security during the Second World War, Jackson wrote, came from the good fortune of not facing the bombardment of our cities or any real threat of invasion. Our institutions were simply never put under the same strain as those of European countries. But after Pearl Harbor, when defense of our soil became a reality, we started, at least in one respect, to look quite European. Roosevelt forbid aliens owing allegiance to Germany, Italy, and Japan from possessing guns, radios, or cameras. Then a flurry of statutes, executive proclamations, and military orders, beginning in February 1942, authorized the creation of "military areas." Soon the entire Pacific coast was declared such an area. This was where most Japanese-Americans lived.

Things were destined to get ugly. Western states had long enforced anti-Japanese laws. On a radio show in 1939, a woman asked Jackson: "Mr. Jackson, there are certain elements who are working to get the Jewish people disenfranchised and forbidden to own property. Does not the Constitution, particularly the Fourteenth Amendment, protect them, or did the legislation against the Japanese act as a precedent which would make this possible?" Jackson replied: "Well, you have given me a very large order." Western governors, lobbying FDR to intervene, pointed to Pearl Harbor, the shelling of oil fields near Santa Barbara by a Japanese submarine in February 1942, countless rumors of sabotage and espionage, and propaganda efforts by Emperor Hirohito in Japanese-American schools. Nevada's governor said that he would accept aliens into his state under "proper supervision," such as in "concentration camps." When some 9,000 mostly Japanese-American citizens headed to Nevada from California by train and car, they were turned back at the state line. The leading state agitator was Earl Warren, who as California Attorney General, in 1942, called the Japanese presence "the Achilles' heel" of the civilian defense effort. By 1943, Japan had wrested Guam, Wake Island, and the Philippines from the U.S. military. That year, a unanimous Court, in an embarrassed and uneasy opinion, upheld a curfew against those of Japanese "extraction." "Espionage by persons in sympathy with the Japanese Government had been found to have been particularly effective in the surprise attack on Pearl Harbor," said the Court, and this properly made loyalty a "matter of grave concern." The curfew, in the Court's strangely ambiguous phrase, was "not wholly beyond the limits of the Constitution."

Soon generals out west declared the curfew inadequate, because it could not segregate the loyal from the disloyal. A week before the Battle of Midway, Fred Korematsu, a 23-year-old, Oakland-born welder, refused to follow a military order to leave his Bay Area home. The decision he provoked, *Korematsu v. United States* (1944), is one of the Supreme Court's preeminent infamies. Justice Hugo Black, a one-time New Deal Senator from Alabama whom FDR appointed, upheld the human impoundment as based, the Court found, on military necessity and not "racial antagonism." Some 5,000 American citizens of Japanese ancestry had refused to renounce their allegiance to the Emperor, wrote Black, and thousands more requested repatriation to Japan. Jackson was one of three justices to dissent on grounds that, as Jackson put it, Korematsu was being punished because he "belongs to a race from which there is no way to resign." The two other dissenters saw conduct smacking of the "despicable treatment of minority groups by the dictatorial tyrannies which this nation is now pledged to destroy." They pointed out, skeptically, that the exclusion order came four long months after Pearl Harbor. As in *Youngstown*, the Justices broke over whether they accepted the truth of the claim of emergency, or not.

Once more Jackson took a third way. His opinion, once more, remains the most famous part of the case. Jackson actually refused to call the military order unconstitutional. He understood, he said, that the army had one job, and that was to win the war at virtually any cost, without irritating lawyers peering over their epaulettes. At the same time, if the Court for this reason deferred to the generals, every order would be constitutional, simply by the fact of being issued. So Jackson, in his legendarily candid and artful prose, reasoned as follows:

> Much is said of the danger to liberty from the Army program for deporting and detaining these citizens of Japanese extraction. But a judicial construction of the due process clause that will sustain this order is a far more subtle blow to liberty than the promulgation of the order itself. A military order, however unconstitutional, is not apt to last longer than the military emergency.... But once a judicial opinion rationalizes such an order to show that it conforms to the Constitution, or rather rationalizes the Constitution to show that the Constitution sanctions such an order, the Court for all time has validated the principle of racial discrimination in criminal procedure and of transplanting American citizens. The principle then lies about like a loaded weapon ready for the hand of any authority that can bring forward a plausible claim of an urgent need.

If the war-making power ever fell into "unscrupulous hands," he concluded, only the "moral judgments of history"—not any court—could condemn the abuses.

A 1988 law signed by Ronald Reagan exemplified the American capacity to recover itself. It made reparations of $40,000 (in today's dollars) to 82,000 people. The law's co-sponsor, Norman Mineta, was sent as a 10-year-old to a Wyoming camp. Later he became the longest-serving Secretary of Transportation in history. (He was in a command center on September 11, 2001, debating the shoot-down of Flight 93.) On arrival guards confiscated Norman's prized baseball bat; years later, elected to Congress, a well-wisher sent him a $1,500 bat once owned by Hank Aaron. He had to return it, as a prohibited gift over $250, remarking: "The damn government's taken my bat again." Daniel Inouye was a Japanese-American who, as a soldier in the Second World War, lost an arm fighting for America, but as a politician, never lost an election. By the end of his 53 years in Congress, he had risen to become the U.S. Senate's president pro tempore—meaning that he was third in line to succeed to the presidency.

No German Jews, by contrast, remained to fight for the nation that had turned on them. This last fact, too, would be a part of Jackson's story. His final service to FDR, who died in April 1945, was to take leave from the Supreme Court to serve as America's Chief Prosecutor of the Nazi war leaders in Nuremberg, Germany. Jackson would call this undertaking the "supremely interesting and important work of my life." Before he arrived in Europe he envisioned a trial that would teach the world about American legal process but also "codify" international law against "aggressive war." Yet a trial of a defeated enemy's chieftains was unheard of. Many were skeptical, including Cordell Hull, Secretary of State for most of FDR's presidency: "If I had my way, I would take Hitler and Mussolini and Tojo and their arch accomplices and bring them before a drum-head court-martial. And at sunrise on the following day there would occur a historic incident." Stalin spoke of shooting 50,000 German officers.

One of the Nuremburg Trial's German defense lawyers (a group which included a few unrepentant Nazis) said that Jackson "struggled in Nuremberg for a new law of nations." This was double-edged: the Nazi leaders' central defense was that Jackson was inventing law by which to punish them — in legal terms, an *ex post facto* law, a law that criminalizes conduct that, when actually engaged in, was not illegal. Crimes committed during war had long been outlawed, but the war-crime doctrine did not extend to the *initiation* of a war. Here Jackson made his argument. "If it is not a crime to start such a war," he insisted, "then there is not much use of talking about the little crimes that occur in the course of a war." His even temper and political finesse helped cement an agreement between the U.S., United Kingdom, France, and Russia, to develop a workable merger of their four very different systems of law. The most difficult co-prosecutors were the Soviets, who, as a member of Jackson's staff quipped to him, only recognized a criminal's right to be present at his own execution.

The Nuremberg Trial, quite rightly, is considered the greatest criminal trial in history. A legal proceeding over a single dead victim can take months; Jackson was face to face with the instigators of a conflagration that killed 60 million. It took place six months after the Nazi surrender, in a necropolis strewn with rubble and putrefying corpses. At night Jackson had to pull down his shades on entering lighted rooms to guard against snipers. He worked, often by candlelight, to prepare arguments based on review of 700 tons of German documents and over 100,000 witness affidavits. Jackson said it was the only case "I have ever tried when I had first to persuade others that a court should be established, help negotiate its establishment, and when that was done, not only prepare my case but find myself a courtroom in which to try it."

One American diplomat said that Jackson's opening and closing arguments "rank with the great state papers of American history." "The wrongs which we seek to condemn and punish," Jackson began, "have been so calculated, so malignant, and so devastating, that civilization cannot tolerate their being ignored because it cannot survive their being repeated." He traced the Nazi Party from its origins in Munich in 1920 to its rise through promises of old-age support or the creation of a strong middle class, as well as its violence, lies, betrayals, and alliances with political opportunists and industrialists. He conducted a climactic cross-examination of Hermann Goering, the second most powerful official in the Reich after Hitler. He proved that though Germany had a bill of rights much like that of the United States, it all went for naught, as Jackson said, because the "German people were in the hands of the police, the police were in the hands of the Nazi Party, and the Party was in the hands of a ring of evil men."

These death-dealers had committed acts that Jackson called "criminal beyond anything that I can dream." The prosecutors showed that Auschwitz's Dr. Rascher took skin from his victims' thighs to make driving gloves for SS officers, and forced humans into ice water or boiling vats to test the fatal limits of organ function. The judges learned of Jewish families lined up to be shot: "The father was holding the hand of a boy about 10 years old and speaking to him softly; the boy was fighting his tears," said an eyewitness. "The father pointed toward the sky, stroked his head, and seemed to explain something to him." "One night we were awakened by horrible cries," said another Auschwitz survivor. "We learned the next day that the Nazis had run out of gas and children were being hurled alive into the furnaces." "If you were to say of these men that they are not guilty," Chief Prosecutor Robert Jackson closed, "it would be as true to say there has been no war, there are no slain, there has been no crime." His old friends from western New York marveled at how far their country lawyer had come; the man who once represented farmers in livestock cases now represented, as close as any American ever has, humanity itself.

❧❀❧

These were harrowing days for Jackson. But there always was something unusually sober about him. Even in grim early 1941 he told a gathering of lawyers that their profession had become accustomed to "speak of 'preserving our freedom' as though it were a pickle to be kept in brine." Nuremberg—his "post-mortem on a totalitarian state," as Jackson saw it—had left him uniquely immune to frantic talk of "slippery slopes" and coming tyranny. Such banter was in the air, especially when it came to free speech. One can trace to the late 1940s our present First Amendment maximalism—the view that any claim of "freedom of speech," however implausible, deserves solicitude, lest we invite despotism. Opposition to this doctrine was Jackson's last great battle and one of the greatest rearguard campaigns in American legal history.

Jackson had undeniable civil-liberty credentials. In the war's early days, despite the ease with which he might have curtailed speech, he instructed federal prosecutors that in "times of fear or hysteria" they had to remember that "[s]ome of the soundest constitutional doctrines were once punished as subversive." Later, in a 1943 Supreme Court decision that struck down a West Virginia school's compulsory flag salute, Justice Jackson laid down an unimprovable statement of the First Amendment's meaning: "no official, high or petty, can prescribe what shall be orthodox in politics, nationalism, religion, or other matters of opinion or force citizens to confess by word or act their faith therein." It was actually his eventual nemeses on the Court, Hugo Black and William O. Douglas, who became converts to the dogma of free-speech transcendentalism only after voting, unlike Jackson, to uphold the removal of Japanese-Americans and the forced flag salute. Jackson believed that his commitment to freedom of speech required him to determine, however hard to do, the point at which an act of expression stopped deserving legal protection but instead came to "endanger the great right of free speech by making it ridiculous and obnoxious."

In 1949, Jackson dissented in a case involving a junior-league Father Coughlin named Arthur Terminiello, who drew to a Chicago speech of his a hostile crowd of 1,500, hurling ice picks and bricks, barely under police control. Terminiello's bizarre rant urged that the New Deal was destroying America, that "Queen" Eleanor Roosevelt was a Communist, and that Jews ought to "go back where they came from." But what concerned Jackson was that Terminiello, aware of the crowd outside, had egged on followers to confront them violently. For this Illinois prosecutors had convicted him of breaching the peace. Justice William Douglas, writing for a 5-4 majority, found a sort of inspiration in Terminiello's harangue: the right to "promote diversity of ideas," he wrote, was "one of the chief distinctions that sets us apart from totalitarian regimes." Jackson found that conclusion interesting, since Terminiello, he said, "followed, with fidelity that is more than coincidental, the pattern of European fascist leaders." Jackson had no quarrel with free speech, he continued. He just denied that immediate incitement to mob violence came within the honored concept. Virtually every lynching, he noted, began with an act of "speech." "No liberty," he warned, in a sentence that he might happily have engraved above the portico of every court, "is made more secure by holding that its abuses are inseparable from its enjoyment."

Jackson's damnation of fascists like Terminiello was nothing compared to what he said about Communists, the next year, in an exposition of literary anti-Sovietism of the highest order. In 1950, the Court held that a federal labor law could withdraw protections from unions whose officers refused to deny that they were Communists. Jackson wrote, separately, to explain why he thought membership in the Communist Party could be treated differently from membership in the Republican, Democratic, or Socialist parties. "This Communist movement," he wrote, "is a belated counter-revolution to the American Revolution, designed to undo the Declaration of Independence, the Constitution, and our Bill of Rights." It was the only party in American history, he said, "controlled by a foreign government," with its Kremlin-directed agents secretly "boring their way into the labor movement" in order to be ready to effect "industrial paralysis." Jackson's job, as he saw it, was to reject appeals "in the name of security" that would "open the way to oppression," to be sure, but just as vigorously to reject claims "in the name of civil liberty" that threatened to "impair authority to defend the existence of our society." Jackson had come a long way since his days of radical repute, during which time he had more than once been accused by members of Congress of having Communist sympathies. (His response to one such attack in 1940: "Senator Bridges is to be forgiven for knowing nothing of the subject of which he talked.")

But Jackson lost these fights on the Court. In *Terminiello* he had been joined by three of the nine justices, one short of a majority. Yet by

1951, he alone cautioned that to disable New York City from stopping "hate-stirring attacks on races and faiths under the protections for freedom of speech" only "belittles great principles of liberty." What neither he nor his opponents on the Court anticipated was how extravagantly the doctrine of free speech would be stretched beyond the traditional guarantee of uninhibited political expression. Today the right takes forms that do not always strike Americans as the sort worth fighting for. In recent years, for instance, courts have wrestled, quite solemnly, with whether the First Amendment protects nude dancing, and, if so, whether that free expression is suppressed by a requirement that dancers wear a G-string; or whether there are free-speech rights to be homeless in public libraries or to flash one's headlights to warn oncoming drivers of police speed traps. In refining the application of these rights—not, one hopes, beyond recognition—Jackson's opinions offer two enduring lessons.

The first is that no right is absolute and so we must always discriminate between justified and unjustified exercises of a "right." Speech loses its protected (or glorified) status when it causes injury, and Jackson was ready to add more categories to list that includes, say, libel, fraud, perjury, intimidation, mislabeling drugs, and exposing military secrets. The second lesson is that there is in fact no such thing as "liberty," but only *liberties*, ever jostling against one another. If nothing else, Jackson wrote, in an unfinished lecture series, the question in "so-called civil rights" cases "simmers down to one of the extent to which the majority rule will be set aside." Clashes over the scope of a "right," then, in this view, are not between a lonely "individual" and a faceless "government," but between one individual, and a far larger group of individuals, whose will the law simply reflects. Each time a court rules for that one individual, and finds a new, uninfringeable "liberty," the majority loses *its* liberty to control behavior that it feels incompatible with society's peace and order. When this happens, does it mean, for most of us, more freedom—or less?

Consider a masterpiece Jackson dissent, in a 1943 case, featuring commercial evangelists who descended, in their words, like "locusts" on small communities like Jeannette, Pennsylvania, and banged on doors and told mothers that they were hell-bound for refusing to buy pamphlets for their children. The Court—Justice Hugo Black again writing—held, in celebratory terms, that a town in western Pennsylvania could not regulate the proselytes. The "authors of the First Amendment," Black wrote, "knew that novel and unconventional ideas might disturb the complacent, but they chose to encourage a freedom which they believed essential if vigorous enlightenment was ever to triumph over slothful ignorance." "I doubt if only the slothfully ignorant wish repose in their homes," replied Jackson, "or that the forefathers intended to open the door to such forced 'enlightenment' as we have here."

Jeannette was a few hours away from where Jackson grew up in Frewsburg. The "Frewsburg" spirit that friends said hovered about Jackson had produced a man who, quite unlike the evangelists in the case, refused even to summon his own staff by buzzer or telephone, instead appearing in their offices with a friendly "Got a minute?" The case seemed to recall to Jackson life before he became a powerful Washington insider. He reminded his fellow justices that they, unlike the unrobed masses, enjoyed "ample shelter from such importunities" as they now were forcing on Americans as a matter of constitutional law. By their decision, fanatics gained the right to pound on unwelcoming doors, and everyone else lost a little of their home's sanctity as a refuge. Jackson's humble, common-sense constitutionalism for a decent society still better reflects the attitude of most citizens, even today.

Robert Jackson died of a heart attack, in October 1954, at age 62. His view of law over an extraordinary career was summed up in a speech he gave on Founders' Day, 1937, a year that marked the Constitution's 150th anniversary. When it came to our institutions, Jackson said, only the "forms" could really be passed on. Their "spirit," by contrast, he continued,

> is perishable and must constantly be renewed. By this process even ancient institutions soon find the level of intelligence, tolerance, honor, and justice of those among whom they flourish. We may well remind ourselves that there is not only a past and a present, there is also a future. And we are among its founders. The opportunity to advance our culture and strengthen our social organization was not exhausted or spent by our forefathers. Our Constitution is always in the making.

ANTONIN SCALIA

9

ANTONIN SCALIA
The Dead Democracy

A few years ago, Mike Papantonio, a former president of the National Trial Lawyers organization, told his talk-radio listeners that the grandfather of the late Supreme Court Justice Antonin Scalia had been the "head of the New York Fascist Party," before adding, sagely, that the "nut does not fall far from the tree." No record exists of such a group, and Scalia's grandfather Antonino, an ex-laborer in Sicily's sulfur mines who arrived in New York in 1920 but who never gained more than a smattering of English, may not have been the most promising *duce* of an American blackshirt movement. Yet a good plaintiffs' lawyer never lets facts get in the way. Besides, if evidence of fascism is what one seeks, there is the telling fact, as Scalia's admirably thorough biographer Joan Biskupic reports, that Antonin was conceived in Mussolini's Florence, in 1935. There was also Scalia's voluble, fist-shaking theatricality and his Führer-like passion for Wagnerian opera. But, for my money, the best proof of the fascism in his soul was that this domestic dictator of nine children forbid them from wearing jeans.

Antonin Scalia, over his long career, faced lesser epithets than fascist, usually drawn from among the following: provocative, combative, incendiary, sneering, caustic, pugnacious, hyperbolic, strident, and surely most woundingly of all, "excessively outspoken." But none of these really stick. They imply an angry curmudgeon, yet Scalia seemed to be having a grand time. "It's fun to push the buttons," he said, describing an unofficial duty of his since roughly 1956, when he became Georgetown University's champion debater. Dissenting in his first case as a judge, in 1982, he informed his seniors on the D.C. Court of Appeals that their decision was "perverse" and "harmful to the national interest." Style makes the man, but with judges, robed in self-effacing black and speaking as depersonalized "courts," the man makes the style.

Scalia was one of the finest judicial stylists on record, and here, too, playfulness reigned. Allusions to Lewis Carroll's Queen of Hearts or Jeremy Bentham's Panopticon or the Babylonian Talmud (though rarely pop culture) testify to wide reading. Thesauruses alone wouldn't have yielded him his references to "incunabula" or "kulturkampf" or Edwardian slang like the "sheer applesauce" of a colleague's position. His fellow Justices, Scalia was sometimes constrained to inform them, were liable to issue rulings of "utterly impossible nonsense" or that "challenge even the most gullible mind," or even, in one terrorism case, that will "almost certainly cause more Americans to be killed." His fusion of earnestness, pizazz, scorn, and comedy made for a tone that is punchier, sharper, and more colorful than that of any other justice in history, with no second place.

Scalia preferred mixing it up publicly, with all comers, instead of the normal judicial quietism. In 2013 alone, for instance, he materialized at the Lanier Theological Library in Houston to give a talk entitled "Is Capitalism or Socialism More Conducive to Christian Virtue?" A month later he debated literary theorist Stanley Fish on textual interpretation at Manhattan's Cardozo Law School. On other occasions, he told the Wild Turkey Federation that as a teenager he used to travel with a rifle on the subway from Queens to Manhattan; he dropped in on legal meetings in Australia, Turkey, and Peru; he spoke at national-security conferences in Canada or on the BBC's "Law in Action" radio program. In these appearances he welcomed the one thing that his day job never permitted: rude questions from hostile interlocutors. He was subject to more recusal motions for his extrajudicial activities than Justices Brandeis, Frankfurter, Fortas, and Douglas, all known for being in the fray, combined. He swatted them away, except when he sat out a case involving the constitutionality of "under God" in the Pledge of Allegiance, after he called the lower court's decision, in a speech for the Knights of Columbus, yet another attempt to "exclude God" from public life.

No justice had his thought so thoroughly sifted—there are more books and articles on Scalia's jurisprudence than any other modern judge—because no other justice so self-consciously claimed to have produced a body of thought worth sifting. Scalia's brand of exasperated common sense stands out in contrast to, say, the self-important mysticism of Anthony Kennedy or the clotted prose of David Souter. (Awaiting the labors of an assistant professor of law are works like *Divided Mind: The Jurisprudence of Anthony M. Kennedy* or *Pen of Granite: The Wit of David Hackett Souter*.) Many justices supplement their salaries, about $250,000 today, with book deals. Clarence Thomas, in *My Grandfather's Son* (2007), chose to recall his days of depression, driving down icy highways with a six-pack in his lap. William Rehnquist wrote trim books on history. Stephen Breyer in *Active Liberty* (2005) wrote gauzily of his philosophy, free from mention of real controversies. John Paul Stevens did criticize actual Court decisions, in *Six Amendments* (2014), but only from the safety of his retirement.

Justice Antonin Scalia, by contrast, for 30 years, was on a mission. That mission was to alert Americans that their Supreme Court, with "almost Czarist arrogance," is slowly usurping their democratic powers. He wrote three books—and remained on a perpetual book tour—two of them more or less devoted to the theme of restraining court authority by identifying its illegitimate forays into republican rule. In area after area—abortion, religion, the death penalty, welfare, free speech, affirmative action, prisons, national security—our justices have declared that the Constitution is conclusive on such questions, which, as Scalia points out, is to say that *they*, the justices, are. It should be said that the Court has always been in the business of elucidating the Constitution on the basis of what it meant to its authors. Chief Justice John Marshall spoke in *Dartmouth College* (1819) of the "view of the framers of the constitution," as did Chief Justice Roger B. Taney, a generation later, in *Dred Scott* (1857). Scalia, moreover, was not the first justice to declare that searching historical inquiry can be a branch of jurisprudence. That view reached an apex in the clashes between Felix Frankfurter and Hugo Black in the 1940s.

Rather, Scalia's contribution was to insist that there is one authentic mode of interpreting the Constitution, sometimes called an "originalist" or "text and tradition" approach, whose only inquiry, he has said, is this: "What was the most plausible meaning of the words of the Constitution to the society that adopted it?" In his official portrait—designed to be hung after his final curtain call—his right hand rests on copies of the *Federalist* and *Webster's Second International Dictionary*, the emblematic sources that Scalia believed had to be used in construing the Constitution, namely, the best Founding-era writings and most non-permissive dictionaries. (His colleagues long since moved on to *Webster's Third*.) Scalia's approach is limited not by judicial "restraint" or "modesty," as the generation of legal conservatives that taught Scalia law in the 1950s put it, but on sheer lack of power. "This Court need not, and has no authority to, inject itself into every field of human activity where irrationality and oppression may theoretically occur," Scalia wrote in one case, "and if it tries to do so it will destroy itself."

Scalia was born in Trenton, in 1936, the only child of Salvatore Scalia and Catherine Panaro. Salvatore arrived on Ellis Island from Sicily before Christmas in 1920. He found work teaching Romance languages at Brooklyn College, specializing in Dante. Young Antonin, growing up in Queens, was preeminently a child of the 1950s, touched by every aspect of that unrebellious, crew-cut decade. At his high school, students were disciplined by being sent to march with a 15-pound rifle in a quadrangle between the school and its church, a rare curricular activity today, unless the school is run by a Montana militia. A classmate recalled that Scalia was so doctrinally faithful to Catholicism that he "could have been a member of the Curia," so Georgetown University, his next stop, was convenient. It had sixteen altars, Daily Mass, and mandatory religious attendance for Catholic students. All around him was a bracingly reactionary spirit, from a history teacher who had tutored the Hapsburg imperial family, to fellow students who in 1954 voted for, as their choice for "Outstanding American," Joseph McCarthy. After Harvard Law School Scalia worked at the law firm of Jones Day, in Cleveland, then entered academia at the University of Virginia.

Scalia quickly grasped that professors constitute the great exception to the maxim that knowledge is power. He soon moved to Washington, D.C., where power is power. After a minor role in the Nixon Administration, he was recruited, following Watergate, to defend a wounded buck of a White House, by Laurence Silberman, later Gerald Ford's Deputy Attorney General. Silberman recalled that many at the time were "afraid of being accused of doing the wrong thing." Not Scalia. He headed Ford's Office of Legal Counsel, which advises the president on constitutional questions. During Ford's 29 months in office he vetoed 66 bills, an extraordinary number comparable to the vetoes by the essentially two-term presidents Theodore Roosevelt, Calvin Coolidge, and Ronald Reagan. The inoffensive Ford distanced himself from Nixon by replacing "Hail to the Chief" with the University of Michigan fight song. But nevertheless he faced a generation of "Watergate baby" Democratic freshmen—Gary Hart, Paul Tsongas, Tom Harkin, Harold Ford—all determined to tie down Gulliver through laws like the War Powers Resolution, the Budget and Impoundment Control Act, and the Ethics in Government Act. Scalia sought to fend them off. "I think you can go back to those who sent you and say you did indeed accomplish your purpose—you stopped the committee for one more day," New York Congressman Otis G. Pike said one day to Scalia, who was testifying on the Hill. "That was not my purpose, Mr. Chairman," replied Scalia. "I think it is worth a couple of hours before you cite a Secretary of State for contempt for the first time in the history of the country."

The tumult of the 1960s was relieved by a sense of being on the cusp of progress. With the 1970s, the decade in which Scalia entered public life, there was a cusp, all right, just in front of the abyss. Americans rang in the bicentennial with a decade of tense and gloomy events like Nixon's resignation, revelations of domestic spying, racial separatism and court-ordered busing (think Boston and "The Soiling of Old Glory"), Gloria Steinem and fights over the Equal Rights Amendment, increased teenage pregnancy and *Roe v. Wade* (between 1974 and 1977 there would be nearly four legal abortions for every ten live births), depressing movies like *Mean Streets, Taxi Driver, Dog Day Afternoon*; urban deterioration and a massive 1977 New York City blackout that saw 1,600 stores looted within five hours; burglary and theft up 76% between 1967 and 1976 and a murder rate at an all-time high (hence cheers for Dirty Harry); four

OPEC price hikes in five months and eventually half of gas stations dry in summer 1979; the fall of Saigon haunting every foreign-policy decision; Iran parading blindfolded Americans; Whip Inflation Now buttons; and the living, breathing person of Jimmy Carter. All Americans got in return for this grim decade were cordless appliances, Miller Lite, and Burt Reynolds.

Antonin Scalia's first and only appearance as an advocate in the Supreme Court, in 1976, was on behalf of the United States in a case over Cuban nationalization. Justice Harry Blackmun noted that Scalia was "plump," another of many qualities in which Scalia remained utterly consistent over the years. He was wide-waisted and jowly, slightly stooped with a large rectangular head and thick hands, like the P.G. Wodehouse character who was poured into his clothes but forgot to say, "When!" By the time of his confirmation hearing in 1986, liberal politicians had used up their powder over Rehnquist's nomination for the Chief Justiceship and did not have time to reload for Scalia. Scalia, who puffed on a thoughtful pipe and joked freely during his hearing, was confirmed 98-0. "The vote I most regret casting out of all the ones I ever cast," recalled then-Senator Joe Biden, was for Scalia, because Scalia, Biden said, "was so effective." But Scalia, it should be said, had never disguised his views. "With neither the constraint of text nor the constraint of historical practice," he wrote in a 1985 case, while still on the D.C. Court of Appeals, "nothing would separate the judicial task of constitutional interpretation from the political task of enacting laws currently deemed essential."

Some anticipated a "consensus builder." "When he's in doubt," said his former judicial colleague Abner Mikva, "he'll look for a middle ground." Many, in a word, saw a conservative version of another judge, also a first-generation son of Catholic immigrants (this time from Ireland), also a New Jersey native (an hour away, in Newark), and the man who became known as the most skilled majority-cobbler in modern Supreme Court history: William J. Brennan, Jr. He was born in 1906 and as a boy delivered milk in a horse-drawn wagon. Later, as an Air Force officer handling labor disputes, Brennan struck one colleague as a man who one might expect would "become the president of one of our great corporations." Scalia would call Brennan the 20th century's most influential justice. But he and Brennan would come to personify the opposing judicial philosophies in interpreting the Constitution that dominate today.

Brennan is the patriarch of the Living Constitutionalists, the school of thought that sees a national charter drafted with deliberate elasticity in order to let judges interpret it to reflect today's sense of justice and wise policy. The Originalists, led by Scalia, if not called into existence by him, denounce this as a form of evolutionism that disregards the Constitution's central purpose, which is to set certain essentials in stone precisely to prevent their effacement by fads or judges. Living Constitutionalism, thoroughly left-leaning, peaked in the 1970s; Originalism was a conservative reaction that began in the mid-1980s. Brennan said that Scalia's approach would leave us with a "stagnant, archaic, hidebound document steeped in the prejudices and superstitions of a time long past." Scalia's response, roughly speaking, was "Damn right." Each tradition puts a different emphasis on the usefulness of historical materials. "[I]t would be comforting to believe," wrote Brennan, "that a search for 'tradition' involves nothing more idiosyncratic or complicated than poring through dusty volumes on American history." But in *casa* Scalia, those volumes never even have time to gather dust.

The crucial difference between Brennan and Scalia was their dispute about the all-important question of *who decides*. Brennan believed himself authorized to do the renovation work. "I put sixteen years into that damn obscenity thing," he said in an interview, referring to the Court's struggle to reconcile obscenity laws with the Free Speech Clause. "I tried and I tried, and I waffled back and forth, and I finally gave up....I reached the conclusion that every criminal-obscenity statute—and most obscenity laws are criminal—was necessarily unconstitutional." This is a remarkable admission: William Brennan, in the comfort of his monastic chambers, deep in a marble palace, decided that 200 million Americans could no longer have obscenity laws, today or ever, even though the men who wrote the First Amendment also wrote obscenity laws. Brennan's decisions could not be reversed, except by a later court. He could not lose his job, no matter how erroneous his opinions. And he could not be overridden even by the united force of Congress, the President, and state legislatures. A formidable power, clearly, and one of the few under our Constitution that knows no hard checks or balances, or any limits, really, beyond the justices' own sense of discretion. A "living-Constitution judge," Scalia said, is a "happy fellow who comes home at night to his wife and says, 'The Constitution means exactly what I think it ought to mean!'"

Both Brennan and Scalia would feel the sting of losses and sound the *cri de coeur*. "The document that the plurality construes today is unfamiliar to me," Brennan wrote in a case shortly before he retired. "When and if the Court awakes to reality, it will find a world very different from the one it expects." Seven years later, it was Scalia's turn. "The Court must be living in another world. Day by day, case by case, it is busy designing a Constitution for a country I do not recognize." Brennan usually despaired when the Court declined to recognize what he believed to be a constitutional right; Scalia mourned when the Court *did* recognize a right that he couldn't find in his copy of the Constitution. Brennan left the bench saying that he hoped that he had helped make the Constitution more "responsive to the needs of the people," the sort of duty one normally associates with politicians, not jurists awarded life tenure precisely to be able to resist those "needs." No surprise, then, writes Joan Biskupic, that Brennan, like any good legislator, cornered colleagues in their offices or sent them cajoling memos to bargain for half-a-loaf outcomes. He did what he needed to get his five votes, including through compromises on law. Scalia, by contrast, was likelier to alienate colleagues with his in-their-face inflexibility.

Scalia, and the movement he led, observed that there was always something suspicious about the claim by Living Constitutionalists that they make the Constitution more "responsive" to citizens. To constitutionalize a new "right"—whether for inmates, welfare recipients, or pornographers—by definition makes the Constitution *less* responsive to voters. For Scalia, this prospect of an "imperial judiciary," bestowing new rights like magnanimous viziers distributing diamonds, was more frightening than a monarchical president or a domineering Congress. Bums can be thrown out, but constitutional decisions, like diamonds, are mostly forever. To pass a federal law, you generally need 218 representatives and 51 senators, plus the president. To reinterpret the Constitution, Scalia notes, you need only "a democratic vote by nine lawyers." Scalia's favorite illustration of how Living Constitutionalism works in practice is also the most heartrending one.

In 1974, Ehrlich Coker escaped from the Georgia prison where he was serving multiple life sentences for raping and stabbing a woman to death and then, within months, raping and bludgeoning a 16-year-old and leaving her to die in a wooded area. That night he entered the home of Allen and Elnita Carver, tied Allen up, and raped Elnita in his presence. The issue in *Coker v. Georgia* (1977) was whether it was "cruel and unusual," under the U.S. Constitution, for Georgians to execute Coker. Justice White, for the Court, held that it was: the punishment was "disproportionate" to the crime. Rape, he wrote, "does not include the death of or even the serious injury to another person.... Life is over for the victim of the murderer; for the rape victim, life may not be nearly so happy as it was, but it is not over, and normally is not beyond repair." After all, he said, "Mrs. Carver was unharmed"—aside, apparently, from the rape. It was a mystery how he knew that Elnita—who was 16 at the time and had given birth three weeks earlier—was so unscathed. Less mysterious was that henceforth, as a result of his opinion, it would be irrelevant that citizens of Georgia or any other state believed that an exceedingly rare execution, or even the threat of it, could deter thousands of rapes; or that a man who rapes three women could inflict as much harm as some murderers; or that sex crimes involve perpetrators notoriously prone to recidivism. There is hard evidence to support all three propositions. How could you possibly decide these questions, Scalia said, except by solemn democratic election? But elections on this issue were now out of the question. That was for the rape of *adults*.

In 1998, an eight-year-old in Louisiana awoke to find her 300-pound stepfather, Patrick Kennedy, on top of her. A pediatric doctor said he found the most grievous injuries he had ever seen from a sexual assault. But the girl didn't get to the hospital right away. Kennedy first called a colleague for advice about getting bloodstains out of a white carpet; his stepdaughter, he said, had "just become a young lady." Then he called a carpet cleaner. Only an hour and a half later, as she bled, did he summon medical help. Beholding this, Justice Anthony Kennedy, in *Kennedy v. Louisiana* (2008), for five justices against four, wrote that it would be "extreme cruelty" to allow Patrick Kennedy to be executed, as Louisiana was preparing to do. Instead, he counseled, society "must embrace and express respect for the dignity of the person," or else it "risks its own sudden descent into brutality."

As it happens, however, jurors had made very few such descents; the last execution of a child rapist was in 1964. In that year, of 36 states that reintroduced the death penalty after the Supreme Court essentially banned it in 1972—before it reversed itself, after popular outrage, four years later—six states chose to permit death for child rapists. The number of states to do so, more importantly, was growing. Justice Samuel Alito, in a dissent that Scalia joined, suggested that this wave of new legislation reflected the fact that society today better understands the permanent harm that sex crimes wreak on the children of a species born almost inconceivably fragile. Psychologists document how sexual abuse, especially by trusted adults, is so damaging that it leads to sociopathic behavior as well as to prostitution, school drop-out, criminality, self-hatred, and suicide. Many victims never recover. This is why those who *commit* such outrages were usually childhood sexual-assault victims themselves. Yet in 2008, the Supreme Court disabled states, under the U.S. Constitution, from ever imposing death on even the most bestial violators of children. In this and other death-penalty cases, Scalia saw the same trick played: the court pretended to defer to state preferences, but in fact permanently froze the anti-death consensus into law. "We are, in effect," Scalia said at the oral argument, "prohibiting the people from changing their mind." Thus a child rapist lived, and a little part of democracy died.

⸎

Al Gore, echoing William Brennan and most Democratic politicians, called the Constitution a "living and breathing document" that was intended to be interpreted, by judges, "in the light of the constantly evolving experience of the American people." What Al Gore got was a living, breathing court decision, after the 2000 presidential election, on the constantly evolving chads of Florida ballots. This was from a court that a majority of Americans feel is shot through with partisanship. The originalist prophecy was that if justices were perceived as highly trained aristocrats annually remodeling the Constitution in their image, the Court would necessarily become the focus of a keen political glare. Sandra Day O'Connor, the daughter of an Arizona cattle rancher who, as a female lawyer in the early 1950s, was rejected by every law firm she applied to, was appointed to the Court by Ronald Reagan, despite a record of support for abortion rights as a legislator. She was confirmed, in 1981, 99-0. But in later years, especially after a series of close abortion cases, America at last arrived at the ritual of court nominees being dutifully asked about their views on *Roe v. Wade*, and then dutifully denying that they have any. Antonin Scalia's position on the abortion debate—like, in fact, his position on most social issues—is that the Constitution is silent on it. "You think there's a right to suicide?" he said in a speech, "Do it the way the people of Oregon did it and pass a law! Don't come to the Supreme Court!"

But come they do. America excels in turning political questions into legal ones. Yet only since the late 1960s have social and cultural questions come to be seen as familiar subjects of court orders. The word Scalia always favored to denote the absorbing vortex of judicial power was "business." In *Webster v. Reproductive Health Services* (1989), an abortion case, Scalia scolded his colleagues for attempting to "prolong this Court's self-awarded sovereignty over a field where it has little proper business." "[F]ederal courts have no business in this field," he said in another case, this time about the right to refuse medical treatment, a question of science and morality "neither set forth in the Constitution nor known to the nine Justices of this Court any better than they are known to nine people picked at random from the Kansas City telephone directory." His suspicion that the Court was ruling the nation through a subjective legal sociology, highly flavored by the left, was heightened in instances when an antagonist like Harry Blackmun, in making a point about religion in schools, could cite Sigmund Freud and James Madison in a single footnote.

Or in a 2005 case on the criminal culpability of a 17-year-old murderer, a brief from the American Psychological Association argued that youngsters under 18 lacked the ability to take moral responsibility for their actions. The same association, years earlier, had said that, by age 14 or 15, youngsters *could* reason about moral dilemmas like adults—that time, however, in a case involving whether juveniles could get abortions without parental consent. Lawyer-crafted amicus briefs give the justices the confidence to conclude on questions that in prior generations were the essence of legislative proceedings. This is why Court arguments today often have the flavor of high-toned Senate hearings. But unlike legislation by real, elected legislators, there is no political accountability. "In practice," wrote Scalia at the end of *Reading Law* (2012), his magnum opus on his method of legal interpretation, "the Living Constitution would better be called the Dead Democracy."

The most persistent criticism of Scalia is that what he called "originalism" was in fact a means—a hypocritical one at that—to achieve conservative policy goals. When Scalia "believes that élite judges or professors are trying to dismantle the moral positions of 'the people,'" wrote Margaret Talbot in a *New Yorker* profile of the justice, his decisions "leave the unavoidable impression that he is speaking not only for originalism but also for his own selective notion of the vox populi." Scalia hasn't always helped avoid this impression. In one opinion he said he "hope[d]" that an extramarital affair was rare; in another, he suggested that government "should" cultivate "respect for the religious observances of others." Despite his protests, pointing out that he has reached decisions that he dislikes politically—usually rulings favoring criminal defendants or making flag-burning a free-speech right—he was never able to shake the impression that, as put by one critic, the Scalia method was to "recite a lot of facts about the framers and then announce a legal conclusion remarkably consistent with [his] own views."

There is truth in this—but not for the reason suggested. To be a conservative judge is naturally to fit in well with the framers. By our standards they were tough on crime, wary of federal power, soft on personal "privacy," and open to prayer in schools (and everywhere else). Chief Justice John Marshall was raised in a frontier of harsh self-sufficiency in which his sisters used thorns for buttons. Would you suppose that these were people sensitive about welfare entitlements? Or that New Englanders, who saw the actual establishment of religion, like penalties for missing Congregationalist services, would be squeamish about a crèche in city hall? No, that steely generation concentrated on the essentials and left the dainty details to us.

When asked about his favorite decisions, Scalia offered the two that he thought most completely reflected his method: *Crawford v. Washington* (2004) and *Heller v. District of Columbia* (2010). *Crawford* reoriented American jurisprudence on the Sixth Amendment's Confrontation Clause, the clause that guarantees a defendant's right to be "confronted with the witnesses against him," in order to make our construction of the clause, wrote Scalia, more "faithful to the Framers' understanding." Previously the Court had said that if witnesses seemed sufficiently reliable, that was enough; *Crawford* required those witnesses to show up in court. "I should be the pin-up of the criminal defense bar," said Scalia of the decision, in which he persuaded the court, by a 7-2 vote, to adopt a defendant-friendly interpretation he had championed for 15 years.

Crawford was correctly decided, but it also illustrates the dangers of originalism, a method that depends on linguistic and historical research largely by partisan advocates. A major question to arise after *Crawford* is whether the statements of medical examiners, the doctors who perform autopsies, also must be confronted in court. It is a momentous question, because if these doctors must testify in court, many murder prosecutions will fail; autopsies often are conducted years before a murder trial, by which time examiners are retired, dead, or otherwise unavailable. Scalia, as part of his argument in *Crawford*, anticipated this important question by analogizing medical examiners to the "coroners" of the common law. But this was historically inaccurate: these coroners were actually elected layman, like sheriffs, whose duty it was to summon juries, exhibit bodies, and interview witnesses—things that modern medical examiners, or pathologists, highly trained doctors who work in labs or hospitals, never do. In 1915, for instance, New York City's scandalizing Wallstein Report revealed that coroners were mostly bribe-hungry political hacks who performed their work with all the ineptitude one might expect of grogshop-keepers given the task of sophisticated medical analysis. (That report led to coroners eventually being replaced by pathologists.) Scalia's bad analogy, however, has misled judges for almost fifteen years now.

But other than the rare misstep, Scalia's method has accounted for scientific or technological developments well, even when these developments require a break with historical practice. Often at issue is the Fourth Amendment, which secures the right to be free of unreasonable government searches and seizures. A constable in, say, 1807, was free to peer into your home's window from a nearby hill, and like any other passerby, he could even use a telescope to do it. But in *Kyllo v. United States* (2001), Scalia wrote, for the Court, that law enforcement's use of high-tech thermal-imaging devices (in that case, to detect marijuana plants) required a warrant. In *Riley v. California* (2014), Scalia joined a decision making it illegal for police to access an arrestee's smartphone without a warrant, even though, until that decision, *anything* in an arrestee's pockets was fair game to officers. A typical smartphone, the Court reasoned, quite persuasively, could have more sensitive information about you—more medical and financial data, or the equivalent of years of letters or photographs—than could be found in your entire house. The rationale behind these decisions was that 21st-century technology transformed a formerly limited privacy intrusion into an unacceptable invasion of constitutional magnitude.

Changed technology was also at the heart of Scalia's opinion in *District of Columbia v. Heller* (2008), a decision Scalia identified as his "legacy" opinion. It was the first decision to construe the Second Amendment's "right of the people to keep and bear arms." Writing it, Scalia said, was "like being John Marshall for a little tiny portion of the Constitution." *Heller* would make it unconstitutional for government to outlaw guns, at least handguns kept in the home. The result was I think correct as a matter of history. To the first generations of Americans under the Constitution, banning firearms for all citizens would have been as puzzling (and tyrannical) as banning stoves. Militia service even presumed private ownership of the tool known as a firearm; to "pass muster" meant to satisfy a state inspection of your household gun.

But now it was Scalia's turn to be accused of denying the people their choice. Justice Stephen Breyer's dissent declared that the decision "threatens severely to limit the ability of more knowledgeable, democratically elected officials to deal with gun-related problems." To this, Scalia replied:

> Undoubtedly some think that the Second Amendment is outmoded in a society where our standing army is the pride of our Nation, where well-trained police forces provide personal security, and where gun violence is a serious problem. That is perhaps debatable, but what is not debatable is that it is not the role of this Court to pronounce the Second Amendment extinct.

The principle, Scalia wrote in his opinion, was that the right to firearms was an application of the natural right of self-preservation. Whether, for Scalia, this principle extends to possession of guns on streets, or in stadiums, or by non-citizens, or in courthouses (I'm guessing not), or whether the right covers 3D-printed guns, banana-clipped fully autos, or bazookas, or how he views any of the thousands of limitations that hedge the reasonable exercise of this (and every other) constitutional right, will never be known.

But when the Court chooses to hear those future gun cases, looming will be decisions, like *Kyllo* and *Riley*, that take account of advancing technology—the very problem, along with mental illness, that makes American gun violence such a painful subject. A Revolutionary War soldier using specially prepared cartridges could load and fire a flintlock three or four times a minute. Not much better was the Kentucky mountain man's musket in 1839, or an Idaho trapper's long rifle in 1894. But in 2012, Adam Lanza, the demon behind the Sandy Hook massacre of 20 schoolchildren and six adults, used a Bushmaster M4, based on military designs, to fire 154 rounds in five minutes, about one every two seconds. "Some have made the argument, bordering on the frivolous," Scalia wrote in *Heller*, "that only those arms in existence in the 18th century are protected by the Second Amendment. We do not interpret constitutional rights that way." Undoubtedly so. But it is equally frivolous to suggest that we must treat 18th-century guns the same way we do 21st-century ones.

Americans revere the framers but leave it to lawyers, not historians, to interpret their handiwork in concrete ways. It was inevitable that lawyers, including judges, trying to prevail in cases, would claim to be the voice of the founders. In *Maryland v. King* (2013), a case on the constitutionality of swabbing the cheeks of arrestees for their DNA, Scalia wrote: "I doubt that the proud men who wrote the charter of our liberties would have been so eager to open their mouths for royal inspection." In fact, the founders would have done very little for royal anything. The real issue in the case, however, was whether those proud men would have submitted *criminal suspects* to the indignity. In *Boumediene v. Bush* (2008), the Court, though not Scalia, decided that foreign jihadists held in Cuba had a constitutional right to challenge their detention in court, since, according to the majority, the "Framers decided that habeas corpus, a right of first importance, must be a part of that framework." Those framers presumably include Thomas Jefferson, who as Secretary of State suggested, in the war against the Barbary pirates, that captured Muslim raiders (not the worst analogue to today's jihadists) be sold in retaliation in the Maltese slave market. "If great lawyers of [that] day—Alexander Hamilton, for example—were sitting with us today," wrote Justice Stevens, in a 2005 case reversing a death sentence, "I would expect them to join Justice Kennedy's opinion for the Court." Here Stevens purported to channel a man who never said a word in opposition to the death penalty, but who did denounce President John Adams's *refusal* to execute the leaders of the Fries Rebellion (1799–1800) as a "dereliction" of his duty to act with "exemplary vigor" against lawbreakers.

Historians of early America like Gordon S. Wood observe, in reaction to Scalia's originalist method, that in deciphering constitutional meaning it is of limited use to speak of a group of people called "framers," as if members of this group weren't endlessly at each other's throats on every important political dispute. Instead there was a generation of men, of varying tempers and perspectives, who served in office or who wrote important documents between 1765 and 1800. They shared a broad consensus of political thought on the limited purposes of government, the divided nature of man, and the need to diffuse power through separate executive, legislative, and judicial branches. But once the Constitution took effect, and the founder-philosophers descended from the heights of Olympus to the battlefields of Thessaly, they fell out, bitterly, on dozens of constitutional questions. By the end of the 1790s, Washington had disowned Madison, Madison believed Hamilton a monarchist, Hamilton felt Madison "perfidious," Adams called Hamilton the most "unprincipled intriguer in the United States," Hamilton thought Jefferson intended the "complete overthrow" of all morality, and Jefferson saw everyone, even his old ally Madison, as traitorously soft on true republicanism.

We have every reason to suspect, in short, that the framers would clash over the major constitutional issues in our day as surely as they clashed in their own. But if lawyers don't seem to respect the complexity of the historians' task, historians at times fail to grasp what it is that lawyers do, which is to resolve real disputes between living people who suffer actual injuries. Solomonic decisions are desirable, wrote Scalia, but Solomon "was not subject to the constitutional constraints of the judicial department of a national government in a federal, democratic system." Scalia, in the end, is right that history, even if it yields us only an approximation, does tremendous good as an objective limit on the free-style philosophizing of the William Brennans and Anthony Kennedys.

◈

For the danger of judicializing American life is that it undermines self-government. Virtually all Americans now believe that the Constitution means what the Court says it does. This is not altogether healthy, but it is understandable. The real danger comes when Americans conclude that they needn't even *bother* thinking about it for themselves. Former House Speaker Nancy Pelosi was soundly mocked for her puzzled response to a journalist who questioned Congress's constitutional authority for the 2010 Affordable Care Act—"Are you serious?" But her response only exemplified a trend long in motion. Former Senate Majority Leader George Mitchell, among the more thoughtful legislators of his time, and a former federal judge, too, once told a professor of mine that no Senator, he felt, ever thought about the constitutionality of the bills he or she was voting on. This spirit of unthinking deference to courts saps America's constitutional soul.

But an astonishing debate that arose around the start of the millennium, now a case study in constitutional change, proved that Americans are still willing, if the occasion is right, to examine the meaning of their basic charter. This was the battle over gay marriage. The progress of moral causes has always been glacial. Between the Seneca Falls Convention in 1848 that demanded female suffrage, and the Nineteenth Amendment that secured it, are 72 long years. African-American fathers in Kansas sought to admit their children to schools on equal terms with white children as early as 1876—78 years before *Brown v. Board of Education* (1954). By contrast, the velocity of the campaign to secure a constitutional right to gay marriage was supersonic. In 1967, the year Scalia became a law professor at the University of Virginia, the Supreme Court upheld the deportation of a Canadian who, as a gay man, was for that reason deemed by Congress "afflicted with psychopathic personality." In 1973, during Scalia's service in the Nixon Administration, the American Psychiatric Association at last declassified homosexuality as a mental disorder. The next year, Kathy Kozachenko, of the Ann Arbor, Michigan, city council, became the first openly gay candidate to win public office in the United States.

Normalization only accelerated. In the 1970s, most gay-rights activists still rejected same-sex marriage, but in 2003 legalization began in Massachusetts. This came in a court decision, and provoked in reaction, within three years, 26 state constitutional *bans* on gay marriage. But then in 2009 Vermont became the first to recognize marriage equality by a democratic vote—and eight states followed suit by 2013. A Gallup poll in mid-2010, around the time that two gay-rights cases that would eventually reach Scalia were filed, found that some 45% of Americans supported gay marriage and 55% were opposed to it. By the time those cases were *decided* by Scalia's court, those numbers had flipped. A 10% change in public opinion means 30 million people—the equivalent of about 3,000 people changing their minds every day.

People did so for many reasons, but all trace to a realization that homosexuality is an incident of nature. Humans are among some 60 species in whom homosexual behavior is known. People are not "born gay," any more than they are born bald, but genetic predispositions are identifiable. Hence the familiar stories of struggle after consciousness, usually in the early teens, of attraction to the same sex—and, later, sham marriages, failed therapy, crises of faith, deception, misery, and suicide. The recognition of a right of gay marriage has been as much the result of advancing scientific fact as of changed moral opinion. To legally circumscribe homosexuality is not "morals legislation," as Scalia called it, outlawing a voluntary but socially harmful "lifestyle," but rather punishing people for what we now know to be their essentially unchosen and unchangeable biology. The gay-marriage battle, then, was a collision between law and the first principle of ethics: do not hold people responsible for what they are powerless to affect. The fight for gay equality thus found its analogy in America's long struggle over racial equality.

In *Hollingsworth v. Perry* (2013), the Justices first heard the case for whether the Constitution secured a right of gay marriage, though ultimately they dodged the issue until 2015. The following exchange occurred between Scalia and Ted Olson, the attorney for two gay couples:

> JUSTICE SCALIA: I'm curious . . . when did it become unconstitutional to exclude homosexual couples from marriage? 1791? 1868, when the Fourteenth Amendment was adopted? . . .

> MR. OLSON: When—may I answer this in the form of a rhetorical question? When did it become unconstitutional to prohibit interracial marriages? When did it become unconstitutional to assign children to separate schools?

> JUSTICE SCALIA: It's an easy question, I think, for that one. At—at the time that the Equal Protection Clause was adopted. That's abso-

lutely true. But don't give me a question to my question. (Laughter.) When do you think it became unconstitutional? Has it *always* been unconstitutional?...

MR. OLSON: ... It was constitutional when we, as a culture, determined that sexual orientation is a characteristic of individuals that they cannot control, and that that—

JUSTICE SCALIA: I see. When did that happen?

MR. OLSON: There's no specific date in time. This is an evolutionary cycle.

JUSTICE SCALIA: Well, how am I supposed to know how to decide a case, then?

Scalia was asking the right questions, but he might have been more cautious. Interracial marriage and mixed-race education were decidedly *not* understood as secured by the Fourteenth Amendment's Equal Protection Clause "at the time" that clause was adopted in 1868. The same Congress that proposed that amendment also funded race-segregated schools in the District of Columbia; leading sponsors of the amendment ridiculed Dixie hysterics about how the clause approved interracial marriage. True equality under law was left to a future generation that better understood the implications of the principle of equality, or were ready to respect those implications—even though, meanwhile, not a word in the Equal Protection Clause had changed.

Antonin Scalia, though personally opposed to gay marriage, said that he believed that the Constitution neither requires nor forbids it—a position consistent with his views on abortion and the death penalty. Yet he was not always content simply to observe that the legal rights of gays were not preeminent subjects of debate at Philadelphia in 1787. In *Lawrence v. Texas* (2003), which invalidated laws criminalizing adult gay sex, Scalia wrote that "[t]oday's opinion is the product of a Court, which is the product of a law-profession culture, that has largely signed on to the so-called homosexual agenda, by which I mean the agenda promoted by some homosexual activists directed at eliminating the moral opprobrium that has traditionally attached to homosexual conduct." Here the decrier of politicization of the Court sought to discredit his colleagues politically in the public eye; here the master of semantic precision would chose to liken homosexuality to bestiality and incest. But Scalia was right about the logical implication: "The Court today pretends that we need not fear judicial imposition of homosexual marriage," he wrote. "Do not believe it."

A decade later, Anthony Kennedy, the author of the *Lawrence* decision, wrote the decision in *Windsor v. United States* (2013), the case that, as a matter of constitutional law, made gay marriage inevitable. That opinion held that Congress could not constitutionally distinguish between gay and straight couples. But the opinion did not rest on equality. Instead the majority reasoned in a confusing way, first suggesting that gay Americans deserved "dignity," then pivoting to say that Congress traditionally "deferred" to states on marriage, so that states could chose to "confer" this "dignity," or, presumably, not. A majority of the Court, however, we know today, believed all along that *no* government, state or federal, could ban gay marriage. The Court once again, as with the death penalty, feigned deference to state authority while preparing to strip them of it—as the Court finally did, two years later, in *Obergefell v. Hodges* (2015).

In 2013, in *Windsor*, Scalia beheld this spectacle of non-candor and produced what after a career of unconcealed irritation with such decisions is striking for its statesmanlike depth of feeling:

> Few public controversies touch an institution so central to the lives of so many, and few inspire such attendant passion by good people on all sides. Few public controversies will ever demonstrate so vividly the beauty of what our Framers gave us, a gift the Court pawns today to buy its stolen moment in the spotlight: a system of government that permits us to rule *ourselves*.... [C]itizens on all sides of the question have seen victories and they have seen defeats. There have been plebiscites, legislation, persuasion, and loud voices—in other words, democracy. Victories in one place for some are offset by victories in other places for others. Even in a single State, the question has come out differently on different occasions.
>
> In the majority's telling, this story is black-and-white: Hate your neighbor or come along with us. The truth is more complicated. It is hard to admit that one's political opponents are not monsters,

especially in a struggle like this one, and the challenge in the end proves more than today's Court can handle. Too bad. A reminder that disagreement over something so fundamental as marriage can still be politically legitimate would have been a fit task for what in earlier times was called the judicial temperament. We might have covered ourselves with honor today, by promising all sides of this debate that it was theirs to settle and that we would respect their resolution. We might have let the People decide.

But that the majority will not do. Some will rejoice in today's decision, and some will despair at it; that is the nature of a controversy that matters so much to so many. But the Court has cheated both sides, robbing the winners of an honest victory, and the losers of the peace that comes from a fair defeat. We owed both of them better.

Scalia's judicial philosophy had many qualities, but arrogance was not among them. That term better fits the *Windsor* majority's characterization of heterosexual-only marriage laws as possible only as the result of anti-gay "animus," the fancy legal word for bigotry. If legislators of recent decades were bigots for being blind to gay rights, so, necessarily, were the framers of the Fourteenth Amendment (on which gay rights now rest), and so, possibly, even the justices' former selves. Their self-righteous name-calling strikes me as the equivalent of a NASA astronomer sneering at the limitations of Galileo. They might, in short, have recognized the modern vantage without condescension toward past ones.

After the *Windsor* decision, the gay-marriage activists who had tramped from door to door were succeeded by lawyers shuttling from court to court. The ten states, and D.C., that, like dominoes, enacted marriage equality before *Windsor* did so democratically—by popular vote, ballot initiative, or legislature. After *Windsor*, however, only two states did so, overshadowed by more than 60 court cases. I have little doubt, for my part, that democratic legalization would have continued—even if the Court ruled that gay marriage was *not* found in the Constitution and so left the question to individual states. This had already happened once before with anti-sodomy laws: in *Bowers v. Hardwick*, decided in 1986, just before Scalia joined the Court, the justices upheld such laws, calling the notion of a right to private, consensual adult gay sex "facetious." By the time the Court got around to de-constitutionalizing such laws, only four states were left who still had such a law on their books, and none really enforced it. In deciding *Obergefell*, the justices made a large withdrawal from the store of goodwill that their predecessors had deposited over generations.

Which brings us back to the core question that Antonin Scalia devoted much of his career to: on constitutional questions, *who decides*? It may be that opposition to gay marriage will appear to future generations the way opposition to interracial marriage does today. But should the credit for the legal victory of marriage equality go to a slow-moving Supreme Court—or to the decades of struggle by gay-rights activists ringing doorbells in dozens of states; or to the three Iowa justices who in 2009 sacrificed their seats by voting for gay marriage and being ousted, as a result, by angry voters; or to San Francisco Mayor Gavin Newsom who in 2004 risked his career to issue defiant gay-marriage licenses, and before him Clela Rorex, the Colorado county clerk who did the same in Boulder in 1975? The real victory of gay marriage was the result not of any court order but of a majority of the American people looking inward and collectively agreeing that there was just no good reason for unequal treatment.

The perhaps unanswerable query for the future is whether Scalia's counsel of patience with the democratic process would have better ensured that when gay marriage was formally constitutionalized, everyday Americans believed that it was because *they* read their Constitution that way, and not life-tenured judges, whose decrees in the end are as much acts of force as of reason. Kim Davis, the Kentucky clerk who briefly became a *cause célèbre* after defying the Supreme Court on issuing gay-marriage licenses, would not have been invited to the 2016 State of the Union, as a sort of folk hero, if she had bucked not the Court but Kentucky's *voters*. At the same time, many politician opponents of gay marriage breathed a faint but noticeable sigh of relief at having the Court put this controversy to rest for them, a response of a piece with a larger trend of lawmakers practically resigning their most divisive social issues into the hands of that eminent tribunal. The Supreme Court majority in *Windsor* and *Obergefell* simply faced an insoluble question, not of law but prudence: judicial justice now or democratic justice later? Their decision not to let the latter process unfold came with a price. We eliminated one harm, but produced another: we lost another piece of our democratic vitality, even unconsciously. Antonin Scalia was right about this, even when he stumbled on the merits. Which I'm sure suited him just fine. "It doesn't prove anything," he said, "that everyone thinks you're wrong."

When Antonin Scalia died in his sleep, in a hunting lodge in Texas, in February 2016, it was international news not only because of his eminence as the greatest American jurist of his generation. It was because, as even a distant observer like London's *Guardian* knew, the identity of his successor would help decide, as the paper put it, the "future direction of the United States." The bitter fight that instantly began over his successor demonstrated that Scalia was correct: the accelerating concentration of power at the courtly palace at One First Street has made the one branch of government originally designed to be immune from partisan politics as politicized as any other. And thus, even in death, Antonin Scalia continues to prove his point.

FINALE

The Experiment Endures

We the People have cast the word "experiment" against our Constitution since the days of our patriarchs. In engineering or medicine, the latest is usually the best. Not so in the law, and especially not American constitutional law, which must always remain an endless contest between centralization and localism, experiment and continuity, liberty and authority, one liberty and other liberties. Thomas Jefferson was in Paris in 1787 and missed that summer's Philadelphia Convention, but decades later he offered this supremely arresting thought on constitutionalism:

> Some men look at Constitutions with sanctimonious reverence, and deem them, like the ark of the covenant, too sacred to be touched. They ascribe to the men of the preceding age a wisdom more than human, and suppose what they did to be beyond amendment. I knew that age well: I belonged to it, and labored with it. It deserved well of its country. It was very like the present, but without the experience of the present. And 40 years of experience in government is worth a century of book-reading. And this they would say themselves, were they to rise from the dead.

The ark of the covenant that Jefferson refers to was the sacred vessel described in Exodus as carrying the tablets on which were engraved the Ten Commandments. We treat our Constitution similarly. We house the original in a shrine at the National Archives. But with the old tablets and the new parchment alike, it has never been the physical object itself, but our allegiance to its contents that matters. The words are what turned out to be the portable truth that overspread the world. If anything could lead me to violate the Mosaic injunction against idolatry, it is the Constitution. But fortunately our holy of holies needs no supernatural reverence. Respect for it can be quite commonsensical and unsentimental.

Cicero, a man yet to be accused of being a redneck or a jingo, had an argument for why patriotism was a perfectly rational duty. He imagined a series of concentric circles reflecting life's central relationships. The first is the family. Parents, he said, tend to their children for the simple reason that it serves us all if parents care for their own, while other parents care for *their* own, and so on. Radiating outward, we take an interest in our city's affairs because it happens to be the city that we live in, though we wish all other cities well. The circle moves outward until you reach the nation: we care for our country because it is our job, not that of foreigners, to promote our interest; we can rest assured that they'll do the same for their nation. Self-interest has a particularly strong claim on us: we have much to gain by preserving the Constitution, and an infinitude to lose by weakening it. We should be proud of our 230-year run as an American republic, even if it's only halfway to the 450 years of the Roman republic that Cicero died serving.

Rome, to stay with that celebrated regime for a moment more, rose because of its appeal to foreigners. So, too, the strongest proof of American success, not to say superiority, remains immigration. People from every corner of the globe pack their suitcases and demonstrate, quite democratically, whose society they believe the most desirable to join. In American cities you find communities descended from virtually every other nation, even from the great empires of yesteryear or today's industrial powerhouses. There are 19th- or 20th-century neighborhoods, for instance, with names like "Japantown" or "Little Italy." Older yet are 17th- and 18th-century communities like "Germantown" or "Stockholm" (of which there are seven in America), and, reaching even further back, an entire region called "New England." I know of no enduring "America-town" in any foreign capital. Americans need not love it or leave it, but they might keep in mind that roughly 100 million people would gladly switch places with them on two days' notice. A British traveler named Andrew Burnaby, in an account of a tour of America that he began in 1759, concluded that humanity was "looking forward with eager and impatient expectation to that destined moment when America is to give the law to the rest of the world." What he didn't realize was that humanity would actually come here to get it.

All the more strange, then, that a persistent part of every American generation considers itself doomed to live in an age of constitutional degeneracy. The fall from purity began, by my calculations, about 600 days into the Constitution's life, when the Virginia legislature, in November 1790, denounced Alexander Hamilton's financial plan as constitutionally blasphemous. The Constitution's first custodians, including James Madison, George Washington, Hamilton, and John Marshall, all expressed, in private, their heartfelt fear that the Constitution was simply born sick and unlikely to survive its first practical tests. We today, given the rather impressive track record, have little right to engage in any such constitutional hypochondria. Our history since the founding may in fact best be captured in the words that William Dean Howells applied to our literary tastes: a "tragedy with a happy ending."

This is not to ignore that there remains much in American history, and in the American present, that is grubby, cheap, and shameful — above all, racial bigotry, the infirmity that has always presented the most painful constitutional questions about what, if anything, our principles mean in reality. The truth that justice will be forever approximated but never achieved is itself constitutionalized in those paradoxical words that gild the Preamble — our "more perfect" Union. That impossibly shrewd phrase suggests that we have a miraculous thing that we must nevertheless strive to make better.

Even if the Constitution is violated in dozens of ways each day, in humble rural courthouses or in lofty Washington bureaucracies, it survives because, at bottom, more hold fast to the law than disobey it. A society under law is like a giant card game. The game can tolerate a few players cheating here and there; but when the game deteriorates so far that there are more flouting the rules than honoring them, it ceases, in point of fact, to be a card game. An insistent majority of Americans must believe in the Constitution for it to work. This is why constitutionalism is not a mere institutional form but a culture, a set of loyalties, sentiments, habits, assumptions, usages, and self-disciplines, a permeating spirit that animates an otherwise lifeless paper scheme. Without this proud and cheerful commitment, the Constitution's checks and balances are barricades of foam and counterweights of butterfly's breath. It is not in *having* a constitution that our strength lies, I conclude, but in cherishing it. So long as we keep the faith, our Constitution will be displaced no sooner than an ant tips over the Statue of Liberty.

The figures in this book, when I reflect on them, blend together in a continuous flow of history. There is Hamilton, scribbling constitutional-economic doctrines late at night. Thirty years later, I see Webster transforming those writings into midday speeches, and forty years after that, Field at his desk in chambers, both Hamilton and Webster's writings at his elbow. Here is James Wilson, looking out at Philadelphia streets with clacking cart-horses, imagining a new beginning for the world. Tocqueville and Bryce arrive to record that new world in all of its roughness, hilarity, and promise. Woodrow Wilson looks out onto Trenton streets with honking Model Ts, imagining a renewed beginning. Here is Wells-Barnett, her blood on fire at seeing newspapers used as weapons to murder her friends. There is Jackson, wondering why his colleagues on the court don't see, as Wells-Barnett did, that speech can kill. And here is Scalia, channeling Jackson's spirit in his high-toned defenses of the people's right to decide on their own laws.

This book has examined the lives of ten worthies, but I hope I don't suggest that the flourishing of our constitutional order has been, even primarily, the work of Platonic guardians. No less important than the few who expounded the Constitution's clauses from high offices, or who led the crucial debates over its meaning in legislatures or in newspapers, are the unheralded millions of Americans who have done nothing more than quietly transmit the inheritance unimpaired. "It is not our duty to leave wealth to our children," wrote John Dickinson, the great Pennsylvania lawyer-agitator, in 1774, "but it is our duty to leave liberty to them."

Late at night I see them, as if in a quick-moving movie, glimpses of Americans in every sort of dress, with every accent, in different ages, all jumbled together, an unceasing procession, having nothing in common but the Constitution—the all-but-English first generation, proud and terrified, leathered pioneers in the Ohio Valley, hacking large oaks, surveying stretches of the Great Plains, plotting routes through the cloud-shredding pinnacles of the west. Hurrying forward in the rush of time, blurred images and indistinct sounds and indecipherable voices, flickering, appearing and disappearing, like an old radio dial being turned, sounds of cannons and daguerreotype images of wounded soldiers on battlefields, slaves trudging to their shacks at sunset, vast convention halls with unsmiling men in bowler hats, Emma Lazarus, lonely cowboys sleeping beneath a saguaro, children laughing past shimmering New England snow, turn-of-the-century Philadelphia laundresses reading under gas light, the Wright Brothers, nervy doughboys on steamers, green-brimmed Manhattan accountants and squawky Lower East Side radicals, a speech from a grinning Franklin Roosevelt, Nebraska prairie boys trudging with M1 carbines through Netherlands, a sweet strain of gospel melody, everything now growing in color and speed, decades passing in a second, Yankee sailors in Asian ports, children in unpainted one-room schoolhouses, tobacco-wreathed journalists, Jackie Robinson, sweat-stained inventors, farmers sipping peach brandy, kisses under bayou moonlight, Beat poets, "I have a dream...," pianists, preachers, televised nominees, bankers, truckers, surfers, engineers, dreamers, patriots, lovers—all these Americans, mingled by the millions, the centuries folding in upon each other, pouring forth, like rushing water, into an overwhelming, deafening roar.

These unknown Americans of all stripes taught and teach their children, even unconsciously, that the Constitution is noble and worthy of our affection and, at times, even our lives. We may not know their names, but we should remember the honorable part they have played, and continue to play, to ensure the passing on of a piece of parchment that set us forth, and continues to sustain us, on the most astonishing experiment in government the world has ever seen.

ACKNOWLEDGMENTS

My thanks, first, to Prof. Christopher Flannery—guide, philosopher, and friend—who made invaluable suggestions on the entire manuscript and whose generosity of soul I can never fully repay. To Prof. Robert Kaczorowski, a master of American law, my thanks also for crucial suggestions on the whole book. I am deeply indebted to Tom Klingenstein for his generous support of this project as well as for his counsel and intellectual fellowship.

Special appreciation to Prof. Richard A. Samuelson for commenting on the Hamilton and James Wilson chapters and to Prof. Andrew Kent for commenting on the Field chapter. My gratitude also to Patrick Collins for his unrivaled skill in fact-checking. (Any errors that remain are, of course, the fault of the critics who pointed them out.)

I thank my agents, Glen Hartley and Lynn Chu, for their very early encouragement, conceptual wisdom, and continuing guidance. I am also deeply in debt to Roger Kimball for his longstanding friendship. And for continuing to give me an intellectual home, I am grateful to Ryan Williams and my many friends and colleagues at the Claremont Institute.

Mark Helprin and Victor Davis Hanson, in their character, in their literary excellence, and in their willingness to yield their time to an eager young admirer, have been a particular blessing for me.

My brothers Adam and Aaron were a source of constant inspiration and encouragement, as were (though they won't understand how much so for some time) my effervescent toddler-age daughters Margot Rivkah and Nava Daisy.

And finally, and most profoundly, I thank my wife, Tahlia, for her love, support, patience, good humor, keen editorial eye, and companionship.

NOTES

OVERTURE

ix   "days of Noah": Thomas Paine, *Writings of Thomas Paine* (1894), ed. Moncure Daniel Conway, Vol. 1, 118–19.

xi   "one clear intent": Clinton Rossiter, *1787: The Grand Convention* (1966), 334.

xiii   "It is not to be wondered": James Madison to Reynolds Chapman, Jan. 6, 1831, Founders Online, National Archives. *See also* James Madison to Thomas Ritchie, Sept. 15, 1821, Founders Online, National Archives (publication of his convention notes should be "delayed till the Constitution should be well settled by practice"); James Madison to Charles J. Ingersoll, Jun. 25, 1831, Founders Online, National Archives (explaining that he signed bill creating Second Bank of the United States in 1817 despite earlier certainty as to its unconstitutionality because it is destabilizing and willful to push prior opinions in the face of a national "common understanding," a "construction reduced to practice, during a reasonable period of time," a "uniform sanction of successive Legislative bodies, through a period of years and under the varied ascendancy of parties," "deliberate & reiterated precedents," "execution throughout a period of 20 years with annual legislative recognitions," and the "entire acquiescence of all the local authorities," which together create a rule of constitutional interpretation like those that bind judges); James Madison to William C. Rives, Oct. 21, 1833, Founders Online, National Archives (explaining that he reversed his position on the constitutionality of the Bank of the United States "on the ground of the authoritative and multiplied sanctions given to it, amounting he conceived, to an evidence of the judgment and will of the nation...[and] that such a sanction ought to overrule the abstract and private opinions of individuals").

xiv   "many defining elements": *See, e.g.*, Alexander Hamilton, John Jay, and James Madison, *The Federalist* (1788) 45 ("no apprehensions are entertained" of commerce power), 78 (courts have "neither force nor will" and suffer from a "natural feebleness").

xiv   "easier to alarm": William R. Davie to James Iredell, Jan. 22, 1788, *Life and Correspondence of James Iredell* (1863), ed. Griffith J. McRee, Vol. II, 217.

CHAPTER ONE — ALEXANDER HAMILTON
A War Ends and a Constitution Begins

3   "half-million souls": Robert Middlekauff, *The Glorious Cause: The American Revolution, 1763–1789* (1982), 563–64.

3 "nearly half the state's population": Alexander Hamilton to Robert Morris, Aug. 13, 1782, *The Papers of Alexander Hamilton*, Vol. 3, *1782–1786*, ed. Harold C. Syrett. Columbia University Press (1962), 132–43 [hereinafter *AH Papers*, various years]; Alexander Clarence Flick, *Loyalism in New York During the American Revolution* (1901), 182 & n.2.

3 "robbing, exiling": Flick 162–68; Maya Jasanoff, *Liberty's Exiles: American Loyalists in the Revolutionary World* (2011), 64–65.

3 "saw their homes burned": Ron Chernow, *Alexander Hamilton* (2004), 76; E. Wilder Spaulding, *New York in the Critical Period, 1783–1789* (1932), 116–17; Edwin G. Burrows and Mike Wallace, *Gotham: A History of New York City to 1898* (1999), 252–55.

4 "duly enacted laws": Spaulding 119–28.

4 "A statute from 1784": "An Act for the immediate Sale of certain forfeited Estates," Apr. 6, 1784, in *Laws of the Legislature of the State of New York in Force Against the Loyalists, and Affecting the Trade of Great Britain and British Merchants, and Others Having Property in that State* (1786), 41–42; *see also* "An Act for the Speedy Sale of the confiscated and forfeited Estates within this State, and for other Purposes therein mentioned," May 12, 1784, *id.* at 43–86; Flick 152–58.

4 "Philipsburg Manor": Middlekauff 568.

4 "disenfranchised most Tories": "An Act to preserve the Freedom and Independence of this State," May 12, 1784, in *Laws of the Legislature of the State of New York in Force Against the Loyalists, and Affecting the Trade of Great Britain and British Merchants, and Others Having Property in that State* (1786), 111–14; Forrest McDonald, *Alexander Hamilton: A Biography* (1979), 73.

4 "1783 Trespass Act": *Law Practice of Alexander Hamilton: Documents and Commentary* (1964), ed. Julius Goebel, Jr., Vol. 1, 282–83.

4 "an alarmed Hamilton": *See Law Practice* 197–223; "New York Assembly. Remarks on an Act for Repealing Part of the Trespass Act, [21 March 1787]," *AH Papers*, Vol. 4, *January 1787–May 1788*, 121–22.

4 "breathing revenge": *See, e.g.*, "To Alexander Hamilton from Robert R. Livingston, 30 August 1783," *AH Papers*, Vol. 3, *1782–1786*, 434–35.

4 "taken our station": "A Letter from Phocion to the Considerate Citizens of New York, [1–27 January 1784]," *AH Papers*, Vol. 3, *1782–1786*, 483–97; "Second Letter from Phocion, [April 1784]," *AH Papers*, Vol. 3, *1782–1786*, 530–58.

4 "world has its eye": *Id.*

4 "meager compensation": Chernow 7–11, 18–19; Richard Brookhiser, *Alexander Hamilton, American* (1999), 14.

4 "other founding fathers": Chernow 8.

4 "regularly witnessed": Chernow 19, 32.

4 "entrusted at age 14": Allan McLane Hamilton, *The Intimate Life of Alexander Hamilton* (1910), 19.

5 "Alexander reporting": *Id.*

5 "managed shipments": "From Alexander Hamilton to Nicholas Cruger, 24 February 1772," *AH Papers*, Vol. 1, *1768–1778*, 27–29.

5 "unmatchable apprenticeship": Brookhiser 18–20.

5 "son of a single mother": Chernow 23.

5 "buy Alexander shoes": Chernow 24–26.

5 "single family member": *Id.* at 148.

5 "pay his way": Chernow 37–38; "To Alexander Hamilton from Hugh Knox, 28 July 1784," *AH Papers*, Vol. 3, *1782–1786*, 573–74.

5 "arrived on the continent": Chernow 39.

5 "bright, ruddy complexion": Hamilton 29–30 (quoting George Shea, *Life and Epoch of Alexander Hamilton* [1879]).

5 "to take command": Chernow 73; "From Alexander Hamilton to William Hamilton, 2 May 1797," *AH Papers*, Vol. 21, *April 1797–July 1798*, 77–80.

5 "write more forcefully": Stanley Elkins and Eric McKitrick, *The Age of Federalism* (1993), 98–99; Chernow 87–91.

5 "artillery notebook": "Pay Book of the State Company of Artillery, [1777]," *AH Papers*, Vol. 1, *1768–1778*, 373–412.

6 "Gouverneur Morris": Gouverneur Morris, *To Secure the Blessings of Liberty: Selected Writings of Gouverneur Morris* (2012), ed. J. Jackson Barlow, xii.

6 "Hamilton's political views": *See, e.g.*, "From Alexander Hamilton to James Duane, [3 September 1780]," *AH Papers*, Vol. 2, *1779–1781*, 400–18; "The Stand No. VI, [19 April 1798]," *AH Papers*, Vol. 21, *April 1797–July 1798*, 434–40; *see also* Morris, *Selected Writings* 53–85.

6 "General Washington's supplies": Middlekauff 347.

6 "Charles Willson Peale": *Id.* at 529.

6 "appears more evident": "From Alexander Hamilton to James Duane, [3 September 1780]," *AH Papers*, Vol. 2, *1779–1781*, 400–18.

6 "like the United Nations": *See, e.g.*, "Undelivered First Inaugural Address: Fragments, 30 April 1789," *The Papers of George Washington*, Presidential Series, Vol. 2, *1 April 1789–15 June 1789*, ed. Dorothy Twohig, University Press of Virginia (1987), 158–73 [hereinafter *GW Papers*, various years, ed. Dorothy Twohig, Mark A. Mastromarino, and Jack D. Warren; David R. Hoth and Carol S. Ebel; Christine Sternberg Patrick; W.W. Abbot and Edward G. Lengel].

6 "thirteen heads": "To Alexander Hamilton from James McHenry, 22[–23] October 1783," *AH Papers*, Vol. 3, *1782–1786*, 472–73; *see also* Karen E. Robbins, *James McHenry, Forgotten Federalist* (2013), 36–37.

6 "captaincy during the war": Jean Edward Smith, *John Marshall: Definer of a Nation* (1996), 4–5, 68–69.

6 "six-part essay series": "The Continentalist No. VI, [4 July 1782]," *AH Papers*, Vol. 3, *1782–1786*, 99–106.

7 "George Clinton": Spaulding 96.

7 "fend for itself": "From Alexander Hamilton to George Clinton, 14 February 1783," *AH Papers*, Vol. 3, *1782–1786*, 255–57.

7 "anticipated with horror": Morris, *Selected Writings* 299.

7 "New York City": Spaulding 8–15, 21, 26.

7 "When Congress relocated": U.S. Department of State, Office of the Historian, citing MS of the Department of State, Continental Congress Papers, No. 127, II, 46, 47.

7 "bravely declared": Spaulding 157, 254.

7 "infuriated Nutmeg State": Spaulding 157.

7 "retaliatory tariffs": Chernow 221; Spaulding 153, 156–57.

7 "farmers at the heart": Spaulding 155.
8 "Eight states": Spaulding 195.
8 "anti-Constitution partisans": Spaulding 194–98 (favored delay); "From
   Alexander Hamilton to James Madison, [8 June 1788]," *AH Papers*, Vol.
   5, *June 1788–November 1789*, 2–4; "From Alexander Hamilton to James
   Madison, [2 July 1788]," *AH Papers*, Vol. 5, *June 1788–November 1789*, 140–41;
   "From Alexander Hamilton to James Madison, [27 June 1788]," *AH Papers*,
   Vol. 5, *June 1788–November 1789*, 91.
8 "state was split": Spaulding 44.
8 "tax gatherers": Spaulding 214.
8 "genuine fear": Spaulding 253–55.
8 "decisive influence": Brookhiser 73–74; Chernow 269.
8 "unluckily placed boulder": "From George Washington to Alexander
   Hamilton, 26 October 1794," *GW Papers*, Presidential Series, Vol. 17, *1
   October 1794–31 March 1795*, 110–11.
8 "serious plot": "Enclosure: [Objections and Answers Respecting the
   Administration], [18 August 1792]," *AH Papers*, Vol. 12, *July 1792–October
   1792*, 229–58.
9 "absorb state war debts": *Id.*
9 "fatal to the existence": "First Report on Virginia Resolutions on the
   Assumption of State Debts," Nov. 22, 1790, Journal of the House of
   Delegates of the Commonwealth of Virginia, Oct. 1790 session (1828), 80;
   Virginia Resolutions on the Assumption of State Debts, Dec. 16, 1790, in
   Laws of Virginia (1823), by William Waller Hening, 234–39.
9 "homegrown monarchy": "Thomas Jefferson's Conversation with
   Washington, 1 October 1792," *GW Papers*, Presidential Series, Vol. 11, *16
   August 1792–15 January 1793*, 182–85; "From Thomas Jefferson to George
   Washington, 23 May 1792," *The Papers of Thomas Jefferson*, Vol. 23, *1
   January–31 May 1792*, ed. Charles T. Cullen. Princeton University Press, 1990,
   535–41 [hereinafter *TJ Papers*, various years; ed. Julian P. Boyd, Charles T.
   Cullen, John Catanzariti, Barbara B. Oberg, and J. Jefferson Looney]; "From
   Thomas Jefferson to George Washington, 9 September 1792," *TJ Papers*, Vol.
   24, *1 June–31 December 1792*, 351–60.
9 "daily pitted": "Thomas Jefferson to Walter Jones, 5 March 1810," *TJ Papers*,
   Retirement Series, Vol. 2, *16 November 1809 to 11 August 1810*, 272–74.
9 "encompassed on all sides": "From George Washington to Thomas
   Jefferson, 23 August 1792," *GW Papers*, Presidential Series, Vol. 11, *16 August
   1792–15 January 1793*, 28–32.
9 "Hamilton was amused": "To Alexander Hamilton from Jean Marie Roland,
   10 October 1792," *AH Papers*, Vol. 12, *July 1792–October 1792*, 545–46; *see also*
   "From Alexander Hamilton to Marquis de Lafayette, 6 October 1789," *AH
   Papers*, Vol. 5, *June 1788–November 1789*, 425–27.
9 "erased from existence": Gordon S. Wood, *The Radicalism of the American
   Revolution* (1991), 231 (citing Charles Downer Hazen, *Contemporary American
   Opinion of the French Revolution* [1897], Vol. 16, 277).
9 "liberty of the whole earth": "From Thomas Jefferson to William Short, 3
   January 1793," *TJ Papers*, Vol. 25, *1 January–10 May 1793*, 14–17.
10 "drag Washington out": "John Adams to Thomas Jefferson, 30 June 1813,"
   Founders Online, National Archives.

10 "Hamilton dreaded": "For the Gazette of the United States, [March–April 1793]," *AH Papers*, Vol. 14, *February 1793–June 1793*, 267–69; "Conversation with George Hammond, [7 March–2 April 1793]," *AH Papers*, Vol. 14, *February 1793–June 1793*, 193–95; "Remarks on the Treaty of Amity Commerce and Navigation lately made between the United States and Great Britain, [9–11 July 1795]," *AH Papers*, Vol. 18, *January 1795–July 1795*, 404–54; "The Defence No. II, [25 July 1795]," *AH Papers*, Vol. 18, *January 1795–July 1795*, 493–501; "From Alexander Hamilton to Oliver Wolcott, Junior, [5 April 1797]," *AH Papers*, Vol. 21, *April 1797–July 1798*, 22–23; "George Washington to James McHenry, [13 December 1798]," *AH Papers*, Vol. 22, *July 1798–March 1799*, 341–53.

10 "cut off the leading Federalists": "From Alexander Hamilton to James A. Bayard, [16–21] April 1802," *AH Papers*, Vol. 25, *July 1800–April 1802*, 605–10.

10 "tottering to its foundations": Gordon S. Wood, *Empire of Liberty: A History of the Early Republic 1789–1815* (2009), 209.

10 "extraordinary event in history": *See, e.g.*, Jeffrey L. Pasley, "1800 as a Revolution in Political Culture: Newspapers, Celebrations, Voting, and Democratization in the Early Republic," in *The Revolution of 1800: Democracy, Race, and the New Republic* (2002), ed. James J. Horn, Jan Ellen Taylor, and Peter S. Onuf, 127–28 (voter participation reached 70% of adult white males in certain states in 1800).

10 "more true to the cause": *See, e.g.*, Conor Cruise O'Brien, *The Long Affair: Thomas Jefferson and the French Revolution, 1785–1800* (1996), 198–202, 223–24.

10 "so unbearably intense": "From Thomas Jefferson to Edward Rutledge, 24 June 1797," *TJ Papers*, Vol. 29, *1 March 1796–31 December 1797*, 455–57.

10 "friend remembered": Michael I. Meyerson, *Liberty's Blueprint: How Madison and Hamilton Wrote the Federalist Papers, Defined the Constitution, and Made Democracy Safe for the World* (2008), 89.

10 "foremost political pamphleteer": Chernow 493.

10 "38-part series": "Introductory Note: The Defence No. I, [22 July 1795]," *AH Papers*, Vol. 18, *January 1795–July 1795*, 475–79; "From Thomas Jefferson to James Madison, 21 September 1795," *TJ Papers*, Vol. 28, *1 January 1794–29 February 1796*, 475–77.

11 "visit Hamilton late": Jeremiah Mason, *Memoir and Correspondence of Jeremiah Mason* (1873), ed. George Stillman Hillard, 33.

11 "I have seen him walk": Allan McLane Hamilton 42–43.

11 "wanted to give government": "From Alexander Hamilton to James Duane, [3 September 1780]," *AH Papers*, Vol. 2, *1779–1781*, 400–18; "The Continentalist No. III, [9 August 1781]," *AH Papers*, Vol. 2, *1779–1781*, 660–65.

11 "rebuked its authors": "From Alexander Hamilton to Oliver Wolcott, Junior, [29 June 1798]," *AH Papers*, Vol. 21, *April 1797–July 1798*, 522–23. *See also* "From Alexander Hamilton to Timothy Pickering, [7 June 1798]," *AH Papers*, Vol. 21, *April 1797–July 1798*, 494–96.

11 "professed Democrat[s]": "From George Washington to James McHenry, 30 September 1798," *GW Papers*, Retirement Series, Vol. 3, *16 September 1798–19 April 1799*, 59.

11 "forfeited an opportunity": "From Alexander Hamilton to James McHenry, 6 February 1799," *AH Papers*, Vol. 22, *July 1798–March 1799*, 466–68.

234 THE LIVES OF THE CONSTITUTION

11 "You are now a king": "To George Washington from James McHenry, 29 March 1789," *GW Papers*, Presidential Series, Vol. 1, *24 September 1788–31 March 1789*, 461–62.

11 "bridled that Washington": Wood, *Empire of Liberty* 83–84.

12 "he was childless": "Undelivered First Inaugural Address: Fragments, 30 April 1789," *GW Papers*, Presidential Series, Vol. 2, *1 April 1789–15 June 1789*, 158–73.

12 "the republican reality": Thomas Twining, *Travels in America 100 Years Ago* (1894), 128.

12 "real danger in our system": "Enclosure: Draft of Washington's Farewell Address, [30 July 1796]," *AH Papers*, Vol. 20, *January 1796–March 1797*, 265–88. *See also* "From Alexander Hamilton to John Dickinson, [25–30 September 1783]," *AH Papers*, Vol. 3, *1782–1786*, 438–58; "The Continentalist No. I, [12 July 1781]," *AH Papers*, Vol. 2, *1779–1781*, 649–52.

12 "Federalist preoccupations": "From Alexander Hamilton to George Washington, [5 August] 1794," *AH Papers*, Vol. 17, *August 1794–December 1794*, 24–58; Thomas P. Slaughter, *The Whiskey Rebellion: Frontier Epilogue to the American Revolution* (1986), 185–88.

12 "wrote detailed advice": "From Alexander Hamilton to George Washington, 2 August 1794," *AH Papers*, Vol. 17, *August 179–December 1794*, 15–19.

12 "ordered army blankets": "From Alexander Hamilton to Samuel Hodgdon, 17 September 1794," *AH Papers*, Vol. 17, *August 179–December 1794*, 239–40; "From Alexander Hamilton to Samuel Hodgdon, 30 September 1794," *AH Papers*, Vol. 17, *August 1794–December 1794*, 292–94; "From Alexander Hamilton to George Gale, 28 September 1794," *AH Papers*, Vol. 17, *August 1794–December 1794*, 285; "From Alexander Hamilton to Tench Coxe, 1 September 1792," *AH Papers*, Vol. 12, *July 1792–October 1792*, 305–10.

12 "martial-romantic streak": "From Alexander Hamilton to George Washington, 19 September 1794," *AH Papers*, Vol. 17, *August 1794–December 1794*, 254–55.

12 "Hamilton took the gun": John Church Hamilton, *History of the Republic of the United States of America, as traced in the Writings of Alexander Hamilton and of his Contemporaries* (1860), Vol. VI, 108.

12 "rebuked Pennsylvania's governor": Slaughter 205–06; "From Alexander Hamilton to Thomas Mifflin, 10 October 1794," *AH Papers*, Vol. 17, *August 179–December 1794*, 317–19; "From Alexander Hamilton to Jared Ingersoll, 10 October 1794," *AH Papers*, Vol. 17, *August 179–December 1794*, 315–17.

12 "President Washington believed": "From George Washington to Thomas Jefferson, 21 January 1790," *GW Papers*, Presidential Series, Vol. 5, *16 January 1790–30 June 1790*, 29–31.

13 "Among the precedents": "To Alexander Hamilton from George Washington, 31 March 1796," *AH Papers*, Vol. 20, *January 1796–March 1797*, 103–05; "Introductory Note: To George Washington, [7 March 1796]," *AH Papers*, Vol. 20, *January 1796–March 1797*, 64–68; "From Alexander Hamilton to Rufus King, 16 March 1796," *AH Papers*, Vol. 20, *January 1796–March 1797*, 76–77.

13 "sought the advice": "To Alexander Hamilton from George Washington, 31 March 1796," *AH Papers*, Vol. 20, *January 1796–March 1797*, 103–05.

13 "Trumped-up accusations": Eugene R. Sheridan, "Thomas Jefferson and the

Giles Resolutions." 49 *William & Mary Quarterly* 4 (Oct. 1992), 589–608;
Leonard D. White, *The Federalists: A Study in Administrative History* (1956),
352–54; Annals of Congress, III, 835 (Jan. 23, 1793), 900 (Feb. 28, 1793).

13 "Hamilton was exonerated": *Belknap Papers: Correspondence Between
Jeremy Belknap and Ebenezer Hazard* (1877), Part II, Collections of the
Massachusetts Historical Society, Vol. III, 323; White 81 & n.20.

13 "advice-and-consent": "The Federalist No. 76, [1 April 1788]," *AH Papers*,
Vol. 4, *January 1787–May 1788*, 633–38; White 82–87.

13 "the Secretary's Reports": Annals of Congress, House of Reps., 2nd Cong.,
2nd Sess. (Nov. 20, 1792), 707.

13 "specific duties": "Report Relative to a Provision for the Support of Public
Credit, [9 January 1790]," *AH Papers*, Vol. 6, *December 1789–August 1790*,
65–110.

13 "Another Congressman": Annals of Congress, House of Reps., 2nd Cong.
2nd Sess. (Mar. 1, 1793), 923.

14 "sacred rights of mankind": "*The Farmer Refuted*, &c., [23 February] 1775,"
AH Papers, Vol. 1, *1768–1778*, 81–165

14 "practical business": "The Continentalist No. I, [12 July 1781]," *AH Papers*,
Vol. 2, *1779–1781*, 649–52.

14 "For forms of government": Alexander Pope, *An Essay on Man* (Epistle
III) (1733–34), lines 303–04. Cf. *Federalist* 68; *The Poems of Alexander Pope*
(1963), ed. John Butt, 534, note to lines 303–04; cf. 2 Farrand 642 ("there
is no form of Government but what may be a blessing to the people if well
administered") (Franklin at close of Constitutional Convention).

14 "governments as exotic": "New York Ratifying Convention. First Speech of
June 21 (Francis Childs's Version), [21 June 1788]," *AH Papers*, Vol. 5, *June
1788–November 1789*, 36–45.

14 "affection of the people": "Conjectures about the New Constitution, [17–30
September 1787]," *AH Papers*, Vol. 4, *January 1787–May 1788*, 275–77. *See also*
"Constitutional Convention. Remarks on the Election of the President,
[6 September 1787]," *AH Papers*, Vol. 4, *January 1787–May 1788*, 243–44;
Constitutional Convention. Remarks on Signing the Constitution, [17
September 1787]; "Notes of a Conversation with Alexander Hamilton, 13
August 1791," *TJ Papers*, Vol. 22, *6 August 1791–31 December 1791*, 38–39.

14 "greatest administrative genius": White 125–26.

14 "largest, richest": White 122.

14 "northern shipyard": White 471.

14 "civilian federal government": White 123, 255–56; "Report on the Salaries,
Fees, and Emoluments of Persons Holding Civil Office Under the United
States, [26 February 1793]," *AH Papers*, Vol. 14, *February 1793–June 1793*,
157–59.

14 "Cleveland's government": City-Data.com, "Cleveland Municipal
Government" (8,743 workers in 2003); John Joseph Wallis, "Table Ea894–
903 Federal government employees, by government branch and location
relative to the capital: 1816–1992" in *Historical Statistics of the United States*
(2006), Millennial Edition Online, ed. Susan B. Carter, Scott Sigmund
Gartner, Michael R. Haines, Alan L. Olmstead, Richard Sutch, and Gavin
Wright.

14 "ten employees": White 136.

14 "paper operations": "IX. Further Memoranda from Henry Remsen, Jr., [ca. 1792]," *TJ Papers*, Vol. 17, *6 July–3 November 1790*, 381–87.

15 "did not grasp": *See also* "The Federalist No. 70, [15 March 1788]," *AH Papers*, Vol. 4, *January 1787–May 1788*, 598–607; "Metellus, [24 October 1792]," *AH Papers*, Vol. 12, *July 1792–October 1792*, 613–17.

15 "Lax enforcement": *See* "Final Version: First Report on the Further Provision Necessary for Establishing Public Credit, [13 December 1790]," *AH Papers*, Vol. 7, *September 1790–January 1791*, 225–36.

15 "customs returns": "Treasury Department Circular to the Collectors of the Customs, 14 September 1789," *AH Papers*, Vol. 5, *June 1788–November 1789*, 373.

15 "considered rather as meritorious": Annals of Congress, House of Reps., 1st Cong., 1st Sess., 311 (May 9, 1789).

15 "tricks by which skippers": White 460–65.

15 "not timid": White 443–47, 464.

15 "pioneered economic interventionism": "Alexander Hamilton's Final Version of the Report on the Subject of Manufactures, [5 December 1791]," *AH Papers*, Vol. 10, *December 1791–January 1792*, 230–340; *see also* "The Examination Number III, [24 December 1801]," *AH Papers*, Vol. 25, *July 1800–April 1802*, 464–68; cf. "Notes on the Constitutionality of Bounties to Encourage Manufacturing, [February 1792]," *TJ Papers*, Vol. 23, *1 January–31 May 1792*, 172–73.

15 "He made your bank": Chernow 353.

15 "called for an institution": H.W. Brands, *The Money Men: Capitalism, Democracy, and the Hundred Years' War Over the American Dollar* (2006), 48–52.

15 "famous legal opinion": "Final Version of an Opinion on the Constitutionality of an Act to Establish a Bank, [23 February 1791]," *AH Papers*, Vol. 8, *February 1791–July 1791*, 97–134; "Second Letter from Phocion, [April 1784]," *AH Papers*, Vol. 3, *1782–1786*, 530–58.

15 "Virginian planter": John C. Miller, *Alexander Hamilton and the Growth of the New Nation* (1959), 272.

15 "Three financial historians": Richard Sylla, Robert E. Wright, and David J. Cowen, "Alexander Hamilton, Central Banker: Crisis Management during the U.S. Financial Panic of 1792," 83 *Business History Review* (Spring 2009), 61–62, 79, 80 n.51.

16 "steadied nerves": *Id.* at 77–84.

16 "fired off missives": *Id.* at 80.

16 "unthinking populace": "From Alexander Hamilton to John Jay, 26 November 1775," *AH Papers*, Vol. 1, *1768–1778*, 176–78.

16 "turbulent and changing": "Robert Yates's Version, [18 June 1787]," *AH Papers*, Vol. 4, *January 1787–May 1788*, 195–202; *see also* Max Farrand, *The Records of the Federal Convention of 1787* (1937), Vol. 1, 424.

16 "enlightened and refined": "New York Ratifying Convention. First Speech of June 21 (Francis Childs's Version), [21 June 1788]," *AH Papers*, Vol. 5, *June 1788–November 1789*, 36–45.

16 "drunken mob": *See, e.g.,* Flick 73.

16 "twice fended": Brookhiser 25–26 (Myles Cooper), 124–25 (Jay Treaty); *see also* James Alexander Hamilton, *Reminiscences of James A. Hamilton: or, Men*

and Events, at Home and Abroad, During Three Quarters of a Century (1869), 7.

17   "great philosophical realists": David Hume, *Essays: Moral, Political, and Literary* (1758; Liberty Fund ed. 1994), 18, 52; Thomas Hobbes, *Leviathan* (1651; Oxford World's Classics ed. 1998), 122.

17   "[T]oo much power": "The Continentalist No. I, [12 July 1781]," *AH Papers*, Vol. 2, *1779–1781*, 649–52.

17   "his preoccupation": *See, e.g.*, "The Federalist No. 1, [27 October 1787]," *AH Papers*, Vol. 4, *January 1787–May 1788*, 301–06; "New York Ratifying Convention. Remarks (Francis Childs's Version), [27 June 1788]," *AH Papers*, Vol. 5, *June 1788–November 1789*, 94–104; "New York Assembly. First Speech on the Address of the Legislature to Governor George Clinton's Message, [19 January 1787]," *AH Papers*, Vol. 4, *January 1787–May 1788*, 3–12; "From Alexander Hamilton to John Dickinson, [25–30 September 1783]," *AH Papers*, Vol. 3, *1782–1786*, 438–58.

17   "true artificers": "Enclosure: [Objections and Answers Respecting the Administration], [18 August 1792]," *AH Papers*, Vol. 12, *July 1792–October 1792*, 229–58; *see also* "From Alexander Hamilton to Edward Carrington, 26 May 1792," *AH Papers*, Vol. 11, *February 1792–June 1792*, 426–45.

17   "an electorate so narrowed": Spaulding 90.

17   "safely dispense": "II. First Annual Message to Congress, 8 December 1801," *TJ Papers*, Vol. 36, *1 December 1801–3 March 1802*, 58–67; "From Thomas Jefferson to James Monroe, 20 June 1801," *TJ Papers*, Vol. 34, *1 May–31 July 1801*, 398–99.

17   "body of neighboring citizens": "II. First Annual Message to Congress, 8 December 1801," *TJ Papers*, Vol. 36, *1 December 1801–3 March 1802*, 58–67.

17   "Hamilton blasted": "The Examination Number I, [17 December 1801]," *AH Papers*, Vol. 25, *July 1800–April 1802*, 453–57.

17   "During the opening decades": Wood, *Empire of Liberty* 301.

18   "Republicans controlling Congress": Wood, *Empire of Liberty* 692.

18   "Jefferson–Madison policy": "From Alexander Hamilton to Rufus King, 3 June 1802," *AH Papers*, Vol. 26, *1 May 1802–23 October 1804, Additional Documents 1774–1799, Addenda and Errata*, 11–16, n.10.

18   "imagine the national destiny": *See, e.g.*, "To Alexander Hamilton from John Jay, 29 December 1792," *AH Papers*, Vol. 13, *November 1792–February 1793*, 384–85.

18   "more *serious* stain": "Printed Version of the "Reynolds Pamphlet, 1797," *AH Papers*, Vol. 21, *April 1797–July 1798*, 238–67 (emphasis added).

18   "If you happen to displease": "From Alexander Hamilton to Angelica Hamilton, [November 1793]," *AH Papers*, Vol. 15, *June 1793–January 1794*, 432.

18   "campaigned against Burr": "Enclosure: Opinions on Aaron Burr, [4 January 1801]," *AH Papers*, Vol. 25, *July 1800–April 1802*, 295–98; *see also* "From Alexander Hamilton to Gouverneur Morris, 24 December 1800," *AH Papers*, Vol. 25, *July 1800–April 1802*, 271–73; "From Alexander Hamilton to James A. Bayard, 16 January 1801," *AH Papers*, Vol. 25, *July 1800–April 1802*, 319–24; "From Alexander Hamilton to ———, 26 September 1792," *AH Papers*, Vol. 12, *July 1792–October 1792*, 480–81.

19 "more rational alternative": Washington Irving, *History, Tales, and Sketches* (1802-1820; Library of America ed. 1983), 42–43 (italics removed).

19 "to justify his decision": "Statement on Impending Duel with Aaron Burr, [28 June–10 July 1804]," *AH Papers*, Vol. 26, *1 May 1802–23 October 1804, Additional Documents 1774–1799, Addenda and Errata*, 278–81.

19 "keep myself in a situation": "From Alexander Hamilton to Robert Troup, 13 April 1795," *AH Papers*, Vol. 18, *January 1795–July 1795*, 328–29.

19 "willingly risk my life": "From Alexander Hamilton to Edward Stevens, 11 November 1769," *AH Papers*, Vol. 1, *1768–1778*, 4–5; *see also* "From Alexander Hamilton to Timothy Pickering, 13 May 1797," *AH Papers*, Vol. 21, *April 1797–July 1798*, 84–85.

19 "odd destiny": "From Alexander Hamilton to Gouverneur Morris, [29 February 1802]," *AH Papers*, Vol. 25, *July 1800–April 1802*, 544–46.

19 "the *Croswell* case": *See Law Practice* 775–806.

19 "equally strong duties": "From Alexander Hamilton to Elizabeth Hamilton, [4 July 1804]," *AH Papers*, Vol. 26, *1 May 1802–23 October 1804, Additional Documents 1774–1799, Addenda and Errata*, ed. 293.

19 "leave in poverty": *Reminiscences of James A. Hamilton* 7–8 (AH couldn't pay debts at death), 41 (JH's poverty in 1810).

20 "another acute concern": "Alexander Hamilton's Explanation of His Financial Situation, [1 July 1804]," *AH Papers*, Vol. 26, *1 May 1802–23 October 1804, Additional Documents 1774–1799, Addenda and Errata*, 287–91.

20 "pistol bullet": Joseph J. Ellis, *Passionate Sage: The Character and Legacy of John Adams* (1993), 62.

20 "ovation": Allan McLane Hamilton 426.

20 "public good": "From Alexander Hamilton to Gouverneur Morris, 26 December 1800," *AH Papers*, Vol. 25, *July 1800–April 1802*, 275; "From Thomas Jefferson to William Branch Giles, 20 April 1807," Founders Online, National Archives.

20 "protect his fame": Morris, *Selected Writings* 356.

20 "To be partisan today": Walter Lippmann, *The Essential Lippmann: A Political Philosophy for a Liberal Democracy* (1982), ed. Clinton Rossiter and James Lare, 207.

21 "abhorrence of monuments": Stephen Knott, "'Opposed in Death as in Life': Hamilton and Jefferson in American Memory," in *The Many Faces of Alexander Hamilton: The Life and Legacy of America's Most Elusive Founding Father* (2009), ed. Douglas Ambrose and Robert W.T. Martin; Kirk Savage, *Monument Wars*, 36–44.

21 "lifelong renter and early Manhattan commuter": Rufus King, *The Life and Correspondence of Rufus King*, Vol. IV, 326.

21 "Monticello": Merrill D. Peterson *Visitors to Monticello* (1989), 2.

21 "no ongoing federal funding": Monticello, "Thomas Jefferson Foundation," https://www.monticello.org/site/about/thomas-jefferson-foundation.

21 "controversial": National Park Service, "Hamilton Grange," http://www.nps.gov/hagr/index.htm; *see also* Sen. Res. 368 (Oct. 6, 2000) ("Whereas no obelisk, monument, or classical temple along the national mall has been constructed to honor the man who more than any other designed the Government of the United States, Hamilton should at least be remembered by restoring his home in a sylvan setting").

21 "generations of vassals": Henry Wiencek, *Master of the Mountain: Thomas Jefferson and His Slaves* (2012), 13; "From Thomas Jefferson to Angelica Schuyler Church, 27 November 1793," *TJ Papers*, Vol. 27, *1 September–31 December 1793*, 449–50.

22 "a child raised every 2 years": "From Thomas Jefferson to Joel Yancey, 17 January 1819," Founders Online, National Archives; *see also* "From Thomas Jefferson to John Wayles Eppes, 30 June 1820," Founders Online, National Archives; "From Thomas Jefferson to Joel Yancey, 17 January 1819," Founders Online, National Archives.

22 "condition in life": Thomas Jefferson, *Notes on the State of Virginia* (1787; 1832 ed.), 148.

22 "want of cultivation": "From Alexander Hamilton to John Jay, [14 March 1779]," *AH Papers*, Vol. 2, *1779–1781*, 17–19.

22 "tinctured with fanaticism": "From Alexander Hamilton to James A. Bayard, 16 January 1801," *AH Papers*, Vol. 25, *July 180–April 1802*, 319–24; *see also* "To Alexander Hamilton from Charles Carroll of Carrollton, 18 April 1800," *AH Papers*, Vol. 24, *November 1799–June 1800*, 412–13.

22 "tree of liberty": "From Thomas Jefferson to William Stephens Smith, 13 November 1787," *TJ Papers*, Vol. 12, *7 August 1787–31 March 1788*, 355–57.

22 "crush these audacious proceedings": "From Thomas Jefferson to Daniel D. Tompkins, 15 August 1808," Founders Online, National Archives.

22 "few prosecutions": "From Thomas Jefferson to Thomas McKean, 19 February 1803," *TJ Papers*, Vol. 39, *13 November 1802–3 March 1803*, 552–55; Leonard W. Levy, *Jefferson and Civil Liberties: The Darker Side* (1963), 50–69.

22 "now-forgotten embargo policy": *Id.* at 93–120.

23 "most perfect system": *Reminiscences of James A. Hamilton* 231; *see also* "From Thomas Jefferson to Pierre Samuel Du Pont de Nemours, 18 January 1802," *TJ Papers*, Vol. 36, *1 December 1801–3 March 1802*, 390–92; Henry Adams, *Life of Albert Gallatin* (1879), 268.

23 "didn't stop Jefferson": *See, e.g.*, "Thomas Jefferson to Benjamin Rush, 16 January 1811," *TJ Papers*, Retirement Series, Vol. 3, *12 August 1810–17 June 1811*, 304–08; "From Thomas Jefferson to William Johnson, 4 March 1823," Founders Online, National Archives.

23 "infected with disease": "Thomas Jefferson to William H. Crawford, 20 June 1816," *TJ Papers*, Vol. 10, *May 1816 to 18 January 1817*, 173–76; *see also* "From Thomas Jefferson to Marie-Joseph-Paul-Yves-Roch-Gilbert du Motier, marquis de Lafayette, 24 February 1809," Founders Online, National Archives.

23 "essays of 1781–82": "The Continentalist No. I, [12 July 1781]," note 2, *AH Papers*, Vol. 2, *1779–1781*, 649–52.

23 "construct a lighthouse": "From Thomas Jefferson to Albert Gallatin, 13 October 1802," *TJ Papers*, Vol. 38, *1 July–12 November 1802*, 486–88; "James Madison to Reynolds Chapman, 6 January 1831," Founders Online, National Archives.

23 "more heroic dimensions": "From Alexander Hamilton to William Jackson, 26 August 1800," *AH Papers*, Vol. 25, *July 1800–April 1802*, 88–91; "From Thomas Jefferson to George Washington, 9 September 1792," *TJ Papers*, Vol. 24, *1 June–31 December 1792*, 351–60; "From John Adams to Benjamin Rush, 25 January 1806," Founders Online, National Archives.

24 "groundswell of opposition": Ana Swanson and Abby Ohlheiser, "Harriet Tubman to appear on $20 bill, while Alexander Hamilton remains on $10 bill," *Washington Post*, Apr. 20, 2016.

24 "In some things": "From Alexander Hamilton to Rufus King, 2 October 1798," *AH Papers*, Vol. 22, *July 1798–March 1799*, 192–93.

24 "I have seen a man": *Reminiscences of James A. Hamilton* 7.

24 "[T]his American world": "From Alexander Hamilton to Gouverneur Morris, [29 February 1802]," *AH Papers*, Vol. 25, *July 1800–April 1802*, 544–46.

CHAPTER TWO — JAMES WILSON
The Philosopher of Philadelphia

27 "cottage industry": *See, e.g.*, Andrew C. McLaughlin, "James Wilson in the Philadelphia Convention," 12 Pol. Sci. Q. 1 (Mar. 1897); William F. Obering, *The Philosophy of Law of James Wilson* (1938); William Ewald, "James Wilson and the Drafting of the Constitution," 10 *U. Pa. J. Const. L.* 5 (2008), 901; Nicholas Pederson, "The Lost Founder: James Wilson in American Memory," 22 *Yale Journal of Law & the Humanities* 2, Art. 3 (2010).

28 "easily topped the list": Mark David Hall, "Justice, Law, and the Creation of the American Republic: The Forgotten Legacy of James Wilson," The Heritage Foundation, *First Principles Series*, citing *America's Forgotten Founders* (2008), ed. Gary L. Gregg and Mark David Hall, 5.

28 "two great figures": Lucien H. Alexander, "James Wilson—Nation Builder (Part IV)," XIX *Green Bag* 5 (May 1907), 276.

28 "strength and determination": Alexander 269.

28 "mysteries of history": William H. Moody, "Oration at the James Wilson Memorial," in 46 *American Law Register* 1 (Jan. 1907), 32; Michael Kammen, *Digging Up the Dead: A History of Notable American Reburials* (2010), 114–17.

29 "James Wilson was born": Charles Page Smith, *James Wilson: Founding Father, 1742–1798* (1956), 3 (Fife), 6 (cattle), 11 (lochs), 5 (education).

29 "By day": Smith 9.

29 "Wilson began": Smith 12 (St. Andrews), 14 (diet), 16 (course materials).

29 "He sailed": Smith 18–20.

29 "uniform, straightforward": Irving, *History, Tales, and Sketches* 198.

29 "struck out": Smith 29 (Reading), 43–44 (Carlisle).

29 "Wilson grew prosperous": Smith 48 (prosperous), 24 (lawyer's practice), 42 (marriage).

29 "Calvinist mother": Smith 42

29 "began as a moderate": Smith 61–62, 81–83 (Congress), 75–76 (report).

29 "broke the Pennsylvania delegation's tie": Smith 87.

30 "American downfall": Max Farrand, *The Records of the Federal Convention of 1787* (1937), Vol. 1, 18.

30 "razing the foundations": 1 Farrand 484.

30 "hand-wringing": *See, e.g.*, 2 Farrand 388 (Gerry warning that differences over Constitution could cause "civil war").

30 "kept up spirits": 2 Farrand 65. For more Franklin humor and good sense, see 1 Farrand 197, 451; 2 Farrand 249 (disparaging call for wealthy president as inviting a greedy president), 641 (saying he doesn't approve of everything but isn't sure he would *never* approve), 643 (advising departing delegates to keep their reservations to themselves).

30 "Seventeen such charters": G. Alan Tarr, *Understanding State Constitutions* (1998), 89; Clinton Rossiter, *1787: The Grand Convention* (1966), 64–65 (17 charters), 146 (20 delegates).

31 "his peculiar study": 3 Farrand 91–92.

31 "Wilson, for instance, knew": James Wilson, *Collected Works of James Wilson* (Liberty Fund ed. 2007), ed. Kermit L. Hall and Mark David Hall, Vol. 1, 649–51 [hereinafter *Wilson's Works*].

31 "second to Madison": Max Farrand, *The Framing of the Constitution of the United States* (1913), 197.

31 "natural law's teaching": *See* Wilson's description in *Wilson's Works* 504, 523.

31 "one man": *Wilson's Works* 574; *see also* 501.

31 "origin of legitimate political power": *Wilson's Works* 445, 639.

32 "enthusiastically democratic": Alexander Graydon, *Memoirs of His Own Time* (1846), ed. John Stockton Littell, 354.

32 "During the debates": *See, e.g.*, 2 Farrand 31 (Mason saying that giving election of president to people is giving a color test to a blind man); 1 Farrand 43 (Sherman: "The people, he said, immediately should have as little to do as may be about the Government. They want information and are constantly liable to be misled"), 359.

32 "like a pyramid": 1 Farrand 49; *see also The Debate on the Constitution: Federalist and Antifederalist Speeches, Articles, and Letters During the Struggle over Ratification, Part One* (1993), ed. Bernard Bailyn, 863.

32 "On most questions": 1 Farrand 132 (legislature should be a "most exact transcript of the whole society"), 141 (all legislative powers should flow "immediately" from people).

32 "elections by popular vote": 1 Farrand 142, 151; 1 *Debate on the Constitution* 848.

32 "direct election of the *president*": 1 Farrand 68 (Wilson "said he was almost unwilling to declare the mode which he wished to take place, being apprehensive that it might appear chimerical. He would say however at least that in theory he was for an election by the people").

32 "xenophobia": 2 Farrand 237, 269 (noting that three members of Pennsylvania delegation were "not natives").

32 "gotten emotional": 2 Farrand 237.

32 "opposed proposals": *See, e.g.*, 1 Farrand 605 ("all men wherever placed have equal rights and are equally entitled to confidence").

32 "representation in the Senate": 1 Farrand 469 (Ellsworth threatens walkout over issue); 2 Farrand 17-18 (Randolph demands day's adjournment to give large states time to reflect on "present solemn crisis"; Patterson says rule of secrecy should be broken and constituents consulted on the question), 19-20 (large states meet privately to consult on situation); 3 Farrand 477 (Madison telling Martin Van Buren that greatest threat to Convention turned on this question).

32 "Small states": *See, e.g.*, 2 Farrand 190 (small states meet separately to strategize about their interests).

33 "suspicion": 1 Farrand 501.

33 "fought more militantly": 1 Farrand 52, 179, 193, 253, 482, 505, 543; 2 Farrand 4, 10 (Wilson saying that a "vice in the representation, like an error in the

first concoction, must be followed by disease, convulsions, and finally death itself").

33 "Quaker State brother": 1 Farrand 180 ("Are not the citizens of Pennsylvania equal to those of New Jersey?.... If New Jersey will not part with her sovereignty it is in vain to talk of government").

33 "Wilson lost": 2 Farrand 15 (vote of Jul. 16).

33 "drew on many sources": 1 Farrand 100 (Catiline, Cromwell), 254 (Caesar); *see also* 1 *Debate on the Constitution* 794 (Wilson: Greek history was "so destitute of that minute detail from which practical knowledge may be derived" that its examples were more "subjects of curiosity" than use).

33 "oddball constitution": Penn. Const. of 1776, Sec. 2 (legislature), Sec 7. (wisdom and virtue), Sec. 9 (annual election), Sec. 3 and 19 (executive council), *The Federal and State Constitutions: Colonial Charters, and Other Organic Laws of the States, Territories, and Colonies Now or Heretofore Forming the United States of America* (1909), ed. Francis Newton Thorpe.

33 "longest running": 1 *Debate on the Constitution* 849 (Wilson saying nothing "perplexed" Convention so much as mode of choosing the president).

33 "single person": 1 Farrand 65.

34 "considerable pause ensuing": The same happened a day earlier when every state was agreed on having two legislative houses, except Pennsylvania, which withheld its support, wrote Madison, in "complaisance to Doctor Franklin." 1 Farrand 48.

34 "point of great importance": 1 Farrand 65–66.

34 "days of debate": 1 Farrand 66 (Randolph calls it fetus of monarchy), 88, 113 (Mason proposes tripartite executive).

34 "single-president position": 1 Farrand 93 (moved for), 97 (agreed to).

34 "man most responsible": *See, e.g.*, William Ewald, "The Committee of Detail," 28 *Const. Comment.*, 196–97 (2012).

34 "counsel for 23 men": Carlton F.W. Larson, "The Revolutionary American Jury: A Case Study of the 1778–1779 Philadelphia Treason Trials," 61 *Southern Methodist University Law Review* 4 (Fall 2008).

34 "double the requirement": Smith 119–23; Willard Hurst, "Treason in the United States," 58 Harv. L. Rev. 395 (1945); *Cramer v. United States*, 325 U.S. 1, 23 n.32 (1945).

34 "400 unpaid soldiers": *Elliott's Debates* (1845), Vol 5., 93; Smith 191–92.

35 "heterogeneous materials": *Wilson's Works* 174; *see also* 1 *Debate on the Constitution* 792 ("spirit of conciliation, resort to mutual concession"), 796 (calling it "unreasonable" to expect plan to be agreeable to all); 834 (1787 Convention's "gloomy" prospect was overcome by "mutual sacrifices").

35 "first to call": 1 *Debate on the Constitution* 91, 832, 874–75; *The Documentary History of the Ratification of the Constitution Digital Edition*, Vol. 2, 260 & n.1 (Wilsonites).

35 "strengthen the deception": 1 *Debate on the Constitution* 91.

35 "class antagonisms": *See, e.g.*, Middlekauff, *The Glorious Cause* 676.

35 "instrument came from them": James Madison, *Writings* (Library of America ed. 1999), 574 (speech on the Jay Treaty, April 1796); *see also* 800 (to Jefferson, 1823), 803 (to Henry Lee, 1824), 816–17 (to Joseph Cabell, 1828); "From James Madison to Thomas Ritchie, 15 September 1821," *The Papers of*

James Madison [hereinafter *JM Papers*, various years], Retirement Series, Vol. 2, *1 February 1820–26 February 1823*, ed. David B. Mattern, J.C.A. Stagg, Mary Parke Johnson, and Anne Mandeville Colony, University of Virginia Press (2013) 381–82.

36 "I am bold to assert": *Wilson's Works* 177.

36 "first public defense": Pauline Maier, *Ratification: The People Debate the Constitution, 1787–1788* (2010), 78.

36 "single most influential": 1 *Debate on the Constitution* 1142.

36 "able, candid, & honest": "From George Washington to David Stuart, 17 October 1787," *GW Papers*, Confederation Series, Vol. 5, *1 February 1787–31 December 1787*, 379–80.

36 "chain reaction": Maier 80–81; *The Documentary History of the Ratification of the Constitution, Digital Edition*, Vol. 2, 337 & n.1.

36 "sporadic at best": Maier 84–85.

36 "not read by either side": *The Documentary History of the Ratification of the Constitution* (1976–), ed. Merrill Jensen, John P. Kaminski, and Gaspare J. Saladino, XV, CC, 134 (letter from Henry Knox to John Sullivan, Jan. 19, 1788).

36 "These included": 1 *Debate on the Constitution* 64, 65 (army), 67 (Senate).

36 "mob attack": 1 *Debate on the Constitution* 101; "To John Adams from Benjamin Rush, 12 October 1779," *The Papers of John Adams*, Vol. 8, *March 1779–February 1780*, ed. Gregg L. Lint, Robert J. Taylor, Richard Alan Reyerson, Celeste Walker, and Joanna M. Revelas, Harvard University Press, 1989, 199–201; John K. Alexander, "The Fort Wilson Incident of 1779: A Case Study of the Revolutionary Crowd," 31 *Wm. & Mary Q.* 4 (Oct. 1974), 589; *see also* Catherine Drinker Bowen, *Miracle at Philadelphia: The Story of the Constitutional Convention, May to September 1787* (1966) 277 (post-ratification mob attack on Wilson).

36 "inferior order": *See, e.g.,* 1 *Debate on the Constitution* 101.

36 "struggle the drafters faced": *Documentary History of the Ratification of the Constitution Digital Edition*, Vol. 2, 565.

37 "recovered by arms": 1 *Debate on the Constitution* 72 (Reply to Wilson's Speech: "A Democratic Federalist," Oct. 17, 1787) (jury trial); *The Documentary History of the Ratification of the Constitution, Digital Edition*, ed. John P. Kaminski, Gaspare J. Saladino, Richard Leffler, Charles H. Schoenleber and Margaret A. Hogan, University of Virginia Press (2009) 592.

37 "deadly shade": 1 *Debate on the Constitution* 812; *see also id.* at 87, 98 (federal taxes would overpower states taxes).

37 "deceptively difficult": 1 *Debate on the Constitution* 90.

37 "master list": Smith 273.

37 "No. 34, 35, 38": *The Documentary History of the Ratification of the Constitution Digital Edition*, Vol. 2, 551–52.

37 "stooping backward": Alexander, "James Wilson—Nation Builder (Part IV)," 268.

37 "lofty carriage": 1 *Debate on the Constitution* 105.

37 "enemies gloated": *The Documentary History of the Ratification of the Constitution Digital Edition*, Vol. 2, 528, 532, 549–50, 551 & n.1; Vol. XIX

480 (New York). Yet Wilson ultimately may have been right. *See, e.g.*, Ruth Ginsburg, "The Jury and the Nämnd: Some Observations on Judicial Control of Lay Triers in Civil Proceedings in the United States and Sweden," 48 Cornell L. Rev. 2 (Winter 1963), 253; Christian Diesen, "The Advantages and Disadvantages of Lay Judges from a Swedish Perspective," *Revue internationale de droit pénal* 1/2001, Vol. 72, 355–63.

37 "North America's first one": *The Bill of Rights and the States: The Colonial and Revolutionary Origins of American Liberties* (1992), ed. Patrick T. Conley and John P. Kaminski, 311 (discussing Penn's "Body of Laws").

38 "not expressly mentioned": 1 *Debate on the Constitution* 808. By contrast, Wilson drafted provisions for the Pennsylvania Constitution's Bill of Rights. *Id.* at 1119.

38 "criterion": 1 *Debate on the Constitution* 805, 809 (Whitehill: "Truly, Sir, I will agree that a bill of rights may be a dangerous instrument, but it is to the views and projects of the aspiring ruler, and not the liberties of the citizen").

38 "would imply power": *See, e.g., Wilson's Works* 206–07; 1 *Debate on the Constitution* 80.

38 "better off complaining": *See, e.g., Minneapolis Star & Tribune Co. v. Minnesota Com'r of Revenue*, 460 U.S. 575, 582 (1983); *Arkansas Writers' Project, Inc. v. Ragland*, 481 U.S. 221, 228 (1987); *Dep't of Revenue v. Magazine Publishers of Am., Inc.*, 604 So. 2d 459, 461 (Fla. 1992).

38 "delay tantamount to victory": Smith 279–80; 1 *Debate on the Constitution* 832 (Wilson's summation and final rebuttal).

38 "my aim rises": "To George Washington from James Wilson, 21 April 1789," *GW Papers*, Presidential Series, Vol. 2, *1 April 1789–15 June 1789*, 111–12.

39 "men of means": Smith 159.

39 "deranged state": "To John Adams from Benjamin Rush, 22 April 1789," Founders Online, National Archives.

39 "toast given": *Chisholm v. Georgia*, 2 U.S. 419, 462 (1793) (Wilson, J.).

39 "still trying to get": *Chisholm*, 2 U.S. at 453 (Wilson, J.).

39 "politically correct": *Yale Book of Quotations* (2006), ed. Fred R. Shapiro, 829.

39 "unlike any other": *Wilson's Works* xiv (Introduction). Wilson did tone it down over time. *Wiscart v. D'Auchy*, 3 U.S. 321, 324 (1796) (Wilson, J.) ("I am desirous of stating, as briefly as I can, the principles of my dissent"); *Ware v. Hylton*, 3 U.S. 199, 281 (1796) (Wilson, J.) ("I shall be concise in delivering my opinion, as it depends on a few plain principles").

39 "own bosom": *Trustees of Dartmouth Coll. v. Woodward*, 17 U.S. 518, 647 (1819) (Marshall, C.J.).

39 "pointing to a clause": Art. III, Sec. 2 ("The judicial power shall extend to all cases ... between a state and citizens of another state). *See Chisholm*, 2 U.S. at 466 (Wilson, J.).

40 "judicial nature": *Hayburn's Case*, 2 U.S. 409, 410 n.1 (Dallas note) (1792).

40 "excited feelings": *Id.*

40 "ambition to displace": *See, e.g., Wilson's Works* 549 (Blackstone contains "seeds of despotism").

40 "simple reason": *Wilson's Works* 1056; *see also id.* at 1054–55 and 1 *Debate on the Constitution* 797 ("though the individual parts with a portion of his natural

rights, yet, it is evident that he gains more by the limitation of the liberty of others, than he loses by the limitation of his own—so that in truth, the aggregate of liberty is more in society, than it is in a state of nature").

41 "freedom infringed by obedience": *Wilson's Works* 1040.

41 "slaves to the law": *Wilson's Works* 415.

41 "the arts, the sciences": *Wilson's Works* 539; *see also* 1 Farrand 605 (arguing that property was not the "primary object of government and society" but that "cultivation and improvement of the human mind was the most noble object").

41 "cannot be exercised": *Wilson's Works* 444.

42 "representative": *Wilson's Works* 557.

42 "single instance": *Wilson's Works* 444.

42 "fifth of adult males": *Wilson's Works* 721; H.T. Dickinson, "The Representation of the People in Eighteenth-Century Britain," in *Realities of Representation: State Building in Early Modern Europe and European America* (2007), ed. Maija Jansson, 20 (total electorate in the late 18th century at 400,000, about 17% of adult males).

42 "law of William III": *Wilson's Works* 736.

42 "England's lordly judges": *See, e.g.*, 1 Farrand 153 ("The British government cannot be our model . . . the whole genius of the people, are opposed to it").

42 "In the attempt": *Wilson's Works* 487.

42 "[U]nion is a benefit": *Wilson's Works* 635.

42 "The legislature": *Wilson's Works* 700.

43 "fragrant and beneficent": *Wilson's Works* 702; *see also* 716 (from consciousness of freedom a person "derives a cheerful and habitual confidence, this pervades and invigorates his conduct, and spreads a noble air over every part of his character").

43 "retire at age sixty": *Wilson's Works* 845.

43 "ancient Locrians": *Wilson's Works* 863.

43 "Privileges and Immunities Clause": *Wilson's Works* 667.

43 "Before ratification": *The Documentary History of the Ratification of the Constitution Digital Edition*, Vol. 2, 63–64, 207.

43 "most peculiar principle": *See, e.g.*, Robert Curry, *Common Sense Nation: Unlocking the Forgotten Power of the American Idea* (2015), 5–9; Shannon C. Stimson, "'A Jury of the Country': Common Sense Philosophy and the Jurisprudence of James Wilson," in *Scotland and America in the Age of Enlightenment* (1990), ed. Richard B. Sher and Jeffrey R. Smitten (1990); Geoffrey Seed, *James Wilson* (1978), 4, 17.

43 "Wilson took from Reid": Compare James Wilson's lecture "Of the Law of Nature," *Wilson's Works*, 513–20, and Thomas Reid, *Inquiry and Essays* (1983), ed. Ronald E. Beanblossom and Keith Lehrer, 314–23. Reid's *Essays on the Active Powers*, bringing together his lectures, was published in 1788, after the Philadelphia Convention, but his ideas already had currency.

43 "manner more analogous": *Wilson's Works* 513; *see also id.* at 509, 520.

43 "feeling of resentment": *Wilson's Works* 510.

43 "Brazilian neuroscientist": Rebecca Saxe, "Do the Right Thing," *Boston Review*, Sept.–Oct. 2005; Jorge Moll, "New imaging evidence for the neural

bases of moral sentiments, prosocial and antisocial behavior," 2nd Annual
Wellcome Lecture in Neuroethics, Cognitive and Behavioral Neuroscience
Unit, D'Or Institute for Research and Education, Rio de Janeiro, Brazil.

44 "mankind are all brothers": *Wilson's Works* 545.

44 "admonished Americans": *Wilson's Works* 538–39.

44 "liked to remind": *Wilson's Works* 532.

44 "In battle": *Wilson's Works* 292.

44 "concern of all": *Wilson's Works* 526.

44 "not in the whole science": *Wilson's Works* 698.

44 "For a people wanting": *Wilson's Works* 703

44 "business deals": *See, e.g.*, Smith 342, 387.

44 "master-plan developer": John Fabian Witt, *Patriots and Cosmopolitans: Hidden Histories of American Law* (2007), 30–31.

44 "house already built": *Wilson's Works* 379 ("On the Improvement and Settlement of Lands in the United States" [mid-1790s]).

45 "flimsy empire": Smith 343. I borrow Smith's apt characterization of his land holdings.

45 "Washington's were successful": Conversation with Prof. Richard Samuelson, December 17, 2010.

45 "judgments from creditors": Witt 77–79.

45 "larder was empty": Smith 384.

45 "Benjamin Rush observed": Benjamin Rush, *The Autobiography of Benjamin Rush* (1948 ed.), 237.

45 "died in August 1798": Smith 386.

45 "just one of ten": Rossiter 316.

45 "man of the people": 1 *Debate on the Constitution* 825; *see also* 2 Farrand 30 (imagines president as "mediator").

46 "great principles of humanity": *Wilson's Works* 242; 241 ("Yet the lapse of a few years, and congress will have power to exterminate slavery from within our borders"); *see also* 1 *Debate on the Constitution* 830 (Wilson declaring, in December 1787, that the Constitution was "laying the foundation for banishing slavery out of this country").

46 "The people and the states": 2 Farrand 150, 152, 163 (reproducing drafts using "We" in Wilson's hand and found in his papers). The Pinckney Plan, which the committee received, still spoke of a confederation of "free and independent States." The Committee of Style and Gouverneur Morris received the "We the People of the States. . . ." 2 Farrand 565; Smith 246.

46 "[T]he force of the introduction": *The Documentary History of the Ratification of the Constitution Digital Edition*, Vol. 2, 556.

46 "citizens who in future ages": 1 *Debate on the Constitution* 791.

46 "adopting this system": 1 *Debate on the Constitution* 868.

46 "A people free and enlightened": *Wilson's Works* 285.

CHAPTER THREE — DANIEL WEBSTER
The First Generation after the Founders

51 "I consider this among": Louis Masur, *1831: Year of Eclipse* (2002), 173.

51 "[We] proceed": "The Character of Washington" (Feb. 1832), in *The Great Speeches and Orations of Daniel Webster* [hereinafter "*Webster's Works*"] (1879), ed. Edwin P. Whipple, 340.

51 "when the smoke first rose": Peter Harvey, *Reminiscences and Anecdotes of Daniel Webster* (1882), 383; Robert Remini, *Daniel Webster: The Man and His Time* (1997), 30 (frontier terrors).

52 "gross domestic product": Daniel Walker Howe, *What Hath God Wrought: The Transformation of America, 1815–1848* (2007), 32.

52 "Small-town storekeepers": Howe, *What Hath God Wrought* 35.

52 "still cheaper to ship": Howe, *What Hath God Wrought* 40.

52 "New England doctor": Howe, *What Hath God Wrought* 32.

52 "mortal disease": Remini 756.

52 "700 lines of Virgil": Remini 41–42.

52 "A 'student at law'": Maurice G. Baxter, *Daniel Webster and the Supreme Court* (1966), 3.

52 "popular entertainment": Harvey 56.

52 "When Mr. Webster began": Harvey 46.

53 "1,700 cases": Remini 90.

53 "inadequate, minor individual": Bruce Cole, "A Heroine of Popular History," *Wall Street Journal*, Mar. 10, 2012.

53 "It gave me": Remini 148.

53 "I was never so excited": George Ticknor Curtis, *Life, Letters, and Journal of George Ticknor* (1876), Vol. 1, 328–31.

53 "demi-god": Remini 29.

53 "tanned complexion": John Burroughs, "Carlyle," in *The Century*, Vol. 26 (May-Oct. 1883), 534.

53 "There was a grandeur": Samuel Griswold Goodrich, *Recollections of a Lifetime* 411–12 (1856).

54 "moved through the streets": Irving H. Bartlett, *Daniel Webster* (1978), 150; Harvey 191.

54 "great, staring black eyes": Remini 28.

54 "There was a solemn grandeur": Jean Edward Smith, *John Marshall: Definer of a Nation* (1996), 435.

54 "Captain Webster": Bartlett 17; Remini 32; Harvey 6.

54 "as if I could see": *Webster's Works* 457.

54 "A number of founders": Harvey 76.

55 "fixed hours for everything": Remini 233.

55 "entered Congress under James Madison": Bartlett 59.

55 "overwhelming": "James Madison to Daniel Webster, 27 May 1830," Founders Online, National Archives.

55 "to judge of the violations": *See* Robert Y. Hayne's Reply to Daniel Webster, Jan. 21 and 25, 1830.

55 "yielded their floor seats": Bartlett 117.

55 "pinch of snuff": Harvey 156.

55 "I felt as if everything": S.P. Lyman, *The Public and Private Life of Daniel Webster* (1852), Vol. 1, 140–41.

55 "You ought not to die": Harvey 153.

55 "Whose prerogative is it": *Webster's Works* 256.

55 "all 24 states individually": *Webster's Works* 258, 260.

55 "the people had created": *Webster's Works* 262–65.

56 "When my eyes": *Webster's Works* 269 ("Reply to Hayne," Jan. 1830).

56 "I never knew": Bartlett 120.

56 "principles of the Revolution": *Webster's Works* 125 ("Bunker Hill Monument," Jun. 1825).

56 "The great trust": *Id.* at 135.

57 "By ascending to an association": *Webster's Works* 26 ("First Settlement of New England," Dec. 1820).

57 "working twelve-hour days": Harvey 372.

57 "fortified him to leave": Bartlett 208 (extent of farm); Harvey 277 (oxen).

57 "New England streams": Remini 62; Harvey 366.

58 "I wish to speak": *Webster's Works* 600 ("The Constitution and the Union," Mar. 7, 1850). *See also* Webster's missive to William Prescott, Nov. 7, 1850, in *The Letters of Daniel Webster* [hereinafter *Webster Letters*] (1902), ed. C.H. van Tyne, 440.

58 "Webster's apostasy": Bartlett 265–69; Craig R. Smith, *Daniel Webster and the Oratory of Civil Religion* (2005), 230.

58 "never failed to denounce slavery": *Webster's Works* 232 ("Reply to Hayne," Jan. 1830); *see also* Remini 664.

58 "I see the smoke": *Webster's Works* 50 ("First Settlement of New England," Dec. 1820); Bartlett 244.

58 "purchased slaves their freedom": Harvey 311.

58 "break up the Union": Letter to John M. Botts, Jun. 3, 1851, on the Buffalo Speech, in *Writings and Speeches of Daniel Webster, National Edition* (1903), ed. Edward Everett, Vol. 16, 615.

58 "But he insisted": *See, e.g.*, Letter from Daniel Webster from G.A. Tavenner, Apr. 8, 1852, in *Webster Letters* 520, and Webster's reply, in *Webster Letters* 522.

59 "hasty, fanatical, and self-defeating": *See, e.g.*, Daniel Webster to Benjamin D. Silliman, Jan. 29, 1838, in *Webster Letters* 211 (saying that it was not worth trying to conciliate an unconciliable South at the expense of offending the anti-slavery movement).

59 "these agitating people": *Webster's Works* 619 ("The Constitution and Union," Mar. 1850).

59 "Webster never forgave": *Webster's Works* 584 ("Speech at Marshfield," Sept. 1848); Howe, *What Hath God Wrought* 688; Bartlett 226; Leslie H. Southwick, *Presidential Also-Rans and Running Mates, 1788 Through 1996* (1984; 2nd ed. 1998), 195.

59 "generation of Whigs": *See, e.g.*, Daniel Walker Howe, *The Political Culture of the American Whigs* (1979), 277–79.

59 "historians echo": *See, e.g.*, Fergus M. Bordewich, *America's Great Debate: Henry Clay, Stephen A. Douglas, and the Compromise That Preserved the Union* (2012), 165–70.

59 "did not even look": Oliver Dyer, *Great Senators of the United States Forty Years Ago* (1889), 239.

60 "Jackson himself was no glad-hander": Remini 587; Bartlett 198; *Webster Letters* 503–04.

60 "a hilarious storyteller": Remini 587.

60 "affectionate father": Letter from C.W. Greene, Dec. 15, 1823, in *Webster Letters* 546.

60 "Peter Harvey recalled": Harvey 321.

60 "chilled by the northern blast": "An Oration," dated Jul. 5, 1802, in *Webster Letters* 7.

60 "He studied Cicero": Remini 90; *Webster's Works* xiii–xiv (Whipple introduction); "Letter to Matthew Carey," May 14, 1833, in *Webster Letters* 182.

60 "ponderous blows": Charles Lanman, *The Private Life of Daniel Webster* (1858), 45.

61 "I war with principles": Harvey 336.

61 "Twentieth-century historians": Howe, *The Political Culture of the American Whigs* 212.

61 "something greater": *Webster's Works* 167.

61 "This oration": Remini 186.

61 "25,000 volunteer militiamen": Howe, *What Hath God Wrought* 404.

61 "laid out precisely how destructive": *Webster's Works* 279, 287 ("Constitution is not a Compact Between Sovereign States," Senate speech, Feb. 16, 1833).

62 "dismemberment": *Webster's Works* 280.

62 "crushes": "James Madison to Daniel Webster, 15 March 1833," Founders Online, National Archives.

62 "168 cases": Baxter viii.

62 "permanent jurisprudence": *See, e.g.*, Baxter 132, 142, 243.

62 "*Charles River Bridge*": *Charles River Bridge v. Warren Bridge*, 36 U.S. 420 (1837); *Swift v. Tyson*, 41 U.S. 1 (1842).

62 "*Dartmouth College*": *Trustees of Dartmouth College v. Woodward*, 17 U.S. 518 (1819).

63 "6,914 employees": John Joseph Wallis, "Table Ea894–903 Federal government employees, by government branch and location relative to the capital: 1816–1992" in *Historical Statistics of the United States* (2006), Millennial Edition Online, ed. Susan B. Carter, Scott Sigmund Gartner, Michael R. Haines, Alan L. Olmstead, Richard Sutch, and Gavin Wright.

63 "power to tax": *McCulloch v. Maryland*, 17 U.S. 316 (1819).

63 "Ohio ignored": Howe, *What Hath God Wrought* 145.

63 "procedure he invented": John C. Calhoun, "South Carolina Exposition and Protest" (1828); Richard Current, *Daniel Webster and the Rise of National Conservatism* (1955), 57.

63 "excellent snipe shooting": *Jeffersonian America: Note on the United States of America Collected in the Years 1805–07 and 1811–12 by Sir Augustus John Foster* (1954), ed. Richard Beale Davis.

63 "sanctity of a *contract*": Current 189.

63 "not to shake": "Basis of the Senate," Dec. 1820, in *The Works of Daniel Webster* (1881), ed. Edward Everett, Vol. III, 16; *see also* his remarks in 1849 to the Sons of New Hampshire in Boston, in Current 150.

63 "Commerce, credit": *Ogden v. Saunders*, 25 U.S. 213, 247 (1827) (brief of Daniel Webster).

64 "You have many": Remini 712.

64 "A banker said": Remini 722.

64 "Shippers, financiers": Bartlett 8.

64 "enjoyed wagering": Howe, *What Hath God Wrought* 329.

64 "monsters": Andrew Jackson to Amos Kendall, Aug. 9, 1835, https://cdn.loc.gov/service/mss/maj/01091/01091_0264_0264.pdf.

64 "It is no matter": *Webster's Works* 450 ("The Credit System and the Labor of the United States," Mar. 1838).

64 "there were only Americans": *See, e.g.*, *Webster's Works* 338 ("The Presidential Veto of the United States Bank Bill," Jul. 1832); *see also* Current 104, 146.

65 "unregulated banknotes": Howard Bodenhorn, *A History of Banking in Antebellum America: Financial Markets and Economic Development in an Era of Nation-Building* (2000), 215; Webster's speech on a redeemable paper currency, Feb. 1834, in *Webster's Works* 362–66.

65 "perfect": *Webster's Works* 310.

65 "history of banks": Remini 410.

65 "What interest": *Webster's Works* 238 ("Reply to Hayne," Jan. 1830).

65 "In war and peace": *Webster's Works* 239.

65 "A study shows": Colleen Dunlavy, *Politics and Industrialization: Early Railroads in the United States and Prussia* (1994), 51–55.

65 "floated twice the cargo": Charles Sellers, *The Market Revolution: Jacksonian America, 1815–1846* (1991), 43.

65 "Long Island oysters": Howe, *What Hath God Wrought* 217.

65 "Do we ever hear": *Webster's Works* 92 ("The Tariff," Apr. 1824).

66 "series of cannonades": *See also* his Senate speeches on Jackson's veto of the bank bill on Jul. 11, 1832; on Jackson's removal of the Bank of the United States deposits on Jan. 31, 1834; on the stability of the banking system and a redeemable paper currency on Feb. 22, 1834; on Jackson's protest against the Senate censure of him on May 7, 1834; and on Jackson's spoils-system abuse of appointment and removal power on Feb. 16, 1835.

66 "Jackson prevailed": *Webster's Works* 337 ("Speech on the Presidential Veto of the United States Bank Bill").

66 "no general power": *Webster's Works* 353–58 (speech at National Republican Convention, Worcester, MA, Oct. 12, 1832).

66 "Jackson had claimed": 2 *A Compilation of the Messages and Papers of the Presidents 1789–1897* (1986), ed. J. Richardson, 582 (veto message Jul. 10, 1832).

66 "If that which Congress": *Webster's Works* 334; *see also id.* at 354 (on executive usurpation and ignoring Indian treaties).

66 "ignored the court's writ": *Cherokee Nation v. Georgia*, 30 U.S. 1 (1831); Howe, *What Hath God Wrought* 354–56, 412; *see also Worcester v. Georgia*, 31 U.S. 515 (1832).

66 "Almost all the business": *Gibbons v. Ogden*, 22 U.S. 1, 9–10 (1824) (brief of Daniel Webster).

67 "prefigure the holdings": *See, e.g.*, *License Cases*, 46 U.S. 504 (1847) and *Passenger Cases*, 48 U.S. 283 (1849).

67 "plenary power": *Heart of Atlanta Motel, Inc. v. U. S.*, 379 U.S. 241, 258 (1964) (Civil Rights Act of 1964 sustained under Commerce Clause); *United States v. Robinson*, 137 F.3d 652, 656 (1st Cir. 1998) (child-pornography possession statute upheld under Commerce Clause); *United States v. Bramble*, 103 F.3d 1475, 1481 (9th Cir. 1996) (Bald Eagle Protection Act upheld under Commerce Clause).

67 "Senators in North Dakota": 62nd Legislative Assembly of North Dakota In Regular Session Commencing Tuesday, Jan. 4, 2011, Senate Bill No. 2309.

67 "In South Carolina": South Carolina Legislature, H. 3101, Session 120 (2013–14). It reached this state after being watered down considerably.

67 "sad and weary": Remini 740.

68 "To dismember": *Webster's Works* 622 ("The Constitution and the Union," Mar. 7, 1850).

68 "miracle": *Webster's Works* 498 ("The Landing at Plymouth," Dec. 1843).

68 "declawed": "Letter to Caroline Webster," Jan. 10, 1836, in *Webster Letters* 198; Remini 444; Howe, *What Hath God Wrought* 440–41.

68 "I am tired": Letter to D. Fletcher Webster, Dec. 29, 1847, in *Webster Letters* 603.

68 "Worst of all": Remini 644; *Webster's Works* 551–568 ("Objects of the Mexican War," Senate speech, Mar. 23, 1848).

68 "He planted": Bartlett 223.

68 "less than three weeks": Remini 742–43.

68 "This fresh and brilliant morning": *Webster's Works* 639 ("The Addition to the Capitol," Jul. 1851).

68 "17 million people": *Historical Statistics of the United States, Colonial Times to 1970, Bicentennial Edition*, Part 1 (1975), 8.

68 "He personally negotiated": Remini 538.

69 "House of Hapsburg": *Webster's Works* 681 ("The Hulsemann Letter," Jan. 1851).

69 "President Washington governed": *Webster's Works* 645 ("The Addition to the Capitol," Jul. 1851); *Historical Statistics of the United States, Colonial Times to 1970, Bicentennial Edition*, Part 1 (1975), 8.

69 "Ralph Waldo Emerson": Ralph Waldo Emerson, *Complete Works* (1904), Vol. XI, "Lecture on the Fourth Anniversary of Daniel Webster's Speech in Favor of the Bill," New York City, Mar. 7, 1854.

69 "28-year-old Abraham Lincoln": Remini 468.

69 "promising young Whig": *Webster's Works* 256 (by the people); 627 (house divided); 300 (last hope); *see also* 134 (last hopes of mankind).

69 "very best speech": Howe, *The Political Culture of the American Whigs* 372; Remini 331.

69 "I profess to feel": *Webster's Works* 588 ("Speech at Marshfield," Sept. 1848).

CHAPTER FOUR — STEPHEN FIELD
Civil War and Uncivil Justice

71 "founding an outpost": Kevin Starr, *California: A History* (2007), 40.

71 "strange and wild": Stephen J. Field, *Personal Reminiscences of Early Days in California* [hereinafter *Field's Reminiscences*] (1893).

72 "moral and geographical opposite": Carl Brent Swisher, *Stephen J. Field: Craftsman of the Law* (1930), 5–7.

72 "The main objection": *Field's Reminiscences* 17–22, 24.

72 "unwashed prospectors": Paul Kens, *Justice Stephen Field: Shaping Liberty from the Gold Rush to the Gilded Age* (1997), 26-28. But see *id.* at 26 n.45 (apparently he didn't know that there *were* two others women in town, also Donner Party survivors).

72 "I knew nothing": *Field's Reminiscences* 27.

72 "drew from his breast pocket": Kens 30.

73 "saved the man's life": *Field's Reminiscences* 28.

73 "ancient Israel": Richard Pipes, *Communism: A History* (2001), 3–7.

73 "Cursed be": Deuteronomy 27:17.

74 "So a red apple": John Locke, *Two Treatises of Government, First Treatise* (1689; 1960 ed.), Ch. 5, 285–88, 300.

74 "Nobody could think": Locke 291.

74 "yellow metal": Locke 294.

74 "age of hoarding": Locke 299–302.

74 "wild woods": Locke 294, 301.

74 "Gold Rush California": Kevin Starr, *Americans and the California Dream, 1850–1915* (1973), 52–68, 73–76, 110–13, 123–25; Josiah Royce, *California: A Study of American Character* (1886; Santa Clara Univ. ed. 2002), 3.

74 "ingathering's peak": H.W. Brands, *The Age of Gold: The California Gold Rush and the New American Dream* (2002), 193; Starr, *California* 80, 86.

74 "In Tuolumne County": Brands, *The Age of Gold* 201; Karen Clay and Gavin Wright, "Order without law? Property rights during the California gold rush," 42 *Explorations in Economic History* (2005), 159–66.

74 "700 of these men": Kens 55–57; Starr, *California* 103–05, 75–76.

74 "quickly got a reputation": *See, e.g.*, the précis of John Norton Pomeroy, a Field confidant in presidential campaign mode, in *Some Account of the Work of Stephen J. Field As a Legislator, State Judge, and Judge of the Supreme Court of the United States* (1881), 17–19.

74 "something shocking": *Biddle Boggs v. Merced Mining Co.*, 14 Cal. 279, 379 (1859).

75 "John Sutter": *Field's Reminiscences* 25; *see also* Starr, *Americans and the California Dream* 136.

75 "David Dudley Field": Gilbert H. Muller, *William Cullen Bryant: Author of America* (2008), 257.

75 "Lincoln saw": Kens 92–96; email correspondence with Allen C. Guelzo, Nov. 22, 2017.

76 "The theory upon": *Cummings v. Missouri*, 71 U.S. 277, 321–22 (1866).

76 "prevent traitors": *Ex Parte Garland*, 71 U.S. 333 (1866).

76 "debtor-relief law": Kens 42.

76 "my limbs": Henry Martyn Field, *Blood Is Thicker Than Water: A Few Days Among Our Southern Brethren* (1886), 50.

77 "transfer the security": *Slaughter-House Cases*, 83 U.S. 36, 77 (1873); "New Orleans Abattoir Decision," *Chicago Daily Tribune*, Apr. 19, 1873; *Davidson v. City of New Orleans*, 96 U.S. 97, 104 (1877).

77 "real character": *Slaughter-House Cases*, 83 U.S. at 85 (Field, J., dissenting).

77 "We hold these truths": *Butchers' Union Slaughter-House & Live-Stock Landing Co. v. Crescent City Live-Stock Landing & Slaughter-House Co.*, 111 U.S. 746, 756–57 (Field, J., concurring) (1884).

77 "patrimony of the poor man": *Slaughter-House Cases*, 83 U.S. 36, 111 n.39 (Field, J., dissenting).

78 "Field, like his brethren": *Bradwell v. Illinois*, 83 U.S. 130 (1872); *Bartemeyer v. Iowa*, 85 U.S. 129 (1873); *Mugler v. Kansas*, 123 U.S. 623, 677–78 (Field, J., dissenting) (1887).

78 "Trinity Church": H.W. Brands, *American Colossus: The Triumph of Capitalism, 1865–1900* (2010), 18, 314.

79 "imagery borrowed": Rudyard Kipling, *From Sea to Sea, Letters of Travel, Part II* (1909 ed.), 235.

79 "name governors": Henry George, "What the Railroad Will Bring Us," *Overland Monthly*, Vol. 1, No. 4, Oct. 1868.

79 "museum": Starr, *California* 115–17.

79 "ardor to serve": *San Francisco Examiner*, Oct. 27, 1879, 1–2.

79 "living human beings": *Santa Clara Cnty. v. S. Pac. R. Co.*, 18 F. 385, 404 (C.C.D. Cal. 1883).

80 "keeps our industries flourishing": *Santa Clara Cnty.*, 18 F. at 405.

80 "killing off our generals": William Graham Sumner, *What Social Classes Owe to Each Other* (1883), 43–57.

80 "rugged individualists": Brands, *American Colossus* 169.

80 "real power lies": "From James Madison to Thomas Jefferson, 17 October 1788," *JM Papers*, Vol. 11, *7 March 1788–1 March 1789*, 295–300.

80 "half of the provisions": *See, e.g., The Federalist* No. 10, Nov. 22, 1787 (speaking of "[a] rage for paper money, for an abolition of debts, for an equal division of property, or for any other improper or wicked project").

80 "Field was outraged": *Stone v. Wisconsin*, 94 U.S. 181, 184 (1876) (Field, J., dissenting).

81 "Does anybody believe": *R.R. Comm'n Cases*, 116 U.S. 307, 344 (1886) (Field, J., dissenting). The majority opinions are found in *Stone v. Farmers' Loan & Trust Co.*, 116 U.S. 307 (1886).

81 "I am aware": *Union Pac. R. Co. v. United States*, 99 U.S. 700, 767 (1878).

81 "conservative men": R. Hal Williams, *The Democratic Party and California Politics, 1880–1896* (1973), 21, 58 (quoting Field to George Ticknor Curtis, Dec. 14, 1884, Grover Cleveland Papers, Library of Congress).

81 "virtual monopoly": *Munn v. Illinois*, 94 U.S. 113, 131 (1876).

82 "harbor of a great city": *Illinois Cent. R. Co. v. Illinois*, 146 U.S. 387, 455 (1892).

82 "monstrous injustice": *Spring Valley Water-Works v. Schottler*, 110 U.S. 347, 367 (1884).

82 "other people's property": *Field's Reminiscences* 166–67.

82 "gold mountain": Brands, *The Age of Gold* 63.

82 "Didn't they build": Brands, *The Age of Gold* 426–27.

82 "four workers": Erika Lee, *At America's Gates: Chinese Immigration During the Exclusion Era, 1882–1943* (2003), 25–26; Roger Olmsted, "The Chinese Must Go!," 50 *Calif. Hist. Q.* 3 (Sept. 1971), 285–94.

82 "Little Yuba River": Stephen E. Ambrose, *Nothing Like It In the World: The Men Who Built the Transcontinental Railroad, 1863–1869* (2000), 150.

83 "I have little respect": *In re Ah Fong*, 1 F. Cas. 213, 217 (C.C.D. Cal. 1874); *see also Chy Lung v. Freeman*, 92 U.S. 275, 277 (1875).

83 "pursuit of their vocations": *In re Quong Woo*, 13 F. 229, 232 (C.C.D. Cal. 1882).

83 "everyone knew": *Ho Ah Kow v. Nunan*, 12 F. Cas. 252, 253–55 (C.C.D. Cal. 1879).

83 "vast hordes": *Fong Yue Ting v. United States*, 149 U.S. 698, 706 (1893) (citing *Chae Chan Ping v. United States*, 130 U.S. 581, 606 (1889); *see also* Solicitor General's Brief for Respondents, *Fong Yue Ting v. United States*, 149 U.S. 698 (1893), No. 92-1345, 92-1346, 92-1347, 55 (May 10, 1893); H.R. Exec. Doc. No. 53-10, 2 (1893).

83 "despotic power": *Fong Yue Ting*, 149 U.S. at 750 (Field, J., dissenting); Field to Don Dickinson, Jun. 17, 1893, in Kens 213. *See also Wong Wing v. United States*, 163 U.S. 228, 243 (1896) (Field, J., dissenting in part).

83 "Later that year": Gabriel "Jack" Chin and Daniel K. Tu, *Comprehensive Immigration Reform in the Jim Crow Era: Chinese Exclusion and the McCreary Act of 1893*, 23 Asian American Law Journal 39 (2016); Lucy Salyer, *Laws Harsh as Tigers: Chinese Immigrants and the Shaping of Modern Immigration Law* (1995), 55–57 and correspondence with author; *United States v. Chum Shang Yuen*, 57 F. 588, 589 (S.D. Cal. 1893) (Attorney General Olney advises Los Angeles's U.S. Attorney of luck of funds from Treasury to enforce Geary Act).

84 "supreme puzzle": Compare *Wong Wing*, 163 U.S. at 243 (Field, J., dissenting in part) and *Virginia v. Rives*, 100 U.S. 313, 330 (1880) (Field, J., dissenting).

84 "These niggers": Leon F. Litwack, *Been in the Storm So Long: The Aftermath of Slavery* (1980), 227.

84 "Black Codes": Litwack 253 (contracts), 284 (punishments); *Laws in Relation to Freedmen*, 39th Cong., 2d. Sess., Sen. Exec. Doc. 6, 170–230 (1866), regarding coerced labor contracts, *see, e.g., id.* at 176–77 (Florida), 181–83 (Louisiana), 190 (Maryland); new forms of bondage out of old apprenticeship or vagrancy statutes, 170–72 (Alabama), 180–81 (Georgia), 190–92 (Mississippi); and regarding replacing the word "slave" with "negro," at 199 (North Carolina).

84 "unregenerate rebel lawyers": *See* Rep. James A. Garfield, in Cong. Globe, 42d Cong., 1st Sess. at 153 (1871).

84 "Colfax Massacre": Charles Lane, *The Day Freedom Died: The Colfax Massacre, the Supreme Court, and the Betrayal of Reconstruction* (2008), 266.

85 "adds nothing": *United States v. Cruikshank*, 92 U.S. 542, 554 (1875).

85 "federal anti-Klan law": *United States v. Harris*, 106 U.S. 629, 640 (1883); *but see United States v. Waddell*, 112 U.S. 76 (1884) (authority to regulate private action under Art. 4, Sec. 3, which gives Congress police power over federal lands).

85 "startling proof": Lawrence Goldstone, *Inherently Unequal: The Betrayal of Equal Rights by the Supreme Court, 1865–1903* (2011), 103.

85 "Sam Hose": Goldstone 4–8; Philip Dray, *At the Hands of Persons Unknown: The Lynching of Black America* (2002), 9–16.

85 "timid, ignorant, and penniless": *United States v. Reese*, 92 U.S. 214, 254 (1875).

86 "finally summoned the will": *See, e.g., Powell v. Alabama*, 287 U.S. 45 (1932) and the later incorporation cases; *Heart of Atlanta Motel, Inc. v. United States*, 379 U.S. 241 (1964) (Civil Rights Act of 1964, enacted under Commerce Clause); *Katzenbach v. McClung*, 379 U.S. 294 (1964); *United States v. Hatch*, 722 F.3d 1193 (10th Cir. 2013) (Shepard-James Hate Crimes Act of 2009, enacted under Thirteenth Amendment).

86 "Equal Employment Opportunity Commission": U.S. Equal Employment Opportunity Commission, Press Release, "BMW to Pay $1.6 Million and Offer Jobs to Settle Federal Race Discrimination Lawsuit," Sep. 8, 2015.

86 "practically a brand": *Strauder v. West Virginia*, 100 U.S. 303, 308 (1880).

86 "drew on a distinction": *Ex Parte Virginia*, 100 U.S. 339, 354 (1880) (Field, J., dissenting); *Strauder*, 100 U.S. at 312.

86 "every day's experience": *Rives*, 100 U.S. at 335.

86 "radically change": *Slaughter-House Cases*, 83 U.S. 36, 78 (1873).

87 "change so radical": *Ex Parte Virginia*, 100 U.S. 339, 362 (1880) (Field, J., dissenting); *Santa Clara Cnty.*, 18 F. at 398, *aff'd*, 118 U.S. 394 (1886) and *aff'd sub nom. San Bernardino Cnty. v. S. Pac. R. Co.*, 118 U.S. 417 (1886) and *aff'd sub nom. People of State of California v. N. Ry. Co.*, 118 U.S. 417 (1886).

87 "unworthy": *Ho Ah Kow*, 12 F. Cas. at 256–57.

87 "humiliation": *See, e.g., Ex Parte Virginia*, 100 U.S. 339, 358–59 (1880) (Field, J., dissenting); *Rives*, 100 U.S. 313; *Strauder*, 100 U.S. 30.

87 "new light": Henry Martyn Field, *Blood Is Thicker Than Water* 50.

87 "fails to explain": Stephen J. Field to John Norton Pomeroy on July 28, 1884, in Howard Jay Graham, *Four Letters of Mr. Justice Field*, 47 Yale L.J. 1100, 1107 (1938); Adam M. Carrington, *Justice Stephen Field's Cooperative Constitution of Liberty: Liberty in Full*, 77–79 (2017).

87 "Field felt": "Mark Twain in Washington. Delayed Letter," *Daily Alta California*, Dec. 23, 1867.

87 "Tilden first": *See, e.g., Daily Alta California*, Vol. 36, No. 12476, Jun. 13, 1884; cf. *Daily Record-Union*, May 15, 1880, and *Daily Alta California*, Apr. 13, 1880; Swisher 314.

88 "petulant letter": Swisher 316–17; Kens 245.

88 "James B. Weaver": Brands, *American Colossus* 490, 483; John D. Hicks, *The Populist Revolt: A History of the Farmers' Alliance and the People's Party* (1961), 266–67; Erik W. Austin, *Political Facts of the United States Since 1789* (1986), 88.

88 "Americans enjoyed": Brands, *American Colossus* 607.

89 "eternal justice": *Legal Tender Cases*, 79 U.S. 457, 670 (1870) (Field, J., dissenting).

89 "pretense": *Cummings*, 71 U.S. at 325; *Slaughter-House Cases*, 83 U.S. at 87; *Union Pac. R. Co.*, 99 U.S. at 756 (Field, J., dissenting); *Ho Ah Kow*, 12 F. Cas. at 254; *In re Quong Woo*, 13 F. at 233; *Santa Clara Cnty.*, 18 F. at 398 (C.C.D. Cal. 1883); *Soon Hing v. Crowley*, 113 U.S. 703, 711 (1885); *Butchers' Union Slaughter-House*, 111 U.S. at 755 (Field, J., concurring); *Powell v. Com. of Pennsylvania*, 127 U.S. 678, 695 (1888) (Field, J., dissenting).

89 "If he perceived": *Powell*, 127 U.S. at 695, 679 (1888) (Field, J., dissenting); *Powell v. Commonwealth*, 114 Pa. 265, 298–99 (1887) (Gordon, J., dissenting); Geoffrey P. Miller, *Public Choice at the Dawn of the Special Interest State: The Story of Butter and Margarine*, 77 Cal. L. Rev. 83, 115 (1989); Paul D. Moreno, *The American State from the Civil War to the New Deal: The Twilight of Constitutionalism and the Triumph of Progressivism* (2013), 78–79; *Jay Burns Baking Co. v. Bryan*, 264 U.S. 504, 513 (1924); *Tip Top Foods, Inc. v. Lyng*, 28 Cal. App. 3d 533, 542 (Ct. App. 1972).

89 "Sometimes he was far-seeing": *Munn*, 94 U.S. at 140 (Field, J., dissenting); *Stone*, 94 U.S. at 186 (Field, J., dissenting).

90 "funeral directors": *St. Joseph Abbey v. Castille*, 712 F.3d 215, 226–27 (5th Cir. 2013); *see also Hettinga v. United States*, 677 F.3d 471, 482–83 (D.C. Cir. 2012).

90 "J.P. Morgan's bank": "Robbery at J.P. Morgan," *Wall Street Journal*, Sept. 29, 2013.

90 "awe-inspiring and dignified": Arthur Brisbane, *New York World*, May 7, 1895.

90 "present assault": *Pollock v. Farmers' Loan & Trust Co.*, 157 U.S. 429, 607 (1895) (Field, J., concurring).

91 "after the New Deal's triumph": *United States v. Carolene Products Co.*, 304 U.S. 144, 152 n.4 (1938).

91 "It should never": Stephen Field, "The Centenary of the Supreme Court of the United States," *American Law Review* 24, 351, 358–68 (1890).

91 "I have long since": Shorb Collection, "Field to J. DeBarth Shorb," Dec. 14, 1884, in Kens 245.

CHAPTER FIVE — ALEXIS DE TOCQUEVILLE AND JAMES BRYCE
Europe Visits at Mid-Century

95 "These nobles": Hugh Brogan, *Alexis de Tocqueville: A Life* (2006), 3–4.

95 "When Alexis's father": Brogan 20.

95 "Four of nine": Alexis de Tocqueville, *Letters from America* [hereinafter *Tocqueville Letters*] (2010), trans. and ed. by Frederick Brown, xi.

95 "lifelong habit": Joseph Epstein, *Alexis de Tocqueville: Democracy's Guide* (2006), 9–10; *The Reign of Terror: A Collection of Authentic Narratives of the Horrors Committed by the Revolutionary Government of France Under Marat and Robespierre Written by Eye-Witnesses of the Scenes* (London 1898), Vol. II, 96–97, 104–06.

95 "opponents warned": Brogan 330.

95 "*juge-auditeur*": Epstein 21.

96 "my inadequacy": Brogan 78.

96 "report young workers": Brogan 103.

96 "I felt": Brogan 127.

96 "When one sees": Brogan 282.

96 "Each nation": Alexis de Tocqueville, *Democracy in America* [hereinafter *DIA*] (2000), trans. and ed. by Harvey C. Mansfield and Delba Winthrop, 6–7, 400, 676.

96 "[I]n America I saw": DIA 13; Tocqueville to Ernest de Chabrol, from Boston, Sept. 17, 1831, *Tocqueville Letters* 190.

96 "My object": Tocqueville to Sylvestre de Sacy, in Brogan 369.

96 "They wore out": Alexis de Tocqueville, *Tocqueville Letters* 50, Letter to Abbé Lesueur, May 28, 1831 (asking for more gloves); Brogan 180 (admiring French-speakers of Boston); DIA 310–11 (Choctaws).

97 "Years later": Brogan 397.

97 "literate pioneers": DIA 445, 699–701.

97 "He chuckled": *Tocqueville Letters* 106 (Beaumont to brother Jules, Jul. 4, 1831).

97 "He scarcely knew": *Tocqueville Letters* 135.

97 "still mix debris": DIA 564 (debris), 673 (only being born).

97 "central fact": DIA 3, 46.

97 "no fire departments": DIA 691 (note to page 90).

97 "pledged to eschew liquor": DIA 492.

97 "When a highway": DIA 180–81.

97 "The lack of such": DIA 391 and especially note 97.

97 "A typical state": DIA 84.

98 "A good government's": Brogan 184.

98 "cushy posts": DIA 604–05.

98 "Enos Throop": *Tocqueville Letters* 117–18.

98 "The President": Brogan 210; *Tocqueville Letters* 264 (Beaumont to his mother, Jan. 20, 1832).

98 "call him *mister*": *Id.*

98 "All dressed the same": Brogan 183.

98 "This turns out": Cf. Beaumont in *Tocqueville Letters* 237–38.

99 "Chevalier also echoed": Michel Chevalier, *Society, Manners, and Politics in the United States: Letters on North America* (1967), ed. John William Ward, trans. T.G. Bradford, 7; cf. DIA 396.

99 "He left that": Gustave de Beaumont, *Marie, or, Slavery in the United States*, trans. Barbara Chapman (1958), xxxiii.

99 "Now I understand": Beaumont, *Marie* 57.

99 "The apparent hypocrisy": James Boswell, *The Life of Samuel Johnson* (1791; 1906 ed.), 771, quoting Johnson's essay 1774 "Taxation No Tyranny." *See also* Sydney Smith, *Edinburgh Review*, Jan.–May 1820.

99 "warlike manifesto": Frances Trollope, *Domestic Manners of the Americans* (1832), 51 (warlike Declaration), 42 (offspring).

99 "Trollope was shocked": Trollope 33.

100 "she was rebuked": Trollope 75.

100 "immediately comfortable": Trollope 110–11.

100 "General Jackson": Trollope 85.

100 "Possible!": Trollope 61.

100 "soil I have trodden": Philip Collins, "Charles Dickens," in *Abroad in America: Visitors to the New Nation, 1776–1914* (1976), ed. Marc Pachter and Frances Wein, 84.

100 "His mind is American": Claire Tomalin, *Charles Dickens: A Life* (2011), 127.

100 "He described": Charles Dickens, *Martin Chuzzlewit* (1844; Oxford World's Classics ed. 1984), ed. Margaret Cardwell, 219 (election), 461 (tobacco), 220 (newspaper).

101 "The only evidence": Charles Dickens, *American Notes for General Circulation* (1842; Penguin ed. 2000), ed. Patricia Ingham (2000), 54–63 (Boston institutions), 78–79 (Lowell).

101 "By the time": Herbert Albert Laurens Fisher, *James Bryce* (1927), 9

101 "independent-minded": James Bryce, *The American Commonwealth* (1888; Liberty Fund ed. 1995) [hereinafter *Bryce*], xiii.

101 "As an Oxford aspirant": Bryce xiv.

101 "A book": Bryce xv.

101 "genocide in Armenia": Merrill D. Peterson, *"Starving Armenians": America and the Armenian Genocide, 1915-1930 and After* (2004), 7.

101 "one of the best informed men": James Bryce, *The American Commonwealth* (1990), ed. Burton C. Bernard, 51.

101 "Americans were charmed": Bryce xxix.

101 "So popular": *See* United States Senate, "James Bryce," https://www.senate.gov/artandhistory/art/artifact/Sculpture_24_00001.htm.

102 "The monument": Bryce xxx; *see also* "Offers Americans Bust of Lord Bryce," *New York Times*, Jan. 28, 1922.

102   "swarm of bold generalizations": Bryce 4; *see also* Morton Keller, "James
      Bryce and America," *Wilson Quarterly* (Autumn 1988).

102   "truth that": Bryce 1546, in Appendix II, "The Predictions of Hamilton and
      de Tocqueville," IX *John Hopkins University Studies in Historical and Political
      Science* (Sept. 1887), ed. Herbert B. Adams, 5th Series.

102   "For Bryce": Bryce 1300 (judges), 436–37 (money bills), 792 (Tammany),
      1546 (middle class).

102   "theories ready made": Bryce 4.

102   "type of institutions": Bryce 1.

103   "genius for prediction": *See, e.g.*, DIA 378, 611, 635 (Civil War will find causes
      in a divided army and the "presence of blacks"); Brogan 265 (Brogan's
      translation) (Civil War will be between rival "peoples" not rival "factions");
      210 (presidential power grows through crisis); 343 (racial relations will
      worsen *after* abolition); 362 (by 1935, America would have 100 million
      inhabitants and 40 states; it was actually 123 million and 48 states); 378, 392
      (war with Mexico would be America's next); 621 (a democratic people has
      trouble both beginning a war and ending one); 142 (nations faces especial
      danger if the Supreme Court is corrupted); 532 (American aristocracy is
      commercial in nature); 557 (workers, alone, will be unable to resist power of
      industrialists); 662–63 (danger of "schoolmaster" government); but see 341
      (impossibility of racial equality); 192 (House might adopt Senate's then-
      mode of election).

103   "self-contradictory": *Compare, e.g.*, DIA 643 (democratic men have no
      time for public affairs) and 232 (democratic men like nothing more than
      meddling in public affairs). Elsewhere, for instance, he writes that Americans
      are impetuous, but also restrained and timid; that Americans love order, but
      also risk; that Americans love tradition, but also innovation.

103   "pensées": *Tocqueville Letters* 19 (Tocqueville's generalizations about
      American appearance begin on his first day in America); Pierson 54.

103   "Show me the books": Letter to Charles Stoffels, July 31, 1834, in Pierson
      744 (emphasis added); *id.* at 740 n.1 (Beaumont on Tocqueville's craft).

103   "His notes": DIA 678–79 (Delaware language); 678 (New World foliage);
      682 (code books of MA and NY).

103   "I talked": Bryce xxv.

103   "rules the country": Bryce 68.

103   "porcelain": Bryce 1418.

104   "unconstitutional in a half-dozen respects": Art. I, Sec. 9, Cl. 8 (federal ban
      on titles of nobility), Art. I, Sec. 10, Cl. 10 (state ban on titles of nobility);
      Art. II, Sec. 1; Art. I, Sec. 2 & 3 (personal election); Art. I, Sec. 2, Cl. 2; Art.
      I, Sec. 3, Cl. 3; Art. II, Sec. 1, Cl. 5 (eligibility qualifications); *see also* Amdt.
      14, § 1 (equal protection of law).

104   "inner circle": Bryce 737.

104   "All adults males": Bryce 976.

104   "Bryce considered": Bryce 765–66.

104   "period of national crisis": DIA 123.

104   "Where else": Bryce 882.

104   "wherein lovers talk": Bryce 869.

104   "could never imagine": Bryce 888.

105 "mores": DIA 275.

105 "singular fixity": DIA 611.

105 "abiding sense": DIA 610 (principal law); 627 (atmosphere); *see* Bryce 275 (on "reverence for the Constitution").

106 "excelled his Gallic rival": Compare DIA 192 (Senate prestige because of double election) and Bryce 105 (Senate prestige because greater constitutional powers and more talented personnel).

106 "What made": *See, e.g.,* Bryce 193–203.

106 "office": Art. I, Sec. 6.

106 "ministers": Art. II, Sec. 2.

106 "This meant inoffensive": Bryce 69–75.

107 "wasn't interested in parties": *See, e.g.,* DIA 166–170.

107 "fraught and irresolvable divisions": *See, e.g.,* Bryce 694–95, 927.

107 "two or three prejudices": Bryce 912.

107 "When an ordinary": Bryce 702.

108 "I have yet": *Tocqueville Letters* 87.

108 "In France": DIA 412.

108 "The burning question": DIA 182–83; Howe, *What Hath God Wrought* 395–410.

108 "Law, custom, and sheer fortuity": DIA 292; Bryce 1267.

108 "Tocqueville noted": DIA 293. For Webster, *see* his "Address at the Completion of the Bunker Hill Monument," in 1843, in *Great Speeches and Orations of Daniel Webster* (1879), ed. Edwin P. Whipple, 144–46.

109 "freedom of expression": 1918 Constitution of the Soviet Federated Socialist Republic, Art. 2, Ch. 5, Cl. 13 and 14.

109 "Tsarist Constitution": Russian Constitution of April 23, 1906, Art. 4, in *Readings in Modern European History* (1908), ed. James Harvey Robinson and Charles A. Beard, Vol. 2, 378–81.

109 "Someone has said": Bryce 271–72.

110 "One exception": Art. I, Sec. 2. ("No Person shall be a Representative… who shall not, when elected, be an Inhabitant of that State in which he shall be chosen.").

110 "If ten great House leaders": Bryce 744.

110 "Tocqueville didn't": Brogan 474. He suggested that voters could judge him from his speeches and votes.

110 "useful in proving": Harriet Martineau, *Society in America* (1962), ed. Seymour Martin Lipset, 57.

110 "even the mules": Plato, *The Republic* (1968), 563c-d, trans. Allan Bloom, 242.

110 "Even the mechanism": Article V requires amendment by three-quarters of the states, acting either through their legislatures or special conventions. You need 38 states to pass one. Thus 13 states—just over one-quarter—could block an amendment. In July 2012 the population of the 13 smaller states was 13,932,743. This many people, conceivably, could block an amendment if it were put to a raw plebiscite in each state. Their will would then prevail over the will of the other 299,348,974 Americans. With a total population of 313,281,717, this means that 4.5% of the population holds sway. And this is only if we measure by states as a whole. But if one vote over 50% is needed,

then you need closer to 7 million to win. That is 2.2%. (These figures are
from Wikipedia, which seemed the democratic choice of source.) So much
for Tocqueville's tyranny of the majority here. As Bryce would say, what
could be more conservative than that? He would also observe, as was his
wont, that states do not vote *en bloc* or by size, so this scenario would never
happen.

110 "not so much": Bryce 273, quoting from an 1886 address by Cooley to the
South Carolina Bar Association.

111 "This was a government": Bryce 273.

111 "What has struck": *Tocqueville Letters* 59.

111 "people make [law]": *See Tocqueville Letters* 97 (Tocqueville in Jun. 1831 to
Kergolay).

111 "Bryce agreed": Bryce 1262.

111 "appeared to feel": *American Notes* 139–40.

112 "fixture of 18th-century thought": Alexander Pope, *An Essay on Man* (Epistle
III) (1733–34), lines 311–12; Adam Smith, *Wealth of Nations* (1776; Modern
Library ed. 2004), Bk 1. Ch. 2, 15.

112 "put a sort of heroism": DIA 387.

112 "The American inhabits": DIA 387–88.

112 "Bryce's landlady": Bryce 1318 n.4.

112 "heroes and leaders": Bryce 1246.

112 "tête-à-tête": *Tocqueville Letters* 72.

112 "Beaumont was struck": Beaumont, *Marie* 227, Appendix I ("Note on
Equality in American Society").

113 "melancholy ghosts": *American Notes* 176.

113 "But they also found": DIA 235–50; Bryce 570–84.

113 "regeneration of man": *Martin Chuzzlewit* 300.

113 "They are proud": Bryce 948

113 "persuade men": Brogan 320 and 666 n.19.

113 "The July Monarchy": Brogan 409.

114 "universal male suffrage": Brogan 507.

114 "You say it": Brogan 428.

114 "active, improving conservative": Brogan 390.

114 "seven revolutions": Epstein 130.

114 "For me the Republic": Brogan 435.

114 "bore very little resemblance": Alexis de Tocqueville, *The Recollections of
Alexis de Tocqueville* (1896) ["*Souvenirs*"] [hereinafter *Tocqueville Recollections*],
trans. Alexander Teixeira De Mattos, 235.

114 "He watched": *Tocqueville Recollections* 241.

114 "electoral college": *Tocqueville Recollections* 252.

114 "bicameralism": *Tocqueville Recollections* 250.

115 "I thought it best": *Tocqueville Recollections* 250, 255.

115 "The Duc de Broglie": Brogan 519.

115 "No longer": Brogan 466.

115 "loss of our aristocracy": Brogan 569.

116 "He thought the coming": DIA 168–69.

116 "His attack on Jackson": *See, e.g.*, DIA 265 ("man of violent character and
middling capacity"), 377 ("General Jackson is the slave of the majority").

116 "duped on arrival": *See, e.g.*, Thomas Hart Benton, who revisited Tocqueville as he wrote his memoirs. Pierson 736.

116 "His class would": *Tocqueville Letters* 22.

116 "Only an aristocrat": Pierson 734 (Francis J. Lippitt, the 22-year-old Brown graduate who assisted Tocqueville in researching *Democracy in America*, recalled that from the *"ensemble* of our conversations I certainly did carry away with me an impression that his political views and sympathies were not favorable to democracy").

116 "Between 1820": Bryce 1105 n.2.

116 "Today 40 million": United States Census Bureau, "The Foreign-Born Population in the United States: 2010," May 2012, 1-2.

116 "two of eight living Secretaries of State": Madeleine Albright (Czechoslovakia) and Henry Kissinger (Germany). The others are George P. Shultz, James Baker, Colin Powell (who has Jamaican parents), Condoleezza Rice, Hillary Clinton, and John Kerry.

117 "great leveler": DIA 273.

117 "The schools": Bryce 1122.

117 "only nation in the world": G.K. Chesterton, "What is America?" in *The Collected Works of G.K. Chesterton: What I Saw in America, The Resurrection of Rome, Sidelights* (Ignatius ed. 1990), Vol. XXI, 41.

118 "Crèvecoeur": J. Hector St. John de Crèvecoeur, *Letters from an American Farmer* (1782; Penguins Classics ed. 1981), ed. Albert E. Stone, 70.

118 "Christopher Hitchens": Christopher Hitchens, *Thomas Jefferson: Author of America* (2005), 188; Christopher Hitchens, *Why Orwell Matters* (2002), 104.

118 "great revolution": DIA 673.

CHAPTER SIX — WOODROW WILSON
The President of the Progressives

121 "He was also the first president": John Milton Cooper, Jr., *Woodrow Wilson: A Biography* (2009), 465 (Pope), 5, 131 (courts).

121 "coached a college baseball team": Cooper, *Wilson* 61.

121 "Wilson the Just": A. Scott Berg, *Wilson* (2013), 20.

121 "*New Republic* speculated": *The New Republic*, Jan. 11, 1919, Vol. XVII, No. 219, 314.

122 "from the throne": "From Thomas Jefferson to Martin Van Buren, 29 June 1824," Founders Online, National Archives.

122 "influence legislation": "Wilson Innovations Excite Washington," *New York Times*, Feb. 28, 1913.

122 "I am very glad": Woodrow Wilson, *Selected Literary and Political Papers and Addresses of Woodrow Wilson* (1926) [hereinafter *Wilson's Selected Papers*], Vol. 2, 25 (special address on the tariff, Apr. 8, 1913).

122 "His trips to Europe": U.S. Department of State, Office of the Historian, "Woodrow Wilson," https://history.state.gov/departmenthistory/travels/president/wilson-woodrow.

122 "palpable violation": Ann Hagedorn, *Savage Peace: Hope and Fear in America, 1919* (2007), 21; Richard J. Ellis, *Presidential Travel: The Journey from George Washington to George W. Bush* (2008), 186–87; "Questions Never Raised Before in Washington," *New York Times*, Nov. 28, 1918.

122 "too much a fashion": Alexander Hamilton, "The Defence No. XXXVI [2
     January 1796]," *AH Papers*, Vol. 20, *January 1796–March 1797*, 3–10.
122 "like a straightjacket": "Wilson Says Elasticity Saves the Constitution," *New
     York Times*, Nov. 20, 1904.
122 "hearing someone pass": *Wilson's Selected Papers*, Vol. 1, 221 ("Abraham
     Lincoln: A Man of the People," Feb. 12, 1909).
122 "His uncle": James B. Miller, "Beyond Non-Contradiction: Lessons from
     the Case of James Woodrow," *Presbyterian Outlook*, Nov. 16, 2009; Cooper,
     Wilson 17 (chemist).
122 "Wilson's father's parents": Berg 27–28.
123 "At age nine": Berg 39 (baseball), 48–49 (yacht), 96 (literary society), 86
     (debate club).
123 "I can see him": Berg 110.
123 "feel like a fire": *Wilson's Selected Papers*, Vol. 2, 46–47 (address to National
     Press Club, Mar. 21, 1914).
123 "After Wilson asked": Berg 438; *see also* George Creel, *Rebel at Large:
     Recollections of Fifty Crowded Years* (1947), 239–40.
123 "I have a passion": Cooper, *Wilson* 51.
123 "He hoped that": Woodrow Wilson, *Congressional Government* (1885), 11
     (introduction by Walter Lippmann).
124 "The men who sat": *Wilson's Selected Papers*, Vol. 2, 30, 36 (address at
     Philadelphia, Oct. 25, 1913).
124 "want to consult": Woodrow Wilson, "Jackson Day Address," Jan. 8, 1915,
     Indianapolis.
124 "not a thorough American": Cooper 28 (Federalist); Woodrow Wilson, "A
     Calendar of Great Americans," *New York Forum*, XVI, Feb. 1894, 715–27, in
     Ronald J. Pestritto, *Woodrow Wilson: The Essential Political Writings* (2005),
     85.
124 "He spoke ill": Pestritto 83–88 (Jackson, Clay, Webster), 88 (Lincoln);
     Wilson's Selected Papers, Vol. 1, 226 ("Abraham Lincoln: A Man of People").
124 "not to remember": Berg 134.
124 "adaptation of English": *Wilson's Selected Papers*, Vol. 2, 89 (adaptation), 85
     (progressive Englishmen) ("Character of Democracy in the United States,"
     Atlantic Monthly, Nov. 1889).
125 "Wilson saw no reason": *Wilson's Selected Papers*, Vol. 1, 126 ("Democracy
     and Efficiency," *Atlantic Monthly*, Mar. 1901); *Constitutional Government* 52-
     57.
125 "One of Wilson's favorite tropes": Woodrow Wilson, *The New Freedom*
     (1913), 23–24.
125 "stump speeches": *The New Freedom* 24.
125 "But it is misleading": Woodrow Wilson to Caleb Winchester, May 13, 1893,
     Papers of Woodrow Wilson, Vol. 8, 211 (master); Woodrow Wilson, "Edmund
     Burke: The Man and His Times," in *Woodrow Wilson: Essential Writings and
     Speeches of the Scholar-President* (2006), ed. Mario R. DiNunzio, 83 (voice).
125 "No president": Drew Maciag, *Edmund Burke in America: The Contested
     Career of the Father of Modern Conservatism* (2013), 143.
125 "by slow modification": DiNunzio 90 ("Edmund Burke: The Man and His
     Times"); *Constitutional Government* 4–5, 25–37, 54.

125 "Wilson wasn't particularly consistent": *Constitutional Government* 56 (Hamilton a Newtonian), 199 (Hamilton a Darwinian); *Wilson's Selected Papers*, Vol. 3, 193 ("A Calendar of Great Americans") (Marshall and Webster "viewed the fundamental law as a great organic product, a vehicle of life as well as a charter of authority; in disclosing its life they did not damage its tissue"). Wilson also uses the metaphor to refer, variously, to the Constitution, "government," and "society," all quite different things.

125 "idea of organic life": Cooper, *Wilson* 62–63; Pestritto 83 (from "A Calendar of Great Americans").

125 "The Darwin metaphor": *New Freedom* 24.

125 "When Wilson decorated": Berg 123.

126 "If I did not believe": *New Freedom* 22.

126 "Historians still struggle": *The Social and Political Thought of American Progressivism* (2006), ed. Eldon J. Eisenach, vii-xi; Robert H. Wiebe, *The Search for Order, 1877–1920* (1967), 11–12; Arthur S. Link and Richard L. McCormick, *Progressivism* (1983), 1–25, 58–66; *The Social and Political Thought of American Progressivism* vii–xi and 262–72 (excerpting Benjamin Parke De Witt, *The Progressive Movement: A Non-Partisan, Comprehensive Discussion of Current Tendencies in American Politics* [1915]).

126 "It enacted Populist priorities": John D. Hicks, *The Populist Revolt: A History of the Farmers' Alliance and the People's Party* (1961), 404–23.

126 "building playgrounds": *See, e.g.*, Theodore Roosevelt's letter to the Washington Playground Association, Feb. 16, 1907.

126 "Many Progressive reformers": Wiebe 118 (Harris), 115–16 (Biggs).

126 "William Bauchop Wilson": Arthur S. Link, *Woodrow Wilson and the Progressive Era, 1910–1917* (1954), 31.

126 "William Randolph Hearst": David Nasaw, *The Chief: The Life of William Randolph Hearst* (2000), 162 (slogan), 169 (pins).

127 "Louisiana Senator's proposal": "Bars Remarriage After a Divorce; Senator Ransdell Fathers an Amendment to the Federal Constitution," *Chicago Daily Tribune*, Feb. 5, 1914.

127 "Men of our day": *Wilson's Selected Papers*, Vol. 1, 189–90 (address to American Bankers' Association, Sept. 1908).

127 "prototypical business": *See, e.g.*, Glenn Porter, *The Rise of Big Business, 1860–1920* (2006), 1–30.

127 "increasingly being displaced": Thomas K. McCraw, *Prophets of Regulation* (1984), 64; Porter 20.

127 "biggest and scariest corporations": Melvin Urofsky, *Big Steel and the Wilson Administration: A Study in Business-Government Relations* (1969), xxix; Richard Ely, *Studies in the Evolution of Industrial Society*, in Eisenach 52–53.

127 "insurance companies": Urofsky 161.

127 "Wilson thought": *Wilson's Selected Papers*, Vol. 1, 285–87 ("The Tariff Make-Believe," *North American Review*, Oct. 1909); *see also* Croly, *Promise* 202–03; Walter Lippmann, *Drift and Mastery* (1914), 79.

128 "put on a policeman's uniform": *New Freedom* 12.

128 "By the end of the 19th century": *Pivotal Decades* 1.

128 "city dweller": Wiebe 14.

128 "worse governed": *Wilson's Selected Papers*, Vol. 1, 115 ("Democracy and Efficiency," *Atlantic Monthly*, Mar. 1901).

128 "supreme Progressive chronicler": Lincoln Steffens, *The Autobiography of Lincoln Steffens* (1931), 208–10.

128 "Steffens's great insight": *New Freedom* 99 ("A boss is not so much a politician as the business agent in politics of special interests"); Steffens 400; *see also* 255, 236 (Richard Croker).

128 "That would work": Steffens 414.

129 "A clash in his 20s": Robert M. La Follette, *La Follette's Autobiography: A Personal Narrative of Political Experiences* (1912; 1968 ed.), 17–22.

129 "he met Senator Philetus Sawyer": La Follette 25.

129 "witnessed land giveaways": La Follette 32.

129 "I have a wife": La Follette 114.

129 "very energetic man": Cooper, *Wilson* 132.

129 "once stumped": La Follette 143–44.

129 "Half a loaf": La Follette 166.

130 "My guess": La Follette 318 (referring, once, to a candidate "who had made a progressive record as governor of New Jersey").

130 "essentially socialistic in principle": "Speech to the Commercial Club of Chicago," Mar. 1908, in DiNunzio 316, 318.

130 "he challenged any politician": Berg 202.

130 "After dealing": Berg 216.

130 "In 1911 he shepherded": Link, *Woodrow Wilson and the Progressive Era* 10; *Pivotal Decades* 167.

130 "He began to call": Cooper, *Wilson* 137.

131 "Even after both": Berg 228.

131 "forced sterilization": Link and McCormick 92.

131 "essay the theoretical improvement": *Smith v. Bd. of Examiners of Feeble-Minded*, 88 A. 963, 966 (N.J. 1913).

131 "weren't so lucky": Edwin Black, *War Against the Weak: Eugenics and America's Campaign to Create a Master Race* (2003), xvi.

131 "Dairymen decried": *See, e.g.*, "Hearings on Oleomargarine Bill," Sen. Comm. on Agriculture and Forestry and the House Comm. on Agriculture (1901), xv; *Oshkosh Daily Northwestern*, Dec. 11, 1902; *Pacific Dairy Review*, Vol. XIV, Sept. 29, 1910.

131 "Chicago's U.S. Attorney": Moreno 92.

131 "When the law": *Hoke v. United States*, 227 U.S. 308, 322 (1913).

132 "The initiative first emerged": Link and McCormick 58; Patrick M. Garry, *The South Dakota State Constitution* (2014) 53–54; Joseph F. Zimmerman, *The Initiative: Citizen Lawmaking* 6; 129–56 (2d ed. 2014).

132 "He thought that": *New Freedom* 100; Woodrow Wilson, "The Issues of Reform," in *The Initiative, Referendum and Recall*, ed. William Bennett Munro, 87–88 (1912). New Jersey to this day does not have the initiative.

132 "Self-government": "The Study of Administration," *Political Science Quarterly*, Vol. II, Jun. 1887, 197–222, in Pestritto 243.

133 "Each candidate": Eugene V. Debs, *Writings of Eugene V. Debs: A Collection of Essays by America's Most Famous Socialist* (2009), 51–52, 59 (home), 99 (TR), 101 (Wilson).

133 "Even the most conservative": Jonathan Lurie, *William Howard Taft: The Travails of a Progressive Conservative* (2012), 196–198.

133 "bigger trust-buster": *Pivotal Decades* 149.

133 "urged Congress": William Howard Taft, First Annual Message, Dec. 7, 1909 (spending); Second Annual Message, Dec. 6, 1910 (matches).

133 "appealed to voters in 1912": William Howard Taft, "The Supreme Issue," *Saturday Evening Post*, Vol. 185, No. 16, Oct. 19, 1912 (essay in days before election, based on his Aug. 1912 nomination-acceptance speech); *see also* Lewis L. Gould, *The William Howard Taft Presidency* (2009), 193–94.

133 "take part in all discussions": Fourth Annual Message, Dec. 3, 1912 (Taft acknowledged that this would resemble parliamentary practice but said that the "rigid holding apart of the executive and the legislative branches of this Government has not worked for the great advantage of either").

133 "Friends described him": *See, e.g.*, Steffens 258, 348.

133 "Roosevelt thought": Berg 6 (clerk), 294 (virile).

133 "great big boy": Berg 458.

133 "To hell with the Constitution": James E. Watson, *As I Knew Them: Memoirs of James E. Watson, Former United States Senator from Indiana* (1936), 63–64; *see also* Theodore Roosevelt, *An Autobiography* (1913; Library of America ed. 2004), 729–34 (TR details his seizure plan).

133 "prime purpose": Theodore Roosevelt, Eighth Annual Message, Dec. 8, 1908.

134 "In TR's case": *See, e.g.*, National Park Service, "Theodore Roosevelt and Conservation," https://www.nps.gov/thro/learn/historyculture/theodore-roosevelt-and-conservation.htm (public lands).

134 "most brilliant American statesman who ever lived": Theodore Roosevelt, Works, Vol. XIV, *New York: A Sketch of the City's Social, Political, and Commercial Progress from the First Dutch Settlement to Recent Times*, 181; Wilson, *Collected Works*, Vol. 3, 188 ("Certainly one of the greatest figures in our history is the figure of Alexander Hamilton").

134 "Free competition and monopoly": Letter from Theodore Roosevelt to William Jennings Bryan, Oct. 22, 1912, Theodore Roosevelt Center, Digital Library.

134 "I do not want a government": Address in Philadelphia on Oct. 28, 1912, in DiNunzio 359.

134 "He thought Roosevelt": Lippmann ch. 4.

134 "Wilson seemed": Lippmann ch. 4 (more advanced).

134 "sweep across our heartstrings": Woodrow Wilson, "First Inaugural Address," Mar. 4, 1913.

135 "If this sounds": Edmund Burke, "Speech on the Sixth Charge," Apr. 21, 1789, Trial of Warren Hastings, in *The Works and Correspondence of the Right Honourable Edmund Burke* (1852), 474 ("If ever there was a cause, in which justice and mercy are not only combined and reconciled...").

135 "Scott Berg calls": Berg 9 (experience), 248 (658 days).

135 "What we Americans": Herbert Croly, *The Promise of American Life* (1909), 5; *see also* Croly, *Progressive Democracy* (1914), in Eisenach, *The Social and Political Thought of American Progressivism* 124.

135 "safeguard": *See also* Roosevelt, *Autobiography* 607 (Lincoln's Republican party was "founded as the radical progressive party of the Nation"), 642–43 (more TR reflections on Lincoln).

135 "He had argued": Wilson, "The Making of the Nation," *Atlantic Monthly*, July 1897 (case for executive leadership); DiNunzio 166–82.

136 "nicely adjusted": *Congressional Government* 28 (supremacy); 141 (silent); 50, 76–78, 23 (preface to 15th printing, 1900).

136 "little more than chief clerks": Wilson, "Cabinet Government in the United States," VI *Int'l Review* (Aug. 1879), 146–63, in Pestritto 127–40.

136 "*compels* cooperation": This clause provides that the President "shall from time to time give to Congress information of the State of the Union and recommend to their Consideration such measures as he shall judge necessary and expedient." At the 1787 Constitutional Convention, "may" became "shall" to make it a presidential obligation. 2 Farrand 405.

136 "sort of President": Arthur S. Link, *Wilson: The New Freedom* (1956), 147.

136 "House Minority Leader": Berg 301 (schoolmaster); Woodrow Wilson, *Constitutional Government in the United States* (1908), 69 (force).

136 "Wilson called the notion": *Constitutional Government*, 179 (absurd); *see also* Link, *Woodrow Wilson and the Progressive Era*, 59 n.11.

137 "right to appeal": *The Independent*, Jan. 24, 1916 (republishing Wilson's letter on the subject).

137 "chief architect": Arthur S. Link, *Wilson: The Road to the White House, Vol. 1* (1947), 489.

137 "helping my mother": Urofsky 10.

137 "hard work of these people": Urofsky 5.

137 "Louis's uncle": Urofsky 18.

137 "He became": Urofsky 73–74 (millionaire), 53 (department store), 88 (liquor), 154 (problems).

137 "counsel to the situation": Urofsky 67–68.

137 "Wilson and Brandeis both": Urofsky 171; *see also* Wilson, "Princeton in the Nation's Service," address at Princeton's Sesquicentennial, Oct. 21, 1896.

137 "opposed the federal regulation of insurance": Urofsky 164.

137 "This meant faith in antitrust law": Link, *Woodrow Wilson and the Progressive Era* 20; Louis D. Brandeis, *Letters of Louis D. Brandeis, Volume II, 1907–1912: People's Attorney* (1972), ed. Melvin I. Urofsky and David W. Levy ("Suggestions for Letter of Governor Wilson on Trusts," Sept. 30, 1912), 688; Brandeis, "The Living Law," 10 *Illinois Law Review* 7 (Feb. 1916); Louis D. Brandeis, *Other People's Money and How the Bankers Use It* (1914).

138 "Massachusetts rail executives": Urofsky 183; Frank Dobbin and Timothy J. Dowd, "The Market That Antitrust Built: Public Policy, Private Coercion, and Railroad Acquisitions, 1825 to 1922," 65 *American Sociological Review* 5 (Oct. 2000).

138 "The notion of fixing prices": *See, e.g.*, Alfred D. Chandler, Jr., *Strategy and Structure: Chapters in the History of the American Industrial Enterprise* (1962) 19–41; David Syme, *Outlines of an Industrial Science* (1876), 56.

138 "Twenty states adopted": Link and McCormick 14–15.

138 "In 1912 Wilson condemned": *New Freedom* 80 (predatory pricing), 78 (refusal to deal); Clayton Antitrust Act of 1914, Pub. L. 63–212, Sec. 2 & 3, Oct. 15, 1914.

138 "But beyond this": McCraw 118–26; H.W. Brands, *Woodrow Wilson* (2003), 37.

138   "This was fitting": McCraw 116, 121.

138   "Wilson also signed": Link, *Woodrow Wilson and the Progressive Era* 38-39 & n.27 ($500,000 in 1913 dollars).

139   "We have in four years": Address at Sea Girt, New Jersey, Accepting the Democratic Nomination for President, Sept. 2, 1916.

139   "A smitten Wilson": Cooper, *Wilson* 285–86 (Lusitania), 298 (2-3 day).

139   "Wilson's passions": Cooper, *Wilson* 306.

139   "President George W. Bush": Dan Eggen, "Bush Says He's Not a Golfer In Wartime," *Washington Post*, May 14, 2008.

139   "His incredible feat": Matthew Larotonda, "Golfer in Chief? Obama Hits 100th Time on the Links," ABC News, Jun. 17, 2012.

139   "greatest conspiracy": Berg 644.

139   "Wilson had years of health issues": University of Arizona Health Sciences Library, "Woodrow Wilson—Strokes and Denial," Secret Illnesses of the Presidents Exhibit, http://ahsl.arizona.edu/about/exhibits/presidents/wilson.

139   "unstable, delusional creature": Cooper, *Wilson* 7.

139   "Dr. Grayson and Edith": Cooper, *Wilson* 536–37.

139   "The Constitution says": Art. II, Sec. 1, Cl. 6.

140   "gaunt and short-tempered": Berg 674.

140   "No cabinet meetings": Cooper, *Wilson* 562.

140   "In 1917": Act of Aug. 29, 1916, ch. 418, 39 Stat. 619, 645; Act of Mar. 21, 1918, ch. 25, 40 Stat. 451, 451; Proc. of Dec. 26, 1917, 40 Stat. 1733 (control); "Can't Pass Rail Bill Before the Recess; But Congress Leaders Expect Wilson to Delay Return of Roads," *New York Times*, Dec. 10, 1919; Wilson, Sixth Annual Message, Dec. 2, 1918; Berg 662–63; Maury Klein, *Union Pacific: Volume II, 1894–1969* 235; Douglas B. Craig, *Progressives at War: William G. McAdoo and Newton D. Baker, 1863–1941* (2013), 206.

140   "His Secretary of State": David Glaser, *Robert Lansing: A Study in Statecraft* (2015), ch. V.

140   "Arabic hieroglyphs": Nasaw, *Hearst* 261 (cartoon).

140   "summon his old creativity": Cooper, *Wilson* 549.

141   "invisible": Cooper, *Wilson* 24; Cooper, *Pivotal Decades* 185.

141   "genteel racism": Berg 578.

141   "Brandeis's 23 years": Urofsky 639.

141   "riding high": Link, *Woodrow Wilson and the Progressive Era* 64.

141   "put up screens": Berg 311.

141   "Atlanta's postmaster": Link, *Woodrow Wilson and the Progressive Era* 65.

141   "William Monroe Trotter": William G. Jordan, *Black Newspapers and America's War for Democracy, 1914–1920* (2001), 11; Berg 347.

141   "most regressive": Eric Yellin, *Racism in the Nation's Service: Government Workers and the Color Line in Woodrow Wilson's America* (2013), 132–74, and his submission to the Princeton Wilson Legacy Review Committee, Jan. 4, 2016, http://wilsonlegacy.princeton.edu/sites/wilsonlegacy/files/media/wilsonlegacy_yellin.pdf (protests).

142   "1913 prophecy": Lippmann, *A Preface to Morals* (1929), ch. 8.

142   "book-length attack": *See, e.g.*, Elihu Root, *Experiments in Government*, iv, 3; *Toward an American Conservatism: Constitutional Conservatism during the Progressive Era* (2013), ed. Joseph W. Postell and Johnathan O'Neill, 4–5, 21, 96, 99–102.

142 "There will be no withdrawal": Elihu Root, "Address to the American Bar Association," 41 Am. Bar. Assn. Rep. 355 (1916), 368–69.

143 "social organism": George Sutherland, "What Shall We Do With the Constitution?" *The Independent*, Oct. 3, 1912, 1003. *See also* William Howard Taft, "Wise and Unwise Extension of Federal Power," address at Johns Hopkins University, Feb. 22, 1917; Charles E. Hughes, "Some Aspects of the Development of American Law," address to N.Y. State Bar Assoc., Jan. 14, 1916.

143 "from banning child labor": John R. Vile, *Encyclopedia of Constitutional Amendments, Proposed Amendments, and Amending Issues, 1789–2010*, 3d. ed., 62 (amendment proposals before and after *Hammer v. Dagenhart* [1918]); Republican Party Platform of 1916, Jun. 7, 1916 (transportation).

143 "more easy and expeditious": *Congressional Government* 163; *see also* Joseph R. Long, "Tinkering with the Constitution," II *Constitutional Review* 1 (Jan. 1918).

143 "nonprofit golf courses": Cal. Const., Art. XIII, § 10.

144 "Well, that is the way": Wilson, address at the City Coliseum in Sioux Falls, South Dakota, Sept. 8, 1919.

CHAPTER SEVEN — IDA B. WELLS-BARNETT
Rights after Reconstruction to the Jazz Age

147 "Parable of the Cobblers": Plato, *The Republic* (2006), trans. R.E. Allen, 151–58 (451B–457B).

148 "no black American": Linda O. McMurry, *To Keep the Waters Troubled: The Life of Ida B. Wells* (1998), xiv.

148 "uncrowned queen": McMurry 233.

148 "better known": McMurry xiv.

148 "Ida's father Jim": Ida B. Wells, *Crusade for Justice: The Autobiography of Ida B. Wells* (1970), ed. Alfreda M. Duster, 8.

148 "The master's childless wife": *Crusade for Justice* 10.

148 "As a little girl": *Crusade for Justice* 9.

148 "After being": *Crusade for Justice* 16.

148 "she rode a mule": *Crusade for Justice* 17–18.

148 "she refused an order": *Crusade for Justice* 18–19.

149 "thought it was right": *Crusade for Justice* 37.

149 "remarkable and talented": McMurry 92.

149 "She wrote for": *Crusade for Justice* 33.

149 "She reaches the men": McMurry 98–100.

149 "There is scarcely": T. Thomas Fortune, "Ida B. Wells," in *Women of Distinction: Remarkable in Works and Invincible in Character* (1893), ed. Lawson Andrew Scruggs, 39.

149 "It was in the movement": Eleanor Flexner, *Century of Struggle: The Woman's Rights Movement in the United States* (1959; 1996 ed.), 38–40.

149 "decided to plot": Elizabeth Cady Stanton, *Eighty Years and More: Reminiscences, 1815–1897* (1898; 2002 ed.), 79–83.

150 "Oh, my daughter": Stanton 20.

150 "She was a rebel": Stanton 72.

150 "Yet she was also": Stanton, preface (housekeeper) and 262–63 (bread and coffee).

150 "Watching her father": Stanton 31.

150 "Her friend Ernestine Rose": *The Concise History of Woman Suffrage: Selections from History of Woman Suffrage* (2005), ed. Mari Jo Buhle and Paul Buhle, 108.

150 "brute who murdered": Stanton 226.

150 "Some women at Seneca Falls": *Concise History* 97.

150 "Stanton was a granddaughter": Stanton 321; ix (Revolutionary War).

150 "comic history": Carrie Chapman Catt and Nettie Rogers Schuler, *Woman Suffrage and Politics: The Inner Story of the Suffrage Movement* (1923; 1969 ed.), 27.

150 "Men actually paid": *Id.*

150 "Stanton was endlessly exasperated": Stanton 196–97.

150 "The many targets": Mia Bay, *To Tell the Truth Freely: The Life of Ida B. Wells* (2009), 72–73; 118–20.

151 "model woman": Ida B. Wells, *The Light of Truth: Writings of an Anti-Lynching Crusader* (2014), 25 (reproduction of "The Model Women," *New York Freeman*, Feb. 18, 1888).

151 "she was pelted": McMurry 214, 222.

151 "she was praised": McMurry 114.

151 "She was as determined": *See, e.g.*, "Our Women," *New York Freeman*, Jan. 1, 1887, in *Light of Truth* 20–21; "The Northern Negro Woman's Social and Moral Condition," in *Light of Truth* 432.

151 "I am an anomaly": McMurry 56.

151 "[W]hen I turn from the arena": Sen. George G. Vest, *Congressional Record*, 49th Cong., 2d Sess., Jan. 25, 1887, 986, in *Up From the Pedestal: Selected Writings in the History of American Feminism* (1968), Aileen S. Kraditor, ed., 194–96.

151 "This argument": *See, e.g.*, George Creel, *Rebel at Large: Recollections of Fifty Crowded Years* (1947), 145–46; Jodie T. Allen, Pew Research Center, Mar. 18, 2009, "Reluctant Suffragettes: When Women Questioned Their Right to Vote."

152 "Suffrage for black men": Stanton 242.

152 "An outraged Stanton": Stanton 256; *Concise History* 254–55.

152 "There is a great stir": *Concise History* 235.

152 "Frederick Douglass rebuked": *Concise History* 258.

153 "changed the whole course": *Crusade for Justice* 47.

153 "This commercial clash": *Crusade for Justice* 48–51.

153 "published searing exposures": Bay 99, 102–06.

153 "Men watched the trains": *Crusade for Justice* 62.

153 "The lynching of Thomas Moss": *Crusade for Justice* 64; McMurry 161.

153 "The near-universal excuse": *Crusade for Justice* 71.

153 "partiality of white Juliets": Bay 103.

153 "one typical frame-up": *Light of Truth* 75 (from *Southern Horrors: Lynch Law in All Its Phases* [1892]).

154 "In response to criticisms": Bay 99.

154 "She pioneered": *See, e.g.*, *Light of Truth* 57–82 (from *Southern Horrors*).

154 "We should be": McMurry 184 (Pinkertons and quote).

154 "What she found shocked": *Light of Truth* 424; *see also* 134 (Wells-Barnett's

*The Reason Why the Colored American Is Not In the World's Columbian
Exposition: The Afro-American's Contribution to Columbian Literature* [1893]).

154 *"The Arkansas Race Riot"*: Robert Whitaker, *On the Laps of Gods: The Red
Summer of 1919 and the Struggle for Justice That Remade a Nation* (2008),
327–29.

154 "At the end of the work": Ida B. Wells-Barnett, *The Arkansas Race Riot*
(1920), 32.

154 "first outsider to arrive": *Crusade* 401–02 (fact-gathering).

154 "Their case": *Moore v. Dempsey*, 261 U.S. 86, 90 (1923).

155 "The next year": *Light of Truth* 267.

155 "These jeers rarely": *Crusade for Justice* 70; McMurry 193; *Light of Truth* 451.

155 "Eventually she came": Stanton 155, 168.

155 "For decades Anthony": Stanton 169–71; Eleanor Clift, *Founding Sisters and
the Nineteenth Amendment* (2003), 67.

155 "Anti-suffrage women for years": Stanton 182; Flexner 81.

156 "For years Anthony watched": Clift 64–65. *See. e.g.*, Majority and Minority
Senate Reports of Jun. 5, 1882, in the 47th Cong., 1st Sess.

156 "Those were precious days": *Crusade for Justice* 229.

156 "Anthony's longtime stenographer": *Crusade for Justice* 229.

156 "Anthony even asked": *Crusade for Justice* 230.

156 "She claimed, plausibly": *Crusade for Justice* 244–45.

156 "chided Wells-Barnett": *Crusade for Justice* 255.

157 "firmly believed": *Crusade for Justice* xxiii.

157 "She was discovered": *Woman Suffrage and Politics* xiii–xiv.

157 "education and agitation": *Woman Suffrage and Politics* 338.

157 "To get the word male": *Woman Suffrage and Politics* 107–08.

158 "unable to give a coherent argument": Quoted in the "Report of a Part
of the Joint Special Committee on Woman Suffrage," made to the Rhode
Island General Assembly, Jan. 1879, 3.

158 "Catt's conclusion": *Woman Suffrage and Politics* viii.

158 "No party adopts": *Woman Suffrage and Politics* xix.

158 "readily made by Algerians": James Grant, *Mr. Speaker! The Life and Times of
Thomas B. Reed, the Man Who Broke the Filibuster* (2011), 181–85.

158 "[W]hen principle and prejudice": *Light of Truth* 451.

159 "Wyoming Territory": Flexner 152–53.

159 "But what really illustrated": *Woman Suffrage and Politics* 83–84.

159 "But in 1887": Flexner 155–56.

159 "pre-suffrage Kansas": *Woman Suffrage and Politics* 121–22.

159 "Only in 1917": Flexner 282, 290.

159 "By 1913": Clift 99.

159 "Yet there was": Clift 176–79.

160 "We have women's greatest right": *Woman Suffrage and Politics* 275; *see also*
Ella Seass Stewart, "Woman Suffrage and the Liquor Traffic," 56 *Annals of the
American Academy of Political and Social Science* (Nov. 1914), 143–52 (examples
of influence).

160 "The liquor opposition": *See, e.g.*, Flexner 292–94.

160 "two most hated elements": Suzanne Pullon Fitch and Roseann M.
Mandziuk, *Sojourner Truth as Orator: Wit, Story, and Song* (1997), 78.

161 "filled with explosive rage": *Woman Suffrage and Politics* 89.

161 "white Southern suffragists": Marjorie Spruill Wheeler, *New Women of the New South: The Leaders of the Woman Suffrage Movement in the Southern States* (1993), 13–20.

161 "We are not afraid": *Woman Suffrage and Politics* 89; Rosalyn Terborg-Penn, "African American Women and the Woman Suffrage Movement," in *One Woman, One Vote: Rediscovering the Woman Suffrage Movement* (1995), 149.

161 "Not one perhaps": *Woman Suffrage and Politics* 233.

161 "Black women had organized": Patricia A. Schechter, *Ida B. Wells-Barnett & American Reform, 1880–1930* (2001), 31, 214–18; McMurry 246.

161 "use their moral influence": McMurry 271.

161 "At one remarkable gathering": McMurry 248.

161 "Alpha Suffrage Club": *Crusade for Justice* 345–46; Wanda A. Hendricks, "Ida B. Wells-Barnett and the Alpha Suffrage Club of Chicago," in *One Woman, One Vote* 263–74.

162 "supported Charles Evan Hughes": McMurry 312.

162 "She recalled that": *Crusade for Justice* 375–76 & n.1.

162 "business card": *Crusade for Justice* xxix.

162 "Alpha Suffrage Club hosted": Schechter 199; McMurry 310.

162 "[T]he winding through": *Crusade for Justice* 360.

162 "She bought": McMurry 310.

162 "Her club even expelled": Schechter 202–03.

162 "far more dangerous": McMurry 318.

162 "It was in working": *Crusade for Justice* 345–46.

162 "The passages in her memoir": *Crusade for Justice* 346.

163 "could no longer sit": McMurry 295.

163 "while our men": Anna J. Cooper, *A Voice from the South* (1892), xxxix (fourth Ph.D.), 75 (logic).

163 "Charlotte E. Ray": Flexner 124.

163 "quietly asked": Rosalyn Terborg-Penn, "African American Women and the Woman Suffrage Movement," in *One Woman, One Vote* 150.

163 "A few years earlier": Bay 290.

163 "Mrs. Barnett's voice trembled": "Illinois Women Feature Parade," *Chicago Daily Tribune*, Mar. 4, 1913.

164 "The movement split": Clift 41; Flexner 146, 167

164 "It is the business": *Concise History* 329–30.

164 "free-spirited West": *See* Beverly Beeton, "How the West Was Won for Woman Suffrage," in *One Woman, One Vote* 99–115.

164 "campaign in Washington": *Concise History* 384–87.

164 "in Well-Barnett's Illinois": *Concise History* 393–94.

164 "In later campaigns": Clift 159.

164 "Mrs. Treadwell": *Concise History* 397–98.

165 "Mrs. Trout": *Concise History* 399.

165 "loud and costly campaign": *Concise History* 401–04; *Woman Suffrage and Politics* 289, 292.

165 "That time they won": *Concise History* 405.

165 "Particularly discouraging": *Concise History* 410–12 (Ohio); Flexner 252 (Michigan); 249 (vaults); *Woman Suffrage and Politics* 185 (Michigan fraud), 205–06 (Ohio fraud).

165 "In Massachusetts": *Historical Journal of Western Massachusetts* (1975), Vol. 7–11, 4.

165 "many Southern suffragists watched": Wheeler 172–86.

166 "I would rather die": *Woman Suffrage and Politics* 471.

166 "Western Governors": *See, e.g., Woman Suffrage and Politics* 376.

166 "women in Carson City": *Woman Suffrage* 379.

166 "World War I had begun": *Woman Suffrage* 357.

166 "Most sordid of all": *Woman Suffrage* 446.

166 "In a last act of desperation": "Vote in Tennessee to Clinch Suffrage Despite Big Bolt," *New York Times*, Aug. 22, 1920.

166 "He left her deathbed": Flexner 283.

166 "That October": Flexner 304.

167 "Dear Son": Carol Lynn Yellin and Janann Sherman, *The Perfect 36: Tennessee Delivers Woman Suffrage* (1998), 104.

167 "My mother": *Perfect 36* 117.

167 "legal challenge": *Leser v. Garnett*, 258 U.S. 130, 136 (1922).

167 "Women began voting": George Gallup, American Institute of Public Opinion, "Analysis of '56 Vote by Groups," Jan. 20, 1957 (quoted in Flexner 318); Nona B. Brown, "Women's Vote: The Bigger Half?" *New York Times Magazine*, Oct. 21, 1956.

167 "Since 1966": Center for American Women and Politics, Eagleton Institute of Politics, Rutgers University, "Gender Differences in Voter Turnout" (2017), White Paper ("Figure 2" and "Voter Turnout in Non-Presidential Elections").

168 "She broke with": Schechter 216.

168 "Third Ward Women's Political Club": Schechter 216–17.

168 "never aggressive": Schechter 232.

168 "daughters of sorrow": W.E.B. Du Bois, *Writings* (Library of America ed. 1987), 953.

168 "mules of the world": Zora Neale Hurston, *Their Eyes Were Watching God* (1937; Library of America ed. 1995), 186.

168 "She gave lectures": Schechter 233.

168 "She groomed": Schechter 239.

168 "traversed Illinois": Schechter 239; McMurry 335.

168 "Few women responded": Schechter 244; *see also* Bay 230–31.

168 "47 long years": Illinois Senate Republican Caucus, "Honoring Illinois' female trailblazers," Mar. 8, 2017, online.

168 "An uncompromising militancy": McMurry 308; Schechter 250.

169 "place of honor": *Light of Truth* 80 (from *Southern Horrors*).

169 "Chicago police shootings": McMurry 333–34.

169 "awakening of the conscience": McMurry 338 (quoting W.E.B. Du Bois, "Postscript," *Crisis*, Jun. 1931, 207).

CHAPTER EIGHT — ROBERT H. JACKSON
New Deals and World Wars

173 "typically American farm life": Eugene C. Gerhart, *America's Advocate: Robert H. Jackson* (1958), 30.

173 "no formal education": Gerhart 34.

173 "He was a prototypical": Noah Feldman, *Scorpions: The Battles and Triumphs of FDR's Great Supreme Court Justices* (2010), 45, 47; Charles S. Desmond, Paul A. Freund, Potter Stewart, and Lord Shawcross, *Mr. Justice Jackson: Four Lectures in His Honor* (1969), 21.

173 "He had an engaging demeanor": Feldman 40, 48–49; Gerhart 59; Robert H. Jackson, *That Man: An Insider's Portrait of Franklin D. Roosevelt* (2003), ed. John Q. Barrett, 6.

174 "In the 1920s": Nathan Miller, *New World Coming: The 1920s and the Making of Modern America* (2003), 151–52, 369; Frederick Lewis Allen, *Only Yesterday: An Informal History of the 1920s* (1931), 155–56 (business books).

174 "My own feeling": *That Man* ix.

174 "winning 38 of 44 cases": Feldman 129.

174 "In three catastrophic years": David M. Kennedy, *Freedom from Fear: The American People in Depression and War, 1929–1945* (1999), 132 (banks), 160 (pipe), 208 (babies); Paul Farhi, "The crash Oct. 29, 1929," *Washington Post*, Oct. 29, 2008 (zoo); Kenneth Whyte, *Hoover: An Extraordinary Life in Extraordinary Times* (2017), 480–82, 501–02.

174 "Herbert Hoover's mistake": *Only Yesterday* 302.

174 "broad Executive power": Franklin D. Roosevelt, "Inaugural Address," Mar. 4, 1933.

174 "Robert Jackson cheered": *That Man* 66–67.

174 "keen political judgments": Gerhart 128; *That Man* 74.

174 "first graced the national stage": *See* Stephen R. Alton, *Loyal Lieutenant, Able Advocate: The Role of Robert H. Jackson in Franklin D. Roosevelt's Battle with the Supreme Court*, 5 *Wm. & Mary Bill Rts. J.* 527 (1997).

174 "bad attack": *That Man* 53.

175 "blow after blow": Robert H. Jackson, *The Struggle for Judicial Supremacy: A Study of a Crisis in American Power Politics* (1941), 124.

175 "Seven major laws": *Struggle* 181.

175 "Burton Wheeler": *Struggle* 352.

175 "I do not want": William E. Leuchtenburg, *The Supreme Court Reborn: The Constitutional Revolution in the Age of Roosevelt* (1996), 109.

175 "he spoke boringly": Franklin D. Roosevelt, "Message to Congress on the Reorganization of the Judicial Branch of the Government," Feb. 5, 1937.

175 "dilute the Constitution": Daniel Webster, *Great Speeches and Orations* (1879), 318.

175 "overwhelm the opposition": Woodrow Wilson, "Government Under the Constitution" (1893), in *Wilson's Selected Works*, Vol. 3, 129.

175 "I was up in Jamestown": Gerhart 105, 107.

175 "Jackson made headlines": Robert H. Jackson, "Address Before the New York State Bar Association," Dec. 29, 1937, 60 N.Y.S.B.A. Rep. 292 (1937) (Jan. 29, 1937), 297–99; "New Dealer Warns the Supreme Court," *New York Times*, Jan. 30, 1937.

176 "The difficulty with the Court": Gerhart 114; *see also* Robert H. Jackson, "A Square Deal for the Court," Address at Boston College Law School, Boston, Mass., Apr. 9, 1940, broadcast on Columbia Broadcasting System.

176 "[s]truggles over power": *Struggle* ix.

176 "Jackson thought more radical": *Struggle* 179–80.

176 "means to make himself": Joseph P. Lash, *Dealers and Dreamers: A New Look at the New Deal* (1988), 298.

176 "frightened many liberals": Joseph Alsop and Turner Catledge, *The 168 Days* (1938), 76.

176 "contrary to the spirit": Senate Jud. Comm., "Reorganization of the Federal Judiciary," S. Rep. No. 711, 75th Cong., 1st Sess. 11 (1937), 9.

176 "astonishing flip-flop": *W. Coast Hotel Co. v. Parrish*, 300 U.S. 379 (1937), cf. *Morehead v. New York ex rel. Tipaldo*, 298 U.S. 587 (1936).

176 "owed much to the pressure": William G. Ross, *The Chief Justiceship of Charles Evans Hughes, 1930–1941* (2007), 125–27; Alsop and Catledge 140–42.

176 "From there on": *See, e.g., Mulford v. Smith*, 307 U.S. 38 (1939); *H.P. Hood & Sons v. United States*, 307 U.S. 588 (1939); *United States v. Bekins*, 304 U.S. 27 (1938); *Graves v. New York ex rel. O'Keefe*, 306 U.S. 466 (1939); *Alabama Power Co. v Ickes*, 309 U.S. 464 (1938); *Electric Bond & Share Co. v. SEC*, 303 U.S. 419 (1938); *Coleman v. Miller*, 307 U.S. 433 (1939); *United States v. Morgan*, 307 U.S. 183 (1939).

176 "Almost 40 years": *Nat'l League of Cities v. Usery*, 426 U.S. 833, 835 (1976), overruled by *Garcia v. San Antonio Metro. Transit Auth.*, 469 U.S. 528 (1985).

176 "The President's enemies": *Struggle* v; *see also That Man* 53.

176 "Jackson emphasized": *Struggle* 235.

177 "constitutional Renaissance": Jackson, "Back to the Constitution," address before the Public Utility Section of the American Bar Association, San Francisco, Jul. 10, 1939.

177 "I have no inclination": Franklin D. Roosevelt, "Letter on the Reorganization Bill," Mar. 29, 1938.

177 "Jackson was suspicious": Jackson, "Democracy Under Fire," 9 Law Soc'y J. 301, 303 (1940), address before Law Society of Massachusetts, Boston, Oct. 16, 1940.

177 "first American to win": Sinclair Lewis, *It Can't Happen Here* (1935; Signet ed. 2014), 385.

177 "Lewis imagined": Lewis 41 (League); 85 (FDR); 133 (Liberia).

177 "Windrip first demands": Lewis 64.

177 "Legislators who balk": Lewis 135.

177 "Before long": Lewis 353 (plantation), 216 (camps), 220 (burnings), 357 (Golden Age).

178 "Lewis was onto something": Lewis 143 (fascists, Twain), 293 (church etc.).

178 "That couldn't happen here": Lewis 17.

178 "That would be Huey Pierce Long": T. Harry Williams, *Huey Long* (1969) 3, 5.

178 "In his own autobiography": Huey P. Long, *Every Man a King: The Autobiography of Huey P. Long* (1933; Da Capo ed. 1996), 3–4.

178 "As a lawyer": Williams 105 (Taft); 429, 694 (buffoon).

178 "Long's techniques": Williams 296 (relatives), 545 (banks).

178 "But what makes Long": Kennedy 234–44.

178 "He eschewed": Williams 16, 209, 327–28, 703, 705 (Klan and race); 413 (demagogue); 262, 857 (pledges); *Every Man a King* xvii-iii; *Harper v. Virginia Board of Elections*, 383 U.S. 663 (1966); Harnett T. Kane, *Huey Long's*

Louisiana Hayride: The American Rehearsal for Dictatorship, 1928–1940 (1941), 9.

179 "Long's plan": Williams 709, 589; Benjamin Stolberg, "Dr. Huey and Mr. Long," *The Nation*, Sept. 25, 1935; *see also Every Man a King* 3–4.

179 "Share Our Wealth": Williams 692–97; Kennedy 238.

179 "When Long began undermining": Williams 793–98.

179 "briefed on the case": Frank John Wilson and Beth Day, *Special Agent: A Quarter Century with the Treasury Department and the Secret Service* (1965), 89.

179 "FDR told associates": Kennedy 276; Williams 812, 836–37; Franklin D. Roosevelt, "Message to Congress on Tax Revision," Jun. 19, 1935 (stealing thunder); Franklin D. Roosevelt, "Message to Congress on Tax Revision," Jun. 19, 1935 (duty to restrict); Amity Shlaes, *The Forgotten Man: A New History of the Great Depression* (2007), 341.

179 "Jackson got to Washington": Gerhart 66.

179 "On a radio program": Debate on "America's Town Meeting of the Air: Is Our Constitutional Government in Danger?" The Town Hall, New York, NBC Radio, Nov. 6, 1939.

179 "Saturday evening": *That Man* 76–77.

179 "Jackson thought": *That Man* 32, 37–39, 42, 45 (experiment).

179 "probably apocryphal quip": Charles F. Downs II, *Calvin Coolidge, Dwight Morrow, and the Air Commerce Act of 1926* (Jun. 26, 2001), Calvin Coolidge Presidential Foundation, online essay.

179 "able to organize": Jackson, "The Undeveloped Strength of American Democracy," address at the Institute of Public Affairs, Charlottesville, VA, Jun. 14, 1940.

180 "Henry Ford": Miller 183 (Ford in 1920); Kennedy 654 (Willow Run).

180 "Jackson's responsibility": *See, e.g.*, Jackson, "A Program for Internal Defense of the United States," 63 N.Y.S.B.A. Rep. 679 (1940) (address before New York State Bar Association, Saranac, NY, Jun. 29, 1940); "Mobilizing the Profession for Defense," 27 A.B.A.J. 350 (1941) (address before American Judicature Society, Washington, D.C., May 7, 1941).

180 "man who today will rifle": *That Man* 72–73.

180 "Private employers asked": Robert H. Jackson, "Address before Federal-State Conference on Law Enforcement Problems of National Defense," Great Hall, Department of Justice, Washington, D.C., Aug. 5, 1940.

180 "What worries me": Franklin D. Roosevelt, *My Own Story: From Private and Public Papers* (2011), ed. Donald Day, 321.

180 "whole world": Richard Langworth, *Churchill by Himself: The Definitive Collection of Quotations* (2008), 5.

181 "trouble must be": *That Man* 90.

181 "Jackson wrote an opinion": Robert H. Jackson, *Acquisition of Naval & Air Bases in Exch. for Over-Age Destroyers*, 39 U.S. Op. Atty. Gen. 484, 486 (1940).

181 "most disputed part": *Id.* at 494.

181 "endorsement of unrestrained autocracy": Edward S. Corwin, "Executive Authority Held Exceeded in Destroyer Deal," *New York Times*, Oct. 13, 1940, 6–7.

181 "strike at an aircraft factory": Kennedy 638–39.
181 "There can be no doubt": Louis Stark, "Roosevelt Explains Seizure; Jackson Cites Insurrection," *New York Times*, Jun. 10, 1941, 1, 16.
181 "A strict observance": "Thomas Jefferson to John B. Colvin, 20 September 1810," *TJ Papers*, Retirement Series, Vol. 3, *12 August 1810 to 17 June 1811*, 99–102.
182 "[M]y oath to preserve": Abraham Lincoln, "Letter to Albert G. Hodges," Apr. 4, 1864.
182 "Yet Jefferson thought": "From Thomas Jefferson to Thomas Paine, 10 August 1803," *TJ Papers*, Vol. 41, *11 July–15 November 1803*, 175–77; "From Thomas Jefferson to John Breckinridge, 12 August 1803," *TJ Papers*, Vol. 41, *11 July–15 November 1803*, 184–86; "From Abraham Lincoln to Erastus Corning and Others," Jun. 12, 1863 (on arrest of Clement Vallandigham); Abraham Lincoln, "Special Session Message," Jul. 4, 1861.
182 "beyond the Constitution": *That Man* 47–48.
182 "Alexander Hamilton's view": "The Federalist No. 23, [18 December 1787]," *AH Papers*, Vol. 4, *January 1787–May 1788*, 412–16.
183 "two gravest possible crises": Art. I, Sec. 8, Cl. 15 ("repel invasions") ("suppress insurrections"); Art. I, Sec. 9, Cl. 2 ("the privilege of the writ of habeas corpus shall not be suspended, unless when in cases of rebellion or invasion the public safety may require it"); Art. IV, Sec. 4 ("shall protect each of them against invasion") ("against domestic violence").
183 "The American people": Franklin D. Roosevelt, "Fireside Chat," Sept. 7, 1942.
183 "The Constitution subordinates": Eric Larrabee, *Commander in Chief: Franklin Delano Roosevelt, His Lieutenants, and Their War* (1987), 15; *That Man* 81.
183 "Americans could take comfort": *That Man* 3.
183 "every time I come to bat": Franklin D. Roosevelt, "Second Fireside Chat," May 7, 1933.
183 "Congress, even in war": Franklin D. Roosevelt, "State of the Union Address," Jan. 6, 1945; Clinton Rossiter, *Constitutional Dictatorship: Crisis Government in the Modern Democracies* (1948; 2002 ed.), 271; FDR's press conference of May 23, 1940 at http://www.fdrlibrary.marist.edu/_resources/images/pc/pc0098.pdf at 22.
183 "work as effectively on spite": Jackson, "Founders Day Address," University of North Carolina, Oct. 12, 1937.
183 "frustration and dissatisfaction": *That Man* 106–07.
183 "summarily deported": *Ludecke v. Watkins*, 335 U.S. 160, 170 (1948); *see also Harisiades v. Shaughnessy*, 342 U.S. 580, 591 (1952) (Jackson, J.); *Chicago & S. Air Lines v. Waterman S. S. Corp.*, 333 U.S. 103, 111 (1948).
183 "postwar rent control": *Woods v. Cloyd W. Miller Co.*, 333 U.S. 138, 146–47 (1948) (Jackson, J., concurring). *See also Shaughnessy v. United States ex rel. Mezei*, 345 U.S. 206, 228 (1953) (Jackson, J., dissenting).
184 "jeopardize": Harry S. Truman, "Executive Order 10340—Directing the Secretary of Commerce to Take Possession of and Operate the Plants and Facilities of Certain Steel Companies," Apr. 8, 1952.
184 "86 steel plants": Maeva Marcus, *Truman and the Steel Seizure Case: The Limits of President Power* (1994), 84.

184 "seizure technique": *Youngstown Sheet & Tube Co. v. Sawyer*, 343 U.S. 579, 586 (1952).

184 "for the Nation's lawmakers": *Id.* at 587–88.

184 "ammunition upon which": *Id.* at 679 (Vinson, C.J., dissenting).

184 "[A]nyone who has served": *Id.* at 634 (adviser), 641 (begins or ends).

185 "one of three categories": *Id.* at 635–38.

185 "lawful economic struggle": *Id.* at 645.

185 "instruction": *Id.* at 641.

185 "His successor": *Id.* at 648–49 (Jackson, J., concurring).

185 "laid at my door": H.L. Pohlman, *Constitutional Debate in Action: Governmental Powers* (2004; 2nd ed. 2005), 214–16.

185 "But he wrote": *Youngstown*, 343 U.S. at 648-49 & n.17 (Jackson, J., concurring).

185 "high-handed": David McCullough, *Truman* (1992), 896–902, 990; Marcus 75–82, 225–26, 251, 256 (no genuine crisis).

185 "I am not alarmed": *Youngstown*, 343 U.S. at 653 (Jackson, J., concurring).

185 "Court simply disbelieved": *See* Kermit L. Hall and John J. Patrick, *The Pursuit of Justice: Supreme Court Decisions that Shaped America* (2006), 118–19; Charles C. Hileman, et al., "Supreme Court Law Clerks' Recollections of October Term 1951, Including the Steel Seizure Cases," 82 *St. John's Law Review* 4 (2008), 1264–89; Marcus 102–03; *Youngstown Sheet v. Sawyer*, 1952 WL 82173, *16 (Brief for Plaintiff Companies).

186 "The Court's rigid opinion": *See, e.g., Youngstown*, 343 U.S. at 588, 589.

186 "Hearings in 2003": National Commission on Terrorist Attacks upon the United States, Public Hearing, May 23, 2003, Testimony of Transportation Secretary Norman Mineta and Major General Larry Arnold; National Commission on Terrorist Attacks upon the United States, *The 9/11 Commission Report* (2004) at 17, 20, 37, 40–41.

186 "America's sense of security": Jackson, "Wartime Security and Liberty Under Law," 104.

186 "Roosevelt forbid aliens": Franklin D. Roosevelt Presidential Proclamation No. 2525 (Japanese), No. 2526 (Germans), No. 2527 (Italians), Dec. 7-8, 1941.

186 "military areas": Franklin D. Roosevelt, "Executive Order 9066 — Authorizing the Secretary of War To Prescribe Military Areas," Feb. 19, 1942.

186 "entire Pacific coast": Lt. Gen. J.L. DeWitt to the Chief of Staff, U.S. Army, Jun. 5, 1943, in U.S. Army, Western Defense Command and Fourth Army, Final Report; Japanese Evacuation from the West Coast 1942 (1943), vii–x.

186 "Western states": *See, e.g., Oyama v. California*, 332 U.S. 633, 684 (1948) (Jackson, J., dissenting); *Takahashi v. Fish & Game Comm'n*, 334 U.S. 410, 428 (1948) (Reed, J., dissenting, joined by Jackson); Maisie and Richard Conrat, *Executive Order 9066: The Internment of 110,000 Japanese Americans* (Cal. Hist. Society ed. 1972), 15–23.

186 "radio show in 1939": Debate on "America's Town Meeting of the Air: Is Our Constitutional Government in Danger?" The Town Hall, New York, NBC Radio, Nov. 6, 1939.

186 "Western governors": William H. Rehnquist, *All the Laws but One: Civil Liberties in Wartime* (1998), 188; *The Oxford Companion to World War II* (2005), ed. I.C.B. Dear, 498 (lobbying); *Personal Justice Denied: Report of U.S. Comm'n on Wartime Relocation and Internment of Civilians* (1992), 102;

Wendy Ng, *Japanese American Internment During World War II: A History and Reference Guide* (2001), 21–22.

187 "The leading state agitator": G. Edward White, *The Unacknowledged Lesson: Earl Warren and the Japanese Relocation Controversy*, 55 Va. Q. Rev. 4 (Autumn 1979).

187 "Espionage by persons": *Hirabayashi v. United States*, 320 U.S. 81, 96 (1943).

187 "not wholly beyond": *Hirabayashi*, 320 U.S. at 101.

187 "Fred Korematsu": Fred T. Korematsu Institute, "Fred T. Korematsu," http://www.korematsuinstitute.org/fred-t-korematsu-lifetime/.

187 "upheld the human impoundment": *Korematsu v. United States*, 323 U.S. 214, 216 (1944).

187 "Some 5,000": *Id.* at 219.

187 "belongs to a race": *Id.* at 243 (Jackson, J., dissenting).

187 "The two other dissenters": *Id.* at 226 (Roberts, J., dissenting); *id.* at 240 (Murphy, J., dissenting) (mistreatment); *id.* at 227 (Roberts, J., dissenting); *id.* at 241 (Murphy, J., dissenting) (skepticism).

187 "Jackson actually refused": *Id.* at 206–07 (Jackson, J., dissenting).

188 "Much is said": *Id.* at 245–46 (Jackson, J., dissenting).

188 "moral judgments of history": *Id.* at 248 (Jackson, J., dissenting).

188 "A 1988 law": John Tateishi, *And Justice for All: An Oral History of the Japanese American Detention Camps* (1984), vii; "Civil Liberties Act of 1988," *Densho Encyclopedia* (2017).

188 "Norman Mineta": Matthew L. Wald, "Norman Yoshio Mineta; A Clinton Holdover, a Reagan Veteran and a Departing Senator," *New York Times*, Jan. 3, 2001.

189 "supremely interesting": Gerhart 441.

189 "Before he arrived": *Report of Robert H. Jackson, U.S. Representative to the International Conference on Military Trials in London 1945* (1947), Letter of Transmittal.

189 "But a trial": Robert H. Jackson, "Liberty Under Law," 77 N.Y.S.B.A. Rep. 207 (1954) (address before the New York State Bar Association, New York, Jan. 30, 1954).

189 "50,000 German officers": George Ginsburgs, *Moscow's Road to Nuremberg: The Soviet Background to the Trial* (1996), 50–51.

189 "struggled in Nuremberg": Gerhart 438.

189 "If it is not a crime": Robert H. Jackson, "A Country Lawyer at an International Court," 58 Va. St. Bar Assn. Proc. 21 (1947) (address before the Virginia State Bar Association, Roanoake, VA, Aug. 8, 1947), 197; Robert H. Jackson, "Nuremberg in Retrospect: Legal Answer to International Lawlessness," 35 A.B.A.J. 813 (1949) (address before the Canadian Bar Association, Banff, Alberta., Sept. 1, 1949).

189 "His even temper": *Four Lectures* 91, 121, 125.

189 "The most difficult co-prosecutors": Jackson, "A Country Lawyer at an International Court," 196.

189 "At night": Gerhart 352.

189 "He worked": Robert H. Jackson, *The Nuremberg Case* (1947; Cooper Square ed. 1971), xviii; Gerhart 427–28.

190 "I have ever tried": Robert H. Jackson, *The Case Against the Nazi War Criminals* xiii.

190 "rank with the great state papers": Gerhart 427.
190 "The wrongs": *The Nuremberg Case* 30–31.
190 "He traced the Nazi Party": *The Nuremberg Case* 38–42.
190 "He conducted": *The Nuremberg Case* 44–46.
190 "criminal beyond anything": Report of Robert H. Jackson, *U.S. Rep. to the Int'l Conf. on Military Trials in London 1945* (1947), 241.
190 "The prosecutors showed": Robert E. Conot, *Justice at Nuremberg* (1983) 287–89; Gerhart 371, 511 n.46.
190 "The judges learned": *The Nuremberg Case* 128 and 167 n.33 (newborns); 169 n.45 (father and son).
190 "One night": Gerhart 376, citing *Trial of the Major War Criminals Before the International Military Tribunal*, Vol. 6, 216.
190 "If you were to say": *The Nuremberg Case* 163.
190 "His old friends": *Four Lectures* 24–25.
191 "preserving our freedom": Robert H. Jackson, address on Accepting Cardozo Award, Mayflower Hotel, Washington, D.C., Feb. 22, 1941.
191 "Nuremberg": *Beauharnais v. People of State of Ill.*, 343 U.S. 250, 304 (1952) (Jackson, J., dissenting); *Dennis v. United States*, 341 U.S. 494, 570 (1951) (Jackson, J., concurring); Jackson, "A Country Lawyer at an International Court," 200 (post-mortem, quoting Judge Parker); Jeffrey D. Hockett, *New Deal Justice: The Constitutional Jurisprudence of Hugo L. Black, Felix Frankfurter, and Robert H. Jackson* (1996), 267–81.
191 "times of fear or hysteria": Robert H. Jackson, "The Federal Prosecutor," 24 J. Am. Jud. Soc'y 18 (1940) (address at Conference of United States Attorneys, Apr. 1, 1940).
191 "no official": *W. Virginia State Bd. of Educ. v. Barnette*, 319 U.S. 624, 642 (1943); *Thomas v. Collins*, 323 U.S. 516, 545 (1945) (Jackson, J., concurring). In the search and seizure context, *see United States v. Ballard*, 322 U.S. 78, 95 (1944) (Jackson, J., dissenting); *Brinegar v. United States*, 338 U.S. 160, 180 (1949) (Jackson, J., dissenting); *Johnson v. United States*, 333 U.S. 10, 17 (1948) (Jackson, J.).
191 "his eventual nemeses": *Korematsu*, 323 U.S. at 216; *Minersville Sch. Dist. v. Gobitis*, 310 U.S. 586, 600 (1940).
191 "endanger the great right": *Saia v. People of State of N.Y.*, 334 U.S. 558, 566 (1948) (Jackson, J., dissenting); *Kovacs v. Cooper*, 336 U.S. 77, 97 (1949) (Jackson, J., concurring) ("Freedom of speech for Kovacs does not, in my view, include freedom to use sound amplifiers to drown out the natural speech of others").
191 "But what concerned Jackson": *Terminiello v. City of Chicago*, 337 U.S. 1, 35 1 (1949) (Jackson, J., dissenting).
192 "promote diversity": *Id.* at 4.
192 "with fidelity": *Id.* 22 (Jackson, J., dissenting).
192 "federal labor law": *Am. Commc'ns Ass'n, C.I.O., v. Douds*, 339 U.S. 382 (1950).
192 "This Communist movement": *Id.* at 425 (Jackson, J., concurring and dissenting in part).
192 "controlled by a foreign government": *Id.* at 427, 428, 430; *see also That Man* 73.

192   "in the name of security": *Id.* at 445 (Jackson, J., concurring and dissenting in part); *see also Hartzel v. United States*, 322 U.S. 680, 683 (1944).

192   "Jackson had come": *That Man* 36; Gerhart 151; *see also Four Lectures* 10.

192   "Senator Bridges": Gerhart 202.

193   "hate-stirring attacks": *Kunz v. People of State of N.Y.*, 340 U.S. 290, 295 (1951) (Jackson, J., dissenting).

193   "a G-string": *City of Erie v. Pap's A.M.*, 529 U.S. 277, 289 (2000); *see also Miller v. Civil City of S. Bend*, 904 F.2d 1081 (7th Cir. 1990), *rev'd sub nom. Barnes v. Glen Theatre, Inc.*, 501 U.S. 560 (1991).

193   "homeless in public libraries": *Lu v. Hulme*, 133 F. Supp. 3d 312, 329 (D. Mass. 2015); *Armstrong v. D.C. Pub. Library*, 154 F. Supp. 2d 67, 69 (D. D.C. 2001); *Kreimer v. Bureau of Police for Town of Morristown*, 958 F.2d 1242, 1264–65 (3d Cir. 1992).

193   "flash one's headlights": Scott Bomboy, "Constitutional right to flash your head lights gains momentum," National Constitution Center, blog post, Apr. 16, 2014; *Elli v. City of Ellisville*, No. 4:13-cv-00711-HEA (E.D. Mo. Feb. 3, 2014); Rene Stutzman, "Sanford judge rules in favor of motorist who flashed his headlights," *Orlando Sentinel*, May 22, 2012.

193   "ever jostling": *Prince v. Massachusetts*, 321 U.S. 158, 177 (1944) (Jackson, J., dissenting).

193   "so-called civil rights": Robert H. Jackson, *The Supreme Court in the American System of Government* (1957), 77.

193   "Clashes over the scope": *The Supreme Court in the American System of Government* 79; *Struggle for Judicial Supremacy* 321–22; *Ry. Exp. Agency v. People of State of N.Y.*, 336 U.S. 106, 112 (1949) (Jackson, J., concurring).

193   "Consider a masterpiece": *Douglas v. City of Jeannette, Pennsylvania*, 319 U.S. 157, 167–68, 172–73 (1943) (Jackson, J., dissenting).

193   "authors of the First Amendment": *Martin v. City of Struthers, Ohio*, 319 U.S. 141, 143 (1943).

194   "I doubt if only": *City of Jeannette*, 319 U.S. at 181 (Jackson, J., dissenting).

194   "Got a minute": James M. Marsh, *The Genial Justice: Robert H. Jackson*, 68 Alb. L. Rev. 41 (2004); *see also* Alma Soller McLay, *That Twinkle in His Eyes*, 68 Alb. L. Rev. 51 (2004).

194   "The case seemed to recall": *Four Lectures* 23 ("always in Jackson there was a lot of Frewsburg"), 31 (Frankfurter said Jackson used "Jamestown jurisprudence"); William H. Rehnquist, *Robert H. Jackson: A Perspective Twenty-Five Years Later*, 44 Alb. L. Rev. 534, 535 (Apr. 1980).

194   "ample shelter": *City of Jeannette*, 319 U.S. at 174 (Jackson, J., dissenting).

194   "By their decision": *Id.* at 157, 177–82 (Jackson, J., dissenting); *Com. of Mass. v. United States*, 333 U.S. 611, 639 (1948) (Jackson, J., dissenting).

194   "When it came to our institutions": Jackson, "Founders Day Address," University of North Carolina, Chapel Hill, N.C., Oct. 12, 1937.

CHAPTER NINE — ANTONIN SCALIA
The Dead Democracy

197   "Mike Papantonio": Jack Coleman, "Liberal Radio Host Mike Papantonio Smears Scalia Elder as Fascist Leader," *Newsbusters.org*, Mar. 4. 2013.

197   "No record exists": Joan Biskupic, *American Original: The Life and Constitution of Supreme Court Justice Antonin Scalia* (2009), 13.

197 "evidence of fascism": Biskupic 14.

197 "domestic dictator": Biskupic 41.

197 "lesser epithets": Bruce Allen Murphy, *Scalia: A Court of One* (2014), 323.

198 "It's fun": Al Kamen, "Justice Scalia fires back at Judge Posner," *Washington Post*, Aug. 2, 2012; Murphy 27 (champion debater).

198 "perverse": *Washington Post Co. v. U.S. Dep't of State*, 685 F.2d 698, 707–08 (D.C. Cir. 1982) (Scalia, J., dissenting from rehearing en banc); Murphy 99–100.

198 "utterly impossible nonsense": *Montgomery v. Louisiana*, 136 S. Ct. 718, 744 (2016), *as revised* (Jan. 27, 2016) (Scalia, J., dissenting).

198 "most gullible mind": *Grutter v. Bollinger*, 539 U.S. 306, 347 (2003) (Scalia, J., concurring in part, dissenting in part).

198 "cause more Americans": *Boumediene v. Bush*, 553 U.S. 723, 828 (2008).

198 "Scalia preferred mixing it up": *See, e.g.*, Stuart Taylor, Jr., "Conservatives Assert Legal Presence," *New York Times*, Feb. 1, 1987 ("It was unusual for any Justice to descend from the Olympian detachment of the Supreme Court to engage in such legal give and take, and Justice Scalia enlivened the session with a bit of self-mockery").

198 "Lanier Theological Library": Cindy George, "At Houston lecture, Scalia explores Christian virtues and economic systems," *Houston Chronicle*, Sept. 6, 2013.

198 "textual interpretation": Cardozo Law School, "Justice Antonin Scalia and Professor Stanley Fish Debate Issues of Interpretation," Press Release, Oct. 16, 2013.

198 "On other occasions": Biskupic 304 (travels); Bill Mears, "Supreme Court justices: They do OK financially," *CNN*, Jun. 20, 2014; Murphy 16, 367, 370.

198 "more recusal motions": Murphy 305.

199 "exclude God": Linda Greenhouse, "Supreme Court to Consider Case On 'Under God' in Pledge to Flag," *New York Times*, Oct. 15, 2003.

199 "days of depression": Clarence Thomas, *My Grandfather's Son: A Memoir* (2007), 134.

199 "almost Czarist arrogance": *Planned Parenthood of Se. Pennsylvania v. Casey*, 505 U.S. 833, 999 (1992) (Scalia, J., dissenting).

199 "In area after area": *See, e.g., Am. Trucking Associations, Inc. v. Smith*, 496 U.S. 167, 201 (1990) (Scalia, J., concurring); *James B. Beam Distilling Co. v. Georgia*, 501 U.S. 529, 549 (1991) (Scalia, J., concurring); *Legal Servs. Corp. v. Velazquez*, 531 U.S. 533, 562 (2001); *Stop the Beach Renourishment, Inc. v. Florida Dep't of Envtl. Prot.*, 560 U.S. 702, 724–25 (2010); *Roper v. Simmons*, 543 U.S. 551, 608 (2005) (Scalia, J., dissenting); *Zuni Pub. Sch. Dist. No. 89 v. Dep't of Educ.*, 550 U.S. 81, 113 (2007); (Scalia, J., dissenting); *United States v. Virginia*, 518 U.S. 515, 567 (1996) (Scalia, J., dissenting); *Dickerson v. United States*, 530 U.S. 428, 465 (2000) (Scalia, J., dissenting); *McDonald v. City of Chicago, Ill.*, 561 U.S. 742, 872 (2010) (Scalia, J., dissenting).

199 "view of the framers": *Trustees of Dartmouth Coll. v. Woodward*, 17 U.S. 518, 644 (1819).

199 "Taney": *Dred Scott v. Sandford*, 60 U.S. 393, 423 1 (1857).

200 "most plausible meaning": Murphy 126 (citing Attorney General's Conference on Economic Liberties, Washington, D.C., Jun. 14, 1986, Appendix C, "A Report to the Attorney General").

200 "In his official portrait": Bruce Allen Murphy, "Scalia's legacy will resonate," *Boston Globe*, Feb. 14, 2016.

200 "This Court need not": *Cruzan by Cruzan v. Dir., Missouri Dep't of Health*, 497 U.S. 261, 300–01 (1990) (Scalia, J., concurring).

200 "Scalia was born": Murphy 7.

200 "teaching Romance languages": Biskupic 15–16.

200 "At his high school": Murphy 16.

200 "A classmate recalled": Murphy 19.

200 "It had sixteen altars": Murphy 21.

200 "All around him": Murphy 22 (Hapsburg); Biskupic 24–25 (McCarthy).

201 "Laurence Silberman": Biskupic 36.

201 "During Ford's 29 months": United States Senate, "Summary of Bills Vetoed, 1789-present," https://www.senate.gov/reference/Legislation/Vetoes/vetoCounts.htm; *see also* Biskupic 46–47 (veto of Freedom of Information Act amendments).

201 "The inoffensive Ford": James T. Patterson, *Restless Giant: The United States from Watergate to* Bush v. Gore (2005), 93.

201 "Watergate baby": Patterson 84.

201 "I think you can go back": Biskupic 53.

201 "Americans rang in": Patterson 52.

201 "depressing movies": Patterson 40.

201 "burglary and theft": Patterson 40–41.

201 "four OPEC price hikes": Patterson 127, 65 (gas stations).

202 "first and only appearance": *Alfred Dunhill of London, Inc. v. Republic of Cuba*, 425 U.S. 682, 684 (1976).

202 "plump": Biskupic 63.

202 "vote I most regret": Biskupic 121 (citing Senate Judiciary Comm. Hearing on nomination of Ruth Bader Ginsburg, July 22, 1993).

202 "With neither the constraint": *In re Reporters Comm. for Freedom of the Press*, 773 F.2d 1325, 1332 (D.C. Cir. 1985).

202 "When he's in doubt": Murphy 132–33.

202 "another judge": Nat Hentoff, "The Constitutionalist," *New Yorker*, Mar. 12, 1990.

203 "stagnant, archaic": *Michael H. v. Gerald D.*, 491 U.S. 110, 141 (1989) (Brennan, J., dissenting).

203 "[I]t would be comforting": *Id.* at 137.

203 "Brennan believed": *See, e.g.*, *O'Lone v. Estate of Shabazz*, 482 U.S. 342, 355 (1987) (Brennan, J., dissenting); William J. Brennan, Jr., "Constitutional Interpretation," Address to the Text and Teaching Symposium, Georgetown University Oct. 12, 1985.

203 "I put sixteen years": Nat Hentoff, "The Constitutionalist," *New Yorker*, Mar. 12, 1990.

203 "living-Constitution judge": Margaret Talbot, "Supreme Confidence," *New Yorker*, Mar. 28, 2005.

204 "When and if the Court": *Michael H.*, 491 U.S. at 141, 157 (Brennan, J., dissenting).

204 "The Court must be living": *Bd. of Cty. Comm'rs, Wabaunsee Cty., Kan. v. Umbehr*, 518 U.S. 668, 711 (1996) (Scalia, J., dissenting).

204 "responsive to the needs": William J. Brennan, Jr., "Letter to the President [on Resignation]," *New York Times*, Jul. 21, 1990.

204 "cornered colleagues": Biskupic 129, 167.

204 "democratic vote": *Stenberg v. Carhart*, 530 U.S. 914, 955 (2000) (Scalia, J., dissenting).

204 "Ehrlich Coker escaped": *Coker v. Georgia*, 433 U.S. 584, 605 (1977) (Burger, C.J., dissenting).

205 "does not include the death": *Id.* at 598.

205 "Mrs. Carver was unharmed": *Id.* at 587.

205 "It was a mystery": *Id.* at 607 n.2.

205 "eight-year-old in Louisiana": David Stout, "Justices reject death penalty for child-rape cases," *San Diego Union Tribune*, Jun. 26, 2008.

205 "pediatric doctor": *Kennedy v. Louisiana*, 554 U.S. 407, 41, *as modified* (Oct. 1, 2008), *opinion modified on denial of reh'g*, 554 U.S. 945 (2008).

205 "But the girl": *Id.* at 415.

205 "extreme cruelty": *Id.* at 419.

205 "must embrace and express": *Id.* at 420.

205 "the last execution": *Id.* at 422.

205 "In that year": *Id.* at 426, 432; *id.* at 461 (Alito, J., dissenting).

206 "The number of states": *Id.* at 455–57, 468–69 (Alito, J., dissenting).

206 "Psychologists document": The literature is large but consider the recent case of Lisa Bridget, a once-happy 21-year-old mother ready to start a career, who said: "The rape destroyed me. I just thought I was a bad person. I turned to drugs, crime. I started going to jail. He didn't just take my body. He took my integrity, my peace, everything a woman can have that makes her her." Twenty years later her rape kit identified her rapist—a fact she *regretted*. "It feels like somebody has opened an old wound and started pouring salt in." "For 2 Cuyahoga County women, rape kits bring answers (and endings)," *Associated Press*, Jun. 1, 2015.

206 "We are, in effect": U.S. Supreme Court, Transcript of Oral Argument, *Kennedy v. Louisiana*, No. 07-343, Apr. 16, 2008, 11.

206 "living and breathing document": "Democratic Presidential Candidates Debate in Los Angeles, California," Mar. 1, 2000.

206 "Sandra Day O'Connor": Ann Carey McFeatters, *Sandra Day O'Connor: Justice in the Balance* (2005), 23 (ranch), 46 (no job), 14–18 (abortion); Linda Greenhouse, *Becoming Justice Blackmun: Harry Blackmun's Supreme Court Journey* (2005), 141.

207 "You think there's a right": Margaret Talbot, "Supreme Confidence," *New Yorker*, Mar. 28, 2005.

207 "prolong this Court's": *Webster v. Reprod. Health Servs.*, 492 U.S. 490, 532 (1989) (Scalia, J., concurring in part and concurring in the judgment).

207 "[F]ederal courts": *Cruzan*, 497 U.S. 261 at (Scalia, J., concurring). *See also Sosa v. Alvarez-Machain*, 542 U.S. 692, 750 (2004) (Scalia, J., concurring); *Lewis v. Casey*, 518 U.S. 343, 362 (1996); *Romer v. Evans*, 517 U.S. 620, 636 (1996); *Crawford-El v. Britton*, 523 U.S. 574, 611–12 (1998) (Scalia, J., dissenting).

207 "single footnote": *Lee v. Weisman*, 505 U.S. 577, 607 n.10 (1992) (Blackmun, J., concurring).

207 "The same association": *Roper*, 543 U.S. at 617 (Scalia, J., dissenting).

207 "In practice": Antonin Scalia and Bryan A. Garner, *Reading Law: The Interpretation of Legal Texts* (2012), 410.

208 "When Scalia": Margaret Talbot, "Supreme Confidence," *New Yorker*, Mar. 28, 2005.

208 "extramarital affair": *Michael H.*, 491 U.S. at 113.

208 "suggested that government": *Lee v. Weisman*, 505 U.S. at 638 (Scalia. J., dissenting); *see also Elmbrook Sch. Dist. v. Doe*, 134 S. Ct. 2283 (2014) (Scalia, J., dissenting from the denial of cert) ("the First Amendment explicitly favors religion").

208 "Despite his protests": Christopher L. Eisgruber, *The Next Justice: Repairing the Supreme Court Appointments Process* (2007), 41.

208 "harsh self-sufficiency": Jean Edward Smith, *John Marshall: Definer of a Nation* (1996), 29.

208 "*Crawford* reoriented": *Crawford v. Washington*, 541 U.S. 36, 59 (2004).

208 "Previously the Court": *Id.* at 68–69.

209 "championed for 15 years": *Maryland v. Craig*, 497 U.S. 836, 861 (1990) (Scalia, J., dissenting).

209 "analogizing medical examiners": *Crawford*, 541 U.S. at 49 & 47 n.2.

209 "historically inaccurate": Daniel J. Capra and Joseph Tartakovsky, *Autopsy Reports and the Confrontation Clause: A Presumption of Admissibility*, 2 Va. J. Crim. L. 62, 89–93 (2014).

209 "thermal-imaging devices": *Kyllo v. United States*, 533 U.S. 27, 30 (2001).

209 "arrestee's smartphone": *Riley v. California*, 134 S. Ct. 2473, 2491–93 (2014).

210 "Changed technology": *D.C. v. Heller*, 554 U.S. 570, 635 (2008).

210 "legacy": Murphy 390.

210 "like being John Marshall": Biskupic 351.

210 "make it unconstitutional": *McDonald*, 561 U.S. at 750.

210 "decision's essential intuition": Nelson Lund, *The Second Amendment, Heller, and Originalist Jurisprudence*, 56 UCLA L. Rev. 1343, 1344, 1354, 1365–66 (2009); Adam Winkler, *Gunfight: The Battle over the Right to Bear Arms in America* (2011), 113–14, 286.

210 "threatens severely": *Heller*, 554 U.S. at 719 (Breyer, J., dissenting); Richard A. Posner, "In Defense of Looseness," *New Republic*, Aug. 26, 2008.

210 "Undoubtedly some think": *Heller*, 554 U.S. at 636.

210 "right of self-preservation": *Id.* at 593–94, 585.

211 "A Revolutionary War soldier": *Heller*, 554 U.S. at 685 (Breyer, J., dissenting), citing James E. Hicks, United States Military Shoulder Arms, 1795–1935, 1 *J. Am. Military Foundation* 23, 30 (Spring 1937); Middlekauff, *The Glorious Cause* 305 (three rounds a minute).

211 "Sandy Hook": *See, e.g.*, Susan Raff, "154 shots in 5 minutes: Sandy Hook warrants released," WFSB-Connecticut, Mar. 28, 2013; see also *Friedman v. City of Highland Park, Ill.*, 784 F.3d 406, 410 (7th Cir. 2015) *cert. denied sub nom. Friedman v. City of Highland Park, Ill.*, No. 15-133, 2015 WL 4555141 (U.S. Dec. 7, 2015).

211 "Some have made": *Heller*, 554 U.S. at 582.

211 "I doubt that": *Maryland v. King*, 133 S. Ct. 1958, 1989 (2013) (Scalia, J., dissenting).

211 "Framers decided": *Boumediene*, 553 U.S. at 798.

211 "captured Muslim raiders": "A Proposal to Use Force against the Barbary States, 12 July 1790," *TJ Papers*, Vol. 18, *4 November 1790–24 January 1791*, 416–22; Joseph Wheelan, *Jefferson's War: America's First War on Terror, 1801–1805* 59.

211 "great lawyers of [that] day": *Roper*, 543 U.S. at 579 (Stevens, J., concurring).

212 "dereliction": "Letter from Alexander Hamilton, Concerning the Public Conduct and Character of John Adams, Esq. President of the United States, [24 October 1800]," *AH Papers*, Vol. 25, *July 1800–April 1802*, 186–234.

212 "Historians of early America": Gordon S. Wood, "The Fundamentalists and the Constitution," *New York Review of Books*, Feb. 18, 1988.

212 "Solomonic decisions": *Thompson v. Oklahoma*, 487 U.S. 815, 878 (1988) (Scalia, J., dissenting).

212 "Scalia, in the end": *See* Antonin Scalia, "Originalism: The Lesser Evil," 57 U. Cinn. L. Rev. 849 (1988–89); *McDonald*, 561 U.S. at 803–05 (Scalia, J., dissenting); *Reading Law* at 399–410.

213 "Former Speaker": Eric Zimmermann, "Pelosi to reporter: 'Are you serious?'" *The Hill*, Oct. 23. 2009.

213 "African-American fathers in Kansas": *Bd. of Educ. of City of Ottawa v. Tinnon*, 26 Kan. 1, 22 (1881).

213 "In 1967": Biskupic 37.

213 "psychopathic personality": *Boutilier v. Immigration & Naturalization Serv.*, 387 U.S. 118, 123 (1967).

213 "Kathy Kozachenko": Ron Schlittler, "Another Legislator Beat Harvey Milk to 'First' Laurel," Letter, *Washington Post*, Nov. 29, 2008.

213 "began in Massachusetts": *Goodridge v. Dep't of Pub. Health*, 440 Mass. 309, 312, 798 N.E.2d 941, 948 (2003).

213 "26 state constitutional *bans*": "A timeline of same-sex marriage in the US," *Boston Globe*, Jan. 9, 2016.

213 "Vermont became the first": Richard Wolf, "Timeline: Same-sex marriage through the years," *USA Today*, Jun. 26, 2015.

214 "numbers had flipped": Justin McCarthy. "Record-High 60% of Americans Support Same-Sex Marriage," *Gallup*, May 19, 2015.

214 "among some 60 species": Deborah Blum, *Sex on the Brain: The Biological Differences Between Men and Women* (1997), 127–57.

214 "born gay": Simon LeVay, *Gay, Straight, and the Reason Why: The Science of Sexual Orientation* (2011); Glenn Wilson and Qazi Rahman, *Born Gay: The Psychobiology of Sex Orientation* (2008); Dean Hamer, *The Science of Desire: The Search for the Gay Gene and the Biology of Behavior* (1994).

214 "morals legislation": *Lawrence v. Texas*, 539 U.S. 558, 599 (2003) (Scalia, J., dissenting).

214 "The following exchange": U.S. Supreme Court, Transcript of Oral Argument, *Hollingsworth v. Perry*, No. 12-144, Mar. 26, 2013, 37–40.

215 "Interracial marriage and mixed-race education": *See, e.g.*, Peggy Pascoe, *What Comes Naturally: Miscegenation Law and the Making of Race in America* (2009), 40–46, 63–69; Charles A. Lofgren, *The Plessy Case: A Legal-Historical Interpretation* (1987), 64–67, 137.

215 "The same Congress": *See, e.g.*, *Pace v. Alabama*, 106 U.S. 583 (1883)

(miscegenation), overruled by *McLaughlin v. State of Fla.*, 379 U.S. 184 (1964); *State of Ohio ex rel. Garnes v. McCann*, 21 Ohio St. 198, 202 (1871); *State v. Duffy*, 7 Nev. 342, 348 (1872); *Ward v. Flood*, 48 Cal. 36, 54 (1874); *Cory v. Carter*, 48 Ind. 327, 356–57, 362–64 (1874); *Bd. of Educ. of City of Ottawa v. Tinnon*, 26 Kan. 1, 16 (1881); *People ex rel. King v. Gallagher*, 93 N.Y. 438, 450–53 (1883); *Bertonneau v. Bd. of Directors of City Sch.*, 3 F. Cas. 294, 296 (C.C.D. La. 1878) (Strong, J.); *Cumming v. Bd. of Ed. of Richmond Cty.*, 175 U.S. 528, 545 (1899) (Harlan, J.) (schools), all overruled by *Brown v. Bd. of Ed.*, 347 U.S. 483 (1954); Alexander M. Bickel, *The Original Understanding and the Segregation Decision*, 69 Harv. L. Rev. 1, 56 (1955); Lofgren, *The Plessy Case*, 172 (Congress sanctioned separate schools in District of Columbia in 1862, 1863, 1864, 1866, and 1873).

215   "neither requires nor forbids": *Romer*, 517 U.S. at 636 (Scalia, J., dissenting) ("Since the Constitution of the United States says nothing about this subject, it is left to be resolved by normal democratic means"); *Lawrence*, 539 U.S. at 603–04 (Scalia, J., dissenting) ("it is the premise of our system that those judgments are to be made by the people, and not imposed by a governing caste that knows best").

215   "[t]oday's opinion": *Lawrence*, 539 U.S. at 602; *Romer*, 517 U.S. at 636 (Scalia, J., dissenting).

216   "The Court today": *Lawrence*, 539 U.S. at 604 (Scalia, J., dissenting).

216   "Instead the majority": *United States v. Windsor*, 133 S. Ct. 2675, 2689–95 (2013).

216   "Few public controversies": *Windsor*, 133 S. Ct. at 2710–11 (2013) (Scalia, J., dissenting) (citations omitted).

217   "The ten states": "A timeline of same-sex marriage in the US," *Boston Globe*, Jan. 9, 2016 (VT, NH, DC, NY, WA, ME, MD, RI, DE, MN).

217   "60 court cases": Wikipedia, "Same-sex marriage in the United States," (last accessed Apr 5. 2016); Lambda Legal, "Post-Windsor Cases Ruling in Favor of Marriage Equality Claims" (as of Jun. 24, 2015).

217   "facetious": 539 U.S. 558.

217   "By the time": *Lawrence*, 539 U.S. at 573.

218   "three Iowa justices": *Varnum v. Brien*, 763 N.W.2d 862, 872 (Iowa 2009); A.G. Sulzberger, "Ouster of Iowa Judges Sends Signal to Bench," *New York Times*, Nov. 3, 2010.

218   "Clela Rorex": "Colo. Clerk Recalls Issuing Same-Sex-Marriage Licenses — In 1975," *NPR Morning Edition*, Jul. 18, 2014.

218   "Kim Davis": *See also Czekala-Chatham v. State ex rel. Hood*, No. 2014-CA-00008-SCT, 2015 WL 10985118, at *3 (Miss. Nov. 5, 2015) (Dickinson, P.J., objecting), *id.* at *12 (King, J., dissenting); *Barber v. Bryant*, 3:16-cv-00442-CWR-LRA (D. Miss.) Jun. 30, 2016; Jonathan M. Katz, "Gay Rights Battle Heats Up in Mississippi and North Carolina," *New York Times*, Apr. 5, 2016; Joe Sterling, Eliott C. McLaughlin, and Joshua Berlinger, "North Carolina, U.S., square off over transgender rights," *CNN*, May 10, 2016.

219   "It doesn't prove anything": Biskupic 145.

219   "future direction": Martin Pengelly, Ben Jacobs, Dan Roberts, and Alan Yuhas, "Supreme court justice Antonin Scalia dies: legal and political worlds react," *The Guardian*, Feb. 14, 2016.

FINALE — THE EXPERIMENT ENDURES

221 "Some men look": "Proposals to Revise the Virginia Constitution: I. Thomas Jefferson to 'Henry Tompkinson' (Samuel Kercheval), 12 July 1816," *TJ Papers*, Retirement Series, Vol. 10, *May 1816 to 18 January 1817*, 222–28.

222 "perfectly rational duty": Cicero, *On Duties* (Loeb ed. 1913), 1:50–58.

223 "looking forward": Andrew Burnaby, *Travels Through the Middle Settlements in North-America: In the Years 1759 and 1760* (1775), 89.

224 "It is not our duty": John Dickinson, *An Essay on the Constitutional Power of Great-Britain Over the Colonies in America* (1774).

INDEX